THE
UNITED STATES
IN
WORLD AFFAIRS
1952

SOME PUBLICATIONS OF THE

COUNCIL ON FOREIGN RELATIONS

FOREIGN AFFAIRS (quarterly), edited by Hamilton Fish Armstrong.

THE UNITED STATES IN WORLD AFFAIRS (annual). Volumes for 1931, 1932 and 1933 by Walter Lippmann and William O. Scroggs; for 1934–1935, 1936, 1937, 1938, 1939 and 1940 by Whitney H. Shepardson and William O. Scroggs; for 1945–1947, 1947–1948 and 1948–1949 by John C. Campbell; for 1949, 1950, 1951, and 1952 by Richard P. Stebbins.

DOCUMENTS ON AMERICAN FOREIGN RELATIONS, 1952, edited by Clarence W. Baier and Richard P. Stebbins.

POLITICAL HANDBOOK OF THE WORLD (annual), edited by Walter H. Mallory.

THE UNDECLARED WAR, by William L. Langer and S. Everett Gleason.

MIDDLE EAST DILEMMAS: The Background of United States Policy, by J. C. Hurewitz.

BRITAIN AND THE UNITED STATES: Problems in Cooperation, a joint report prepared by Henry L. Roberts and Paul A. Wilson.

TRADE AND PAYMENTS IN WESTERN EUROPE: A Study in Economic Cooperation, 1947–1951, by William Diebold, Jr.

THE CHALLENGE TO ISOLATION, by William L. Langer and S. Everett Gleason.

THE ECONOMICS OF FREEDOM: The Progress and Future of Aid to Europe, by Howard S. Ellis.

WAR AND THE MINDS OF MEN, by Frederick S. Dunn.

PUBLIC OPINION AND FOREIGN POLICY, by Lester Markel and Others.

THE PRICE OF POWER, by Hanson W. Baldwin.

OUR FARM PROGRAM AND FOREIGN TRADE, by C. Addison Hickman.

THE FOREIGN AFFAIRS READER, edited by Hamilton Fish Armstrong.

THE STUDY OF INTERNATIONAL RELATIONS IN AMERICAN COLLEGES AND UNIVERSITIES, by Grayson Kirk.

THE PROBLEM OF GERMANY, by Hoyt Price and Carl E. Schorske.

FOREIGN AFFAIRS BIBLIOGRAPHY, 1932–1942, by Robert Gale Woolbert.

THE UNITED STATES IN A MULTI-NATIONAL ECONOMY, by Jacob Viner and Others.

THE FAR EASTERN CRISIS, by Henry L. Stimson.

THE STRUGGLE FOR AIRWAYS IN LATIN AMERICA, by William A. M. Burden.

LIMITS OF LAND SETTLEMENT, prepared under the direction of Isaiah Bowman.

SURVEY OF AMERICAN FOREIGN RELATIONS (in four volumes, 1928–1931), prepared under the direction of Charles P. Howland.

DOLLARS IN LATIN AMERICA, by Willy Feuerlein and Elizabeth Hannan.

NEW DIRECTIONS IN OUR TRADE POLICY, by William Diebold, Jr.

INTERNATIONAL AIR TRANSPORT AND NATIONAL POLICY, by Oliver J. Lissitzyn.

AMERICAN AGENCIES INTERESTED IN INTERNATIONAL AFFAIRS, compiled by Ruth Savord.

THE
UNITED STATES
IN
WORLD AFFAIRS
1952

By Richard P. Stebbins
and the Research Staff of the
Council on Foreign Relations
with an introduction by
William L. Langer

Published for the
COUNCIL ON FOREIGN RELATIONS
by
HARPER & BROTHERS
NEW YORK
1953

The Council on Foreign Relations is a non-profit institution devoted to study of the international aspects of American political, economic and strategic problems. It takes no stand, expressed or implied, on American policy.

The authors of books published under the auspices of the Council are responsible for their statements of fact and expressions of opinion. The Council is responsible only for determining that they should be presented to the public.

COUNCIL ON FOREIGN RELATIONS

ACKNOWLEDGMENTS

THE cooperative effort which produced this volume has laid its
author under heavier obligations than can be fully acknowledged here. Of those whose varied abilities have been placed
at my disposal, only a few can be singled out for individual
mention: Inez Viterbo for aid with printed materials; Gustav
Schweizer of the American Geographical Society for the maps
and charts; Else Greulich for help with the index; and especially Elaine P. Adam, who has not only had a hand in every
phase of the work but has proved to the author that such an
undertaking can be positively enjoyable.

My colleagues of the research staff have been as generous
with help and constructive criticism as have the various outside
authorities to whose experience I have appealed. Ruth Savord,
Donald Wasson and the library staff have patiently solved our
reference problems as they arose; administrative difficulties
have vanished under the skillful hands of Frank D. Caruthers,
Jr. and Patrick Tanner. Professor Langer's introduction permits
an inadequate acknowledgment of various obligations extending far beyond the limits of this book.

But perhaps my chief debt is to those who are maintaining
the Council on Foreign Relations as an institution devoted to
the serious and objective study of international questions. As
time goes on I have learned to value increasingly the encouragement and support of such men as Percy W. Bidwell, Hamilton Fish Armstrong, George S. Franklin, Jr., and Dr. Henry
M. Wriston and the members of the Committee on Studies.
Though wholly without responsibility for the contents of the
volume, they have never wavered in the determination that it
should be written with all the honesty our situation demands.

R. P. S.

INTRODUCTION

BY WILLIAM L. LANGER

THIS latest volume in the series of annual surveys of world affairs and United States foreign policy is presented to the public
at a time when uncertainty and perplexity as to the future have
reached a point almost without precedent in recent times. The
outcome of the presidential election on the one hand and the
death of Stalin on the other have wrought fundamental changes
in the regimes of the two major world powers whose mutual
antagonism underlies and conditions every development of importance in international relations. Whether and how the
United States and its Western allies will regain the initiative
and be able to replace the policy of containment with a more
positive program are questions comparable in importance only
to the problems of the succession to Stalin and the future stability of the Soviet system. The men who have taken control in
the Kremlin have been profuse in expressions of their desire
for a settlement of the many outstanding differences between
East and West. On the American side there is a tendency to attribute this ostensible conciliatoriness to the firmer line of the
new Republican administration, but actually it is impossible to
say whether Moscow's new line is sincere or is designed primarily to gain time and forestall a crisis until the Soviet situation has been clarified and consolidated. Meanwhile it is fully
recognized by the leaders of the Western powers that Soviet
gestures may be intended above all to arouse false hopes among
the peoples of the free world and to create dissension among
their governments which will delay if not frustrate further efforts at rearmament and unity.

The answers to these fateful questions can only be provided
by time, but they can certainly be influenced by the reaction of

the Western governments and peoples. The greatest danger no doubt lies in the perfectly understandable yearning of the average citizen for an end of crisis and hostility, and in his disposition to ignore the infinite complexity of the issues involved in the national security. Ignorance and even indifference to foreign affairs are characteristic not only of the American public, but of the common man everywhere. They lead to emotionalism and prejudice in the formation of public opinion and to a strong inclination to attribute difficulties or setbacks to personal stupidity or even malevolence on the part of responsible officials. The popularity of the glib and sensational commentator provides frightening evidence of the readiness of many to seek refuge in a flight from reality.

It is, of course, unreasonable to suppose that the average citizen should acquire an intimate knowledge and understanding of foreign issues and world relationships, since these matters are among the most involved, the most difficult and the most baffling of all social problems. The ever growing complexity of the modern world and the ever increasing tempo of human affairs is such that even the expert despairs of his efforts to grasp the many interlocking aspects of the global situation. He must do as best he can, but in any event he cannot hope to be successful unless he has a substantial measure of public understanding and support, expressed through the multitudinous organs of public opinion and ultimately translated into action by the Congress. This in turn means that outside the sphere of officialdom there must be intelligent, educated and consistent leadership to shape and guide the public response.

The Council on Foreign Relations has, since its inception a generation ago, pursued the objective of making generally available reliable information on foreign affairs and thereby furthering understanding of the problems and policies of the United States Government. The publication of an annual volume surveying the developments of the year is one of its major contributions and, beginning with the present volume, will be supplemented by a companion volume of *Documents on American Foreign Relations,* published with the help of the

World Peace Foundation, which has for some years been providing this excellent and highly valuable collection of texts.

The composition of the annual survey is an arduous undertaking, for great knowledge and skill are required to shake down the huge volume of "news," to sift out the essential data and to effect a reasoned synthesis of much disparate material. Ten years hence it will be easier to get perspective on these matters and arrive at a fair evaluation. But ten years hence it will be too late to do anything about them. Our great need is a present need, for if we are to keep our bearings and judge soundly of the requirements of national security and welfare, if we are to understand our current policies and gauge the probable course of future developments, it is essential to look back from time to time, to review the position, to take stock and to plan for the future. *The United States in World Affairs* performs an important function in this respect by providing an authoritative, succinct review linking current events with finished history.

The year 1952, to which the present survey is devoted, was one of continued tension and deadlock between West and East. While the Soviet bloc refrained from further aggressive moves, Europe remained weak in defense. Not even the costly program of American aid, economic and military, seemed capable of producing the unity of purpose and action that seemed essential in face of the continuing Communist threat. The German problem remained wide open and even the plan for integrating the West German Republic with the European Defense Community continued problematical in view of the constant accentuation of Franco-German difficulties. In Africa and the Middle East the position of the Western powers underwent progressive deterioration as the impact of nationalism made itself increasingly felt and the flood of anti-imperialism rose higher and higher. So also the Far East continued in turmoil. The negotiations to end hostilities in Korea dragged on without real prospect of agreement, while in Indochina the Communist offensive remained a standing threat.

It was perhaps inevitable that under these trying and dis-

heartening circumstances there should have developed in
Europe a growing impatience with the Korean War and indeed
with the entire program of rearmament sponsored by the
United States. If anything more ominous was the dissatisfaction
of the American people as reflected in the presidential campaign. It was impossible to overlook the fact that the country
was tiring of the heavy burden of rearmament, of foreign aid
and of actual combat in Korea, and that a large part of the
electorate favored a more positive policy if not an effort to
force a decision, notably in Asia. However, the question still
remains how, without resort to general war and failing a genuine turn in Soviet policy, an international settlement is to be
attained. This broad, over-all question in turn cloaks innumerable, concrete and specific questions of a political, military, economic or psychological nature. It involves questions as to the
real aims and intentions of the Kremlin, of the unity and
strength of the new Soviet leadership, and of the extent and
firmness of Moscow's control over the satellites and Communist China. In like fashion it raises issues of American and
NATO capabilities, of European confederation, of Western
relations with the Moslem world, of common action through
the United Nations, and of world strategy in the political and
military spheres.

These and other problems are reviewed and analyzed in the
present survey, which provides factual material and the evaluation of the present situation without which it would obviously
be sheer folly to embark upon a new and more positive course.
It is decidedly in the public interest that this sound and altogether competent volume should meet with the attention and
should inspire the study which it richly deserves.

PREFACE

THE year 1952 marked a culminating phase in the evolution of America's global policy and crystallized a world situation whose future development might well prove decisive for the future of civilized man. Its salient characteristic was the continued stalemate between the hostile forces of East and West and a growing fear of total war as the armaments available to both sides increased in quantity and destructive power. While the Western governments strove for increased military security against the Communist threat, Soviet leaders advertised anew their heavy reliance on divisive forces operating within the non-Communist world. Some basis for their apparent confidence could be found in the widespread murmuring against the policies of the Atlantic alliance, the growing revolutionary ferment in colonial and underdeveloped countries, and the tendency in the United States toward a more limited definition of American responsibilities in international matters.

The present volume attempts to describe these developments in terms appropriate to a series which aims at dispassionate analysis of American world policy as it develops from year to year. Like its predecessors, it makes no pretense at definitive history nor at exhaustive treatment of any particular segment of our foreign relations. What it does attempt is to aid in the understanding of contemporary affairs through a balanced interpretation that brings recent happenings into focus and relates them to the broad underlying tendencies that are reshaping the modern world.

To reduce the welter of daily events to a coherent pattern is, of course, no easy task, and not everyone will be equally satisfied with the results achieved in any one year. The growing interrelation of developments in all parts of the world poses extraordinarily difficult problems of interpretation, organization, and space allotment. To keep the treatment within manageable bounds requires rigorous condensation at all points; often no more than a sentence or a footnote can be devoted to matters which may at the time have filled many columns of newsprint. The compensating advantage, if any, lies in the fact that the really decisive forces in the world situation stand out more prominently in the absence of encumbering detail.

If the main purpose of the volume is to present a reasoned interpretation of a year's developments, the author has been conscious that it will also be used as a work of reference and specialized study. Accordingly, he has endeavored wherever possible to provide both the essential factual information and a bibliographical listing of additional source materials. The most pertinent official texts and illustrative data are conveniently available in the 1952 volume of the annual *Documents on American Foreign Relations* (published by Harper & Brothers for the Council on Foreign Relations), to which footnote references have been included wherever appropriate.

At a time when foreign policy remains the most vital issue before the American public, it is appropriate to remind the reader that these volumes eschew identification with the views of any particular individual, administration, or political party. Avoiding both apologetics and gratuitous faultfinding, they endeavor to assess the actual record in the light of what would seem to be the permanent interests of our nation and of the larger civilization in which we form a part. Some readers undoubtedly will feel that despite his effort to avoid narrow partisanship the author has occasionally leaned too far in the direction of one or another recognized school of thought on foreign policy matters. If so, the fault arises not from any desire to accentuate current disagreements but rather from a conviction that our survival as a free nation quite literally depends on better understanding of the aims, methods, capabilities, and global implications of our national foreign policy.

R. P. S.

New York, June 1953

CONTENTS

MAPS AND CHARTS

THE
UNITED STATES
IN
WORLD AFFAIRS
1952

CHAPTER ONE

WORLD IN TURMOIL

THAT OUR era is a time of unprecedented crisis in human affairs is a notion so repugnant to the natural optimism of Americans that it is not always easy to focus attention on the larger significance of the events through which we are living. Few readers of this volume, it is true, will be inclined to question the statement that the experience of the United States in world affairs in the years around 1952 possessed an historical importance extending far beyond our nation's territorial limits. Providentially or otherwise, this country's emergence as a principal arbiter of the world's destinies occurred at a time when men everywhere were beset by heavy doubts and fears for a civilization built up through countless generations. Yet the full implications of this development are not to be grasped without a considerable mental effort. Only by serious reflection will it be recognized how great were the responsibilities, and the opportunities, which history had conferred on Americans of the mid-twentieth century. For the sequence of events which had begun with the discovery of America in 1492 had actually given to them, barely four and one-half centuries later, the principal voice in determining whether or not humanity—themselves included—was going to triumph over a set of forces that threatened quite literally to destroy the bases of civilized life.

In the years that followed World War II it became conventional in many circles to identify these forces with the handful of individuals who exercised dictatorial power in the Union of Soviet Socialist Republics—men whose conduct undoubtedly was motivated by a determination to extend their perniciously revolutionary influence throughout the world. Even among those who hesitated to believe that the sources of the contemporary crisis could be so narrowly circumscribed, there were many who interpreted current history in terms of a power struggle or ideological conflict in which the chief protagonists were the Soviet Union, as the embodiment of revolutionary Marxist imperialism, and the United States of America as the upholder of a more conservative position identified with the traditional values of Western culture. It was certainly true, moreover, that the world situation in the late 1940's and early 1950's was dominated by this "East-West conflict" or "cold war," the effects of which were strongly felt in all parts of the globe and in every department of human affairs. Yet to equate it with the world crisis as such would be yielding to a dangerous oversimplification. That crisis was, and is, more profound and universal than any competition among sovereign states. Unless some of its deeper causes are recognized, it is useless to try to understand how the behavior of a dozen men in Moscow could become a source of fascinated apprehension to the entire free world and determine, at least indirectly, the foreign policy of a great power like the United States.

To describe this deeper crisis in all its complexity is neither possible nor, happily, is it necessary to the present purpose. For the student of international affairs it is perhaps best understood as a major transitional period in world history, marked by the widespread collapse of established institutions and beliefs and by a necessity for massive readjustment to novel conditions on the part of nearly all of the earth's population. Rapid and tremendous changes were occurring not only in economic and social life but also in the fields of political organization, military affairs, and even religion and morals. The story of our age is that of a gigantic effort to keep pace with the transformations of a world that year by year was taking on a more unfamiliar and, on the whole, more menacing aspect. What lent this process its unique character was, first, its world-wide nature and, second, the immense disparity between the technical resources at hand and the experience of the race in consciously shaping its own destiny. The technology of the more "advanced" nations had virtually annihilated the barriers of time, space, and geography, suddenly making neighbors of distant peoples who stood at totally different levels of development and in many cases were forced to sustain expanding populations with inadequate or imperfectly developed resources. In effect, "one world" was being created in a physical sense at a time when mankind as a whole was unprepared to appreciate, much less cope with what was happening.

The ideas which accompanied and stimulated this process were generally of the crudest sort and did little to mitigate the prevailing confusion. The breakdown of the Europeanized international system which had imposed a semblance of "world order" in earlier decades was paralleled by a breakdown of many of the ideas, attitudes, and values which in the past had given human relations some measure of stability. The contracting influence of the European nations was matched, especially among the educated classes of European culture, by a growing skepticism and pessimism that sometimes verged on nihilistic rejection of all intellectual and moral values. Thus the way was opened for such ideological aberrations as Italian Fascism and German National Socialism and, at a somewhat later stage, for the uncritical acceptance of Soviet Communism.

In this atmosphere of rapid change, the notion of "progress" was embraced with general enthusiasm, but often with limited understanding of the nature or preconditions of progress in any real sense. Material advance was stressed at the expense of spiritual values, and sometimes in complete disregard of actual possibilities; national self-assertion was cultivated irrespective of concrete national interests; there was a widespread demand for economic and social "democracy," without much concern for developing the individual qualities which alone can make democracy work. In the colonial or until recently colonial sections of the world, there was a tremendous revulsion against everything associated with foreign domination, economic "exploitation," real or fancied, and all the other negative features which had characterized the European "imperialism" of the

preceding era. Both in Asia and, to a lesser extent, in parts of
Africa and Latin America, this reaction against the leading
Western countries dominated the outlook of politically influential groups. In their obsession with old grievances against the
West, they tended to ignore the advantages of continued collaboration with the Western nations and to disregard the genuine values which the latter still claimed to uphold.

The peril inherent in these conditions was accentuated by a
new factor which unquestionably threatened not only the established pattern of political and social relations but the whole
material basis of modern civilization, together with the lives of
incalculable numbers of human beings. In discovering the means
of releasing atomic energy, man had reached a culminating
point in his struggle to control the forces of nature. At one
bound he had acquired powers, both constructive and destructive, which bore no relation to his previous state of intellectual
and ethical development. In the best of cases, control over this
formidable new potential would have represented an awesome
responsibility. In actual fact, its early availability to the two
principal contenders in the East-West conflict raised fears that
sooner or later it would be unleashed as an incident of their
political struggle, and without due appreciation of the long-
range consequences to humanity at large. The distribution of
political and military power in the twentieth century was scarcely
proportionate to the moral and social responsibility of those who
wielded it. The incalculable possibilities of destruction that on
one side were entrusted to responsible democratic statesmen
were also at the command of persons whose boast it was to
recognize no authority, human or divine, except the rule of
expediency and the advancement of their own fanatical cause.
Such men could have few scruples about the means they employed to undermine the power of the "imperialist" nations
and hasten the victory of what they were pleased to call the
"world proletariat." Nor was it certain that the Western peoples on their side, confronted with an ideological and military
challenge as formidable as it was unfamiliar, would develop

the patience and resolution that would be needed if the peril was to be successfully outfaced.

It was the concurrence of all these factors, rather than the mere reality of Soviet power and irresponsibility, that caused such justified concern to all who were solicitous for preserving the essentials of the human inheritance and maintaining a basis for organized international life in the new age. The Soviet Union was formidable not simply because it represented the greatest single concentration of economic and military strength outside the United States. It was formidable above all because it stood in the midst of a radically unstable world situation—a situation, moreover, which it was almost ideally equipped to exploit for its own purposes, and which the Western powers were no longer able to control effectively. From the point of view of Soviet objectives, there were definite limitations on the usefulness of actual military aggression against the outside world. In any large-scale use of its military power, the U.S.S.R. would always have to reckon with the likelihood of severe and possibly fatal punishment by the United States—a danger which could be only partially offset by the wealth of the European and Asiatic countries that might be overrun in the meantime. But by associating themselves with the world-wide social and ideological ferment of the twentieth century and turning its corrosive force against the bases of Western power, the men in the Kremlin might hope to undermine the world position of their antagonists and, perhaps, to avoid a head-on military collision until they were strong enough to be sure of winning.

1. Struggle of Cross Purposes

That this had been from the beginning the general outline of Soviet world policy seems evident both from the writings of Soviet authorities and from the practice of the Soviet Government and the world Communist movement. Without in the least minimizing the importance of military power and international war as elements in their unconditional struggle with "world capitalism," Soviet and Communist spokesmen laid even heavier stress on other aspects of this all-absorbing contest. As one Soviet theoretician wrote in 1952, in significant reiteration of well-defined Soviet views:

"The struggle between the two systems takes on the most diverse forms: economic, political, ideological, diplomatic. In all spheres of economic, public-political and cultural life a constant historical contest is in progress between the capitalist system and the socialist. In this contest the socialist system will inevitably prevail over the capitalist. . . ." [1]

Within this framework of a "constant historical contest," Soviet authorities attached special importance to stimulating and exploiting the conflicts of economic, social, and political interest which they observed among their antagonists. Particularly relevant to the conditions which had developed as a result of World War II was their long-standing policy of encouraging the efforts of colonial and "backward" peoples to free themselves from influence or control by Western governments and their nationals. This interest on the part of the Soviet rulers was prompted not by sentiment but by a conviction that the "emancipation struggle" in colonial and semicolonial areas had the effect of weakening the Western "imperialist" powers and thus supplemented the revolutionary agitation of their own "proletariats" at home. Years earlier, J. V. Stalin himself had emphasized in unequivocal terms the doctrine that colonial emancipation was to be regarded as an integral and essential part of the process of world revolution:

"In order to win a war one must not only triumph at the front but also revolutionize the enemy's rear, his reserves. Hence the victory of the world proletariat revolution may be regarded as assured only if the proletariat is able to combine its own revolutionary struggle with the movement for emancipation of the toiling masses of the non-sovereign nations and the colonies against

[1] G. V. Kozlov, "The General Crisis of Capitalism and its Aggravation at the Present Stage," *Voprosy Ekonomiki*, No. 4, April 1952, 68-86 (*Current Digest of the Soviet Press*, IV, No. 31, September 13, 1952, 9).

the power of the imperialists and for a dictatorship of the proletariat." [2]

And again:

"Most probably, the world revolution will develop along the
line of a number of new countries breaking away from the system
of the imperialist countries as a result of revolution, while the
proletarians of these countries will be supported by the proletariat
of the imperialist states." [3]

Observation of Soviet tactics in the period after World War
II permits little doubt that Stalin and his associates continued
to adhere to this general conception. While sparing no effort
to protect and advance what they considered the interests of
the Soviet state, the homeland and center of the "socialist"
revolution, they seemed convinced that the general trend of
world affairs was working irresistibly to further the revolutionary cause. On the one hand, the division of the world into two
camps, "imperialist" and "socialist," had become more clear-
cut; on the other, they considered that the "general crisis of
capitalism" was intensifying as the imperialist camp was torn
by ever more serious internal conflicts between national governments, between capital and labor, and between "imperialist
powers" and colonial peoples. Thus the postwar policies of the
Soviet Government seemed guided by two main considerations
directly corresponding to this outlook: (1) the possibility
of outright war with the "imperialist" camp headed by the
United States; and (2) the opportunities for accentuating the
"general crisis of capitalism" by playing upon and exploiting
the numerous conflicts or "contradictions" that were supposedly
undermining their opponents' base.

Of the two lines of action, it is reasonable to assume that the
second was the more congenial to the Soviet mentality. Unlike
the leaders of Nazi Germany, the men in the Kremlin were not

[2] J. V. Stalin, "New Features of the National Question" (1921), in *Marxism
and the National Question* (New York, International Publishers, 1942), 115.
[3] Stalin, "The October Revolution and the Tactics of the Russian Communists"
(1924), in *Problems of Leninism* (Moscow, Foreign Languages Publishing
House, 1940), 115.

88

particularly concerned with military glory and armed conquest for its own sake. Their interest was in promoting the triumph of "socialism" in accordance with supposedly scientific maxims which relegated international war to the status of merely one instrument among many which could be used as circumstances demanded. At the same time, their own dogma had also convinced them of the immutable enmity of the capitalist states, with which they expected "a series of frightful clashes" as a prelude to the ultimate triumph of their own system. Their interpretation of Western actions seemed to them to bear out this expectation. Thus they felt compelled to maintain a formidable military establishment and an advanced state of military preparedness, even while seeking to influence world events in a favorable direction through such nonmilitary instrumentalities as the apparatus of the world Communist movement. If war came, they would be prepared to make the most of it; meanwhile, their military power would usefully reinforce their action in the political and diplomatic fields.

The peculiar dualism that pervaded Soviet postwar policy was not unserviceable to Soviet aims. Behind a façade of military strength which largely fixed the attention of the outside world, the Soviets intensified their tactics of subversion and infiltration against the weak spots of the societies they had marked for eventual capture and destruction. With the assistance of local Communist movements and sympathizers, and with variations dictated by local conditions, these methods were applied not only in the Soviet-occupied areas of Eastern and Central Europe but also in the more industrialized countries of the West and in the "colonial and semicolonial" regions of Asia and the Middle East. As a smoke screen for these aggressive activities, the propaganda apparatus of world Communism ascribed the most atrocious of warlike intentions to the United States and its democratic allies and extolled the Soviet Union— actually the world's most heavily armed state—as the unshakable guardian of world peace.

It cannot be denied that these tactics were well suited to the unsettled conditions that had prevailed in many parts of the world as the tide of Axis aggression receded. Marxism-Leninism, with all its fallacies, gave the men in the Kremlin a quicker understanding of some features of the postwar world than prevailed in some non-Communist quarters. Trained in the analysis of revolutionary situations, they gauged the significance of the prevalent instability and began turning it to their advantage at a time when the Western nations were almost entirely occupied with the problems of their own demobilization and reconstruction. In several instances, favorable conditions originating in the circumstances of war enabled Soviet agents and Communists loyal to Moscow to capture the leadership of local antifascist and nationalist movements and subordinate their action to the over-all Communist strategy. In Greece and Yugoslavia, and later in China and Indochina, revolutionary-type movements whose local appeal was largely independent of Soviet aims were thus converted, at least temporarily, into spearheads of the Soviet drive against the West.

Over a still wider area the theories of Marx and Lenin, vulgarized and adapted to local situations, exercised considerable attraction for minds no longer fixed in a traditional pattern but still largely unfamiliar with the realities of world affairs. To those who were engaged in spontaneous, uncoordinated reaction against foreign domination, poverty, and social and economic oppression, a movement which professed to be both patriotic and democratic—and which was certainly skilled in revolutionary tactics—was a welcome ally. Communist propaganda, with its constant, implacable attribution of every evil to the so-called capitalist and imperialist West, lent support and confirmation to many who saw in the conservatism of Western governments the principal enemy of their own aspirations. Revolutionary agitation directed from Moscow, and uncontested by any comparable effort by the Western nations, thus supplemented other influences that were tending to shake the world position of the United States and the other Western powers. In the process, the Soviet Union gained at least passive supporters even in circles which had no particular interest in forwarding the aims of Soviet imperialism.

The United States and its democratic allies, while not insensible to the menace of Soviet-Communist actions, tended to view the problems of postwar instability and East-West tension in a somewhat narrower and more conventional way than the Soviet leaders. The sociological approach to international relations aroused little interest in the West, where the relations among states were traditionally thought of in terms of power, national interest, and legal relationships rather than of clashing economic and social interests that cut across national lines. Thus a good deal of attention was devoted to the undesired possibility of armed conflict with the Soviet Union, but comparatively little notice was taken of the broader and more revolutionary aspects of Soviet strategy. Of the two sides of the Soviet threat, the military and the world-revolutionary, the Western nations from the beginning focused their attention on the former to a degree that severely handicapped them in coping with the widespread revolutionary tendencies their adversary was trying to exploit. "In the face of this general revolutionary unrest," as one critic complained, "the West is actually behaving like a typical *ancien régime*." [4]

As a comparative newcomer to the field of high politics, the United States was perhaps especially prone to oversimplified views about the East-West conflict and the world situation generally. Public opinion in this country, which had hesitated to believe in Soviet hostility toward the United States itself, was even more reluctant to undertake responsibility for combating Soviet influence in other lands. The United States, it was argued, had no quarrel with the Soviet Union, and desired nothing better than to live in peace with its old ally and fellow member of the new United Nations organization. If the Kremlin really harbored aggressive designs against this country, it was felt that our monopoly of the atomic bomb (not breached until 1949) provided an adequate defense. What was the necessity, people asked, for getting involved in local wars and poli-

[4] Hermann Rauschning, *Ist Friede Noch Möglich?* (Heidelberg, Vowinckel, 1953), 45.

tics in countries where the U.S.S.R. might have a genuine interest to defend but where we clearly had little or none? The unpreparedness of most Americans to think in terms of a global policy commensurate with that of the Soviet Union could be gauged by the bewilderment that greeted President Truman's famous message of March 12, 1947, which combined the recommendation of a limited amount of financial and military aid to Greece and Turkey with a series of far-reaching propositions about the general responsibilities of the United States in the postwar world. As an early attempt to define the basic principles of American postwar policy, the key sentences in this pronouncement retain permanent interest:

". . . Totalitarian regimes imposed upon free peoples, by direct or indirect aggression, undermine the foundations of international peace and hence the security of the United States. . . .

"I believe that it must be the policy of the United States to support free peoples who are resisting attempted subjugation by armed minorities or by outside pressures.

"I believe that we must assist free peoples to work out their destinies in their own way.

"I believe that our help should be primarily through economic and financial aid which is essential to economic stability and orderly political processes. . . .

"The seeds of totalitarian regimes are nurtured by misery and want. They spread and grow in the evil soil of poverty and strife. They reach their full growth when the hope of a people for a better life has died.

"We must keep that hope alive.

"The free peoples of the world look to us for support in maintaining their freedoms.

"If we falter in our leadership, we may endanger the peace of the world—and we shall surely endanger the welfare of our own Nation."

This pronouncement was broadly enough conceived to challenge comparison with the most authoritative Soviet utterances on the world situation. Though animated by a totally different spirit, it resembled them in its recognition of the importance of individual small nations in the modern world, in the weight it attached to economic and psychological as well as military factors, and above all in its implied recognition that the conflict between "freedom" and "totalitarianism" was world-wide and not susceptible of limitation to particular geographic areas. Here in embryo was a program which, if applied with resolution and discrimination, might deprive the Kremlin and its agents of the revolutionary initiative they had captured in so many parts of the globe.

Given the temper of the postwar United States, however, the underlying ideas of the "Truman doctrine" were destined to loom larger in the theory than in the practice of American foreign policy. The next few years saw the United States extending large amounts of economic and financial as well as military aid to a wide variety of "free peoples." The effect on the recipients, however, was conditioned by the fact that the aim of countering Soviet ambitions by direct means invariably received more emphasis than the more general objective of "assisting free peoples to work out their own destinies in their own way." As Americans gradually awakened to the reality of the Soviet challenge, they continued for the most part to view the problem in a bilateral rather than a global perspective, and to think in terms of military solutions more than of purposeful action on the economic, social, and psychological plane. This bias, reflected in the choice of the military term "containment" to describe the broad policy of resistance to Soviet expansionism, was evident in all the monumental foreign policy actions of the next few years: the Greek-Turkish aid program, the Marshall Plan for European economic recovery, the North Atlantic Treaty and the accompanying military aid program, and even the Point Four program of assistance to economically underdeveloped areas.

It is no disparagement of these unprecedented efforts to point out that they seem in retrospect to have rested on a somewhat incomplete appreciation of Soviet aims and methods. Nor can the responsibility for any imperfections in conception or execution be realistically ascribed entirely to particular individuals or branches of government. Such shortcomings as can be dis-

covered in America's postwar record were rooted in a national
state of mind—one that adjusted itself with difficulty to conditions which, in effect, were forcing this country to undertake
a global foreign policy even before the new challenge to American interests could be adequately evaluated.

Two problems implicit in any attempt at the "containment"
of Soviet expansionism seem in particular to have been imperfectly grasped by the nation at large and perhaps by some
of the responsible authorities. The first of these concerned the
possible effect of the new policies on the Soviet Union itself.
Whether or not the promulgation of the Truman doctrine actually stimulated the U.S.S.R. to greater aggressiveness must
remain an open question. It seems clear, however, that the
determination of the Soviet leaders, and the difficulty of induc-
ing them to moderate their ambitions, were widely underesti-
mated in the United States. Even those who conceded the necessity for vigorous action by this country tended to assume that
the expenditure of a few millions or billions of dollars in the
right places would suffice to bring Soviet ambitions within
bounds. The possibility that this might not occur—that United
States-Soviet relations might go on deteriorating, and even drift
rapidly in the direction of a new world war—was seldom
squarely faced. Years afterward, when Americans had theoretically accustomed themselves to the possibility of war with the
Soviet Union, American policy was still troubled by confusion
about the relationship between (a) our attempts to frustrate
Soviet designs by measures short of war, and (b) the possibility
of precipitating the total war which most Americans still hoped
ardently to avoid.

A second major source of confusion had to do with the identity and function of those "free peoples . . . resisting attempted
subjugation by armed minorities or by outside pressures" whom
the President had said it must be the policy of the United States
to support. This broad definition might include almost any
people not already subject to Communist rule, since few if any
nations in the modern world could count on permanent immunity from Communist pressure. Yet obviously the United States

was in no position to safeguard the liberties of every nation threatened by Soviet imperialism. In 1947, Hungary, Rumania, and Czechoslovakia were already within the paws of the Russian bear. China was torn by a civil war in which few Americans desired this country to become involved. Clearly, more definite criteria were needed to determine which nations best qualified for American support. Were they to be those that seemed to have the best chance of preserving their independence? those most determined to fight for it, if necessary, in association with the United States? those whose form of government was most acceptable to particular groups of Americans? or those whose geographical position was of greatest concern from the viewpoint of American strategic interests?

On this question there was little evidence of national agreement, in 1947 or afterward—all the less so because even the postwar strategic interests of the United States were not susceptible of exact and generally satisfactory definition. Some few Americans, indeed, appeared confident that this country, with its powerful strategic air force and growing stockpile of atomic bombs, could face the Soviet challenge without troubling itself unduly about any of these smaller powers with their limited military potential. Others made an exception only in the case of Great Britain and its associates in the Commonwealth of Nations. Others again, while conceding that political and strategic ties with various countries might be necessary under modern conditions, concentrated their solicitude on particular governments or regions in a manner that contrasted sharply with the global outlook of the U.S.S.R. Nearly all Americans assumed that any non-Communist country to which the opportunity was offered would automatically line up with the United States. Imputing our own abhorence of Communism to the world at large, we reasoned that this factor alone would sufficiently ensure the responsiveness of other non-Communist nations to American leadership.

This assumption may have been justified in the sense that Communism on the Soviet pattern was not a very popular movement anywhere outside of the Soviet Union, if there. What it

overlooked was the fact that many of the world's peoples were
influenced by other preoccupations, some of them equally
powerful, which made them hesitate to throw in their lot with
one major power or bloc against another. General war-weari-
ness and fear of a new conflict, widespread belief in the supposed "reactionary" tendencies of American capitalism, admira-
tion and sympathy for the U.S.S.R. as the self-proclaimed
champion of "peace" and of "progressive" movements everywhere, made some men skeptical of the American position
and loath to commit themselves in a struggle from which they
felt that they themselves had little or nothing to gain. This
attitude was conspicuously prevalent in the so-called colonial
and underdeveloped countries, where the reaction against "imperialism" affected the standing of the United States almost as
much as it did that of Great Britain, France, and smaller
colonial powers whose rights the American government often
felt bound to uphold. Not altogether deservedly, the United
States was regarded in many quarters not as the champion of
threatened democratic freedoms but as the upholder of an
obsolete status quo.

Such reactions, however superficial and ill-founded, helped
to account for the fact that the line of policy initiated by this
country in 1947 failed to achieve as much as some Americans
had expected of it. The next four years saw Greece, Turkey,
and the nations of Western Europe restored to their feet without any full-scale armed conflict between the two camps, but
also without any diminution of Soviet power and aggressiveness. On the contrary, relations with the Soviet world continued
to worsen. A series of aggressive Soviet actions culminated in
1950 in the armed attack (by proxy) on the Republic of Korea
—an act of open aggression carried out, endorsed, and supported in complete defiance of non-Communist world opinion
as expressed through the United Nations. Meanwhile the
U.S.S.R. was known to have exploded its first atomic bomb.
China, the world's most populous nation, had fallen almost
entirely under the control of a Communist government which
was already attempting to exploit the revolutionary ferment

throughout the Far East in its own interest and that of Stalinist Communism.

Contrary to popular expectations, moreover, other non-Communist governments not only had failed to react to these events in harmony with the United States but were showing a good deal of discontent with some aspects of this country's world policy. This was especially true of Washington's refusal to consider any concessions, diplomatic or otherwise, to the new Chinese Communist regime in Peking. Communist China's bid for acceptance into the United Nations, followed by its intervention in the Korean conflict at the end of 1950, not only resulted in the gravest international crisis of the postwar period but also disclosed an astonishing insensitivity to American wishes on the part of this country's allies and associates. Nearly all of the latter voiced strong opposition to any military measures against the aggressors in Korea which could result in extending the area of hostilities in the Far East. A considerable number indicated that they were not without sympathy for a Chinese government which, despite the barbarity of many of its actions in both the domestic and foreign fields, claimed to represent the live forces in Asia in their battle against Western imperialism and its "reactionary" native instruments. Among the latter, some non-Communists insisted on classing the Chinese National Government which had taken refuge on Formosa early in 1950 and was still recognized and supported by the United States.

For the United States, the effect of these developments was to confirm and intensify the emphasis on the purely military aspect of the Soviet-Communist threat. Paradoxically, the evaporation of any remaining illusions about the hostility of the Communist governments was accompanied by the evaporation of most of the interest in programs for combating Communism on its own chosen battleground through economic, social, and political measures. America's primary response to the Korean war was a large-scale, international rearmament program aimed at putting this country and its North Atlantic allies in a better condition to deter or fend off any sudden military attack by the

Soviet Union. Concurrently, the rehabilitation of the fallen enemies of World War II was expedited in the hope of fitting Western Germany and Japan into a global scheme of anti-Soviet defense. This general line of policy seemed to accord with the preferences of articulate public opinion in the United States; yet its pursuit was hampered by manifestations of growing popular discontent. From an object of bipartisan cooperation, foreign policy had gradually developed into a leading issue of party politics and was subordinated in a considerable measure to partisan interest. A series of chaotic "debates" took place in which existing policies were drastically criticized and largely denuded of popular support, yet in which no agreement could be reached on alternative lines of action.

So far as the national administration under President Truman and Secretary of State Dean Acheson was concerned, the outbreak of war in the Far East entailed no modification of the underlying principles of American postwar policy. That policy, they emphasized, was unequivocally dedicated to the pursuit of peace—not, however, through an attempt to reach immediate agreements with the U.S.S.R., which was deemed unpromising in the existing state of world power relations, but by trying to balance the military power of the Soviet Union through the creation of a "deterrent force" in Western Europe and of "situations of strength" in threatened areas throughout the world. The success of these efforts, it was hoped, would eventually induce the Kremlin to renounce its aggressive aims and negotiate outstanding issues on a basis of equality.

The objections raised to this line of action made much of its alleged weakness but were not easily reduced to any clear-cut system of alternatives. The principal ground of difference with the official policy appeared to concern not so much the administration's reluctance to risk general war as its alleged subservience to the opinions of other non-Communist governments. Americans of extreme "neo-isolationist" temper, indeed, seemed equally ready to applaud demands for vigorous military action against the Communist states or a strategic retreat to the Western Hemisphere. Their distinctive outlook appeared

less clearly in their positive ideas than in their impatience with
the United Nations and the North Atlantic alliance, their
readiness to "go it alone" if necessary, and their virtual inac-
cessibility to arguments in which world opinion figured as a
critical element in the shaping of American policy.

Many who hesitated thus to reject the basic principles
of the national policy were none the less dismayed by its complexity and heavy material demands and eager to find ways of
limiting the nation's foreign commitments. Such individuals
were conspicuously partial to schemes for achieving American
objectives through simpler and less costly means—perhaps by
reliance on air and sea power and atomic weapons, to the exclusion of ground forces; perhaps by a "psychological" offensive
aimed at fomenting revolutionary disturbances behind the Soviet
"Iron Curtain"; perhaps by an expanded "campaign of truth"
which would dispel foreign misapprehensions about America
and neutralize the hostile propaganda of the Kremlin; possibly
even by concentrating on the elimination of anything that
looked like Communist influence at home. Such persons did not
necessarily question America's need of allies, but were disposed
to insist on a more nearly "equal" relationship with them, and
to overlook the factors that prevented even the most powerful
friendly countries from putting forth an effort commensurate
with that of the United States. Other nations, these Americans
felt, should exert themselves much more; the United States
should limit its assistance to them more severely and reserve
the right to shape its policies with less regard for their separate
interests and sensibilities.

But the critics of the official policy and those who supported
it were alike in one respect. With few exceptions, both groups
continued to think of relations with the Soviet world in essentially military terms. The question remained, though it was seldom asked in America, whether this approach was really adequate and whether at least some part of the effort devoted to
preparing for an undesired war might not be better applied to
strengthening the general economic and social position of the
non-Communist world. No one knew, of course, whether or

not the Soviet Union was actually planning to attack the West, although the state of its military preparations left little doubt of its capacity to do so. But many observers, especially in Europe, continued to believe that Premier Stalin and his associates desired to avoid a showdown as long as possible, and would not attack unless they felt compelled to do so by the growing pressure of Western armaments and United States policy.

Naturally, these broader aspects of the East-West struggle had not escaped notice in the country where the Truman doctrine had been promulgated. It had often been pointed out that the revolutionary tradition of the United States was itself an important element of strength in a world so largely concerned with liberation from traditional restraints. In earlier postwar years there had been much talk of "recapturing the revolutionary initiative" which was in danger of being misappropriated by the antidemocratic revolutionaries of Moscow. American policy toward dependent areas, the Point Four program, even the Marshall Plan, with its emphasis on the elimination of trade barriers and the creation of a single market in Western Europe, had possessed distinctly revolutionary implications. But with the triumph of revolutionary Communism in China and with the Korean war and the rearmament program, revolutionary and even progressive ideas in foreign policy had lost much of their appeal in America. Little remained except a popular notion, conservative rather than progressive in its sociological implications, of fomenting disturbances within the Soviet domain itself. American policy in other areas of the world—Europe, Asia, Africa, Latin America—still clothed itself in the progressive language of the past but in practice was almost wholly subordinated to the practical exigencies of the rearmament program.

Thus it seemed that the opportunity to exercise a dynamic leadership of world opinion was being largely surrendered to the U.S.S.R.—at a time, moreover, when the revolutionary tendencies which had been latent in many parts of the world were constantly becoming more manifest. A couple of years earlier a high Soviet dignitary, reputed to be the leading candidate to succeed the aging Stalin, had called attention to the stimulating effect of the Chinese Communist victory on the revolutionary movements in other lands. "The national liberation struggle of the peoples of Asia, the Pacific and of the entire colonial world," he had declared, "has reached a new and considerably higher level." [5] Even for those who seldom agreed with Soviet pronouncements, this claim had been amply confirmed by subsequent developments in Asia and Africa. No one could realistically differ with the Soviet view that the deteriorating conditions in these parts of the world were hurtful to the West and advantageous to the Soviet Union. As the Western rearmament programs swung into high gear, any apprehensions felt by the Soviet leaders on military grounds might well have been balanced by satisfaction over what looked like a growing cleavage between the leading nations of the West and the peoples of the other continents.

2. Enter Nineteen Fifty-Two

The early months of 1952 provided further evidence of the general instability of the world situation and of the effectiveness with which the Kremlin enlisted the most varied interests in support of its permanent campaign to discredit the United States and encourage the latent differences within the non-Communist world.

As always in recent years, the dominant factor of international affairs was the condition of complete diplomatic deadlock that existed between the Soviet Union and the Western governments, excluding any settlement of the issues remaining from World War II or of the more recent differences which stood in the way of establishing tolerable relations between the two power groups. This situation, continuously recalled by the harsh words and actions in which both sides freely indulged, spelled a permanent threat of war which

[5] G. M. Malenkov, November 6, 1949, quoted in *The United States in World Affairs, 1949,* 422.

tended to become constantly more oppressive with the rising level of military preparedness in both East and West. This was the unpromising atmosphere in which men struggled to cope with the varied situations that claimed international attention in the winter of 1951–1952:

In the Far East, a series of local wars between Communist and anti-Communist forces, of which the campaign in Korea remained the largest in scale and the most complex in its international ramifications;

In Western Europe, a climactic effort to build a unified defense organization that would combine the strength of the United States and its European allies with that of the Federal Republic established in the western portions of Germany;

In the underdeveloped and colonial or formerly colonial countries of Asia, Africa, and Latin America, an agitation of revolutionary scope aimed at securing a more independent and supposedly happier status in defiance of policies espoused by leading Western governments.

Among the various armed conflicts that absorbed much of the attention of East and West, the war in Korea stood out as the one instance in which an armed aggression, supported by the major Communist governments, had actually been resisted —and successfully, though at heavy cost—by armed forces acting in the name of the United Nations organization and under the leadership of the United States. In the eighteen months since the initial attack had been launched across the 38th parallel in Korea, the invaders had been repulsed and a defensible line established across the peninsula; but the military casualties incurred in this effort were officially estimated at 192,960 for the Korean Republic and 113,110 for the participating members of the United Nations (including 103,739 for the United States), to say nothing of the further 1,569,069 casualties sustained by the North Korean and Chinese Communist aggressors and of the untold destruction of civilian life and property throughout the Korean peninsula.[6] Negotiations looking toward a cease-fire and an armistice in Korea had been going on

[6] Cf. *The United States in World Affairs, 1951,* 403.

intermittently since July 1951. Their eventual outcome, however, remained highly uncertain; and meanwhile Communist China's status as an aggressor in Korea ruled out any discussion of its wider political demands, including admission to represent China in the United Nations and the recognition of its claim to the island of Formosa. These demands, which represented a major source of conflict in the Far East and a cause of acute division among the non-Communist nations, were certain to be renewed whenever the fighting in Korea was brought to a halt. Recently, moreover, the Far Eastern picture had been further darkened by indications that the Peking authorities, having failed in their hope of conquering all Korea, planned to intervene more actively in support of the various Communist insurrectionary movements in Southeast Asia. Military revolts against the established order were already in progress in Burma, in Malaya, and especially in Indochina, where the French and their Indochinese associates had for years been barely holding their own against a native Communist army that looked to China for weapons, supplies, training, and other forms of support.

Although their resistance to advancing Communism in the Far East had been largely uncoordinated and only partially successful, the major Western governments—France, Great Britain, and the United States—had achieved a remarkable degree of unity in the attempt to erect solid defenses against a possible Communist aggression in Western Europe. There they had joined with other threatened governments in a daring experiment designed to place the future of Western Europe on a sound basis (and, simultaneously, to exorcise the fear of a revived German militarism) by bringing about the rearmament of Western Germany within the framework of a unified administration of European heavy industry and a unified European army. By the beginning of 1952, negotiations to this end were nearing completion, and the governments concerned would soon have to reach final decisions as to whether their common interest in Western Europe's defense and future prosperity was great enough to justify the limitations on their freedom of action which were implicit in the acceptance of such novel institutions. Success of the European Coal and Steel Community and of the projected European Defense Community would require not only the full participation of France, Western Germany, Italy, and the Low Countries but also the full support of Great Britain and the United States.

Of the many obstacles to be surmounted before these plans could be put into effect, the most immediate arose from the lack of mutual confidence that still persisted between the Western Allies and the German Federal Republic. A precondition to the establishment of any European army was an agreement between Germany and the Western powers on a "Peace Contract" which would liquidate the nominal state of war, regulate the status of the Allied forces remaining in Western Germany, and provide the basis for peacetime Allied-German relations. Behind this problem loomed a still more formidable difficulty in the pointed objection of the Soviet Government to the whole scheme of West German rearmament, and the likelihood that it would use its position as the occupying power in Eastern Germany to obstruct Allied plans. Since many if not all Germans tended to regard the reunification of their own divided country as a more important objective than association with the West, the U.S.S.R. might be able to turn German opinion against the Western concept merely by posing as an advocate of German national unity on any superficially reasonable terms.

The situation in the underdeveloped and colonial world, unlike that in the Far East and in Europe, was not officially and formally at issue between the U.S.S.R. and the West.[7] Nevertheless the primary effect of developments in these areas was to weaken the position of the Western democracies and create new opportunities for Soviet-Communist encroachments. This was particularly true in the strategically vital Middle East, which within recent months had witnessed a series of violent anti-Western outbursts in connection with (1) the ex-

[7] The U.S.S.R. did, however, officially object to the recently announced Western plan for establishing a Middle East Command. Cf. *The United States in World Affairs, 1951,* 292-293 and the Soviet protest note of January 28, 1952 (text in *Relazioni internazionali,* XVI, July 19, 1952, 787).

propriation of the huge British oil company in Iran; (2) the commencement of guerrilla warfare against the British contingents in the Suez Canal Zone as a sequel to the denunciation by Egypt of its basic agreements with Great Britain concerning the garrisoning of the Canal Zone and the status of the Anglo-Egyptian Sudan; and (3) the growing demand for independence from French control on the part of nationalist elements in Tunisia and Morocco. In January 1952, while Iran seemed to be drifting gradually toward bankruptcy and chaos, Egyptian and Tunisian centers were convulsed by bloody and destructive rioting of an openly anti-Western character and on a scale which at moments approached revolutionary dimensions.

These developments, which were closely and sympathetically watched by the Arab and Asian nations as well as by the Communist world, had produced a tremendous echo in the Sixth Session of the United Nations General Assembly, held in Paris from November 6, 1951 to February 5, 1952. As the principal international gathering of the winter, this meeting provided a sounding board for most of the conflicting tendencies in contemporary world affairs. One of its most significant features was the concentrated fervor and the unprecedented solidarity shown by delegates from the Arab, Asian, African, and Latin American states in championing each other's nationalistic claims, demanding audience for the opponents of "imperialism," especially in French North Africa, and condemning the social, economic, and above all the colonial policies of the Western governments. On most issues directly concerned with resistance to Soviet imperialism, a majority of these delegates still supported the official Western position as they had done in earlier sessions. On other matters they not only insisted on going their own way but heaped abuse on the Western governments—including the United States—in a manner that scarcely reflected any strong sense of common purpose or interest. On the contrary, their performance called attention to what seemed a widening, potentially dangerous gulf between the wealthy and long-established nations of Western Europe, North America, and the British Commonwealth and the much less wealthy, predominantly non-

white, and technically less advanced nations of the other continents.[8]

That this revelation of divergent purposes in the non-Communist world was not unnoticed in the Kremlin could be inferred from the continuing efforts of Soviet spokesmen to dramatize and accentuate it, in and outside of the General Assembly.
Possibly the most sensational utterance at the Paris meeting
was the apparently unrehearsed remark of Soviet delegate
Yakov A. Malik on February 2 with reference to that much-
discussed question, the possible imminence of a third world
war. A few weeks earlier Winston Churchill, Britain's new
Prime Minister, had told American newspapermen that he, at
any rate, regarded the prospects for peace in 1952 as "solid
. . . provided we take prudent measures." Foreign Minister
Robert Schuman of France had also declared himself "sure that
war is not now imminent or inevitable," adding that "we have
now in our hands the elements to permit us to prevent it."
President Truman, on the other hand, in appealing to Congress
to continue its heavy appropriations for defense and mutual
security in the free world, had warned that the Soviet Union
was increasing its armed preparedness in such a way that the
threat of world war remained "very real." But Mr. Malik, in
Paris, brushed aside considerations of this order. Not only was
the "Anglo-American bloc" engaged in preparing for a third
world war, he said, but

"this world war *has in fact begun* . . . war is being waged against
Korea, China, Malaya, Egypt, Tunisia and Morocco. . . . The
three imperialistic colonial powers—this coalition of colonizers—
are waging war against the peoples of Africa and Asia, who are
striving for independence and freedom." [9]

Although this remark was not reproduced by the Soviet press
in its coverage of the Assembly session, its emphasis on the split
within the non-Communist world was typical of the strategy

[8] For fuller discussion cf. the chapter entitled "The Revolt of the Underprivileged" in *The United States in World Affairs, 1951*, especially pp. 406-415.
[9] *New York Times*, January 6, 7, 10, and February 3, 1952. (Emphasis supplied.)

pursued by Soviet representatives and their colleagues from the Soviet satellite states in all phases of United Nations business. In matters concerned with the administration of dependent areas, the economic development of underdeveloped countries, the formulation of a world covenant on human rights, they consistently threw their weight on the side of the more intransigently anti-Western element among the non-Communist governments. Whether this impromptu coalition won or lost on particular votes, its activities kept attention continuously focused on the basic cleavage among non-Communist states. Even where the debate centered on matters of immediate concern to the Soviet Union, the latter sometimes won over enough discontented non-Communist delegations to defeat the orthodox position favored by the United States and its close associates. Failing this, it at least contrived to emphasize the difficulty experienced by this country in holding together an adequate majority.[10]

Soviet agitation in and around the General Assembly was not, of course, confined to this indirect form of attack. Like theatrical technicians, Communist operatives kept their spotlights in motion over the entire international scene, illuminating one situation after another in lurid anti-American colors. In the last weeks of 1951, immense effort had been devoted to publicizing and misrepresenting the first tentative American steps in the field of "psychological warfare" as a plan for fomenting wholesale armed rebellion in the Soviet satellite states and the U.S.S.R. itself.[11] At the beginning of 1952, similar tactics were applied in reference to the already much more touchy situation in Southeast Asia. Soviet Foreign Minister

[10] Two prime examples occurred on February 1, when a Soviet resolution on U.N. membership which was opposed by the U.S. received 22 affirmative votes to 21 against and 16 abstentions, thus failing of adoption only because it passed by less than a two-thirds majority. On the same day a watered-down version of a U.S.-supported Chinese Nationalist resolution, charging the U.S.S.R. with failure to carry out its 1945 treaty with China (General Assembly Resolution 505 [VI], reprinted in *Documents on American Foreign Relations, 1952*, No. 35 [b]), secured only 25 affirmative votes to 9 opposed and 24 abstentions.
[11] Cf. *The United States in World Affairs, 1951*, 395-401. These Soviet charges were formally rejected by the Assembly on January 11, 1952 by a vote of 5 in favor, 42 against, and 11 abstentions.

Andrei Y. Vyshinsky told the delegates at Paris on January 3 that the United States was actually transporting Chinese Nationalist military forces into Thailand and Burma for operations against Communist China, and, furthermore, was preparing to accuse the Peking government of resorting to aggression "whenever events begin to take their course [!] on the southern borders of China, in Thailand, Burma, and Yunnan Province." [12]

Such accusations, immediately echoed by hundreds of Communist spokesmen despite categorical denials from authoritative quarters in Washington and elsewhere, were not merely unfavorable publicity for the United States; they were a source of real uneasiness to all who were concerned with the intentions of the U.S.S.R. and its Chinese Communist ally. What better smoke screen could be laid down for an impending aggression in Southeast Asia by the Communists themselves? Almost equally disturbing was the manner in which Vyshinsky repeatedly tried to involve the Assembly in a debate on the Korean problem, which supposedly was being dealt with by the accredited armistice negotiators at Panmunjom. On this same January 3, Vyshinsky proposed that the matter of restoring peace in Korea be entrusted to a special "periodic" meeting of the United Nations Security Council, in which, of course, the U.S.S.R. possessed a veto power. A few days later (January 12), when this plan had been rejected as a source of mere confusion and delay, Vyshinsky unfolded a new scheme whereby the Assembly would endorse a set of principles for a Korean armistice which coincided with familiar Soviet views but took no account whatever of the military and political realities on the Korean peninsula.[13]

Those who detected in such maneuvers a possible prelude to new acts of Communist aggression in the Far East could find additional cause for uneasiness in a New Year's message addressed by Stalin to the people of Japan. Far from congratu-

[12] New York Times, January 4, 1952.
[13] As in his proposals of November 8, 1951 (The United States in World Affairs, 1951, 383-384), Vyshinsky continued to advocate an armistice at the 38th parallel and the withdrawal of all foreign troops and "volunteer forces" from Korea within three months. For further discussion cf. below, pp. 179-193.

lating the Japanese on the peace treaty they had recently concluded with forty-eight non-Communist governments, the Soviet
Premier commiserated them on what he called their continued subjection to "foreign occupation" and wished them success in the struggle "for independence of their homeland" and
"for the preservation of peace." Thus he served notice that the
Kremlin had by no means resigned itself to Japan's inclusion
in the strategic and political orbit of the United States in accordance with the peace treaty and related agreements. Any expression of Soviet interest in Japan's future was a reminder to
both Japanese and foreigners that the U.S.S.R. remained keenly
interested in Japanese developments, and, moreover, that its
1950 alliance treaty with Communist China provided a basis
for common action against Japan in practically any eventuality
in which the two Communist allies found it to their interest to
act together.

But the most novel and in some ways the most significant
features of the Soviet political strategy for 1952 were still
to disclose themselves. One of these, which concerned the
possible reunification of conquered Germany, will require detailed treatment elsewhere; for to the U.S.S.R., which in the
case of Japan could content itself for the moment with a more
or less offhand expression of good wishes, the countering of
Western Allied plans for Germany was a matter of such importance as to transcend the ordinary rules of political warfare.
The Soviet note of March 10, 1952 to the United States, Britain,
and France, which seemed to many like a recognition of the
growing strength of the Allied position in Western Europe,
was to open an entirely new phase in the relations of the four
powers in German matters.[14] But that phase cannot be properly
understood except in conjunction with two other primary developments in Soviet political warfare which helped to establish
the atmosphere for the German negotiations as well as for all
other international business of the year. The first was an intensification of the perennial Soviet "hate America" campaign
through the dissemination of charges that the United States was

14 Cf. below, pp. 138-146.

resorting to bacteriological warfare in the Far East. The second was a renewal of the concurrent effort to portray the Soviet Union as a guarantor of international peace and prosperity.

The former of these two developments carried the vilification of America to new depths of scurrility; the second, which reached its climax in connection with the International Economic Conference held in Moscow at the beginning of April, served mainly to focus the dissatisfaction which current United States economic policies had aroused in various parts of the world. Both of them, like the other Soviet maneuvers which have been cited, aimed at mobilizing widely prevalent emotions of fear and irritation—the almost universal apprehension of war, the "poor-relation" complexes of Europeans, the touchy self-consciousness of the Asian nations—and turning their full force against the United States. If continued long enough, the Soviet leaders evidently reasoned, such tactics were the surest means of dissolving that coalition of anti-Communist forces of which the United States was the center and which, in fact, represented the only serious external obstacle to the achievement of their own far-reaching ambitions.

3. Atoms, Ants, and "Peace"

"There can be no breathing space in ideological warfare," wrote an important Soviet literary man in 1947.

"On the ideological front, we must and we shall fight not by passive resistance but by an active and unceasing attack on our enemies. This is what the party of Lenin and Stalin teaches. This is in accordance with our traditions. . . . Let the enemy consider us nasty people. From the mouth of the enemy this is praise." [15]

People reared in the Soviet way of thought did not share the Western democratic view of ideological or political warfare as a specialized activity that might occasionally reinforce the effects of national policy in other fields. On the contrary, they looked on and used it as an integral part of Soviet policy and

[15] K. Simonov, "Drama, Theater and Life," *Pravda*, November 26, 1946, quoted in *The Kremlin Speaks: Excerpts from Statements Made by the Leaders of the Soviet Union* (Department of State Publication 4264, Washington, 1951), 15.

as one of the most important means of undermining "imperialism" and consolidating what Soviet spokesmen shrewdly if inaccurately called the "camp of peace and democracy." No Soviet move on the international scene was made without careful calculation of its psychological effects. Propaganda was never for a moment permitted to become divorced from political tactics. If Soviet and foreign Communists devoted themselves year after year to lauding the "peace-loving" Soviet Union and denouncing the United States as a monster of bellicose iniquity, that was because Soviet policy ascribed central importance to the attitude of world opinion and reckoned heavily on the possibility of turning that opinion against the United States.

The surprising feature in this situation was not the aim or the methods by which it was pursued but the mixture of indifference and incredulity with which many Americans watched this determined assault on their international credit. It was doubtless true that the U.S.S.R. might be having its own difficulties with public opinion and popular attitudes behind the Iron Curtain—a possibility which, however, in no way diminished the aggressiveness of its political warfare against the outside world. It was also true that the anti-American stereotypes disseminated by the globe-girdling Soviet propaganda machine were often so crude that they could appeal only to the most naïve. But those who laughed at such efforts sometimes forgot that falsehoods may gain wide acceptance even in "enlightened" communities, and that the exaggerations and distortions of Communist propaganda were not necessarily an impediment to its acceptance by millions of those "backward" peoples in whom the Kremlin obviously took a particular interest.

Soviet political warfare tactics, moreover, were framed with an eye to the partly sophisticated as well as to the politically inexperienced. The recurrent denunciation of the United States on the score of "barbarity" in the conduct of the Korea war seemed principally aimed at the great body of Asian opinion, which would naturally tend to be dubious about any Western country that found itself engaged in warfare against people of Asian blood. For the more critical European audience, on the other hand, the Soviet Union could capitalize on the general longing for peace not only by its patronage of various "peace" organizations but also by citing its long-standing agitation in favor of a particular plan of disarmament which allegedly had been blocked by the Western governments under the dictation of the United States. At least some Europeans could be trusted not to grasp the fact that the disarmament and "peace" proposals put forward by the U.S.S.R. were invariably designed in such a way that their acceptance by the West would work to Russia's direct military advantage, while their rejection would tend to encourage the erroneous opinion that the Western powers, rather than the U.S.S.R., were primarily responsible for the ever-present danger of war.

To critical observers of the annual disarmament and "peace" debates in the United Nations, it was no secret that these exercises had in recent years belonged rather to the realm of political warfare than to that of practical diplomacy. Conscious of the overwhelming popular concern for peace and yet completely without confidence in each other's intentions, the major governments of East and West could have little expectation that any mutually satisfactory plan for disarmament and general pacification would be agreed upon unless and until one side or the other radically modified its general outlook. Thus the various proposals advanced by either side were shaped with more concern for their effect on public opinion than for their acceptability to the adversary. Soviet disarmament and peace programs, as a rule, were transparently demagogic and impractical; those of the Western powers, on the other hand, aimed at technical practicability as well as propagandistic appeal, and could actually have been put into effect if only the Soviet regime had been willing to submit to the same rules and regulations as other governments.

The difference of approach was clearly evident in the rival disarmament plans which had been laid before the United Nations General Assembly late in 1951, in what was admitted on both sides to be primarily a contest for the approval of world opinion. Superior tactics had enabled the Western powers to secure prior consideration by the Assembly for their plan for the "regulation, limitation and balanced reduction of all armed forces and all armaments," which was formally approved—after due discussion and amendment, and over the objections of the Soviet bloc—on January 11, 1952. Based on the principle of "progressive disclosure and verification on a continuing basis of all armed forces . . . and all armaments including atomic," this comprehensive plan provided for the setting up of a new United Nations Disarmament Commission and looked forward to an eventual disarmament conference at which the detailed proposals to be worked out by the commission would be taken under advisement by the world's governments.[16]

To the Soviet Government, which had shown no interest in subjecting its own armed forces and armaments to "progressive disclosure and verification," this program was quite unacceptable—the more so since it wholly failed to support the Soviet propaganda line concerning the bellicose intentions of the West. Foreign Minister Vyshinsky's Moscow-made disarmament and "peace" program, which he had brought to Paris in the autumn of 1951 in the obvious expectation of enjoying a propagandistic field day, had been thrust to one side while the Western plan was under consideration. Now, however, he furbished it up once more and undertook to reassert the Soviet view not only on disarmament but on all the other leading issues of the time. On January 12 he presented the General Assembly with an eight-point draft resolution [17] repeating, with some few modifications, all the points he had failed to drive home at the beginning of the session.

Some of Vyshinsky's typically provocative recommendations for United Nations action were of a broadly political nature—a condemnation of the "aggressive Atlantic bloc," a new demand for a Korean armistice at the 38th parallel, and a repetition of the stock Soviet demand for a "peace pact" among the

[16] General Assembly Resolution 502 (VI), adopted January 11, 1952 by a vote of 42-5-7 (reprinted in *Documents on American Foreign Relations, 1951,* 222 ff.). For background cf. *The United States in World Affairs, 1951,* 380-389.
[17] U.N. Document A/C.1/698, January 12 (*Department of State Bulletin,* XXVI, January 28, 1952, 127).

five major powers. These the Assembly presently voted down by varying but sizable majorities, preferring to adopt the American view that the Korean problem was being handled elsewhere and that Vyshinsky's other proposals, in the light of the U.S.S.R.'s own record of performance under existing international agreements, were sheer impertinence.

The Soviet proposals in the specific field of disarmament inspired slightly greater deference, although they differed only superficially from the generally unconvincing scheme Vyshinsky had offered two months before.[18] Their principal feature, as always, was the sweeping demand for immediate and "unconditional" prohibition of atomic weapons and for a one-third reduction in the armaments and armed forces of the Big Five. However appealing these familiar ideas might be in the abstract, it required only a little reflection to see that their effect (even supposing they were to be faithfully carried out by the U.S.S.R. itself) would be disastrous to any idea of restoring the defensive position of the West and thus rectifying the existing global imbalance of military power. The Western lead in the field of atomic weapons would be nullified; the Soviet Union, meanwhile, would preserve its relative superiority in other departments of military strength, while the considerable armies of its European satellites could be maintained or even increased. The fact that the Bulgarian, Hungarian, and Rumanian military establishments had already been built up in disregard of peace treaty limitations was proof in itself that no confidence could be placed in any disarmament plan which rested on the unsupported faith of the Soviet Government.

Under such circumstances the Western governments were bound to oppose the Soviet plan, even at the risk of disappointing that section of world opinion which insisted on taking Soviet schemes at their face value. On this occasion, however,

[18] Cf. *The United States in World Affairs, 1951*, 386. Allegedly in the interest of meeting Western views, Vyshinsky's earlier proposals were modified so as to provide for (1) institution of international control of atomic weapons simultaneously with their prohibition, and (2) inspection by the international control organ "on a continuing basis," but without the right to "interfere in the domestic affairs of states." For a critical analysis by Secretary Acheson (January 16) cf. *Department of State Bulletin*, XXVI, January 28, 1952, 126-127.

it was not necessary to vote down the plan outright as had been customary in the past. "The testing ground for Soviet good faith—and our own," said the American delegate in Paris, "is and should be the Disarmament Commission." Accordingly, the Assembly voted on January 19 to hand the whole problem to that new group, which was thus assured of having a wide choice of practicable and impracticable alternatives to work upon. After completing its other business and making provision for a special session in New York in case of an armistice or other significant developments in Korea, the Assembly concluded its Sixth Session on February 5.

Nearly six weeks elapsed before the Disarmament Commission was ready to begin substantive work at the new United Nations Headquarters in New York. In the meantime the armistice negotiations in Korea had not moved perceptibly closer to a point at which it would be worth while for the General Assembly to reconvene. Military operations, on the other hand, though limited in scale, had exacted a continuing toll of casualties on both sides and maintained an atmosphere of tension which was further accentuated by the violently anti-American outpourings of the Chinese and Korean Communist propaganda machines.

It was during the interval that followed the adjournment of the General Assembly that Communist sources began to put forward systematic intimations to the effect that the United States was resorting to bacteriological warfare in Korea. Similar groundless charges from the same quarters had been heard occasionally in the past, along with complaints over the mass bombing of civilian centers and other "atrocities" allegedly perpetrated by the United Nations command. But there had been nothing to compare as yet with the circumstantial statement broadcast on February 22, 1952 in the name of Pak Hun Yong, Foreign Minister of the North Korean Communist government. Its text merits liberal quotation:

"According to authentic data available to the headquarters of the Korean People's Army and the Chinese People's Volunteers, the American imperialist invaders have, since January 28 of this year, been systematically spreading large quantities of bacteria-carrying insects by aircraft in order to disseminate contagious diseases over our front-line positions and our rear. On January 28, enemy military aircraft dropped three types of infected insects over the Yonsodong and Yongsudong areas to the southeast of Ichon such as have never been seen before in Korea. The first type resembles black flies, the second fleas, and the third ticks. . . . On February 11, enemy aircraft dropped large numbers of paper tubes and paper packets filled with fleas, spiders, mosquitoes, ants, flies, and other bacteria-carrying insects over our front-line positions in the Chorwon area, a large quantity of flies over the Sibyonni area, and a large quantity of flies, mosquitoes, and grasshoppers in the Pyongyang area. . . . Bacteriological tests show that these insects . . . are infested with plague, cholera, and germs of other infectious diseases. This is irrefutable proof that the enemy has planned to employ bacteria on a large scale to slaughter the men of the Korean People's Army, the Chinese People's Volunteers, and peaceful Korean civilians. . . . In perpetrating these ghastly crimes, the American imperialists have been openly collaborating with Japanese bacteriological war criminals. . . . We resolutely protest against this new crime that the interventionists are perpetrating by spreading deadly germs in Korea. We appeal to the people of the whole world to check the outrages of the interventionists, and to hold the organizers of the use of bacteriological weapons responsible internationally." [19]

As in previous instances, "the people of the whole world"—or, at any rate, that portion of them that lived under Communist orders—were quick to respond to this appeal. Protest meetings were held throughout the Communist domain. Countless letters and telegrams denounced the American "interventionists." Chou En-lai, Premier and Foreign Minister of Communist China, issued a statement fully supporting the North Korean protest and adding the new complaint that "hundreds of thousands [sic] of the captured personnel of the Korean People's Army and the Chinese People's Volunteers have been victims of experimentation with . . . bacteriological weapons." [20]

By March 4 this agitation, carried on "through every device known to Communist propaganda," had prompted Secretary of

[19] Peking broadcast, February 23, 1952.
[20] Peking broadcast, February 25, 1952.

State Acheson to deny "categorically and unequivocally" that
the United Nations forces had used or were using any sort of
bacteriological warfare. Apparently, said the Secretary, the
Communists' inability to care for the health of the people under
their control had resulted in a serious epidemic of plague which
they were now trying to blame on the United Nations. He
challenged them to submit their charges to the test of truth by
authorizing an impartial investigation by an international
agency such as the International Committee of the Red Cross.[21]
Denials were likewise issued by the United Nations commander,
General Matthew B. Ridgway, and by Trygve Lie, the Secretary-
General of the United Nations. Within a few days Acheson
had secured the agreement of the International Red Cross to
investigate the nature and causes of the supposed epidemic—
provided the Communists would submit to direct inspection as
the United Nations command had promised to do. Mr. Lie announced the readiness of the World Health Organization to
provide technical assistance in controlling the outbreaks.[22]

But the Communists, who invariably shrank from international investigations on their own territory, showed no interest
in these proposals. Their main concern was obviously to blacken
the character of the United States. Already they had broadened
their allegations against the Americans to embrace Manchuria
as well as North Korea. On March 8, Chou En-lai officially affirmed that between February 29 and March 5 the "American
aggressive forces" had sent "sixty-eight formations of military
aircraft, in a total of 448 sorties, to invade China's territorial
air in the Northeast," spreading "large quantities of germ-
carrying insects" as well as bombing and strafing residential
areas. A prominent Chinese jurist offered a legal opinion to the
effect that both the air crews that penetrated over Chinese territory and the "American politicians, militarists, and financial
magnates, and the Japanese 'germ experts'" who shared re-

[21] *Department of State Bulletin*, XXVI, March 17, 1952, 427-428.
[22] *Ibid.*, XXVI, March 24, 1952, 452-453; *United Nations Bulletin*, XII, April
15, 1952, 323.

sponsibility for the alleged attacks should be dealt with as war criminals.[23]

Evidence which later became available in the United States indicated that the Chinese regions in question actually had been suffering at this time from severe epidemics of influenza and other diseases, although up to the moment of Mr. Chou's statement these had been ascribed entirely to natural causes.[24] But even if the epidemics themselves were real, it was hardly to be expected that the Communists would react favorably to the repeated offers of outside intervention. To accept aid from the World Health Organization would have looked like an admission of medical incompetence; investigators from the International Red Cross Committee would have been bound to expose the falsity of the Communist propaganda charges. Instead, the Communists ignored all offers from outside and eventually sponsored their own, supposedly more "impartial" investigation by representatives of a Communist-front group known as the International Association of Democratic Lawyers. Their observations not unexpectedly resulted in a finding that "American forces in Korea" had committed "crimes against humanity as defined by the Nuremberg Charter," violated the United Nations Genocide Convention, and "should be brought to the bar of world justice to answer for these crimes." [25]

The world-wide agitation over the bacteriological warfare charges was at its height when the Disarmament Commission convened in New York in mid-March, with Mr. Malik present to represent the Soviet Union notwithstanding the fact that his government had voted against the Western plan under which the commission had been set up. For the U.S.S.R., with its permanent interest in agitating the disarmament issue, the raising of the question of bacteriological warfare was not inopportune, whether or not it had been done with the Kremlin's prior knowledge. The charges themselves, fantastic as they might seem to reputable scientists, were clearly of a nature to cause

[23] Peking broadcasts, March 8 and 13, 1952.
[24] *People's World* (Peking), February 25, cited in *New York Times*, April 20, 1952.
[25] U.N. Document S/2684/Add.1, June 30, 1952, 34 (dated March 31, 1952).

uncertainty in the popular mind. Their repetition would help to neutralize the psychological advantage gained by the West in the disarmament debate in Paris. Bacteriological warfare, moreover, already had a place in the Soviet agitation against the atomic bomb and other "weapons of mass destruction," and could readily be used as an additional means of denigrating the United States. Even if American military authorities had not dropped plague-infected insects in the Far East, it was well known that they were devoting a good deal of attention to the problems of bacteriological attack and defense. Something could also be made of the fact that the United States had never ratified the Geneva Protocol of 1925, which had outlawed the use of bacteriological weapons but failed to provide for any type of enforcement. Here, then, was a fresh opportunity to keep the United States on the defensive by misrepresenting its attitude and decrying its unwillingness to agree to the immediate prohibition of all weapons of mass destruction, bacteriological as well as atomic.

Under such circumstances, the outlook for early agreement on the nominal business of the Disarmament Commission was scarcely propitious. In line with the recommendations of the General Assembly, the United States and its allies proceeded to advance cautious, practical proposals looking toward the ascertainment and eventual reduction of world armament levels; the U.S.S.R., on its side, continued its denunciation of such proposals simply because they did not begin with a prohibition of weapons of mass destruction plus a one-third reduction in the armed forces of the Big Five. But the early history of the Disarmament Commission was largely shaped not by this familiar disagreement but by Mr. Malik's wholehearted repetition of the germ warfare charges and by the resultant clashes with the American delegate (Benjamin V. Cohen) and those of the other governments represented on the commission. On March 28 this battle reached its climax as Mr. Malik enumerated the following items of infected material which he said had been dropped or fired by the Americans into specified localities in Korea and northeastern China between March 6

and 12: insects; spiders; wild birds; yellow leaves; a paper
bag containing spiders; infected food products, rusks and
tinned foods; fleas; sacks of infected pork; birds resembling
crows; bacterial shells giving forth white smoke and infected
flies; mosquitoes; ants; grasshoppers; duck and goose feathers;
and three sacks containing a poisonous white substance and a
yellow powder.[26]

At this point in his recital Mr. Malik was ruled out of order
on the ground that the Disarmament Commission was not a
proper forum for making specific charges of bacterial or any
other form of warfare. So irrepressible a spokesman could not
be completely silenced, but at subsequent meetings the subject
was not allowed to interfere seriously with the more prosaic
tasks of the commission. Yet the ruling could hardly be termed
a serious blow to Communist quarters, which had innumerable
other ways of keeping the agitation alive and seemed wholly
unimpressed by proofs of the scientific impossibility of the
charges made. As its novelty wore off, the germ warfare campaign was not allowed to die out but gradually ceased to
monopolize the limelight. In Korea, a new field for propaganda had been discovered meanwhile in the situation of Communist prisoners of war held by the United Nations; in Moscow, a suitable atmosphere had been created for new efforts to
dramatize the role of the Soviet Union as the principal influence allegedly making for world peace and prosperity.

4. Moscow's Feast of Reason

To balance the stigma of criminality it was endeavoring to
attach to the United States, the Soviet-Communist apparatus
made unusual efforts during the spring of 1952 to highlight
the supposedly virtuous and constructive role of the Soviet
Union and its Eastern European satellites, the countries of so-
called "people's democracy." These efforts had at best an in-
verse relation to the facts of Soviet policy, which remained in
essence as egoistic and hostile to free governments as in the

[26] U.N. Document DC/PV.8, March 28, 1952, 5-6.

past. But the continuing drive to build up the Soviet military potential, as reflected once again in the new budget adopted by the Supreme Soviet in March,[27] did not prevent Soviet propagandists from representing Moscow as the chief guardian of world peace. Similarly, the Soviet policies which were largely responsible for the artificial and uneconomic pattern of postwar world trade, particularly the low level of trade between Eastern and Western Europe, did not deter them from using the resultant unsatisfactory situation as an additional stick with which to beat the United States.

Soviet attempts to exploit the propagandistic potentialities in the field of international economics rested on a somewhat more solid factual basis than did the germ warfare campaign. It was an undoubted fact that the numerous artificial restrictions on trade between the Eastern and Western countries were economically disadvantageous to both sides. The U.S.S.R. and its satellites had to get along without machinery, machine tools, and other items which could have been readily procured in the countries of Western Europe; the latter, largely cut off from trade with the East, were compelled to turn to the dollar area for some of the raw materials, foodstuffs, and semifinished products which under more normal circumstances would have been imported from Eastern Europe. In recent years the economic inconvenience of this situation had been aggravated to some extent by the insistence of the United States on preventing the shipment Eastward of so-called strategic commodities which might serve to strengthen the Soviet military machine. The necessity for such restrictions was officially acknowledged by all of the Western governments allied with this country; but considerable dissatisfaction had been expressed with what were considered the unnecessarily rigid methods by which the American government, especially its legislative branch, sought to circumscribe their trade with the Eastern bloc.

[27] The budget for the fiscal year 1952, unanimously approved by the Supreme Soviet at its session on March 6-8, allocated 23.8 percent of all expenditure to defense purposes as compared with 21.3 percent in 1951. Actual defense expenditure was generally assumed to account for a far larger proportion of the Soviet national product.

This discontent had attracted the notice of authoritative Communist quarters as early as November 1950, when the "Second World Peace Congress," held under Communist auspices in Warsaw, had launched an appeal for the "restoration of normal economic relations among all states." With the subsequent tightening of American export controls, the institution of closer surveillance over the foreign trade of countries receiving American aid, and the revocation of tariff concessions previously accorded to Soviet-bloc countries under the Reciprocal Trade Agreements Program,[28] Communist agitation against the "discriminatory" trade policies of the United States had grown in volume. As a part of this agitation, plans had been announced many months earlier for a "world economic conference" in Moscow which would ostensibly endeavor to lay the basis for a larger volume of international trade, uninfluenced by political considerations.

The chief inspiration of this project was clearly political and propagandistic. True, the U.S.S.R. and its satellites would benefit materially if the level of East-West trade could actually be raised; but this was highly unlikely so long as the Kremlin maintained the hostile attitude which had forced the Western countries to subordinate their economic advantage to the necessities of defense. The propagandist aim of the proposed conference was sufficiently evidenced by the fact that it was sponsored by the "World Peace Council," one of the leading international Communist-front organizations. That the Soviet bloc could really offer concrete inducements for a revival of East-West trade had seemed all the more doubtful in view of the repeated postponements of the conference, which finally met in Moscow on April 3-12, 1952.

Soviet propaganda, however, did not need to be closely geared to the facts in order to achieve its purpose; it was enough if it focused attention on some existing grievance and encouraged the impression that all the trouble was somehow the fault of the United States. Secretary Acheson correctly ap-

[28] Cf. *The United States in World Affairs, 1951,* 227-233 and *Department of State Bulletin,* XXVI, June 16, 1952, 946-947 and June 30, 1952, 1018-1019.

praised the objectives of the Moscow gathering three weeks in advance when he told the press that the organizers were out "to confuse and weaken our unity of purpose," "to organize pressures in non-Communist countries against current restrictions on the export of strategic materials to the Soviet bloc," and generally to discourage efforts at creating the strength essential for independence and peace.[29]

A similar aim, moreover, could be discerned in efforts which the Kremlin was making at the same period to encourage the idea of East-West negotiation on political as well as economic problems. A considerable section of world opinion was obsessed by the notion that a meeting among the heads of the major governments could lead to a settlement of outstanding issues and inaugurate an era of world tranquillity. This idea was invariably resisted in official Washington, where it was argued that no personal contact among heads of states could produce good results unless and until there was convincing evidence that the Soviet Government had changed its viewpoint. Washington's realistic stand undoubtedly reflected a truer understanding of Soviet methods, but it also had the incidental effect of assisting the Kremlin in its effort to cast this country in the role of the principal obstacle to world peace.

So keen was the general interest in any prospect of a reduction in East-West tensions that it required only a word from Stalin to bring it to the boiling point. Great, therefore, was the sensation produced by some rather general comments of the Soviet Premier which were made public on April 2, the day before the International Economic Conference assembled. In laconic replies to a series of leading questions, Stalin expressed the opinion that a third world war was actually no closer than two or three years ago; that a meeting of the heads of the great powers "possibly" would be helpful; and that the present was an opportune moment for the unification of Germany—an aim which the Soviet Government had meanwhile been actively pursuing, in accordance with its own ideas, through diplomatic

[29] Statement of March 14, *ibid.*, XXVI, March 24, 1952, 447-448.

channels. Asked on what basis the coexistence of capitalism and Communism was possible, Stalin replied:

"The peaceful coexistence of capitalism and Communism is fully possible, given the mutual desire to cooperate, a readiness to perform obligations which have been assumed, observance of the principle of equality, and non-interference in the internal affairs of other states." [30]

The emphasis on the principles of equality and noninterference, a novelty in Soviet statements on the theme of "peaceful coexistence," was obviously meant to imply an unfavorable contrast between the practices attributed to the United States and those which the U.S.S.R. claimed to follow.

This same contrast between the supposed Soviet and American attitudes was destined to be the main theme of the International Economic Conference itself. And, if the basic aims of the gathering were indeed of a propagandist nature, the sponsors had taken extraordinary pains to prevent the fact from emerging too obviously. Every effort had been made to give the conference a businesslike rather than a propagandist atmosphere, and to secure the participation of bona fide business and labor representatives from as many countries as possible. Although more than 150 invitees from the Western nations declined to attend in view of the unsympathetic attitude of their governments, a total of 471 persons from forty-nine countries took part in the proceedings, among them a small handful of American businessmen who attended in an individual capacity. One of the more "respectable" figures in the Communist world, Dr. Oskar Lange of Poland, emerged from obscurity to act as chairman; his remarks and those of the principal Soviet delegate were remarkably free from political overtones and even from hostile references to the United States.

The principal speech was delivered by the president of the Chamber of Commerce of the U.S.S.R., M. V. Nesterov, who read the delegates a lecture on the benefits of international trade and told them that the first requirement for its resumption and expansion was the renunciation of all "discrimination"

[30] *Documents on American Foreign Relations, 1952,* No. 8.

such as "the American trade blockade against China." Soviet policy, he asserted, was based on the principle that foreign trade was an affair of mutual economic advantage, since it enabled all countries to make a more productive use of their economic potentialities and thus contributed to all-round economic development and general prosperity, irrespective of differences in political systems. Implying that the Soviet economy had entered a period when more attention could be devoted to satisfying the need for consumers' goods, he intimated that the U.S.S.R. was currently in a position to double or treble its commerical exchanges—on a "nondiscriminatory" basis—with "the countries of Western Europe, the Americas, Southeast Asia, the Middle East, Africa and Australia." Among desired imports he mentioned "textiles, leather goods, food products and articles of general consumption." [31]

In addition to passing resolutions about the possibility of expanded international trade and its importance for all countries, the conference had been designed to permit actual business transactions between Western firms and the foreign trade representatives of the Communist countries. Several days were devoted largely to bargaining on a bilateral basis. Although no comprehensive picture of the resultant deals could be obtained, Western observers estimated that their total value might be no higher than $250 or $300 million and in any case was far below the $3,000 million at which the sponsors had aimed. There was, moreover, no assurance that the Communist agencies concerned would not fall down on the execution of these contracts as they had often done in the past. Some of the British representatives were described as enthusiastic over the arrangements, totaling £28 to £34 million, which they had concluded with Communist China and other Eastern countries. Officials in London, however, treated their reports with skepticism and pointed out that any shipments made under the new agreements would be subject to the usual licensing requirements. Since Eastern spokesmen had not concealed their interest in securing consignments of finished steel, machinery, and other

[31] For excerpts see *Documents on American Foreign Relations, 1952,* No. 9.

products of potential military value, the caution was highly pertinent.

But the significance of the Moscow gathering was not to be gauged by the paucity of immediate economic results. More important was the way in which it dramatized the Soviet Union as a supposed champion of liberal international economic policies, disdainful of the narrow political and strategic considerations which allegedly determined the economic policy of the United States. Thus, in a rough way, it offered to the comparatively sophisticated what the germ warfare campaign presumably gave the illiterate masses—a reason for looking more favorably on the Communist states and more dubiously, if not with outright abhorrence, on the policies of their chief adversary. "If the conference had propagandistic aims," wrote one West German journalist, "it must first of all be noted that it was not entirely without effect. The discussion of East-West trade was without doubt greatly stimulated." Moreover, this observer added, "An invigoration of trade with the Eastern bloc is certainly preferable to a further deterioration in the hostile atmosphere between East and West, and need not endanger the military security of the West." [32]

A curious bit of byplay which occurred in Moscow during the conference served to strengthen the impression in some quarters that the Soviet Government was really free from aggressive aims and favorable to a reasonable settlement of international differences. The Ambassador of India, Sir Sarvepalli Radhakrishnan, who represented a government well known for its interest in promoting East-West accommodation, was received by Stalin in a farewell interview on April 5, the eve of his return to New Delhi to seek the Indian vice-presidency. Foreign Minister Vyshinsky was also present, and the impression was conveyed that there had been a broad review of world issues and possibly even a discussion of a four-power conference. "There is no outstanding problem now dividing the world which could not be settled by discussion and negotiation," said

[32] *Süddeutsche Zeitung*, April 25, 1952, quoted in *Europa-Archiv*, VII, May 20, 1952, 4934.

the ambassador next day. ". . . Every effort should be made to
get top people together." In India's Communist press it was
reported that Stalin had actually invited Prime Minister Jawaharlal Nehru to act as arbiter between East and West.[33] All
such tales were presently denied both in New Delhi and in
Moscow; but meanwhile the original story had offered fresh
encouragement to all who wanted to believe in the Politburo's
good intentions.

Secretary Acheson, who habitually took the most skeptical
view of maneuvers of this kind, was asked at a press conference
on April 16 whether the current Soviet "peace offensive" had
led to any change in the United States policy of "negotiating
from strength"—a policy often interpreted as one of avoiding
negotiation with the U.S.S.R. until the strength of the West
had attained a more persuasive level. His reply indicated that
recent events had brought no change in the American position:

"I think that we have always taken the view that one who is in
a stronger position is much more able to negotiate than one who
is in a weak position. We never changed our view on that. We
always have negotiated—we have been negotiating for years with
the Soviet Union. . . . The question is not whether you are willing
to negotiate, but what you can negotiate about, and whether there
is any real desire to negotiate."

As to the supposed "peace offensive," the Secretary found the
term somewhat inappropriate in view of the fact that charges
of germ warfare were still being made through all Communist
propaganda media, in disregard of repeated proposals for an
impartial investigation. The International Economic Conference, he said, had merely confirmed his original impression:

"The whole thing seems directed toward raising doubts as to
whether the defense of the West is an urgent matter, and should
be carried forward with the zeal that we all believe is necessary.
I don't think that maneuver has succeeded in any way."[34]

Here, undoubtedly, was a realistic over-all appreciation of
Communist political warfare efforts during the past few months,

[33] New York Times, April 7 and 13, 1952.
[34] Department of State Bulletin, XXVI, April 28, 1952, 666-667.

one that directed attention both to their basic insincerity and to their failure to offer any real opening for fruitful negotiation between East and West. What the Secretary's remarks failed to provide, perhaps, was an answer to those who wondered what constructive measures the United States itself might have in view for dealing with the various unsatisfactory situations the Soviet-Communist apparatus had been exploiting. How did this country propose to alleviate the real economic problems that beset its allies as a result of the rearmament program, the limitations on East-West trade, and the various impediments to trade with the dollar area? What did it intend to do about the impasse in the Far East and the numerous areas in which not only Soviet and Western but also Western and Asian aims were in conflict? Was it possible that the avoidance of contact with the Soviet Union, coupled with constant reminders about the urgency of rearmament, cost more than it gained in terms of the effect produced on world opinion? What, in short, was being done by the United States to contest the Soviet-Communist initiative on the political, economic, and psychological levels and convince the world that the United States, despite the slanders of the Communists, was still the leading force working for international peace and human progress?

To have expected from the United States and its allies a concerted political warfare effort like the germ warfare campaign or the "peace offensive" would have been to overlook both the practical limitations of democratic institutions and their ethical basis, to which the concepts of a uniform "party line" and of untruth as an instrument of policy are deeply repugnant. It is in the nature of democracy that its strength and superiority must be demonstrated concretely and in action if the lies of its detractors are to be effectively refuted. Political warfare as such can play only a marginal role, and is effective only in so far as it reflects an underlying reality. The American "Campaign of Truth," to quote a contemporary State Department publication, "brings out the psychological effect of the political, economic, military, and diplomatic measures taken by the U.S.

Government to strengthen world freedom." [35] If its purpose is to be achieved, the measures themselves must be attuned to the requirements and expectations of those they are designed to influence.

How far the operations of American foreign policy and of the American democracy during 1952 were governed by a recognition of this truth is a question which may arise obliquely in the course of this narrative, but to which a final answer must be sought elsewhere. So far as conscious efforts to influence foreign opinion are concerned, the observer is struck less by their comparatively limited scope than by what seems their incomplete adaptation to the actual world situation and the strategy of the Communist high command. A good deal of attention was being given to technical improvements such as the fitting out of a floating radio transmitter, capable of relaying the message of the Voice of America from points close to the Iron Curtain. [36] American diplomats were alert to refute Soviet misrepresentations against the United States,[37] and to seize the opportunity for prodding the Soviet Union about its flagrant delinquencies in such matters as the unfinished Big Four treaty with Austria, the failure to return or account for World War II prisoners under its control,[38] and the refusal to conclude a satisfactory settlement of its wartime lend-lease account with this country.[39] Occasionally a well-earned diplomatic rebuke was administered to one or another of the Soviet satellite govern-

[35] *Our Foreign Policy 1952* (Department of State Publication 4466, Washington, 1952), 73.
[36] *Department of State Bulletin*, XXVI, February 25, 1952, 306; March 17, 1952, 421-422.
[37] See, e.g., the "Answers to Soviet Distortions and Misrepresentations of U.S. Economy" presented by Isador Lubin to the U.N. Economic and Social Council on June 11 (*Department of State Bulletin*, XXVI, June 30, 1952, 1032-1036). Somewhat less alertness was apparently displayed by Defense Department authorities in failing to brand as Communist forgeries certain extremely bellicose passages allegedly copied from the private diary of Major Gen. Robert W. Grow, former U.S. military attaché in Moscow. Cf. Demaree Bess, "The Truth About General Grow's Moscow Diary," *Saturday Evening Post*, CCXXV, September 27, 1952, 22-23, 47-58.
[38] U.S. note, January 8, and Soviet reply, January 21, in *Department of State Bulletin*, XXVI, January 21, 1952, 90-91 and February 11, 1952, 228.
[39] U.S. note, January 7, and previous correspondence, *ibid.*, January 21, 1952, 86-89.

ments in Eastern Europe.[40] But in spite of numerous speeches by officials of the State Department's International Information Program, comparatively little interest was shown in more positive steps to rally world opinion to the side of the United States.

The somewhat negative state of mind that appeared to govern this phase of American policy in early 1952 found a better reflection in restrictive measures taken against Soviet interests and personalities. Some of these were imposed in retaliation for similar restrictions instituted by the U.S.S.R., others in response to the will of Congress. All of them, however, seemed inspired by a more or less defensive attitude which had no visible connection with America's traditional self-confidence and faith in the power of democratic ideas and institutions. This was a marked departure from the spirit of the 1940's, when the United States had striven vigorously, if unsuccessfully, to promote a free exchange of persons and ideas with the Soviet Union. As recently as 1951 Congress had declared:

"That the American people deeply regret the artificial barriers which separate them from the people of the U.S.S.R., and which keep the Soviet peoples from learning of the desire of the American people to live in friendship with all other peoples, and to work with them in advancing the ideal of human brotherhood; and . . . believe the Soviet Government could advance the cause of peace immeasurably by removing those artificial barriers, thus permitting the free exchange of information between our peoples. . . ." [41]

But these overtures had been rebuffed by the Kremlin; and American practice in the 1950's showed no inclination to act unilaterally on the views that had inspired them. On the contrary, persons suspected of radical opinions found it increasingly difficult either to enter or leave the United States to participate in international gatherings, whether official or private, Communist or non-Communist. Americans were forbidden to visit Communist-controlled countries without specific au-

[40] Cf. *ibid.*, March 31, 1952, 496-498.
[41] Senate Concurrent Resolution 11, 82nd Congress, 1st Session (*Documents on American Foreign Relations, 1951*, 548).

thorization by the State Department.[42] Travel by Soviet officials in the United States was restricted, though less stringently than that of American diplomats in the U.S.S.R.[43] In July the State Department, having been compelled to give up its long fight for the free circulation of its Russian-language magazine *Amerika* in the U.S.S.R., retaliated by requiring the Soviet Embassy in Washington to suspend the *USSR Information Bulletin,* the principal outlet for official Soviet documents and propaganda in the United States.[44]

Individually such actions, like the concurrent withdrawal of trade concessions from the U.S.S.R. and its satellites, could easily be justified in terms of diplomatic policy, internal security, or administrative convenience. Taken together, however, they could almost be viewed as the expression of an ideological "Maginot complex"—a kind of intellectual isolationism which not only shunned contact with the enemy but, perhaps even more important, refused to compete with him in important sectors of the ideological battlefront. This general impression was not greatly lessened by the prevalent and mainly theoretical talk of weakening Soviet rule in the Iron Curtain countries by "psychological warfare" aimed at assisting internal revolutionary movements. That was a separate program which its advocates had not yet related to the totality of American aims, interests, and commitments.

If America's global policy was indeed hampered by an overly narrow approach to the problems of political and ideological conflict, the defect could not be ascribed entirely to any one element in our political system. Like other aspects of foreign policy, it was a product of the complicated political and administrative processes through which the judgment of the American people as a whole was brought to bear on world affairs. "A foreign policy," as the successful candidate for the

[42] Announcement of May 1, *ibid.,* XXVI, May 12, 1952, 736. Further statements designed to clarify the State Department's policy in issuing or denying passports to American citizens appear *ibid.,* XXVI, June 9, 1952, 919-920; XXVII, July 7, 1952, 12 and 40-42; September 15, 1952, 417-418.
[43] U.S. note of March 10 and explanatory comment, *ibid.,* March 24, 1952, 451-452.
[44] *Ibid.,* XXVII, July 28, 1952, 127-132; August 18, 1952, 263-264.

presidency was to remark in the course of 1952, "is the face and voice of a whole people. . . . It expresses the character and the faith and the will of [the] nation." [45] Those who perceived a need for more decisive efforts to recapture the allegiance of world opinion were constrained to work within the general outlines of American foreign policy as it emerged from the interplay of conflicting domestic ideas, interests, and pressures. Some salient aspects of this process, as it affected America's impact on the general world crisis during 1952, must be examined more closely in the following chapter.

[45] General Dwight D. Eisenhower, quoted in *New York Times*, October 25, 1952.

CHAPTER TWO

THE HEADQUARTERS OF FREEDOM

THE CIRCUMSTANCES of early 1952 were not particularly favorable to calm analysis of America's world position and foreign policy. Public attention was focused almost entirely on the coming presidential election and the activities of the dozen or so men who aspired to carry the standard of one of the major political parties. Personalities loomed larger than principles in the speculation and maneuvering that began months in advance of the July conventions. Foreign policy, when it entered the picture at all, was more often considered in terms of its relation to individual and party fortunes than in its bearing on the national destiny as a whole.

Lacking the stimulus of any external event like the Communist aggressions in Korea, American action in world affairs proceeded meanwhile along a groove already well established by previous decisions. Despite an unsuccessful attempt by ex-President Herbert Hoover to revive the "great debate" on United States world policy which he had precipitated the winter before,[1] the year saw no new frontal attack on any major administration program and only sporadic attempts to assess the larger implications of existing programs. Congress, where such discussion usually centered, was chiefly intent on having its business wound up by the time the Republican convention assembled in Chicago early in July. The foreign policy actions which it took—or failed to take—in the time available followed a pattern which had become increasingly familiar

[1] Radio address, January 27, 1952; cf. *The United States in World Affairs, 1951*, 48-57.

through the years of Democratic government in Washington: on the one hand, grudging acceptance of most of the recommendations made by the incumbent administration; on the other, manifestations of sharp dissent from some of the principles by which the administration professed to be guided. Not infrequently this dissent was expressed in actions which tended to give American foreign policy a somewhat different direction from that intended by the President and his advisers.

That Congress and the executive should have responded in noticeably different ways to the conditions that faced the United States under the Truman administration—or, perhaps, under any administration—was natural in view of the differing backgrounds and preoccupations of the men involved. At bottom it was less a question of party or constitutional relationships than of the differing speeds with which different groups of Americans adjusted their thinking to the exigencies of America's new position. Of the two coordinate branches, it was probably the administration that showed the more consistent appreciation of world realities and of the demands they imposed upon the United States; Congress, on its side, presented what may have been a truer reflection of public attitudes in a nation which recognized that times were changing but remained unenthusiastic about many of the obligations this country had assumed.

For the turn of mind which had formerly produced the phenomenon known as "isolationism" was still a powerful influence on the American scene, greatly as some of its specific manifestations had altered. Few Americans denied that such a movement as international Communism directly menaced the safety and welfare of the United States and required vigorous counteraction on the part of this country; but there still remained a vast disinclination to combat it by such elaborate and difficult methods as those developed under the Truman administration. Those methods, closely adapted to the Soviet-Communist strategy though they claimed to be, were widely felt to be too indirect in their operation, too uncertain in their results, and, above all, too costly in terms of their impact on the national life and economy. The more closely any aspect of the national policy affected the daily existence of individual Americans, the more strenuously was it resisted by a large and influential section of opinion. Some features of that policy, notably the proposal to establish a system of universal military training, had repeatedly been rejected outright; others, like the resistance to aggression in Korea and the various programs of economic and military assistance to free nations, continued to meet with vigorous opposition in detail even though their broad principles had apparently won general acceptance.

Americans who shrank from following the administration lead in matters of global policy often showed zeal for more specialized causes which might seem peripheral to the East-West conflict but which offered a ready outlet for the sense of frustration engendered by Communist successes abroad. The exposure and restriction of Communist activities at home—obviously an important if limited aspect of the struggle with international Communism—did not in itself run counter to administration purposes except in so far as it might threaten to confuse the public mind, to handicap the legally constituted security agencies of the government, to become perverted for political ends, or to encroach on legitimate democratic freedoms.[2] Rather more difficult to reconcile with the bases of postwar foreign policy was a related tendency, noticeable both in and outside of Congress, which seemed to reject the whole concept of modern internationalism and aimed directly at restricting American participation in the United Nations and other phases of organized international life. This latter trend, which had grown conspicuously in recent years, seemed largely independent of political parties and looked like a resurgence of

[2] The principal developments in this field during 1952 centered around the activities of the Internal Security Subcommittee of the Senate Judiciary Committee. Its investigation of the affairs of the Institute of Pacific Relations (see bibliography) was followed by the suspension on December 15 of John Carter Vincent, U.S. Minister to Tangier, on grounds of doubtful loyalty and by the indictment on December 16 of Professor Owen J. Lattimore on perjury charges. (For background cf. *Department of State Bulletin*, XXVI, February 18, 1952, 274-275; March 3, 1952, 351; XXVIII, January 19, 1953, 121-123.) On the committee's later investigation of Communist infiltration of the U.N. Secretariat cf. below, pp. 378 ff.

true isolationism, fed by disappointment with the United Nations and by a fear of Communist and other "insidious alien influences" toward which the administration was accused of showing undue complacency.

To recognize that many Americans in and out of Congress differed sharply with the administration on these matters is not to claim that either their approach or the administration's was invariably right or wrong in the specific instance. Nor should it be assumed that either Congress or the administration was wholly fixed or consistent in its own attitude. Congressmen of both parties often played a constructive and forward-looking part in working out policies developed in the executive branch; the administration sometimes modified its own position substantially in deference to congressional opinion. Even when their attitudes were diametrically opposed, both sides remained conscious of their ultimate responsibility to the people and seemed anxious to discharge it in a way that would do justice to the popular will as well as to the hard facts confronting them. Both the officials of the administration and the dissenting members of Congress obviously regarded themselves as vigorous and effective champions of the national interest.

But what, in fact, was the national interest? That was the decisive question which many reflective Americans were asking themselves in 1952. Did it consist, as at least some congressmen appeared to think, in choosing those courses of action that seemed to offer this country the biggest immediate advantage at smallest cost? Was it promoted simply by the application of individualistic, "businesslike" principles in international life? Or was the national interest something broader and more elusive, which could not be rightly grasped by thinking of the United States as a self-contained unit but became clearer if this country was seen as part of a larger organism whose health depended on the harmonious functioning of all its members? Some Americans—not excluding members of Congress—believed that the interdependence of nations had reached a point where this country's interests were no longer sharply separable from those of the world community as a whole.

This latter view was clearly in the mind of one official of the State Department who suggested early in 1952 that "we can serve our national interest in these times only by a policy which transcends our national interest." American purposes, this official declared, required the collaboration of other nations; and the latter "will not work along with us solely on the basis of our national interest. The collaboration must be founded on an identity among their interests and ours. The primary responsibility for discovering and developing that identity of interests is ours because we are in the position of greatest strength." [3]

It was just here, perhaps, that the thinking of most administration officials diverged most sharply from that of most members of Congress. The administration had chosen to base American foreign policy for the most part on multilateral courses of action which were designed to promote the interests of this country in concert with those of other friendly nations. Congress, with some notable exceptions, still tended to act upon the older view which conceived this country's interests as separate from, if not actually antagonistic toward, those of the outside world. The effects of this underlying difference could be traced in virtually every act of postwar foreign policy which had involved collaboration between the executive and Congress. Whether concerned with national security, foreign aid, commercial policy, diplomatic relations, or political warfare, the original administration concept had almost invariably been subjected to modifications aimed at "correcting" the internationalist bias of the administration and securing maximum *direct* advantages for this country in return for any benefits extended to outsiders. Under the traditional view of national interest, these departures from the administration concept were obviously improvements, even if they entailed some loss of flexibility and caused inconvenience abroad. How far they really advanced the interests of the United States depended

[3] C. B. Marshall, in *The National Interest: Alone or With Others?* (*Annals of the American Academy of Political and Social Science*, CCLXXXII, July 1952), 89.

on how far their underlying principle remained valid under the conditions of today's interdependent world.

1. Principles and Programs

For thoughtful observers, questions of this kind loomed especially large during the 1952 session of Congress because there were indications that the nature of America's future participation in international life might provide the main issue of the forthcoming presidential campaign. Whether or not President Truman became a candidate for reelection—a possibility that remained open until his negative decision was announced at the end of March—it was practically a foregone conclusion that the Democratic party would uphold the foreign policy record of his administration and invite the country to persevere in the main lines of action already initiated. On the Republican side, the prospects were less definite. Although many features of the existing foreign policy had been initiated with bipartisan support, a segment of Republican opinion now professed to favor a rather more drastic limitation of this country's international commitments. The leading early contender for the Republican nomination, Senator Robert A. Taft of Ohio, plainly shared this outlook and insisted, in particular, that "peacetime" expenditures for national defense and foreign aid must be considerably reduced. That such views would be officially embraced by the Republican organization remained a possibility even after General of the Army Dwight D. Eisenhower, the head of the North Atlantic Treaty Organization's defense forces in Europe, emerged as the favored candidate of the more "internationalist" wing of the Republican party and thus provided an alternative to major revision of the existing policy.

Even without the stimulus of the coming campaign, the second session of the Eighty-second Congress would have found many legislators unusually preoccupied with the costs, both material and human, of the policy the nation had been pursuing during the past few years. On one side, they were confronted with another in a long, almost unbroken series of unbalanced national budgets; on the other, they saw a world still racked by insecurity and instability after more than five years of large-scale foreign assistance, nearly two years of large-scale rearmament at home, and over 100,000 casualties in Korea. Who could wonder that the question "Can we afford our present foreign policy?" was raised more insistently than ever before? It was not surprising that Congress showed an unusual determination to reduce the administration's estimates for new expenditure and to insist that every dollar spent must promote the direct advantage of the United States, irrespective of the effect on allied and friendly nations. As total American expenditures for postwar foreign aid crept toward the $35 billion mark, Congress was hardly to be blamed for wanting to hasten the day when such subsidies could be discontinued. More noteworthy was its lukewarm interest in measures designed to provide increased trade opportunities for foreign countries as an alternative to American grants and loans. This comparative indifference to the long-range problems of commercial policy was the most conspicuous of several indications that Congress for the most part still thought in terms of a self-contained America whose interests were essentially distinct from those of the outside world.

The central influence on the development of American foreign policy during the first half of 1952 was, then, a continuing battle between the administration and Congress in which the national legislature resisted the administration's views on fiscal and other matters with more than ordinary determination and success. The struggle, of course, was not one of pure principle on either side. In an election year, political factors were bound to play an important role, and the virtual breakdown of bipartisan cooperation had relieved the Republican opposition of any obligation to support policies in which it did not fully believe. Opposition to the administration program, however, was by no means confined to Republicans. The conflict is not fully explained either by the lapse of bipartisanship or by the sometimes not very effective tactics of the administration. The truth is that a profound lack of confidence between the two branches exaggerated the differences arising from their divergent evaluation of foreign problems.

Several incidents which occurred early in 1952 provided illustrations of the deep distrust with which many in Congress regarded the operations of the executive, and of their determination to limit the field of executive action as far as possible. Winston Churchill, the new British Prime Minister, crossed the Atlantic in company with Foreign Secretary Anthony Eden at the beginning of 1952 on an official visit which included conferences at the White House and ended with an address to a special session of Congress on January 17. Various Anglo-American problems were exhaustively discussed, and agreements were announced on several matters pertaining to arms standardization, command problems in the North Atlantic Treaty Organization, and the allocation of scarce materials. The tone of the proceedings indicated a distinct improvement in Anglo-American relations on the executive level.[4]

In the legislative bodies of the two countries, however, this rapprochement was viewed with suspicion. In London, a section of the House of Commons feared that the Prime Minister had been too acquiescent in his judgment on American policies in the Far East.[5] In Washington, a majority in the House of Representatives feared, or professed to fear, that the President had entered into secret undertakings which might require the dispatch of additional American forces abroad or involve them "in armed conflict on foreign soil"—perhaps in the strife-torn Suez Canal Zone, where the Prime Minister had suggested that the presence of "token forces" from other allied powers would have a helpful moral effect. Despite assurances in the negative from the State Department and an adverse recommendation from its own Foreign Affairs Committee, the House insisted

[4] See especially the joint communiqués (January 9 and 18) and Churchill's address to Congress (January 17) in *Department of State Bulletin*, XXVI, January 21, 1952, 83-84 and January 28, 1952, 115-120.
[5] A motion of censure criticizing Churchill's "failure to give adequate expression" to British policy during his American visit was defeated on February 26 by a vote of 318-285.

on voicing a formal demand for "full and complete information" on any "agreements, commitments or understandings"
which might have been reached.[6] Such a resolution, though it
amounted to a vote of no confidence in the President and the
Secretary of State, was without legal effect. Nevertheless its
passage, and the monosyllabic "No" with which the President
confirmed the absence of secret commitments, were significant
reflections of the state of mind in which the two coordinate
branches of government were going about their responsibilities.

Somewhat similar in inspiration, but considerably more far-
reaching in its implications, was the action of the Senate in
formally repudiating the Yalta agreement on the Far East
which President Roosevelt had concluded with Messrs. Churchill and Stalin in February 1945. For practical purposes that
agreement had long been considered a dead letter. The new
Treaty of Peace with Japan, concluded in 1951 without the
participation of the U.S.S.R., had been deliberately drawn in
such a way as to ignore the Soviet claim to the various territories (Southern Sakhalin, the Kuriles, and adjacent islands)
which Soviet forces had occupied at the close of the war in
conformity with the Yalta provisions. Such an omission could
only mean that the United States no longer considered itself
bound by the Yalta understanding, which, moreover, had never
received Senate approval and in recent years had figured chiefly
as a political war cry and an unsavory reminder of one of the
least successful passages in American diplomatic history. John
Foster Dulles, the principal architect of the Japanese treaty,
described it to the Senate Foreign Relations Committee as "the
first formal act which the United States will have taken which
involves a clear abandonment of Yalta . . . [and] recognizes
our total freedom from any obligations that stem from Yalta."[7]

But Mr. Dulles was not a permanent member of the ad-

[6] House Resolution 514, 82nd Congress, adopted February 20, 1952 by a vote
of 189-143.
[7] *Japanese Peace Treaty and Other Treaties Relating to Security in the Pacific:
Hearings*, Senate Foreign Relations Committee, 82nd Congress, 2nd Session
(Washington, 1952), 56-57. For background cf. *The United States in World
Affairs, 1951*, 186-188.

ministration, and this assurance was not enough for those to
whom the very name of Yalta had become identified with
"softness" toward Communism. Before recommending approval of the treaty by the Senate, the Foreign Relations Committee agreed on an interpretive statement which made the
rebuke to Russia (and incidentally to the administration) explicit. It not only disallowed any rights the Soviet Union might
claim under the Japanese treaty but also declared that nothing
in the treaty or in the Senate's approval of its terms implied
recognition by the United States of the "provisions in favor of
the Soviet Union contained in the so-called Yalta agreement
regarding Japan of February 11, 1945." [8] This language was
unopposed by the administration and was included in the resolution by which the Senate gave its advice and consent to ratification on March 14. The affirmative vote of 66 to 10 could not
alter the actual situation in the Pacific, but might conceivably
strengthen the hand of the United States in diplomatic negotiations at some future date. Meanwhile it enabled the Senate to
give emphatic expression to its feelings about the Yalta agreement and, more generally, about the whole concept of diplomatic concessions to Communist governments. The mood that
prompted the repudiation of Yalta would also go far to determine the American position on more current issues.

A third incident, different in detail but not dissimilar in its
underlying significance, arose in connection with the President's nomination of General Mark W. Clark to be the first
American Ambassador to the Vatican. Although the anti-Communist outlook of the Holy See was well known, the proposal
to designate a permanent American diplomatic representative
aroused opposition even in strongly anti-Communist circles on
the ground that it ran counter to the American principle of "the
separation of church and state." In the face of indications that
it would fail to gain the approval of the Senate Foreign Relations Committee, the nomination was withdrawn in the course

[8] Senate Executive Report 2, 82nd Congress, 2nd Session, February 14, 1952
(Washington, 1952), 8-9. For text of the Senate declaration see *Documents on
American Foreign Relations, 1952*, No. 25 (b).

of January; yet the incident continued to agitate congressional circles. When the House of Representatives approved the State Department Appropriation Act on April 4, it included a provision designed to prevent the President from making a recess appointment to the Vatican post by prohibiting the use of State Department funds to support any new diplomatic mission until its chief had been confirmed by the Senate. The vote was 159-82.[9]

But expressions of this kind were more or less incidental to the main function of Congress in the sphere of foreign relations. That function was to provide such legislative authority and such sums of money as might be necessary to achieve the broad international purposes of the United States in what all agreed would be a crucial year—perhaps a turning point—in the long struggle with Communist totalitarianism. The general aim and outlook, as they appeared to the administration, had been freshly stated by President Truman on January 9 in his State of the Union message:

"The United States and the whole free world are passing through a period of grave danger. . . . Faced with a terrible threat of aggression, our Nation has embarked upon a great effort to help establish the kind of world in which peace shall be secure. Peace is our goal—not peace at any price, but a peace based on freedom and justice. We are now in the midst of our effort to reach that goal. . . . If we falter, we can lose all the gains that we have made. If we drive ahead with courage and vigor and determination, we can by the end of 1952 be in a position of much greater security. The way will be dangerous for years ahead, but if we put forth our best efforts this year—and next year—we can be 'over the hump' in our effort to build strong defenses." [10]

[9] The provision was later dropped at the instance of the Senate—not because the prevailing attitude had changed but because it was felt that "religious issues should not be interjected into an appropriation bill." See *Congressional Record,* Daily Edition, June 26, 1952, 8243. Meanwhile the move to restrict the powers of the executive in the field of foreign relations had culminated in the introduction of a Senate resolution (S.J. Res. 122, 82nd Congress, 2nd Session, in *Department of State Bulletin,* XXVI, June 16, 1952, 953) designed to limit the use of executive agreements except as authorized by Congress. The resolution did not come to the floor during the 1952 session.
[10] *Documents on American Foreign Relations, 1952,* No. 1.

Building defenses for peace, the President reminded his hearers, was a many-sided undertaking that could not be completed overnight. The Soviet Union, too, was still expanding its military production and increasing its "already excessive" military power. It was still producing more war planes than the free nations; recently it had "set off two more atomic explosions." Faced with this menace, said the President, the free nations "may have to maintain for years the larger military forces needed to deter aggression"; but at the same time they must work toward "political solidarity and economic progress among the free countries in all parts of the world." If an adequate level of defensive armaments was to be attained, American industry would have to double its output of military items during 1952 and maintain a peak rate of military production until sometime in 1954. Abroad, the United States "must continue to strengthen the forces of freedom throughout the world"—through military and economic aid in Europe and Asia, through the Point Four program, and through such activities as the Voice of America, which bore America's message of hope and truth even to the oppressed peoples behind the Iron Curtain.

How would this program for building strength at home and abroad affect America's national life in the years just ahead? Some of the answers were indicated more precisely in the Budget Message which the President sent to Congress a few days later, setting forth the estimated receipts and expenditures of the Federal Government during the fiscal year July 1, 1952-June 30, 1953.[11] The number of men and women actually serving in the Armed Forces would not, it appeared, be greatly increased: as the President had explained in his earlier message, we were not attempting to build "an active force adequate to carry on a full scale war" but were "putting ourselves in a position to mobilize very rapidly if we have to." The present active strength of the armed services was just short of 3,500,-000; during the next eighteen months it was scheduled to increase by only 200,000, to a total of 3,700,000. Obviously,

[11] Excerpts *ibid.*, No. 2.

however, a much greater expansion would be required in the event of war, and meanwhile it seemed likely that "we shall have to maintain relatively large military forces for a long time to come." To provide a broader basis for mobilization of American manpower in any required degree, it was proposed to expand and reorganize the reserve components of the Armed Forces and—if Congress provided the necessary statutory authority—to institute promptly a system of Universal Military Training which would gradually be expanded until it provided six months of military training for every able-bodied young man.

A more spectacular feature of the program was the mobilization of resources and skills which was considered necessary to sustain the build-up of our own and allied armed forces. For the leaders of the free nations relied ultimately on two factors in their contest with the Soviet world: the superior moral strength and resiliency of democratic societies, and the industrial and technical superiority which, it was hoped, would overbalance the advantage in manpower possessed by the U.S.S.R. and its allies. Thus the main emphasis of the defense program was placed on the development and large-scale production of the most modern weapons and equipment required for both atomic and conventional warfare. This was the undertaking which, ever since the Korean outbreak, had been transforming the face of America as more and more of the nation's expanding productive capacity was devoted to turning out airplanes, bombs, tanks, ships, guns, ammunition, and the hundreds of other items required by men who were facing the Soviet military threat at close quarters.

This, too, was the factor responsible for the steadily increasing annual expenditure of the Federal Government and the heavy tax burden sustained by the American people. Financial outlays of the United States Government were scheduled to attain a peacetime record of $85.4 billion dollars in the fiscal year 1953 and to remain at comparable levels for at least one and possibly two years longer.

"More than three-fourths of the total expenditures included in this budget," the President pointed out, "are for major national security programs—military services, international security and foreign relations, the development of atomic energy, the promotion of defense production and economic stabilization, civil defense, and merchant marine activities. Major national security programs not only dominate this budget but also account for practically all of the increase in total budget expenditures since the attack on Korea."

Other United States Government programs, the President's figures showed, were actually costing fewer dollars than before Korea, when total budget expenditures had amounted to only $40.1 billion. The more than twofold increase since that time was directly traceable to increased expenditures on the defense establishment (from $12.3 billion in 1950 to an estimated $51.2 billion in 1953), foreign aid (from $4.6 billion in 1950 to $10.5 billion in 1953), and related security programs of smaller financial scope. During this same period receipts from taxes and other sources had almost doubled; but there remained a considerable gap between receipts and expenditures, which was expected to widen to $14.4 billion in the next fiscal year.

The President did not attempt to deny that this program represented a heavy burden for the American taxpayer, whether or not Congress reversed its stand of the year before and granted an additional $5 billion in tax revenue in order to put the defense effort more nearly on a pay-as-we-go basis. Such consolation as there was would have to be found in the knowledge that British and French taxpayers, among others, were sustaining even heavier burdens; that even though $85 billion was about a fourth of America's gross national product, output had been expanding rapidly enough to ensure an almost uninterrupted supply of consumers' goods of all kinds; that it was hoped to reduce the level of Federal expenditures, world conditions permitting, after the fiscal year 1954, when most of the currently planned military expansion would have been completed; and that the objective being sought was, after all, nothing less than the survival of the United States as a free nation. "In the current world crisis," said the President, "the price of peace is preparedness. In terms of the sacrifices which this involves, it is a heavy price, but when freedom is at stake, it is a price which all of us will gladly pay."

Although no member of Congress would have questioned this declaration, many of them were more strongly impressed by the President's figures than by the exhortations that accompanied them. Preparedness, some congressmen believed, might perhaps be sought along somewhat different lines and on a different scale from those envisaged in the presidential blueprint. For the next five and one-half months, Senators and Representatives were to labor almost unceasingly to adapt the President's conception to their own views concerning the national interest and the ways of serving it.

2. The Price of Preparedness

Although the "major national security programs" outlined by the President included various activities outside the military field, the largest item by far was the proposed appropriation of $51.2 billion to expand and strengthen the Armed Forces of the United States. Accompanying this estimate was a request for an additional $52.4 billion in obligational authority to permit a beginning on other projects for which specific appropriations would be requested in subsequent years. These estimates, the President explained, reflected some increases in the level of preparedness envisaged a year earlier:

"These new goals contemplate an Air Force of 143 wings, an Army of twenty-one divisions, a Navy with 408 major combatant vessels in the active fleet and sixteen large carrier air groups, a Marine Corps of three divisions and essential supporting elements for all these services. . . . More than half of the expenditures for major procurement in the fiscal year 1953 will be for aircraft. . . ."

Other projects included in the Defense Department program were the construction of the giant aircraft carrier *Forrestal*, commencement of a second 60,000-ton carrier, construction of two atomic-powered submarines, and the expenditure of some

$3.5 billion on "military construction" projects, chiefly air bases, in the United States and abroad.

What was the general philosophy behind this program, and how did it relate to the broad position of the United States in world affairs? In what degree, if at all, had it been influenced by one or another of the prevailing schools of thought on questions of world politics and strategy? In a field where technical considerations were often decisive and where secrecy was all-important, it was difficult to generalize about the inspiration and implications of the various lines of action recommended by the Defense Department. Yet some attempt in this direction was unavoidable for anyone who sought to understand the course of American world relations in the middle of the twentieth century.

It required no particular insight to perceive that American military policy through the postwar years had not relied on any single, clearly thought out concept. On the contrary, it had seemed to oscillate between two distinct concepts—both based on the idea of a global deployment of American military power aimed at discouraging (or punishing) the aggressive tendencies of the U.S.S.R., but radically different in other respects. According to one theory, the principal guarantee of American security lay in this country's ability to strike promptly against an aggressor state and overwhelm its war-making capacity by the use of strategic air power and atomic bombs. This view, which emphasized the importance of direct, vigorous, and unilateral action by the United States in the event of aggression, commended itself to an influential school of military thought and, among civilians, proved especially congenial to those whose outlook had been shaped by the philosophy of isolationism. Its application, however, was limited by the influence of an alternative concept which had perhaps played an even larger part in the development of America's postwar policy. This, broadly speaking, was the concept which underlay the containment policy, the North Atlantic Treaty, and the resistance to aggression in Korea. Its object, too, was to protect American (and world) security against potential or actual aggression—not, however, by full-scale action against the aggressor's heart, but by localized defensive efforts in the areas actually threatened with aggressive action. Where one school hoped to forestall Soviet aggression by the threat of total war with the United States, the second hoped to accomplish the same end by strengthening the local forces which were presumed to share the same interest.

While the defense organization envisaged by the North Atlantic Treaty had been taking shape through 1950 and 1951, these two concepts had remained somewhat imperfectly reconciled on the military and diplomatic levels as well as in the public mind. On one hand, the United States had assumed a variety of new commitments involving direct participation in the resistance to Soviet-Communist aggression in both Europe and the Far East. On the other, it appeared to be leaning increasingly toward reliance on its own specialty, the long-range application of strategic air power directed against the Soviet Union more or less independently of what happened in the Soviet borderlands. This emphasis, which became strongly marked after the aggression in Korea, was dictated partly by the necessity of maintaining a strong air arm to supplement the still inadequate protective forces being built up in Europe, partly by concern over the unexpectedly rapid progress of the U.S.S.R.'s own atomic program. It was also powerfully furthered by pressure from the Air Force itself and from political circles which had become increasingly dissatisfied with the results achieved by the alternative policy.

Thus, as early as the spring of 1951, the development of a ninety-five-group Air Force had become the acknowledged aim of an administration which only eighteen months earlier had refused to sanction an increase beyond forty-eight groups. Before the end of 1951 this goal had been raised by 50 percent, to 143 air groups or wings. While Air Force circles talked of an ultimate goal of 188 wings, the target date for the 143-wing program was fixed at July 1, 1955—a year later than the date recommended by the Joint Chiefs of Staff. For the fiscal year 1952–53, the sum of $22.6 billion was requested as the first installment of what was intended to be a three-year program of further growth. Meanwhile, planned expenditure on the Army and Navy in the new budget had been cut back from the level of the previous year, although it still remained much higher than pre-Korean levels. To all appearances the United States had abandoned the principle of "balanced" forces and was entrusting primary responsibility for its security to the youngest of the three services. Closely related to this growing reliance on air power was the expanded work of research and development on which the Atomic Energy Commission had been engaged since the presidential instruction of January 20, 1950 "to continue its work on all forms of atomic weapons, including the so-called hydrogen or super-bomb." Estimates for the Atomic Energy Commission in fiscal 1953 totaled $1.78 billion for immediate expenditure and were presently revised to include a $3.19 billion expansion program.

Without denying the importance of air power in modern war, some voices nevertheless had warned against undue reliance on atomic weapons and strategic bombardment. Apart from certain persistent ethical doubts, critics of the prevailing trend had noted that the deterrent effect of our atomic bomb stockpile on a potential aggressor would tend to diminish as the U.S.S.R. approached atomic parity with this country or achieved sufficient strength to carry out a damaging surprise attack. Even from the standpoint of economy, the wisdom of undue concentration on air power was questioned in view of the fact that aircraft not only were exceedingly expensive to build but became obsolete much more rapidly than naval and ground force equipment. Considerable doubt was expressed about the feasibility of attaining the present Air Force goals within the next several years unless production could be speeded up by still larger allocations of government funds. Already there had been complaints over failures to meet delivery schedules for aircraft and other equipment consigned to United States forces as well as to allied nations participating in the Mutual Security Program.

General Omar N. Bradley, the Chairman of the Joint Chiefs

of Staff, added his own words of caution in a speech at Pasadena on March 20, 1952:

"Because we Americans prefer quick and easy solutions to difficult problems, we are very vulnerable to any theory of defense which catches our imagination. It's the will-o'-the wisp call of air and sea power projected from this hemisphere, which is a military concept popularly known as the 'Gibraltar theory.' This concept unbalances our forces by placing reliance mainly on air power and sea power. It contemplates the withdrawal of our ground forces from the continent of Europe to our own North American 'Gibraltar.' . . .

"Air power is the mighty weapon of the 20th Century. Coupled with the atomic bomb it is the most violent weapon of retaliation and attack that the world has known. At the moment, our allies in the North Atlantic Treaty Organization have largely entrusted their chances for a continued peace to this American-owned deterrent to aggression. But *they* know, and *we* know, that air power and the atomic bomb are not enough. . . . In the event of war, Americans will have to fight on the ground 3,000 miles from home if we are to provide an ultimate protection to New York, St. Louis and Pasadena." [12]

Though there were soldiers as well as civilians who disagreed with this opinion, it was certainly true that while the emphasis within the American military program had been shifting toward heavier concentration on air power and atomic weapons, direct American military obligations overseas had remained in effect and several new ones had been assumed. In addition to the 250,000 men in Korea, six divisions of American troops were now deployed in Europe as an integral part of the NATO defense organization. Greece and Turkey, largely on American insistence, had recently been brought within the defensive scope of the Atlantic Pact, and it was anticipated that some similar commitment would soon have to be undertaken toward Western Germany in connection with its membership in the proposed European Defense Community. In the Middle East, the United States had lately joined with other powers in proposing a regional defense organization which, if and when accepted by the Arab nations, would assume similar

[12] *Vital Speeches of the Day,* XVIII, May 1, 1952, 446.

responsibilities in another area exposed to possible Soviet aggression. In the Pacific, new reciprocal engagements had been entered into with Japan, Australia, New Zealand, and the Philippines. In the United Nations and in the Organization of American States, the United States had been pressing for the development of collective military planning which would enable those organizations to face up more successfully to any new aggression on the Korean pattern. The purpose of all these arrangements was a broader distribution of the responsibility for resisting Soviet-Communist aggression; but their success would clearly require the direct support, and in most cases the active participation, of the United States.

There was, perhaps, no real inconsistency in promoting broad-scale collective defense efforts with one hand while laboring with the other to build up overwhelming atomic and air superiority for the United States. Yet it was difficult to escape the impression that in practice the two policies were still inadequately coordinated. Even within the North Atlantic Treaty Organization, whose collective defense efforts had thus far been unequivocally supported by the American government, there was lingering uncertainty about this country's long-term intentions. Was the new emphasis on air power directed merely to more effectual fulfillment of America's responsibilities within NATO, or did some of its proponents look on it rather as an eventual substitute for NATO? The eagerness with which the Air Force was establishing new facilities in French Morocco, Greenland, and the Azores and negotiating for additional bomber bases in Spain could be taken, perhaps incorrectly, as a sign of comparative indifference toward the fate of West-Central Europe. On the other side of the world, no complete reconciliation had yet been worked out between the policy of multilateral defense in Korea through the United Nations and the policy of protecting Formosa against capture by the Chinese Communists as a unilateral American responsibility, dictated by strategic considerations of a purely national character.

In short, American military policy as developed since the

Korean aggression carried with it political and psychological implications which might have nothing to do with its strategic and technical merits but which, under the circumstances, inevitably complicated the pursuit of other policy objectives. This was not simply because the State Department and other civilian agencies were largely occupied in trying to carry out the requirements of the military. More fundamentally it was because the concentration on air power, overseas bases, and atomic weapons stood out so prominently that for the superficial observer American policy had begun to take on a militant and even "aggressive" appearance that was entirely out of harmony with the existing temper of world opinion and with the real aims of the United States. It was undoubtedly true, as the President and others repeatedly stressed, that this formidable array of weapons was being built up in order to deter aggression, not to commit it. Nevertheless, long-range aircraft and atomic bombs were offensive weapons *par excellence*. Individual Americans had occasionally suggested that they should actually be employed offensively (or "preventively") without waiting for the Soviet Union to attack first. As the national strength increased, it was conceivable that other Americans might come to feel the same way. Meanwhile it was an unfortunate fact that the more American preparedness advanced, the greater became the superficial resemblances to the stock picture of an "aggressive" America, bent on unleashing a third world war and achieving world domination, which Soviet propaganda had been laboring for years to build up.

We do not know what the Soviet leaders themselves may have thought about America's decision to concentrate primarily on weapons which could, theoretically, be used against the U.S.S.R. in offensive as easily as in defensive warfare. But we are in no uncertainty about the reaction in non-Communist parts of the world, where fear of war tended to outweigh even the fear of Soviet imperialism. Neutral statesmen like Prime Minister Nehru of India made no attempt to hide their concern over the trend of American military policy. Even in Western Europe, the sense of strategic dependence on the United States

was joined with lively distress over the form American protection was taking. Apart from their dread of anything that
could bring war closer, non-Communist Europeans had special
reasons to dislike the new emphasis on air and atomic operations. American atomic attacks launched from air bases in
Britain or on the Continent might expose them to direct retaliation by the U.S.S.R. From their point of view, this would be
no better than immediate submersion by the Soviet Army—
which might occur anyway unless the United States gave all
necessary support to their defense efforts on the Continent itself. Such worries helped to explain the number of otherwise
rational Europeans who accepted the Soviet "peace" propaganda at face value, as well as the larger number who remained
dubious of American intentions and somewhat cool toward the
large numbers of American personnel stationed in their countries.

The effect of congressional action on the national defense
program was not to curtail but rather to accentuate from year
to year this leaning toward the unilateral use of air power as
the main pillar of national and world security. In 1948 and
1949, Congress had insisted on approving considerably larger
Air Force estimates than the administration had thought justified. By 1952 this particular difference of opinion had largely
disappeared. Congress, however, continued to display its partiality for the Air Force, even while vigorously criticizing the
waste and inefficiency that were being brought to light in related phases of the mobilization program such as aircraft
procurement and especially the construction of overseas bases.
The leniency with which it treated the Air Force budget contrasted sharply with its handling of other defense matters that
were politically more delicate.

However deep its concern with "preparedness," the record
of the 1952 session suggested that Congress as a whole was
still thinking almost exclusively in terms of a war that the
United States would win promptly with atomic weapons delivered by land-based and carrier-based bombing planes. Comparatively little was done about preparing the nation for any

other kind of war, or even for the defensive phases of an
atomic war. Although Selective Service remained in effect, Universal Military Training was buried for another year on March
4 when the House of Representatives voted 236-162 to recommit a training bill recommended by its Armed Services Committee. The problem of protecting the civilian population
against enemy atomic attacks was treated with conspicuous indifference. A year earlier, the President's request for funds for
civil defense had been cut by 86 percent; in 1952 the cut was
93 percent, from $600 million to $43 million. On the defense
mobilization front, controls against inflation were weakened
and the budget of the Economic Stabilization Agency was reduced from $103 million to $60 million—"another case," said
the President, "of reckless slashing without regard to the consequences to our people or to defense." [13]

But Congress was more amenable when it came to supporting that side of the defense program that had to do with preparedness for the active waging of atomic war. Here, too, administration estimates—which Defense Secretary Robert A.
Lovett had described initially as "the very thin edge of an acceptable calculated risk"—were subjected to considerable prun-
ing. Some features were eliminated or drastically changed, but
the broad characteristics of the administration plan were not
materially altered. After the administration request for the Department of Defense had been scaled down from $51.2 billion
to $46.6 billion, there still remained $21.1 billion for the Air
Force, $12.8 billion for the Navy, and $12.2 billion for the
Army. These sums, together with an additional $4 billion left
over from previous appropriations and still available because
of delays in placing and executing defense contracts,[14] would
enable the services to go ahead with all major programs.

[13] Supplemental Appropriation Act, 1953 (Public Law 547, 82nd Congress, approved July 15, 1952), and presidential statement printed in New York Times,
July 16, 1952.
[14] Primarily as a result of these delays, the fiscal year 1952 ended on June 30
with a deficit of only $4 billion instead of the $8.2 billion forecast in the
President's budget message. Estimates of expenditure during fiscal 1952–53 were
likewise revised downward as a result of delayed procurement and other factors.
For details cf. Department of State Bulletin, XXVIII, January 19, 1953, 96-97.

The same was true of the appropriations for the Atomic Energy Commission, which eventually reached a total of $4.1 billion for fiscal 1953. This figure included a special grant of $2.9 billion to cover the initial costs of a five-year atomic expansion program that was laid before Congress during the spring. Finally, another $2.89 billion was made available to the Defense Department for the construction of airfields, posts, camps, and other facilities at home and abroad. Again the lion's share ($1.2 billion) was awarded to the Air Force, the bulk of it for projects outside the United States.

In so far as the object of national military expenditure was to promote the general security of the free world, there was no basic distinction between these appropriations and the separate allocation of $7.9 billion which Congress was asked to provide for the Mutual Security Program of military and economic aid to other free nations. One set of funds would be used to build up the military strength of the United States itself; the other would be devoted to strengthening the defenses and, to a much smaller extent, the general stability of countries whose situation was deemed important to American security. Though large in themselves, the sums requested for these purposes were hardly to be compared with the tremendous appropriations voted for the direct defense build-up. But, just because the requirements of "national" security were so great, Congress was even less inclined than usual to accept the administration estimates of what was necessary for the "mutual" security of the United States and its allies.

By far the largest part of the Mutual Security estimates laid before Congress—almost $5.96 billion out of the total of $7.90 billion—was intended to support the rearmament effort of the NATO countries in Western Europe, partly by direct military aid in the form of arms and equipment ($4.15 billion) and partly by economic aid or "defense support" geared directly to defense needs ($1.82 billion). The balance of the program envisaged smaller allotments of military aid and economic and technical assistance in Asia and the Pacific ($1,019 million), the Near East and Africa ($802 million), and the American

Republics ($84 million), plus about $30 million for miscellaneous economic assistance through United Nations and other channels. In all areas of the globe, the military aspect of the program predominated. Military aid constituted roughly 60 percent of the entire program for Asia and the Pacific, 70 percent for Europe, and 75 percent for the Near East, Africa, and the American Republics. (See Table 1.)

That Congress approved this general emphasis was evidenced by the fact that it ultimately appropriated 78 percent of the

TABLE 1

THE MUTUAL SECURITY PROGRAM, FISCAL YEAR 1953

(*In millions of dollars*)

	Requested	Authorized	Appropriated
Europe (total)	5,964.20	4,698.05	4,410.65
Military	4,145.00	3,415.61	3,128.22
Defense Support	1,819.20	1,282.43	1,282.43
Near East and Africa (total)	802.37	741.43	680.23
Military	606.37	560.32	499.12
Economic and Technical	196.00	181.11	181.11
Asia and the Pacific (total)	1,019.23	931.22	811.38
Military	611.23	564.81	540.81
Economic and Technical	408.00	366.41	270.57
American Republics (total)	84.40	78.01	72.01
Military	62.40	57.69	51.69
Technical	22.00	20.33	20.33
Miscellaneous Economic (total)	53.80	44.02	27.67
Multilateral Technical Cooperation....	17.00	15.71	9.17
European Migration	10.00	9.24	9.24
Ocean Freight—Relief Packages	2.80	2.59	2.59
U.N. International Children's Emergency Fund	24.00	16.48	6.67
Combined Total	7,924.00	6,492.73	6,001.95

Source: Column 1, *Mutual Security Act Extension: Selected Tables* (Committee print, House Foreign Affairs Committee, 82nd Congress, 2nd Session, Washington, May 15, 1952), 2-4; Column 2, Mutual Security Act of 1952 (Public Law 400, approved June 20, 1952); Column 3, Supplemental Appropriation Act, 1953 (Public Law 547, approved July 15, 1952).

Note: Because of rounding, columns do not necessarily add to totals shown.

funds requested for military assistance and only 71 percent of those asked for economic aid—$4.22 billion of military and $1.78 billion of economic assistance, for a total of just over $6 billion in new money. (Also available for expenditure in the new fiscal year was about $9 billion in earlier appropriations which had been committed but not yet expended.) But the detailed allocation of the new funds differed in important respects from the administration's recommendations. In addition to cutting down the size of the entire program and strengthening its military emphasis, Congress expressed its doubts about the general orientation of American policy by cutting most heavily into just those parts of the program which the administration considered most vital to American security interests. These were the sections aimed at promoting the defense build-up of the North Atlantic Treaty Organization in Western Europe.

In open disregard of the administration's advice, the total Mutual Security allocation for Europe was reduced by more than one-fourth, from $5.96 billion to $4.41 billion—some 26 percent less than the $5.94 billion appropriated the year before. Of the saving of $1.5 billion as compared with the President's estimates, two-thirds was taken from the military side of the ledger and one-third from the "defense support" or economic aid funds which were intended, as the President had explained, "to enable other countries to sustain and increase their military efforts, where that type of support produces greater returns in military strength than would an equal amount of direct military aid." [15] The contention that raw materials, commodities, machinery and the like were as necessary as tanks and guns if Europe was to make full use of its defensive potentialities found Congress hardly more receptive than it had been in 1951,

---

[15] Message of the President on the Mutual Security Program, March 6, in *Documents on American Foreign Relations, 1952*, No. 3 (a). As in the legislation for fiscal 1952, 10 percent of the $3,128 million appropriated for European military aid could be used in the President's discretion to supplement the $1,282 million provided for defense support. For the text of the Mutual Security Act, cf. *Documents on American Foreign Relations, 1952*, No. 3 (b).

the first year of post-Marshall Plan aid to Europe. But for a cautionary statement from General Eisenhower,[16] the reduction in both military and defense support aid for Europe might have been even greater. As it was, the President declared in signing the appropriation bill in mid-July:

"By virtue of the cuts made by the Congress in the military equipment program and in defense support, the European forces will have less equipment and consequently less fire power and less air cover. As a result, our own forces in Europe become both more vulnerable and less effective in the defense tasks they might be called on to perform. I think the American people should clearly understand that every dollar which has been cut from the amount requested represents a loss of much more than a dollar's worth of strength for the free world." [17]

Various other features of the Mutual Security legislation for 1953 will require consideration at later stages of this narrative. Enough has been said here to indicate that as a phase of American military policy it failed to command the same measure of congressional assent as did, for example, the expansion of the United States Air Force and the atomic energy program. In the eyes of Congress, Mutual Security evidently ranked somewhere between the programs for direct enhancement of the national striking power, which deserved general support, and those, like universal military training and civil defense, that aimed at a more rounded development of American defense potential but were wholly unacceptable under the conditions of 1952. The significance of the Mutual Security Program, however, was not confined to the sphere of defense. Some attention must now be devoted to its other aspect as one of the important factors in America's relation to the world economy.

[16] Replying on May 5 to a cable from Senator Tom Connally, General Eisenhower declared that "in terms of impact on our military programs, an aggregate reduction of the order of a billion dollars would be heavily and seriously felt. Any cut materially greater than this would create such difficulties that a drastic revision of the whole program might well be indicated. . . ." (*Department of State Bulletin*, XXVI, May 26, 1952, 840.)
[17] Statement of July 15, *ibid.*, XXVII, August 4, 1952, 200.

3. The Economic Dilemma

If the foreign aid program was one of the main elements in the system of world security that the United States was endeavoring to build up, it played what may have been an even more vital role in the economic relations between this and other nations of the non-Communist world. In the seven years since World War II, the United States had already extended some $28 billion in economic and military assistance to Western Europe and its dependencies and approximately $10 billion in aid to other areas; the total postwar foreign aid bill as of mid-1952 (deducting repayments of about $3 billion) stood at just over $35 billion, including $9.6 billion in reimbursable credits and $25.4 billion in outright grants or gifts (see Table 2). These figures, aggregating rather less than 2 percent of the gross national product of the United States during the same period, represented the value of goods and services which this country had made available to other countries in the interest of recovery and security abroad. The advantages of this transaction for the foreign beneficiaries were obvious; but there had been advantages for the United States as well. Notwithstanding the economically critical situation of much of the outside world, American foreign trade and general prosperity during these years had stood at record levels. Without the help of the government-financed foreign aid program, it was difficult to see how American farmers and manufacturers could have placed their products on such an abundant scale in the hands of people abroad who needed them but had been deprived by war and other factors of the normal means of paying for them.

Admittedly, however, this use of governmental funds to supplement the dollars earned by foreign countries through their own efforts was a roundabout and, in the long run, would prove a demoralizing way of maintaining the flow of American goods to foreign markets. The various American foreign aid programs of the postwar period had not been designed for permanency but were conceived as emergency, short-term oper-

TABLE 2

U.S. FOREIGN AID (GRANTS AND CREDITS)

July 1, 1945—June 30, 1952

(Fiscal years. In millions of dollars)

	Gross Foreign Aid				Returns	Net Foreign Aid
	1946–1950	*1951*	*1952*	*Total*	*1946–1952*	*1946–1952*
Western Europe	20,422	3,633	3,646	27,702	1,907	25,795
Other Europe	1,160	...	...	1,160	69	1,091
Near East and Africa.	130	75	174	379	143	235
Asia and Pacific	5,139	828	924	6,892	530	6,362
Western Hemisphere.	657	153	196	1,004	420	584
Undesignated	744	148	66	958	1	957
Grants utilized	17,810	4,418	4,347	26,575	1,182	25,393
Credits utilized	10,441	419	659	11,519	1,890	9,629
Totals	28,251	4,837	5,006	38,094	3,072	35,022

Source: U.S. Department of Commerce, *Survey of Current Business,* XXXII, No. 10, October 1952, 8 and 10-11.

Note: Because of rounding, columns do not necessarily add to totals shown. Figures do not include payments of $635 million to the International Bank for Reconstruction and Development and $2,750 million to the International Monetary Fund. "Western Europe" includes Western European dependencies and Yugoslavia; "Undesignated" includes aid furnished through international organizations. "Grants utilized" excludes $1,256 million in grants subsequently converted into credits.

ations, to be administered in a way that would help the beneficiaries to become self-supporting as quickly as possible. Particularly in Western Europe, the area whose recovery was considered of preeminent importance, emphasis had been laid on measures aimed at increasing the productivity of European industry and agriculture and promoting closer economic relations among the Western European countries themselves. By this means, it was hoped, their long-term dependence on imports from the dollar area would be lessened; at the same time, thanks to lowered costs, their own exports would be able to compete more effectively in world markets. Thus their accounts with the dollar area would gradually be brought into balance and the period of emergency assistance would be followed by one of freer multilateral trade and convertibility of world currencies.

For a brief moment toward the end of 1950, this objective had actually appeared to be coming into view, despite unforeseen difficulties resulting from the cold war and the restriction of economic intercourse between the Soviet and non-Soviet worlds. Thanks partly to the initial impact of hostilities in Korea, the "dollar gap"—the excess of United States exports over imports on current account, including "invisibles"—had narrowed from $11.5 billion in 1947 to $2.3 billion in 1950. Production in Western Europe had surpassed prewar levels in most fields. The balance-of-payments position of the United Kingdom, the largest single recipient of American grants and loans, had improved to such an extent that economic aid from this country could be suspended through most of 1951. Unhappily, however, the inauguration of large-scale rearmament reversed these tendencies, imposed new burdens on the European economies, and necessitated large new increments of United States assistance, now predominantly though not exclusively military in character. In 1951 the dollar gap reopened. For the year as a whole it stood at $5 billion; during the last quarter it actually reached an annual rate of $7.5 billion, the highest since 1947. Three-fifths of this new world-wide deficit with the United States was incurred by the countries of Western Europe, largely as a result of new economic trends initiated by the rearmament program.

Despite these disappointing developments, there remained on both sides of the Atlantic a strong desire to get away from the existing system by which each reappearance of European payments difficulties was met with a new installment of American aid. Military assistance to Western Europe might, indeed, be necessary for a considerable time to come; economic aid might also be required in special circumstances like those besetting Austria, Yugoslavia, and Greece. But Congress had already shown its dislike of the general principle of economic aid or "defense support" as a means of balancing Europe's accounts with the dollar area. European governments, for their part, would have every reason to welcome the termination of American subsidies—provided, however, that alternative means were available to secure the American products without which Western Europe could hardly hope to defend its territory and maintain its way of life.

By itself, the reduction or cessation of American aid would obviously solve few problems. Further curtailment of their supply of dollars would simply mean that the countries affected must further restrict their imports from the United States, as Great Britain and the Commonwealth countries were already doing. Most authorities believed it preferable to maintain or even increase the supply of dollars—not in the form of gifts or loans, but in the form of increased American investment abroad and especially of increased opportunities for Europe to earn dollars in trade with the dollar area. Already the dollar earnings of the Western European group of countries had more than doubled since 1949; but they still remained well below the level at which accounts with the dollar area would balance. "Trade, not aid" was the formula hit upon by Britain's Chancellor of the Exchequer, R. A. Butler, to describe his country's principal economic need in the post-recovery period—a need it shared with the other countries of Western Europe, the Commonwealth and sterling area, and, in general, with all countries that looked to the United States for the satisfaction of some of their import needs. Dollar aid was already decreasing and was likely to shrink further; the logical counterpart of this shrinkage, it was felt, should be a better chance to earn dollars by furnishing more goods and services to the American market.

With this general line of reasoning the American administration had always shown considerable sympathy. Although certain protectionist laws like the "Buy American" statutes of the depression era still remained in effect, administration efforts under the Reciprocal Trade Agreements Act and the General Agreement on Tariffs and Trade (GATT) had been explicitly directed toward the lowering of barriers to international trade in the belief that intensified trade relations were economically advantageous to all parties. Political and military exigencies since the war had occasioned some noteworthy deviations from this principle, but leading administration spokesmen had often reaffirmed the general aim. In particular, they had recognized again and again that the future economic viability of Western Europe was bound up with its ability to increase its exports to the United States, despite the fact that this would undoubtedly require some modifications of existing American law and procedure and a measure of readjustment in some sections of the American economy.

But here as in so many other fields, the impact of administration thinking was limited by the more reserved and skeptical outlook predominating in the Congress. In its dealings with economic matters, Congress had not infrequently shown a tendency to focus on relatively simple, clear-cut objectives which seemed meritorious in themselves and could be pursued without overmuch regard for broader consequences and implications. Thus it had been sharply hostile to any large-scale trade between Western Europe and the Soviet bloc, but comparatively unconcerned with the economic problems which resulted for allied countries; strongly favorable to the lowering of trade barriers abroad, but distinctly cooler toward the idea of reciprocal tariff concessions by the United States. In its periodic renewals of the Reciprocal Trade Agreements Act, Congress had been increasingly insistent on limitations of the administration's freedom to implement the basic principle of mutual tariff reductions. Other administration efforts in the same general direction had fared even less well. The Charter for an International Trade Organization, one of the early postwar fruits of administration enterprise, had never reached the floor of Congress; the bill to simplify United States customs procedures, sent up to Capitol Hill in May 1950, had passed the House but never come before the Senate. On the other hand, Congress had been quite resourceful in devising measures, such as the famous "Cheese Amendment" to the Defense Production Act of 1951,[18] which aimed at shielding particular American interests from foreign competition.

That this approach was not furthering a solution of the basic problems of United States economic relationships seemed evident from the statistics on United States foreign trade during 1951 and the first half of 1952. During that period both imports and exports attained extraordinarily high levels in value terms, but the relation between them failed to improve significantly, and the chronic disequilibrium between the United States and Western Europe was in some respects accentuated. On the export side, military aid shipments and other factors kept the dollar total steadily rising; imports, on the other hand, actually fell off during the latter half of 1951 and made only a partial recovery in the following six months. In terms of the hoped-for increase of European shipments to this country, this trend was especially disquieting. Far from increasing, imports into the United States from Western Europe fell from $1.1 billion in the first half of 1951 to less than a billion in each of the two succeeding periods. By the first half of 1952, moreover, the efforts of European governments to conserve their scarce dollar resources had occasioned a marked drop in Western European imports (other than military) from the United States. This trend, if continued, would spell discomfort for American businessmen as well as for European consumers.

Most authorities agreed that a correction of this relationship would require action along several lines, both in Europe and in the United States. European countries would have to intensify their search for improved production and marketing techniques; the United States would have to act more vigorously in clearing away unnecessary obstacles to the entry of foreign goods into the American market. One such obstacle to which Europeans attached great importance was the complex and baffling structure of customs regulations and procedures which remained in effect pending adoption by Congress of the Customs Simplification Act. Another was the uncertainty created

[18] Section 104, Public Law 96, 82nd Congress, approved July 13, 1951; cf. *The United States in World Affairs, 1951,* 227, 229.

by the "escape clause" provision which Congress had written into the Trade Agreements Extension Act of 1951. Under this provision, tariff concessions granted by the United States on any product could be revoked if the Tariff Commission found that it was being imported in such increased quantities as to "cause or threaten serious injury to the domestic industry producing like or directly competitive products." Such a finding could be disregarded by the President, who, however, was required to report his reasons to Congress.[19] Immediately following the enactment of this provision, a large number of American producers had begun to besiege the Tariff Commission with demands that the escape clause be invoked in their favor. A recommendation from the Commission that higher duties be imposed on certain grades of hatter's fur, a product imported chiefly from Belgium, France, and Italy, had actually been accepted by the President at the beginning of 1952.[20]

These developments, which seemed to reflect a growing protectionist trend in the United States, proved highly disturbing to those European governments which had been so strongly encouraged by American officials to build up their exports to this country. Italy presently submitted to the State Department what amounted to a polite but comprehensive indictment of current American trade policies. Pointing to this country's growing recourse to restrictive devices, the Italian Government asserted that "the inconsistencies between principle and practice . . . are once more increasing" and invited attention to "the serious economic, social and psychological repercussions that recent United States restrictions have had in Italy and other friendly countries of Europe." Great Britain, in a similar communication, referred to "a most disturbing increase" in the number of applications for special protection against British imports. Loose interpretation of the escape clause provision, London suggested, could not fail to aggravate the difficulties

---

[19] Sections 6 and 7, Public Law 50, 82nd Congress, approved June 16, 1951; cf. *Department of State Bulletin*, XXVI, January 28, 1952, 143-148.
[20] White House press release, January 7, *ibid.*, January 21, 1952, 96-97.

of other governments and lessen their ability and willingness to cooperate with the United States.[21]

In reply, the State Department could say little except that the United States remained dedicated to the principle of free multilateral trade. But meanwhile a more comprehensive test of administration intentions was being prepared in the form of further recommendations from the Tariff Commission which called for restrictive quotas on imports of garlic, increased import duties on dried figs, and, most important, a 50 percent increase in customs duties on imported watches and parts. Presidential action in these cases was awaited with an interest by no means confined to Italy, Greece, and Switzerland, the three countries principally affected.

When the President's decisions were made known in the course of the summer, they amounted to an emphatic reaffirmation of the administration's basically anti-protectionist philosophy. As a temporary measure, the duty on figs was allowed to go up two cents a pound; but the recommendations on garlic and watches were rejected. In neither case, said the President, had "serious injury" to American producers been shown; and, he added, the escape clause had not been intended either as a protection against changing domestic demand or as "an escape from normal, healthy competition." Recent events, the President continued, had heightened the apprehension abroad concerning the future course of United States trade policy. This did not mean that we must never use the escape clause again. It did mean that "if we wish to avoid a serious loss of confidence in our leadership, any new restrictive action on our part must be clearly justified." [22]

Although these decisions were generally considered to establish a precedent of fundamental importance, their impact was

[21] Italian note verbale (January 15) and U.S. reply (April 15), *ibid.*, April 28, 1952, 660-666; British aide-mémoire (April 9) and U.S. reply (May 12), *ibid.*, May 12, 1952, 737-738 and June 2, 1952, 858.
[22] *Ibid.*, XXVII, August 25, 1952, 303-305 (garlic, July 21) and 305-307 (watches, August 14); September 1, 1952, 337-338 (figs, August 16). The decision in the watch case is reprinted in *Documents on American Foreign Relations, 1952*, No. 4.

lessened by the realization that Congress had meanwhile done little if anything to support administration views. Of the two legislative actions which the administration had considered most urgent for psychological as well as economic reasons, neither was accomplished at the 1952 session. The Customs Simplification Act (H.R. 5505) failed for a second time to obtain clearance from the Senate Finance Committee. And the Cheese Amendment—which, as the *New York Times* observed, "has probably caused as much bad feeling toward the United States in Western Europe as any single legislative action since the war"—was not repealed. After lengthy discussion, it was reenacted in a form that made possible some relaxation of import quotas on cheese and other dairy products, but failed to ward off the threat of retaliation by the countries affected or to bring it into harmony with American obligations under the General Agreement on Tariffs and Trade.[23]

Likewise unsupported by specific congressional action at this session was the program of negotiating bilateral treaties of friendship and commerce to provide a modernized basis for American commercial relations with other countries. Five such treaties—with Colombia, Denmark, Ethiopia, Greece, and Israel—remained in the Senate Foreign Relations Committee when Congress adjourned.[24] The Senate's only important gesture in a liberal direction was its rejection of a House-approved bill (H.R. 5693) to establish temporary import duties on tuna fish, which had already occasioned a formal protest by Peru and caused apprehension in Japan and elsewhere.[25] To balance this concession to foreign dollar-earners, House and Senate joined to strengthen the competitive position of another Ameri-

---

[23] Section 103, Public Law 429, approved June 30, 1952. The Senate had voted to repeal the amendment outright but the House refused by a 105-25 vote on June 19. Cf. the *New York Times* editorial of June 21 and the critical comments of Secretary Acheson and Assistant Secretary Thorp in *Department of State Bulletin*, XXVI, March 31, 1952, 517-519 and May 19, 1952, 800-802.

[24] Cf. *ibid.*, XXVI, June 2, 1952, 881-883. Congress did include in the Mutual Security Act a provision (Section 514, Public Law 400) calling on the State Department to "accelerate" the negotiation of commercial treaties.

[25] *Ibid.*, March 3, 1952, 352-354 and May 26, 1952, 821. The adverse vote in the Senate on June 24 was 43-32.

can industry by enacting a Long-Range Shipping Bill which provided more liberal subsidies for the construction of American vessels engaged in foreign trade.[26]

The impression of relative unconcern with problems flowing from this country's creditor position in world trade was strengthened by congressional actions in related fields of economic policy. As we have seen, the reluctance of Congress to provide enlarged opportunities for trade with this country did not prevent it from sharply limiting the prospective flow of "unearned" dollars abroad by its curtailment of military and economic or "defense support" aid, particularly to Western Europe. On another front, it narrowly refrained from action which would have further aggravated the situation of this country's European allies by raising fresh barriers to what remained of their trade with areas behind the Iron Curtain.

Congressional pressure for stringent limitation, amounting to a virtual embargo, on trade between Western and Eastern Europe was obviously motivated more by concern for security factors than by precise calculation of the military and economic effects on the two camps. The Mutual Defense Assistance Control Act (Battle Act) of 1951,[27] which provided for automatic termination of American aid to any country that shipped strategic goods to Communist countries unless the President found that such action would clearly be detrimental to the security of the United States, had been a compromise between two groups in Congress: (1) those who preferred to abolish East-West trade altogether rather than let any strategic item slip through the Iron Curtain, and (2) those who insisted that the economic disadvantages of such a procedure outweighed the potential military gains. In practice the administration had found it necessary to apply the Battle Act with liberal exceptions in favor of those countries whose trade with the East was particu-

---

[26] Public Law 586, approved July 17, 1952.
[27] Public Law 213, 82nd Congress, approved October 26, 1951; cf. *The United States in World Affairs, 1951,* 230-232 and *Export Controls and Free World Security* (Department of State Publication 4626, Washington, August 1952).

larly important.[28] Many members of Congress, on the other hand, remained altogether dissatisfied with a system of selective and discretionary controls and continued to hanker for the iron-clad prohibitions that had been prescribed in the abortive "Kem Amendment" to the Mutual Security Act of 1951. On May 28, 1952, the Senate actually voted to repeal the Battle Act and reinstate the coercive machinery of the Kem Amendment. The forty Senators who supported this decision (later reversed in Senate-House conference) appeared just as unimpressed by the administration's representations as they had been by the Soviet attempt to exploit the issue at the International Economic Conference.

Still another phase of economic policy in which Congress appeared somewhat indifferent to foreign susceptibilities, as well as to the over-all economic requirements of the non-Communist world, concerned the allocation of scarce raw materials by international agreement through the International Materials Conference set up in 1951. Acting with purely advisory powers, this group had done much to promote the rational and equitable distribution of available raw material supplies [29] and, incidentally, had helped to mitigate the irritation caused by American procurement policies in the early stages of the rearmament boom. But certain members of Congress remained highly critical of this particular type of interference with the free market, the more so as they believed (erroneously, according to the administration) that it was limiting the supply of copper and other imported materials available to the civilian economy in the United States. Several sharp attacks against the I.M.C. were mounted during the 1952 congressional session. In extending

[28] For details cf. *Department of State Bulletin*, XXVI, May 5, 1952, 720-721; XXVII, July 14, 1952, 75-77; August 4, 1952, 198-199; XXVIII, January 12, 1953, 79-83; also *Mutual Defense Assistance Control Act of 1951: First Report to Congress* by the Mutual Security Administrator (Washington, 1952), 47-57; *Second Report* (Washington, 1953), 20-21 and 77-86.

[29] See especially the *Report on Operations of the International Materials Conference, February 26, 1591 to March 1, 1952* (Washington, I.M.C., 1952) and the evaluations of Manly Fleischmann, Defense Production Administrator, in *Department of State Bulletin*, XXVI, February 25, 1952, 297-302 and in *Annals of the American Academy of Political and Social Science*, CCLXXXII, July 1952, 31-35.

the Defense Production Act, both houses approved rather complicated amendments whose frank purpose was to evade the
principle of international allocation of raw materials—perhaps that of domestic allocation under the Controlled Materials
Plan as well. Defenders of the I.M.C. managed to draw the
sting of these provisions before the final text of the law was
adopted; [30] but the anti-I.M.C. forces succeeded in writing into
the State Department Appropriation bill the unusual stipulation that none of that department's funds should be used to
meet any of the expenses of participating in the organization.[31]

Taken as a whole, the record of United States foreign economic policy in the first half of 1952 was thus inconclusive at
best. The definite aims of the administration had been largely
nullified by congressional opposition or inertia; Congress, unwilling to take its cue from the executive and lacking clear inspiration from any other source, had shied away from general
principles but generally leaned toward the type of solutions
associated with economic nationalism and protectionism. If the
immediate direction was uncertain, moreover, the outlook was
further obscured by the approaching election and the possibility
that under a Republican president and Congress this latent protectionist trend might become more explicit. Whatever the outcome in November, all these issues would plainly require fresh
examination in the light of changing world conditions and of
the realization that no early solution of the problems created
by the East-West struggle was in sight.

Shortly after Congress adjourned, therefore, the President
commissioned the Public Advisory Board for Mutual Security—
a bipartisan body that included representatives of business,
labor, agriculture, education, and the public—to undertake a
comprehensive survey of United States foreign trade policies.
Daniel W. Bell, a banker and former Under-Secretary of the

[30] Section 102, Public Law 429, approved June 30, 1952 stipulated only that in
accepting I.M.C. allocations the U.S. must reserve the right to buy up any unused stocks allocated to other countries.
[31] Section 113, Public Law 495, approved July 10, 1952. This amendment,
orginated in the Senate, had been eliminated in Senate-House conference, but
on July 3 the House voted 184-157 to insist on its retention.

Treasury, was appointed acting chairman of the board for purposes of this study, which presumably would be completed in
time for consideration by the next Congress. In his letter of instructions the President sharply focused the issue which the
board, and the nation, would have to face:

"I am asking the Board to undertake this assignment because
I fear that recent developments affecting our trade policy may
work at cross purposes with the basic objectives of the Mutual
Security Program. . . . On the one hand we are insisting that our
friends expand their own world trade; on the other hand we seem
to be raising new barriers against imports from abroad. This poses
a very real dilemma for our whole foreign policy. In my judgment,
the first step toward clarifying this situation is for a responsible
public group to study this problem and recommend to the President and the Congress the course we should follow in our trade
policy." [32]

One aspect of the problem that the Board would presumably
take into account had recently been given startling emphasis by
another White House-appointed group, the International Materials Policy Commission headed by William S. Paley.[33] This
was the growing dependence of the American economy on foreign sources of raw materials, as industrial requirements grew
and domestic sources approached exhaustion. Though primarily
concerned with other aspects of the raw materials problem,
this five-volume study brought out a number of facts directly
relevant to foreign trade policy. The United States, it pointed
out, was currently consuming 10 percent more raw materials
than it produced, and if present trends continued would need
to import more and more foreign materials as time went on.
Already, out of seventy-four separate categories of strategic and
critical materials, it was relying wholly on imports in more

[32] *Department of State Bulletin,* XXVII, July 21, 1952, 104-105. The report of
the Public Advisory Board, released March 5, 1953 under the title *A Trade
and Tariff Policy in the National Interest,* recommended tariff reductions and
other measures designed to increase U.S. imports by $700 million to $1 billion
annually over a period of three to five years. A summary appears *ibid.,* XXVIII,
March 23, 1953, 436-438.
[33] *Resources for Freedom: A Report to the President by the President's Materials Policy Commission* (5 vols., Washington, 1952). The major conclusions
are summarized in *Department of State Bulletin,* XXVII, July 14, 1952, 54-60.

than forty. The time might come when increased purchases of foreign raw materials and the investment necessary to develop new sources of supply would play a major part in solving the world's dollar problem. Meanwhile the Paley report would provide a wealth of ammunition to those who questioned the adequacy of economic policies inspired by the venerable ideal of national self-sufficiency.

4. The Politics of Self-Containment

Half way through its labors, on April 3, Congress paused to hear a remarkable address by Queen Juliana of the Netherlands. In it, appreciation of this country's constructive role in world affairs was mingled with good-humored but unambiguous references to the serious responsibilities borne by Congress—"both toward your voters and toward the general well-being of your country, and consequently, especially in our modern interwoven conditions, toward the world at large." Each member of Congress, the Queen declared, carried "the full burden of a responsibility nobody will envy you, as your decisions have enormous repercussions all through the world." Notwithstanding the close ties of kinship and experience between the United States and the Netherlands, she insisted, "there is still always need to deepen our understanding for each other. Because . . . as contact among mankind is growing ever closer, we have never before been so keenly aware that in this world of ours we need cooperation as intimate as that among the cells of one body." [34]

So far as cooperation among the countries of Europe was concerned, Congress was in hearty agreement. Its annual enactments dealing with European economic recovery had manifested an urgent interest in the movement toward closer association among the Western European democracies. The Mutual Security Act of 1952 was even more explicit than earlier legislation in its insistence on "the necessity for further vigorous efforts" toward "political federation, military integration, and economic unification in Europe." To this end Congress pro-

[34] Text in *Department of State Bulletin*, XXVI, April 14, 1952, 580-582.

vided not only that funds voted for aid to Europe could be made available directly to international bodies like NATO, the European Coal and Steel Community, and the prospective European Defense Community, but also that assistance should be *withheld* from any country that failed to "take decisive action to marshal its resources collectively, or individually where more suitable, with integration and unification plans in the appropriate area." [35]

But the principle of collective action, political, military, or economic, was not one that Congress seemed willing to apply in any comparable degree to the United States itself. The objective of "building strength, establishing security, and preserving peace in the North Atlantic area" might call for unrelenting pressure on European governments to relinquish some of their sovereignty to a supranational organization. It might justify criticism or, possibly, even economic "sanctions" against a power like Great Britain which had thus far refused to do so. But Congress clearly did not feel that the United States was called upon to surrender its own freedom of action, except in a very minor way, in any of the fields of common international concern. On the contrary, the trend in Congress and the country in the early 1950's was toward a definite reassertion of national autonomy and thus away from the principles of multilateral, cooperative action which had guided American policy in recent years.

This tendency operated with varying force in different areas of foreign policy. It was least noticeable, perhaps, in connection with the development and implementation of the North Atlantic Treaty and its new Pacific counterpart. In contrast to the sharp misgivings exhibited at the time of the "great debate" on troops for Europe, the Senate showed little hesitation in approving the various new political commitments which this country had recently assumed in its endeavor to round out a world-wide system of mutual security pacts. The protocol bringing Greece and Turkey into the North Atlantic

[35] Preamble and Sections 7(h) and 8(b), Public Law 400, approved June 20, 1952 (*Documents on American Foreign Relations, 1952*, No. 3 [b]).

Treaty system was overwhelmingly approved on February 7.[36]
In March the Senate ratified the Treaty of Peace with Japan,
the Security Treaty between the United States and Japan, the
Security Treaty between the United States, Australia, and New
Zealand, and the Mutual Defense Treaty between the United
States and the Philippines.[37] Late in the session approval was
given to two more significant agreements affecting United
States interests in the European-North Atlantic area: the Convention on Relations Between the Three [Western] Powers
and the Federal Republic of Germany, signed at Bonn on May
26, and a new protocol to the North Atlantic Treaty, signed
at Paris on May 27, which extended the treaty's guarantees to
all members of the new European Defense Community.[38]

In its acceptance of these additional undertakings, the Senate
may have been influenced by the recollection that some members of Congress had been well ahead of the administration in
advocating the rearmament of Germany, the inclusion of Greece
and Turkey in NATO, and the conclusion of a Pacific defense
pact. In each of these matters the administration and the other
governments most immediately concerned had ultimately come
a good way toward accepting the congressional viewpoint. But
there were other matters concerning which congressional views,
whether positive or negative, did not command general acceptance away from Capitol Hill. In these instances Congress

[36] Senate Executive E, 82nd Congress, 2nd Session, approved by a vote of 73-2
(text in *Documents on American Foreign Relations, 1952,* No. 14). The protocol was first approved by voice vote on January 29 but was later brought up
for reconsideration in view of the perfunctory nature of the initial discussion.
[37] Senate Executives A, B, C, and D, 82nd Congress, 2nd Session, approved by
the Senate March 20 and ratified by the President April 15, 1952 (texts in
Documents on American Foreign Relations, 1951, 262 ff. and 470 ff.) The votes
on the two Japanese treaties were 66-10 and 58-9 respectively; the other two
treaties were approved without a record vote. In furtherance of the policies underlying the Japanese settlement, the Senate later approved a North Pacific Fisheries Convention concluded by the U.S., Japan, and Canada for regulation and
conservation of high seas fisheries (Senate Executive S, approved July 4, 1952),
and both houses passed legislation authorizing the loan of 18 patrol frigates
and 50 landing craft to Japan for five years with provision for a five-year extension (Public Law 467, approved July 8, 1952).
[38] Senate Executives Q and R, approved July 1, 1952 by votes of 77-5 and 72-5
respectively (texts in *Documents on American Foreign Relations, 1952,* Nos.
19 [b] and 20 [b]); for details cf. below, pp. 150-168.

asserted its opinions with equal vigor, though with less prospect of contributing to the harmony of national and international life.

One such case was that of Spain. By 1952 the long-standing desire of Congress (and the military) for closer ties with the Franco regime had been reluctantly embraced by the administration, but still produced only a negative echo from most of the other North Atlantic governments. Undeterred either by international skepticism or by the slow pace of this country's negotiations with the Spanish Government, Congress followed up its unsolicited and still unutilized 1951 appropriation of $100 million for "military, economic, and technical assistance" to Spain [39] with a further appropriation of $25 million for the same purpose.[40] A second case was the refusal to approve the appointment of a diplomatic representative to the Vatican; a third was the refusal of the Senate to approve the 1941 agreement to join with Canada in carrying out the St. Lawrence seaway and power project—an undertaking that had been endorsed by every President since Woodrow Wilson, but was considered to threaten domestic interests which some congressmen had much at heart.[41]

All these actions, so diverse in appearance, had one feature in common irrespective of their individual technical merits. In these as in many other instances, Congress had faced a choice

[39] *The United States in World Affairs, 1951,* 236. Secretary Acheson reported on March 12, 1952 that the use of these funds would be discussed with the Spanish Government in forthcoming negotiations looking toward U.S. use of military facilities in Spain. Cf. below, pp. 421-422.

[40] Section 3(d), Public Law 400. This amount was to come out of the total appropriation of $4.4 billion for European aid.

[41] S.J. Res. 27, 82nd Congress, reported without recommendation by the Senate Foreign Relations Committee and recommitted by a 43-40 vote of the Senate on June 18, 1952; for background cf. especially the presidential statements reprinted in *Department of State Bulletin,* XXVI, February 11, 1952, 232-234 and May 5, 1952, 719-720. On June 30 the U.S. and Canada asked the International Joint Commission to authorize certain engineering works for power development in the International Rapids section of the St. Lawrence, on the assumption that the seaway would be built by Canada alone while the power project would be carried out jointly by the Province of Ontario and an appropriate agency of the U.S. This application was approved October 29. Cf. *ibid.,* XXVI, February 11, 1952, 234-235; XXVII, July 14, 1952, 65-67 and December 29, 1952, 1019-1024.

between one course of action that involved broad cooperation for common ends and an alternative that emphasized freedom of national action and minimum involvement with any kind of foreign interests and influences. From a study of the entire record it is difficult to escape the conclusion that Congress, unlike the administration, valued the comparative independence of unilateral procedure as something desirable in itself which frequently outweighed any advantages that might flow from a different course.

The tendency to minimize American involvement in the concerns of the outside world was nowhere more obvious than in the affairs of the United Nations, the institution which administration spokesmen had described again and again as the very cornerstone of American postwar foreign policy. True, in its actions affecting the world organization Congress did not openly dissent from the principles of the Charter which the Senate had ratified, with only two dissenting votes, in 1945. Yet its tendency, increasingly as time went on and the United Nations became a familiar feature of the American landscape, had been to interpret those principles in a more restrictive spirit than most Americans had anticipated at the time the Charter was adopted. The tendency could be seen both in the pressure occasionally exerted on the United Nations to support policies favored by the Congress [42] and in the resistance of Congress to large parts of the United Nations program which were unrelated to immediate United States policy objectives.

This cooling of congressional sentiment toward the United Nations cannot be fully understood unless it is recognized as part of a broader transformation in American public attitudes which resulted directly from the conditions of the cold war. In the emotional climate of the 1950's, it was not surprising that some of the prevalent hostility toward the Soviet Union and its partisans should have transferred itself to an institution in which the Soviet Government continued to enjoy privileges equal to those of the United States. The facilities available to

[42] Cf. *The United States in World Affairs, 1951,* 88 and 121.

Soviet and satellite representatives to denounce and conspire against the United States on our own territory were felt by some to be not only offensive but actually dangerous to a country already deeply concerned about its own internal security. Nor were Americans uniformly sympathetic even to those nonpolitical phases of United Nations activity which the Soviet Union and its satellites customarily ignored or denounced. By some subconscious process, a growing number of Americans were coming to look on the United Nations as the foremost embodiment of insidiously "un-American" tendencies that were felt to be endangering the national way of life. In some extreme cases, hostility to the United Nations and all its works appeared to outweigh even the preoccupations aroused by Soviet-Communist imperialism in the world outside.

Contributing to this hostile trend was a mounting wave of uneasiness about the implications of such United Nations efforts as the unratified Convention on Genocide and the prospective International Covenant on Human Rights. Such treaties, it was argued, tended to subvert the rights of American citizens by subjecting them to the jurisdiction of an international body; in addition, the "socialistic" emphasis on equal rights and non-discrimination which characterized United Nations undertakings was felt in some quarters to threaten well-established social patterns in this country.[43] In recent months these fears had been powerfully accentuated when a California court invalidated that state's alien land law as being inconsistent with the "equal rights" provisions of the United Nations Charter. They were only partially allayed when the Supreme Court of California ruled that the Charter provisions, although they did *not* supersede domestic legislation, nevertheless represented "a moral commitment of foremost importance" and were "entitled to respectful consideration by the courts and Legislatures of every member nation." [44]

[43] For a powerful statement along these lines cf. Frank E. Holman, "The Constitution and the United Nations: The Foundations of the Republic are Threatened," *Vital Speeches,* XVIII, September 1, 1952, 678-684.
[44] Sei Fujii v. State of California, April 17, 1952, 242 Pac. (2d) 617 (reprinted in *American Journal of International Law,* XLVI, July 1952, 559-573; com-

If Congress as a whole was free from the more extreme manifestations of this outlook, its members found many ways of showing that their own enthusiasm for United Nations activities was not unqualified. This, for example, was one of the phases of American foreign policy where Congress felt freest to economize, since the sums involved were comparatively small to begin with and their relation to the military security of the United States was at best indirect. Thus, in line with its general reduction of funds for the Point Four program of aid to underdeveloped areas, Congress reduced the appropriation for multilateral technical assistance (primarily through the United Nations) in 1952–53 from $17 million to $9.17 million. For the International Children's Emergency Fund, the $24 million requested by the President was cut to $6.67 million. Although $60 million of new money was appropriated for the relief of Palestine refugees, a request for $45 million for the United Nations Korean Reconstruction Agency was eliminated on the theory that sufficient funds to take care of immediate needs were available from previous appropriations.[45] A more definite index to congressional attitudes was a strong reaffirmation of the principle that henceforth the contribution pledged by the United States for the general support of any international organization must not exceed one-third of that organization's total budget.[46]

But these enactments were dictated more by prudential considerations than by hostility to United Nations endeavors as such. Thus their implications were hardly to be compared with those of certain resolutions introduced into the 82nd Congress with the apparent object of redefining the whole relationship between the United States and the United Nations. The most noteworthy of these efforts was a resolution introduced by

ments *ibid.*, October 1952, 682-690). The Supreme Court held that the land law nevertheless was invalid because it violated the Fourteenth Amendment to the U.S. Constitution.

[45] Public Law 547, approved July 15, 1952. For the President's appeal in behalf of UNICEF cf. *Department of State Bulletin*, XXVI, March 24, 1952, 477.

[46] Public Law 495, approved July 10, 1952. An exception was made for inter-American organizations. For background cf. *The United States in World Affairs, 1951*, 373 and 409.

Republican Senator John W. Bricker of Ohio, on behalf of fifty-eight Senators, in the form of a constitutional amendment that would in effect assert the supremacy of United States law over the provisions of any international treaty, including the United Nations Charter.[47]

The administration was not asked for its views on the Bricker resolution, but expressed consternation at the restrictions such an amendment would impose on the routine conduct of the nation's foreign affairs as well as on participation in the United Nations. "The importance of the issues raised cannot be over-estimated," said the President; "[they] have a bearing on the welfare of every state and every person in our country." The State Department submitted detailed arguments purporting to show that the proposed amendment was unwarranted, would "prevent many treaties which have been beneficial to the United States and to its citizens," prevent the Government from entering into "beneficial and humanitarian treaties," and alter the division of powers "which is the basic structure of our constitutional system." [48] The crowded calendar of Congress prevented more detailed consideration of an issue that seemed certain to excite discussion and controversy for some time to come.

Meanwhile there were other developments to indicate the trend of congressional feeling on some of the issues involved. In approving the constitution by which the people of Puerto Rico proposed to govern themselves under the tutelage of the United States, Congress demonstrated a belief in the principle of self-determination for dependent peoples but insisted on deleting an enumeration of economic and social rights which echoed the Universal Declaration of Human Rights approved by the United Nations General Assembly in 1948.[49] More noticed at the time was a sharp attack on the much-criticized

---

[47] S.J. Res. 130, 82nd Congress; text and discussion in *Documents on American Foreign Relations, 1952*, No. 5.

[48] *Department of State Bulletin*, XXVI, June 16, 1952, 952-961.

[49] Public Law 447, approved July 3, 1952; for background cf. especially the President's message of April 22 (*ibid.*, May 5, 1952, 721-723) and the Senate's discussion in *Congressional Record*, Daily Edition, June 23, 1952, 7969-7970 and 7972-7974.

United Nations Educational, Scientific and Cultural Organization (UNESCO). This body, which was boycotted by the Soviet bloc because of its alleged subservience to the United States,[50] was equally unpopular with a section of the American public which believed it aimed at doing away with national sovereignty and establishing a world government and world citizenship in the literal sense. Notwithstanding categorical denials of this allegation from many quarters, Congress undertook to discourage any possible tendency in such a direction by writing into the State Department Appropriation Act the following prohibition:

"None of the funds appropriated in this title shall be used (1) to pay the United States contribution to any international organization which engages in the direct or indirect promotion of the principle or doctrine of one world government or one world citizenship; (2) for the promotion, direct or indirect [presumably by the State Department], of the principle or doctrine of one world government or one world citizenship." [51]

The sponsor of this amendment, Democratic Senator Pat McCarran of Nevada, was prominently identified with several efforts aimed at protecting the United States from internal subversion or foreign contamination. Leading advocate of ties with Spain, chairman of the Senate Judiciary Committee and of its Subcommittee on Internal Security, author of the Internal Security Act which Congress had passed over a presidential veto in 1950, he was also the principal sponsor of the famous Mc-Carran-Walter Immigration and Nationality bill which became law—once again in disregard of a presidential veto message—in June 1952.[52] This important enactment was essentially a codification of earlier statutes on immigration and naturalization, and liberalized existing law in several respects. The outright ban on immigration from eight Asiatic countries, for

[50] Czechoslovakia, Hungary, and Poland, the three Soviet-oriented members of UNESCO, ceased to participate in the organization in 1950 and resigned during the winter of 1952–53.
[51] Section 112, Public Law 495, approved July 10, 1952; for background cf. the remarks of Senator Pat McCarran in *Congressional Record,* Daily Edition, June 26, 1952, 8243.
[52] Public Law 414, enacted June 27, 1952.

example, was replaced by annual quotas of 100 for each country. The most prominent single feature of the new law, however, and the basis of much of the criticism directed against it both before and after enactment, was its retention of the system of immigration quotas based on national origins which had been in effect since 1924.

The effect of this system was twofold. First, it sharply limited the total volume of new immigration into the United States. Quota immigration was limited by law to approximately 154,-000 persons a year; in practice, since some of the larger quotas were never filled, it never exceeded 95,000 and in most years fell well below that figure. In addition, certain classes of persons (mainly relatives of United States citizens and natives of independent Western Hemisphere countries) were permitted to enter the country as nonquota immigrants; their number varied between 60,000 and 100,000 a year. The actual number of immigration visas issued in both categories during the seven fiscal years 1946–1952 amounted to only 1,129,894, or an average of slightly more than 161,000 per year.[53]

Secondly, the quota system had been set up in such a way as to exclude most persons of non-European origin and, among Europeans, to give preferred status to immigrants from Great Britain, Germany, Ireland, and other countries of Northwestern Europe while discouraging immigration from the populous countries of Eastern and Southern Europe. Of the total of 154,277 quota immigrants admissible in the fiscal year 1952, the British Isles and Germany were assigned no fewer than 109,531; quota immigration from the rest of the world was limited to 44,746, including a bare 14,394 from countries behind the Iron Curtain. In practice, moreover, the perpetuation of the existing quota system would mean that future immigration from Eastern European countries would be even more limited than the figures suggested. Most of these countries'

[53] These figures, which include 95,785 special nonquota immigrants admitted in 1946–48 under the War Brides Act of December 28, 1945, are derived from official data presented in *Hearings before the President's Commission on Immigration and Naturalization* (Committee print, House Judiciary Committee, 82nd Congress, 2nd Session, Washington, 1952), 1892 and 1898-1899.

quotas were already partially mortgaged for years to come, since nearly 400,000 persons admitted ahead of schedule under the Displaced Persons Act of 1948 had been charged off against future annual quotas of their countries of origin.[54] Thus the Polish quota of 6,524, which was among the most heavily oversubscribed, would not be clear until the year 2000; the Latvian quota of 236 was partially encumbered until A.D. 2274. Under these circumstances, total immigration from Eastern Europe in the coming years might not exceed half the figure nominally authorized.

In contrast, the quotas assigned to Great Britain, Ireland (Eire), and certain other countries of Northern and Western Europe were chronically undersubscribed. Quota immigration visas from the British Isles in the seven years 1946–1952 numbered only 406,438, as compared with an authorized total of 585,018. The unused portion of the British and Irish quotas actually exceeded the *total* quotas of all Iron Curtain countries by a margin of more than 75 percent. The obstacles to immigration from the latter areas could thus have been largely circumvented by merely authorizing the President to transfer the unused portion of any national quota to other areas where the quotas were oversubscribed. But no such provision was included in the McCarran-Walter bill, which provided for only such modification of existing quotas as was necessary to accomodate a few hundred yearly immigrants from areas previously denied any quota at all.[55]

The original aim of the quota system had been to maintain the historical balance among white persons of different national origins in the American population. Its retention in 1952 was ascribed by critics of the bill, including the President, to

[54] Under the Displaced Persons Act as amended, annual quotas were absorbed to the extent of 25 percent through the fiscal year 1954 and 50 percent thereafter. As of June 30, 1952, admissions under this act totaled 393,524, including 337,244 displaced persons, 53,448 German expellees, and 2,850 orphans and adopted children. Operations in this and related fields are summarized in *Memo to America: The DP Story—The Final Report of the United States Displaced Persons Commission* (Washington, 1952).

[55] The new quotas proclaimed under Public Law 414 on June 30, 1952 (*Department of State Bulletin*, XXVII, July 14, 1952, 83) totaled 154,657; for most countries they were slightly smaller than the quotas previously in effect.

religious and racial bias against people of Eastern and Southern European origin. Whether or not this charge was justified, the bill had evidently been drawn with little or no reference to general foreign policy objectives and would provide little assistance toward solving the world's pressing population and migration problems. A theoretical yearly total of 154,657 immigrants was in no way commensurate with the 773,465 intending immigrants already registered at American consulates abroad, to say nothing of the 3,750,000 persons who, it was estimated, ought to leave Europe for overseas destinations within the next five years if that continent was to regain economic balance and stability.[56] Nor would the quotas established by the bill do much to relieve population pressure in those countries (apart from Germany) where it was strongest. The combined quotas of Italy, the Netherlands, and Greece, three allied countries which happened to be among the most heavily overpopulated in Europe, totaled 9,089.

The importance of encouraging the emigration of surplus manpower from Western Europe, and of encouraging individual defection from "Iron Curtain" areas, had been stressed in previous congressional enactments; funds for these purposes were provided in the Mutual Security appropriations for both 1951–52 and 1952–53.[57] But there had been less interest in attracting such migrants to the United States. In March 1952

[56] *Department of State Bulletin*, XXVI, June 23, 1952, 980 and 996-997. As of August 1, 1952 the number of applicants registered at U.S. consulates was 877,047. (*Hearings Before the President's Commission*, cited, 1900.)

[57] A $10 million appropriation in 1951 (followed by a second appropriation of $9.2 million in 1952) was the basis for U.S. participation in the Intergovernmental Committee for the Movement of Migrants from Europe, which was endeavoring to move a total of 137,500 emigrants overseas in the course of 1952. Of this number, 28,000 were destined for admission to the U.S. under the Displaced Persons Act. (For details cf. *Department of State Bulletin*, XXVI, February 4, 1952, 169-173; April 21, 1952, 638-640; June 23, 1952, 996-997; XXVII, July 21, 1952, 107-108.) Under another provision of the Mutual Security Act of 1951, the President had allocated $4.3 million (plus $2.9 million from other sources) "to improve the reception and treatment and to secure the resettlement [not necessarily in the U.S.] of qualified persons who escape from the Iron Curtain area." (White House release, March 24, *ibid.*, XXVI, April 14, 1952, 602; see further *ibid.*, XXVII, August 18, 1952, 261-262.)

the President, as an emergency measure, proposed the admission over a three-year period of 300,000 additional immigrants from Italy, Germany, Greece, the Netherlands, and Communist-dominated Eastern Europe.[58] Bills to this effect were introduced in Congress but failed to reach the floor of either house. Any immigration into the United States, Congress decided in effect, must conform to the quota and other requirements established by the McCarran-Walter bill.

The objections to that legislation, however, were not confined to the fact that it did not come to grips with actual population problems abroad. There was also criticism of numerous detailed provisions which were felt to be unduly restrictive in character and to place unwarranted difficulties in the way of bona fide immigrants, visitors, and even loyal Americans. "Seldom has a bill exhibited the distrust evidenced here for citizens and aliens alike," remarked the President, expressing a view which was by no means confined either to the executive branch or to interested sections of the public. Already four members of the Senate Judiciary Committee had withheld their approval from the bill, declaring that it not only failed to correct many existing defects in the immigration laws but also included many provisions inconsistent with "our democratic traditions of justice and equality." Specifically, they said,

"the bill would inject new racial discriminations into our law, establish many vague, and highly abusable requirements for admission, impede the admission of refugees from totalitarian oppression, incorporate into law vague standards for deportation and denaturalization, and would deprive persons within our borders of fundamental judicial protections.

"In addition, the bill . . . fails to modify present arbitrary restrictions on immigration, fails to modernize our anachronistic quota system, and fails to establish administrative procedures consonant with our democratic tradition of fair play. Such provisions, if enacted, would seriously weaken American internal strength, would antagonize friendly peoples, and would subject many American citizens to unreasonable hardship. . . ." [59]

[58] Message of March 24, *ibid.*, April 7, 1952, 551-555.
[59] Senate Report 1137, 82nd Congress, Part 2, March 13, 1952, 1-2.

Such warnings, however, failed to impress a majority in either house of Congress. After a sharp legislative battle, the alternative bills offered by opponents of the measure were defeated and the McCarran-Walter bill was passed by sizable majorities. The expected presidential veto message, transmitted on June 25, noted with approval the fact that the bill removed all racial bars to naturalization and provided at least minimum immigration quotas for each of the free nations of Asia.

"But," said the President, "this most desirable provision comes before me embedded in a mass of legislation which would perpetuate injustices of long standing against many other nations of the world, hamper the efforts we are making to rally the men of East and West alike to the cause of freedom, and intensify the repressive and inhumane aspects of our immigration procedures. The price is too high, and in good conscience I cannot agree to pay it." [60]

The vote to override the President's veto was 278-113 in the House and 57-26 in the Senate.

Confronted with this unequivocal rejection of administration thinking, the President took the same course he had adopted in response to the growing protectionist trend in the economic field. "I do not believe that the matter should remain where the Congress left it," he declared on September 4. "The problems of immigration policy grow more pressing, and the inequities fostered by the new law require careful examination." Accordingly, he announced, he was appointing a commission of seven leading citizens to "study and evaluate" the nation's immigration and naturalization policies and make a report in time for consideration by the next Congress. In addition to examining pertinent conditions both at home and abroad, the new Commission on Immigration and Naturalization was directed to consider the relation of our immigration laws and procedure to the general conduct of American foreign policy. "The United States," said the President, "must remain true to its great traditions and have an immigration policy that

[60] Message of June 25, in *Documents on American Foreign Relations, 1952,* No. 6.

strengthens our nation at home and furthers our world leadership." [61]

It is to be assumed that the members of Congress who had voted to override the President's veto shared his concern with both of these objectives. True, Congress had often seemed willing to subordinate the furtherance of world leadership to the pursuit of what looked like strength at home, without overmuch concern for the effect its actions might produce in relations with the outside world. Yet it would be quite wrong to imagine that Congress was indifferent to foreign opinion or overlooked the desirability of mobilizing international support for American aims. "Psychological strategy," as this field of endeavor was now called, played a considerable part in its deliberations; the Senate even adopted a resolution insisting on the need for "greatly expanded and far more effective operations in this vital area of foreign policy." [62]

But meanwhile, existing agencies for political warfare could count on no assured congressional support. While estimating that the Soviet Union and its satellites were spending some $1.4 billion a year on activities of this kind, Congress reduced the appropriation for the United States international information and educational program for the next twelve months from $133 million to $87 million,[63] and flatly refused to appropriate funds for additional radio facilities to help overcome Soviet jamming of American broadcasts. Such actions, however, seemed less significant than the prevalent tendency to look upon psychological strategy as a special type of activity which

[61] White House release, September 4, in *Department of State Bulletin*, XXVII, September 15, 1952, 407-408. The report of the President's Commission on Immigration and Naturalization, released January 1, 1953 under the title *Whom We Shall Welcome*, held "that our present immigration law has a detrimental effect upon our foreign relations in a variety of ways" (p. 70) and "should be reconsidered and revised from beginning to end" (p. 263). Excerpts from the report appear in *Department of State Bulletin*, XXVIII, January 19, 1953, 97-102.

[62] Senate Resolution 74, 82nd Congress, adopted June 30, 1952 (text in *Congressional Record*, Daily Edition, June 30, 1952, 8716-8717).

[63] Public Law 495, 82nd Congress, approved July 10, 1952. The estimate of Soviet propaganda expenditure appeared in the *New York Times* of December 12, 1951 and was repeated in various congressional documents.

might produce great results if properly organized but had little or nothing to do with the ordinary conduct of government. Few Congressmen seemed ready as yet to embrace the concept, so relevant to their own endeavors, which General Eisenhower was to outline in a campaign speech a few months later. "We must realize," the former Supreme Allied Commander in Europe would say, "that as a nation, everything we do, and everything we fail to say or do will have its impact in other lands. It will affect the minds and will of men and women there." [64] Recognition of this truth would be worth many millions of those dollars which Congress was justifiably anxious to save for the American taxpayer.

[64] Address of October 8, excerpted in *Documents on American Foreign Relations, 1952*, No. 7 (e).

CHAPTER THREE

EUROPE AND THE GERMAN PROBLEM

THE DIFFICULTY experienced by the United States in balancing
its duty to itself with its obligations toward the rest of the
world was not a unique phenomenon. Throughout the Western
world, other national groups were struggling with problems
that were essentially similar even if their historical implications
were not always so far-reaching. The issue everywhere was
fundamentally the same. Technologically, economically, militarily, Western man had arrived at a point where few important problems could be satisfactorily solved within the
boundaries of a single nation. "The logic of larger groups and
association," as General Eisenhower put it in his first annual
report as Supreme Allied Commander in Europe, "is becoming
increasingly impelling." [1] Psychologically, however, the vast
majority among the Western peoples continued to think of
the national state as the ultimate and exclusive basis of secular
existence. The growth of international organizations during the
postwar period testified to a widespread recognition that coordinated effort was desirable in many areas of public life. But
traditional aims and attitudes persisted within the new machinery and largely governed the way it operated—or failed
to operate.

Such an interaction of new and older tendencies was especially noticeable in the affairs of Western Europe, an area
where the proliferation of novel international institutions was

[1] Gen. Dwight D. Eisenhower, *First Annual Report of the Supreme Allied Commander, Europe,* April 2, 1952, in *Documents on American Foreign Relations,
1952,* No. 13.

one reflection of the quite extraordinary difficulties the European peoples had inherited from World War II. For Europe, in the few short years between 1939 and 1945, had lost its centuries-old political, economic, and military preeminence and experienced a catastrophe that left it small hope of regaining its former material position and only a limited prospect of reasserting its cultural and intellectual leadership. Its chances of postwar recuperation, already limited by serious impairment of its economic and spiritual life, had been further prejudiced by the successful revolt of many of its former colonial territories, the sharpening world-wide antagonism between the United States and the U.S.S.R., and especially the predatory tendencies exhibited by the Soviet Union on the European Continent itself. Stalin's success in advancing the frontiers of the Soviet empire into the heart of Europe had compelled the Western European nations not only to live in unnatural isolation from their neighbors in the East but also to face a continuing threat of interference by a power whose intentions appeared as unfriendly as its military potential was overwhelmingly superior.

Within the Western or "Atlantic" world this basically unfavorable situation had given rise to three main tendencies which together offered at least some hope of enabling Western Europe to survive as a positive influence in Atlantic and world affairs. First, Great Britain, France, and the other democratic allies of World War II in Western Europe had drawn closer together and made some tentative efforts toward pooling their economic and military resources as the best means of defending their common interests and ideals. Second, a closer association had been established with the kindred democracies of the United States and Canada, and had acquired a more or less permanent and official character with the conclusion of the North Atlantic Treaty in 1949 as the basis for a collective effort to ensure the military defense of Western Europe. Since the Communist aggression in Korea, finally, increasing stress had been laid on the rehabilitation of Germany—or, rather, of those portions of the former Reich that were not under Soviet occupation—as an essential element in any Western European-North Atlantic combination that might hope to maintain itself as a whole in face of the continuing Soviet threat.

All of these efforts had, of course, been pursued amid the violent and mounting tensions of the cold war. All of them, and especially the attempted revival of Germany as an associate of the West, had been denounced by the U.S.S.R. in the most menacing terms as steps toward the unleashing of a new world conflagration for the benefit of American "monopolists." And, although this characterization of Western aims was wholly false, the proposed inclusion of Western Germany in the Western coalition had raised issues of peculiar difficulty which gave the German problem special importance both in the context of the East-West struggle and in the relations among the Western nations themselves.

That German rearmament should be under consideration at all was a measure not only of the decisive influence of the United States but also of the extent to which old grievances had been forced aside by the antagonisms of the cold war. No nation that had gone through the whole bitterness of World War II could be expected to view the project with much enthusiasm. For the U.S.S.R. and its Eastern European satellites, rearmament of Germans under any auspices except their own was bound to be distasteful in the extreme. Not only did it seem likely to strengthen the West, but it also threatened to establish a strong and potentially dangerous military power in their immediate neighborhood. Several of the Western countries, moreover, found the prospect almost equally objectionable. For them, too, any rearmament of Germany would carry with it the threat of a revived German militarism; at the very least, therefore, they felt that it would require elaborate safeguards to ensure that no new German military force could become the instrument of an aggressive policy. For the Germans themselves, finally, rearmament in a form acceptable to the West had many drawbacks. It might eventually add to the over-all strength of Western Europe, including Western Germany. In the meantime, however, it would expose the West Germans to an imminent threat of Soviet retaliation, compel them to accept a somewhat inferior position among their former enemies in the West, and presumably entail the indefinite postponement of any hope they might have for the reunification of their own country through agreement with the Soviet Government.

Since there was no possibility of reconciling all these conflicting views, the Western Allies and the West German government of Dr. Konrad Adenauer had determined to disregard the objections of the U.S.S.R. and to work out a procedure by which it was hoped that the Federal Republic could participate in Western European defense without doing unnecessary violence to popular sentiment either in Western Germany or in Western Europe. The essence of their plan, which had first been put forward by French statesmen in the fall of 1950, was the creation of a unified "European Defense Community" with an international military force that would eventually take the place of the existing national armies in Western Europe (excluding Great Britain and the Scandinavian states), and in which German components would be included on much the same basis as those of other nationalities. By this means it was hoped not only to secure the advantages of German participation in European defense but also to consolidate the progress toward a unified Western Europe, including Western Germany, which had been going forward for some years within the framework of the Organization for European Economic Cooperation, the Council of Europe, and, more recently, the preparatory commission of the "Schuman Plan" or European Coal and Steel Community.

By the beginning of 1952 the basic principles which were to govern this consolidation had been worked out and it remained only to regulate the final details and secure their acceptance by the appropriate parliamentary bodies in Germany and in the North Atlantic Treaty countries. This final stage, however, promised to be exceptionally difficult. Arrangements which had been fashioned by diplomats and technicians had now to be passed upon by men whose concern was primarily political rather than technical and who were necessarily much more responsive to the various currents of popular opinion. And popular opinion in non-Communist Europe could not be described as wholeheartedly in favor of the far-reaching policies espoused by the Western governments. Quite aside from the widespread skepticism regarding German matters, there was considerable dissatisfaction with the whole trend of Atlantic affairs as they had developed under United States leadership since the Korean aggression. Not only the Communist and fellow-traveling element, which bulked especially large in France and Italy, but persons of the most varied political affiliations—nationalist, socialist, neutralist, conservative, and "moderate"—objected to the scale of the post-Korean rearmament programs, questioned some of the motives and implications of current American policy, resented the pressure from their own governments to accept higher taxes and static living standards, and showed particular reluctance to believe that the intentions of the U.S.S.R. were really so unfriendly as to require all these unpleasant measures.

This somewhat negative atmosphere helped to shape the issues which would confront the statesmen of the European-North Atlantic community in the early part of 1952 as the various projects for the preservation and recreation of Western Europe neared fruition. The basic design was reasonably clear —a reinforcement and extension of the North Atlantic Treaty Organization through a continued build-up of its existing military forces and the inclusion of Western Germany as part of an integrated nucleus of continental states. The chances of its realization were prejudiced mainly by three factors: (1) the hostile attitude and uncertain intentions of the U.S.S.R., particularly with respect to the rearmament of Germany; (2) the threats to economic and political stability inherent in large-scale rearmament; and (3) the particularist inclinations which predisposed so many Frenchmen, Germans, Britishers, and Americans—to name only the four principal nationalities concerned—to give the over-all program less than full support or even to see their main advantage as lying outside the framework of common action.

1. Elements of Atlantic Policy

Such formal responsibility as existed within the Western world for the consideration of problems of this order rested with the North Atlantic Council, comprising the foreign, defense, and finance ministers of the twelve governments which were signatory to the North Atlantic Treaty.[2] Of necessity, however, this body concerned itself mainly with concrete administrative, military, and economic problems rather than with these broader and subtler issues whose solution, if any, lay primarily in the diplomatic or even in the psychological realm. At its meeting in Rome in November 1951, the Council had been chiefly interested in finding ways by which the European governments could sustain the economic impact of the rearmament program while the prospective European Defense Community was being fitted into the structure of the Atlantic alliance. Major decisions had been put off to a later meeting which was to convene in Lisbon early in 1952, and at which it was expected that NATO's functions and purposes would be reviewed against a broader background of European and world developments.

From the beginning of NATO's existence in 1949, the basic aim of its twelve participating governments had been to develop in Europe a joint military force sufficiently powerful to "deter" (i.e., discourage) the Soviet Union from resorting to aggression against them, either directly or through its satellites. It had, of course, been perfectly conceivable that the Kremlin did not seriously contemplate military aggression in Western Europe but was relying on the "contradictions of capitalist society," aided by Communist propaganda and subversion, to keep the area in a state of weakness until it was ripe for conquest. It could even have been argued that no defense effort

2 The original members of the North Atlantic alliance were Belgium, Canada, Denmark, France, Iceland, Italy, Luxembourg, the Netherlands, Norway, Portugal, the U.K., and the U.S. The protocol extending the treaty to include Greece and Turkey (in *Documents on American Foreign Relations, 1952*, No. 14) entered into force on February 15 and the two countries formally acceded to the treaty on February 18, 1952.

undertaken in Western Europe had any real chance of success, and that attempts along this line would be more likely to provoke a Soviet attack than to deter it. Nevertheless, all of the North Atlantic governments had been agreed that it was essential to create a more adequate counterpoise to the military forces the Soviet Union had been and was still maintaining in Central and Eastern Europe. Those forces, comprising some thirty Soviet divisions with supporting aircraft and another sixty divisions organized by the satellite states, had appeared sufficient by themselves "to try, with fair prospect of success, to thrust far into the weaker West." Behind them lay the whole armed might of the Soviet Union—175 divisions, one-third of them mechanized or armored; 20,000 military aircraft; twenty cruisers and some 300 submarines; an industry geared to war and already capable of turning out atomic weapons.[3]

Against such an array of military power—primarily land power—American superiority in atomic bombs had offered at best a partial and imperfect defense. Yet the forces locally available to the West for the defense of the European Continent had at first been pitifully inadequate. As late as April 2, 1951, when General Eisenhower formally took command of the Allied Forces in Europe, the total strength at his disposal had amounted to "fewer than fifteen NATO divisions adequately trained and equipped for war" and "fewer than 1,000 operational aircraft," many of them of obsolescent types. In the course of 1951 the situation had been considerably improved, thanks to the commencement of large-scale deliveries of American-made arms and equipment and the arrival of six additional divisions—four American and two British—to reinforce the American, British, and French units already stationed in Germany as occupation forces. At the same time the accelerated European defense programs adopted since the Korean aggression had begun to show results, and the coordination of allied effort through SHAPE (Supreme Headquarters Allied Powers Europe), General Eisenhower's headquarters near Paris, had proceeded at a good pace. Conscription periods were

[3] Eisenhower, *First Annual Report,* cited.

lengthened, communications and training were increasingly standardized, joint exercises were held, and General Eisenhower's broad concept of Western Europe as "an ultimate stronghold flanked by two defended regions: One comprising Denmark and Norway and the other comprising Italy" began to take on some measure of strategic reality. By the end of 1951 there existed for the first time an allied force, concentrated primarily in Germany, which despite its numerical inferiority could offer serious resistance to any aggressive move originating behind the Iron Curtain.

It was also in 1951 that the NATO members definitely resolved to broaden the scope of their alliance by inviting Greece and Turkey and (indirectly) Western Germany to share the burdens and benefits of participation in Europe's defense. This expansion, undertaken largely on American initiative, promised to place additional divisions under SHAPE's over-all command—possibly twenty-five from Greece and Turkey, and eventually twelve from Western Germany. In the nature of the case, however, it could contribute little to the solution of immediate strategic problems in the crucial central sector of the European front. Most observers agreed that Western Germany had to be defended, if only because it was the key to the defense of Denmark, Norway, the Low Countries, and France. It was also acknowledged that Western Germany could not be adequately defended without the assistance of the West Germans themselves. But the method adopted for enlisting West German assistance would take time to work out, and there would certainly be an awkward transitional period while the new European army designed to "contain" the German units was being organized and learning to function. As for Greece and Turkey, they were geographically isolated and, despite amply demonstrated military qualities, lacked the kind of strength required for modern mechanized warfare. Although they might occasion some redeployment of the Soviet and satellite forces, they could offer little direct aid in the defense of Western Europe, nor could they undertake by themselves to prevent a Soviet breakthrough to the Mediterranean.

If the strategic pattern of European defense thus remained somewhat hazy, more tangible difficulties confronted the NATO governments in the material burdens inseparable from their military program. As their defense forces grew in strength and effectiveness, the economic cost of developing and maintaining them was having an increasingly serious impact on national economies and government finances. There was some reason to fear that the ambitious rearmament effort on which most of the NATO countries had embarked since Korea—to which were added extensive requirements for airfields, communications, and other facilities to be used in common by the NATO forces in Western Europe—might need to be reconsidered and perhaps scaled down if serious economic disturbances were to be avoided. Economic dislocations and the political unrest that usually accompanied them might undo all that was being accomplished in the military sector. Few European governments were stable enough to disregard the domestic implications of the regime of sacrifice that NATO defense planning entailed.

In recognition of the seriousness of this problem, the NATO Council in 1951 had authorized a committee of high-ranking experts to survey the economic and military programs of the individual member governments and formulate detailed recommendations which would be considered at Lisbon. Meanwhile there were multiple indications of difficulty ahead. The British Government had already conceded that there would be delays in carrying out the three-year, £4.7 billion rearmament program projected not many months earlier; a powerful faction within the Labor opposition was going further and challenging the whole concept of large-scale rearmament under existing world conditions. France was in the grip of similar difficulties. The chronic French financial and political crisis, aggravated by the costs of the war in Indochina, was to bring about the collapse of Premier René Pleven's government shortly before the Lisbon conference. Italy, on the contrary, had managed to exceed its original rearmament goals; but those who noted the privations endured by the bulk of the Italian people and the continued

vitality of the pro-Soviet political parties in the peninsula were
not wholly satisfied with the surface stability maintained by
the Christian Democratic party under Dr. Alcide De Gasperi.

The fact was that the countries of Western Europe, despite
the monumental economic recovery achieved under the Marshall Plan, were not yet in a position to rearm themselves by
their own efforts on the scale deemed necessary by NATO
planners. Without outside assistance, they could meet their
minimum defense targets only by imposing a degree of aus-
terity which their peoples were psychologically unable to accept. That was why the United States, in addition to maintaining a substantial part of its armed forces in Europe, felt
compelled to go on providing military and "defense support"
aid to its allies even after Western Europe's postwar "recovery"
was considered virtually complete. True, official Washington
looked with disfavor on suggestions from Europe that each
NATO nation, including the United States, should contribute
to the common effort in proportion to its actual economic and
financial strength. But Congress had nevertheless appropriated
$5.8 billion for aid to Europe in 1951–52 and, as we have seen,
would eventually appropriate another $4.4 billion for 1952–53.
Shipments of military end-items and other supplies under the
Mutual Security Program—some of them coming directly from
the United States, others paid for by this country but manufactured abroad and made available through "offshore procurement"—remained an indispensable element in Europe's
revival. Yet even such assistance had not entirely closed
the gap between what was considered necessary for European
defense and what could be provided by the nations of Western Europe as presently organized.

This situation gave added importance to the postwar effort
to bring about a larger measure of international cooperation
or "unity" in Western European economic, political, and military affairs. What the European nations could not accomplish
individually, it was argued, they should be able to accomplish
collectively if they would only get away from the restrictions
and inhibitions inherent in a system of sovereign, national

states. A merging of national economies and the creation of a unified European market would bring a realignment and rationalization of economic life and encourage the large-scale production without which Western Europe could not hope to maintain itself in the contemporary world. Replacement of national armies by an all-European defense establishment with a common military budget would not only provide a safe framework for the rearmament of Western Germany but also impose a further measure of economic and political unification throughout Western Europe. The common interest of the European peoples, it was maintained, could then find its supreme embodiment in a European political union.

This order of ideas, though endorsed from the beginning by the United States administration and Congress and supported in some degree by most of the Western European governments, had never been officially approved by the NATO nations as a group. In recent months, however, the concept of European unity had become increasingly involved in NATO's defense planning through the negotiations for the European Defense Community, which directly concerned five of the twelve NATO governments, as well as through its relation to the general objective of increased productivity and defense potential. The cause of European union was, moreover, explicitly supported by NATO's principal military authority, a soldier whose personal position was such that he could undertake to inspire policy as well as executing it. "As time goes on," General Eisenhower observed in an important press conference on January 21, 1952, "it seems obvious that [Europe] cannot gain strength and stability if it is to remain split up in a number of independent economies. There must be progress toward the unification of Western Europe if the objective of permanent security and peace in the western world is to be realized . . . . The whole thing [the European army, political unification of Europe and the North Atlantic Treaty Organization] must succeed because there is no satisfactory alternative for any of us." [4]

[4] New York Times, January 23, 1952.

To emphasize the earnestness of his conviction, General Eisenhower on this occasion went on to suggest the early summoning of a European constitutional convention "to examine and actually cope with the problems of a greater economic and political unity." Although this proposal went somewhat beyond the immediate plans of European governments, at least six of the latter were already moving rapidly in the direction indicated. Not many weeks previously the ministers of the six countries involved in the Schuman Plan and the European Defense Community (France, Western Germany, Italy, Belgium, the Netherlands, and Luxembourg) had agreed that the ultimate goal of their efforts must be "a European organization of a federal or confederal character" which would, eventually, take over the responsibilities exercised by both of those organizations. Already plans were on foot for merging the representative assembly of the Coal and Steel Community with that of the projected Defense Community, and for linking both bodies with the existing institutions of the Council of Europe. Other "pools" were contemplated for European agriculture and transportation. Something very like a European constitution seemed likely to result within the next few years from the organic development of institutions already in process of formation.

But if a kind of European unity was actually taking shape amid the pressures of the cold war, it was as yet neither solid nor complete. The only true supranational bodies thus far under consideration were the Coal and Steel Community and the Defense Community, both limited to the same six countries; and there was no real assurance as yet that even in these six countries the people would support their governments in the final steps necessary to put them into effect. The Schuman Plan had, indeed, been endorsed by the French Assembly late in 1951, and received a further impetus on January 11, 1952 when the West German Bundestag approved the treaty by a margin of better than three to two; these actions cleared the way for ratification by the other countries concerned and the treaty's entry into force on July 25. But the treaty constituting the European Defense Community had still to be negotiated in final form, and its ratification might prove considerably more difficult in view of its more sensitive nature and its more direct bearing on the vital issues of national and European security.

Progress toward European unity on a six-government basis also raised difficult questions about the future position of Great Britain and the Scandinavian members of NATO, as well as of other NATO members like Greece, Turkey, and Portugal and "neutral" or unaffiliated countries such as Ireland, Sweden, Switzerland, Austria, and Spain. In particular, it brought up in acute form the problem of Great Britain's relationship to a movement for which the British Government professed warm sympathy but with which it had refused any form of direct association.

British insistence on avoiding commitments which could weaken Britain's special ties with the Commonwealth and the United States was perfectly comprehensible to British opinion. "This is something which we know, in our bones, we cannot do," Anthony Eden had told an American audience.[5] But the British attitude had proved highly unsatisfactory to much of the Western world. British aloofness, it was argued, not only deprived the prospective union of a major element of strength but also impaired the chances of an effective union even among the continental states.

The desire for more active British participation in European affairs was directly related to the mutual fears and suspicions of the continental countries. The rapid recovery of Western Germany had produced apprehensions, particularly in France, that the new European association might actually come to be dominated by Germany unless British influence was somehow brought in as a counterweight to German influence. Germans appeared equally unenthusiastic about staking their future on the new experiment unless they were at least assured that Britain (and the United States) would continue to take an active interest in the defense of continental Europe. One of the pre-

[5] *New York Times,* January 12, 1952.

conditions for the success of the European Defense Community, and thus of the whole venture in European unification, thus appeared to involve the establishment of suitable links with Great Britain, either directly or through NATO and other bodies like the Council of Europe. In addition, the United States would certainly be asked to associate itself with the new institutions more directly than Washington had thus far contemplated.

The compulsions of Britain's position as a world power influenced other aspects of Western defense planning, not only in the heart of Europe but also in adjacent areas of the North Atlantic, the Mediterranean, and the Middle East. The organization within NATO of a system of military and naval commands for the North Atlantic and the Mediterranean had been delayed for months by disagreements between London and Washington over the division of command responsibility between the two nations, as well as by differing political and strategic conceptions affecting principally the Mediterranean area. Not until Mr. Churchill's January visit to the United States was a compromise solution for the North Atlantic worked out, along lines which in effect represented a substantial triumph of the American viewpoint. The American Admiral Lynde D. McCormick, Commander-in-Chief of the United States Atlantic Fleet, was designated Supreme Allied Commander, Atlantic (SACLANT), with headquarters at Norfolk and with responsibilities coordinate to those of General Eisenhower as Supreme Allied Commander, Europe (SACEUR). Two British admirals were assigned to serve under McCormick, the one as Deputy Supreme Commander for the Atlantic and the other as Commander-in-Chief of the Eastern Atlantic. British coastal waters were to remain under exclusively British command.[6]

This subordination of British to American officers in the Atlantic was frankly distasteful to the British Prime Minister and intensified his determination that in the Mediterranean,

[6] White House communiqué, January 18, in *Department of State Bulletin*, XXVI, January 28, 1952, 116; *New York Times*, January 31, 1952.

at least, British naval units should serve independently rather than under American command. But this dispute was only one of several factors in the confusion that surrounded NATO's role in the Mediterranean. Nominally the southern flank of General Eisenhower's European command, the Mediterranean was actually a focal point of uncoordinated and to some extent conflicting policies affecting both NATO members and outside countries. At one extremity, the United States was contemplating independent dealings with Spain in the hope of obtaining naval and air facilities in exchange for economic and military assistance. In the center, France worried about the security of its North African possessions while Italy divided its attention between its obligations as a NATO member and its perennial quarrel with Yugoslavia over the future of Trieste and other Adriatic problems. Farther east, where Greece and Turkey were in the process of formalizing their accession to NATO, uncertainty prevailed as to how their special situations would be fitted into the NATO program and how Turkey's new status would affect its position as a guardian of the Middle East and co-sponsor of the recent proposal to set up a Middle East Command outside of NATO.

This whole area, from Italy eastward to the Suez Canal and the Caucasus, presented strategic and political problems which were even farther from solution than those involving Germany and Western Europe. If Soviet expansionism was to be effectively contained, it was obviously necessary not only to hold the Rhine or the Elbe but also to establish solid defenses embracing the Alpine areas of Northern Italy, Austria, and Yugoslavia and extending through the southern Balkans to Turkey and the Middle East. But such an undertaking would be technically difficult and politically not less so. Western Austria at the moment was lightly held by Western occupation troops, but these would have to be withdrawn if ever the Soviet Government consented to conclude a treaty restoring Austrian sovereignty. Yugoslavia, though it was receiving Western economic and military aid and gradually establishing closer relations with Greece and Turkey, occupied a highly vulnerable position vis-à-vis the Soviet bloc and adhered to a political outlook which made cooperation with NATO difficult and exaggerated the obstacles to an understanding with its neighbor Italy. Greece and Turkey, geographically isolated and situated directly on the frontiers of the Soviet empire, could contribute little to the defense of other areas and could expect little immediate help if they themselves were attacked. All this would leave many problems for the NATO governments even if the meeting at Lisbon succeeded in dealing with more pressing issues.

2. NATO Comes of Age

The principal task of the thirty-five foreign, defense, and finance ministers who converged on the Portuguese capital from fourteen countries in the last week of February was to work out a schedule for the continuing build-up of NATO defense forces in Western Europe during 1952 and the two following years. In so doing they would have at their disposal for the first time not only the estimates of strategic requirements provided by General Eisenhower's headquarters but also the assessment of economic capabilities carried out by NATO's Temporary Council Committee and its three-man executive bureau (informally known as the "Three Wise Men") under the American chairmanship of W. Averell Harriman and later of William H. Draper, Jr. To arrive at a workable adjustment between military and economic imperatives, the NATO ministers would also be obliged to make certain assumptions about future developments in those fields that bore most directly on their problem. Particularly significant in this respect would be the level of future American aid to Europe and the success of the current effort to secure West Germany's participation in Europe's defense.

In both of these matters the North Atlantic governments were almost forced to take an optimistic view. To have done otherwise would have been tantamount to acknowledging defeat at the outset and setting in motion a chain of negative consequences which might have shaken the alliance to its foundations. Thus it was tacitly assumed that American aid would continue at a level not lower than in the past; further, that the treaty constituting the European Defense Community would be concluded and duly ratified within the next few months, and that German units would begin to take their places in a European army under SHAPE's over-all command by early 1953 at latest.

In retrospect it is obvious enough that these expectations were oversanguine. Even in February 1952, signs were not wanting that neither the Mutual Security estimates being prepared by the American administration nor the detailed arrangements for the European Defense Community that were being worked out by the technicians in Paris would be readily accepted by the legislative bodies concerned. Already the West German Bundestag and the French National Assembly had gone on record with what looked like mutually irreconcilable conditions for their acceptance of the future Defense Community.[7] As negotiations on the technical level neared a successful issue, the atmosphere was being increasingly clouded by the tendency of the Germans to demand additional advantages and concessions, such as full membership in NATO—which France, for one, would not hear of—and a reversal of French policies in the German-speaking Saar territory. Behind these Franco-German quarrels loomed the larger question of how German opinion would react to the preparations being made by the Soviet Government to try to block Germany's integration with the West by intensifying the popular agitation over German national unity.

But there had also been favorable developments which debarred the Lisbon gathering from taking too dark a view. The major governments—or at least the ministers principally concerned—remained grimly determined to make the experiment succeed. On February 18 and 19, Secretary Acheson and his French and British colleagues (Anthony Eden and Robert Schuman) had met with Chancellor Adenauer in London and resolved with him a number of issues which had to be dealt

[7] *Chronique de politique étrangère*, V, March 1952, 197-200.

with before the European army treaty could be put in final form. Most of these concerned the so-called "Peace Contract" which was being simultaneously negotiated between Western Germany and the Western Powers with the object of ending the Allied military occupation in Germany, giving the Federal Republic full sovereignty in most matters, and thus removing the legal and psychological obstacles to German participation in the European Defense Community. A complex argument about how much Western Germany could and should contribute financially to Western defense was settled on the basis of a compromise figure suggested by the "Three Wise Men." The four ministers also studied the prospective relationship between the E.D.C. and NATO, reaffirmed their governments' determination to preserve and strengthen their "partnership for peace," and adjourned in the expressed conviction that their meeting had "removed the obstacles which have hitherto delayed the conclusion of the negotiations." [8] Of equal importance to those who looked to Britain and the United States to ensure the success of the E.D.C. experiment was a separate communiqué in which the three Western ministers declared their "abiding interest" in the project and announced that their governments intended to "find appropriate means of giving the community the desired cooperation and support."

The ninth session of the North Atlantic Council was convened in Lisbon immediately following the London meeting and continued from February 20 to February 25. After the formal welcome to Greece and Turkey, the endorsement of the E.D.C. project was the first item of completed business. At Rome, three months earlier, Secretary Acheson had been unable to secure from the Council an unequivocal pronouncement in favor of the E.D.C. Now, however, the authorized spokesmen of all fourteen governments agreed that its underlying principles "conformed to the interests" of the NATO partners. To assure the new community of the requisite international sup-

[8] Communiqué, February 19, in *Department of State Bulletin*, XXVI, March 3, 1952, 325-326. On the German financial contribution cf. *ibid.*, March 17, 1952, 423-426.

port, it was further agreed that "reciprocal security undertakings" between the members of NATO and E.D.C. should be worked out and submitted for ratification by the governments—in other words, that Great Britain, the United States, and the other NATO countries which were not participating directly in the E.D.C. should assume toward the members of the Defense Community (including Germany) the same obligations they had already assumed toward their fellow-members of NATO (including all E.D.C. countries except Germany). These reciprocal obligations and relationships, the Council declared, "should be based on the concept of two closely related organizations, one working, so far as this [security] objective is concerned, within the framework of, and reinforcing the other." [9]

While awaiting the establishment of the E.D.C. and the recruitment of twelve hypothetical German divisions, the NATO members would be fully occupied in trying to carry out their own military programs as adjusted—upward, in most cases—in light of the recommendations put forward by the Temporary Council Committee. Through its impartial scrutiny and frank criticism of the defense plans and budget of every member country, the T.C.C. operation had provided a far more comprehensive and reliable view of NATO military and economic problems than had ever before been available. No longer did the demands of the military have to be judged solely in terms of political acceptability; for the first time they had been carefully weighed against the realistic economic capabilities of the individual NATO countries. The T.C.C. report was anything but "soft" in its recommendations. It insisted, as vigorously as ever the military had done, on the reality of the Soviet threat and the urgency of a more rapid build-up of forces, backed by a more rational and efficient utilization of all the resources at the disposal of the Atlantic partners. But the impartiality of the procedure, the high competence of the survey group, and its concern for maintaining the defense effort on a sound economic base assured its findings of respect. Not only

[9] Communiqué, February 26, in *Documents on American Foreign Relations, 1952,* No. 15 (a).

were its suggestions adopted as official goals, but it was decided to make such an "annual review" a regular feature of NATO procedure.

In the general satisfaction over this achievement the Council went so far as to abandon its usual reticence and publish a statement which included detailed military target figures:

"By its resolution on the T.C.C. report, the North Atlantic Council agreed on specific policies and plans for building NATO defensive strength during the present year. NATO nations agreed to provide approximately 50 divisions in appropriate conditions of combat readiness and 4,000 operational aircraft in Western Europe as well as strong naval forces.[10] It further provided a definite program for taking measures this year necessary to increase the defensive power of NATO in following years. This defensive force does not include the contributions of Greece and Turkey."

Goals for subsequent years were not made public, but it later became known that the Council had fixed a target figure of 75 divisions and 6,500 aircraft for 1953 and 96 divisions with 9,000 aircraft for 1954.

The public intimation that NATO expected to dispose of fifty divisions "in appropriate conditions of combat readiness" by the end of 1952 provoked immediate expressions of skepticism, and it was presently explained that nearly half of these forces would actually consist of "ready reserves" which could be mobilized within three to thirty days after the outbreak of hostilities. Even with this qualification, however, the Council felt able to state that such an increase in defensive power would constitute "an important increased deterrent to aggression"—particularly when account was taken of the fact that Allied strategic air power, though not specifically covered by the Council's action, was "already a powerful deterrent to aggression

[10] According to later information, these were to include 704 major combatant vessels and 925 smaller combatant types. Cf. *The Mutual Security Program for Fiscal Year 1953: Basic Data Supplied by the Executive Branch* (Committee print, House Foreign Affairs Committee and Senate Foreign Relations Committee, 82nd Congress, 2nd Session, Washington, 1952), 7. The NATO release on the T.C.C. report (February 24) appears in *Documents on American Foreign Relations, 1952*, No. 15 (b).

and in the event of attack would be a most valuable addition to the defense of Western Europe."

In its consideration of the financial and economic aspects of European defense, the Council also agreed "on the financing of a further portion of the infrastructure program, for airfields, communications and headquarters." This program, involving the construction of an elaborate system of defense installations intended to be used in common by the NATO forces defending Western Europe, had been begun by Great Britain, France, and the Benelux countries in 1950; subsequently they had been joined by the United States and Canada and, more recently, by Italy, Denmark, and Norway. Like other aspects of Western defense, development of the "infrastructure" had been complicated not only by arguments about the division of financial responsibility but also by the impossibility of securing long-term financial commitments from any of the governments concerned. Thus the work was being carried out in successive "slices," each one of which was separately financed. The first "slice," undertaken by five European governments in 1950, had been designed to cost $92 million; the second, in which the United States and Canada joined in September 1951, amounted to $221 million. At Lisbon the ten governments which were by then participating agreed on a "third slice" program of $425.6 million, and the United States share of the combined second and third slices was set at $288 million.[11] This would not include United States expenditure on other installations intended solely for the support of United States forces in Europe, such as the supply line that stretched across France from the port of Bordeaux.

These Council actions would affect primarily the Central sector of General Eisenhower's command in Europe. In addition, the Council had to deal with a variety of organizational problems which involved both the definition of command responsibility under NATO and the unwieldy structure of NATO itself. The presence of Greek and Turkish representatives at

11 *Second Report to Congress on the Mutual Security Program,* June 30, 1952 (Washington, 1952), 14; *Third Report,* December 31, 1952 (Washington, 1953), 2.

Lisbon increased the urgency of establishing a permanent Mediterranean command to replace the existing unsatisfactory arrangement, under which the nominal American commander (Admiral Robert B. Carney, Eisenhower's Commander-in-Chief, Southern Europe) was deprived of authority over the British forces in the area and had only partial control over those of the other allies. But the problem created by Anglo-American disagreements on the over-all command in the Mediterranean was further complicated by the reluctance of Greece and Turkey to place their armies under the Italian general who was Admiral Carney's deputy commander for ground forces. In the absence of any agreement between the principal powers concerned, the Council could only commission an expert study of the whole problem for consideration at its next meeting. In the meantime, it said, Greek and Turkish ground and air forces assigned to NATO would operate under General Eisenhower's over-all command "through Commander-in-Chief, Southern Europe," thus by-passing the Italian subcommander; naval forces would remain under national command but operate "in close coordination with all other naval forces in the Mediterranean."

Spain's relationship to Mediterranean defense lay outside the Council's official purview, although Portugal's foreign minister seized the occasion of the Lisbon meeting to plead once again for the admission to NATO of a country with which his own government had special ties and whose exclusion he termed a "strategic absurdity." Western relations with Yugoslavia were likewise handled outside the NATO framework, through the bilateral channels of the American military aid program and through special procedures set up by the United States, Great Britain, and France to deal with Yugoslavia's economic aid requirements. On the northern approaches to Europe, however, NATO was in a better position to assume direct responsibility. At Lisbon the Council announced the establishment of a new Channel Command, responsible for naval and "maritime air" operations in the Channel and the southern North Sea, under a British admiral who would also be in charge of defending British coastal waters. Unlike the Mediterranean command, the

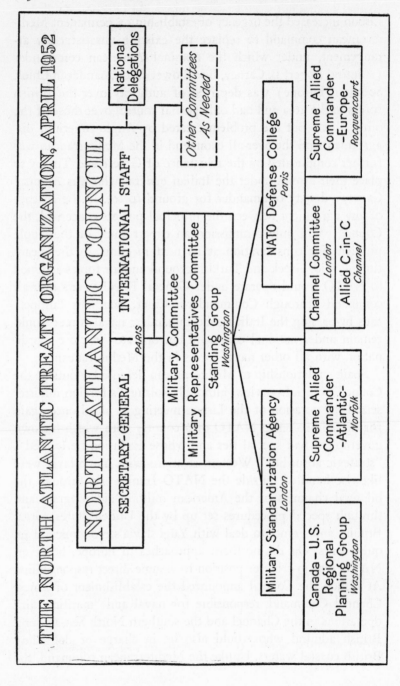

THE NORTH ATLANTIC TREATY ORGANIZATION, APRIL 1952

NORTH ATLANTIC COUNCIL

SECRETARY-GENERAL
PARIS

INTERNATIONAL STAFF

National Delegations

Other Committees
As Needed

Military Committee

Military Representatives Committee

Standing Group
Washington

NATO Defense College
Paris

Channel Committee
London

Allied C-in-C
Channel

Supreme Allied Commander -Europe- *Rocquencourt*

Military Standardization Agency
London

Supreme Allied Commander -Atlantic- *Norfolk*

Canada – U.S. Regional Planning Group
Washington

Channel Command would not be under SHAPE but would be made responsible to a special "Channel Committee" representing Belgium, France, the Netherlands, and the United Kingdom and situated in London.

So far as the civilian organization of NATO was concerned, it had long been recognized that the complex bureaucracy developed over the past three years required overhauling and realignment, both for efficiency and in order to give more effective representation to civilian as distinguished from military interests in the association. SHAPE, with its definite views on military requirements, had tended in the past to dominate the entire organization; a strengthening of the civilian element would tend to reassert the principle of civilian control as the organization emerged from the "planning" into the "operational" stage and prepared to face the difficult trials ahead. Accordingly, NATO's highest civilian authority, the North Atlantic Council, was now endowed with a regular status, enlarged and continuing responsibilities, and the facilities needed to discharge them. Periodic ministerial meetings would be held as in the past, the communiqué announced, but in the intervals the Council would "function in permanent session through the appointment of permanent representatives" and would take over the functions previously exercised by the Council Deputies, the Defense Production Board, and the Financial and Economic Board. To assist in the fulfillment of its increased responsibilities, it would be provided with a permanent executive or Secretary-General and a "unified international secretariat."

It was further agreed that the civilian activities of NATO, which had heretofore been scattered over two hemispheres, would now be concentrated in the same area as those of other international agencies with which it was desirable to maintain "close administrative connection"—in other words, in Paris, the seat of the Organization for European Economic Cooperation (O.E.E.C.) and of the group in charge of planning for the future E.D.C. Great Britain's reluctant consent to this arrangement was aided by an informal understanding that a British national would receive preference in the choice of a

Secretary-General. But Sir Oliver Franks, the preferred candidate, turned out to be unavailable, and the Council was unable to announce its selection before the close of the Lisbon meeting. Eventually, in March, the post was accepted by Lord Ismay, the British Secretary of State for Commonwealth Relations and former Secretary of the War Cabinet. Ambassador Draper, the United States Special Representative in Europe and European head of the Mutual Security Agency, stepped naturally into the post of permanent United States delegate on the reorganized Council.

Before concluding its Lisbon meeting the Council also adopted the report of a special committee which had been set up to study the problems of cooperation among NATO members in nonmilitary fields. Its conclusions reinforced those of the Temporary Council Committee in their emphasis on the importance of economic cooperation in general, and of the expansion and liberalization of trade in particular, as essential bases of a healthy Atlantic community. Special consideration was also given to the development of closer cooperative arrangements with the O.E.E.C. and kindred bodies, and to the desirability of more effective use of the manpower resources available to the NATO nations as a group.

Finally, the Council endeavored to place its decisions in a favorable public light and counteract the denunciations of the Soviet-Communist propaganda apparatus by adopting a "Declaration of Aims" which recalled that all of the actions contemplated, including those relating to the European Defense Community and the rearmament of Western Germany, were the reflection of an unwavering dedication to peaceful and progressive purposes:

". . . The members of the North Atlantic Council . . . wish once more to emphasize that this association was forged as a shield against aggression. Its first aim is peace, and the armed strength which is being built up by the united efforts of the member nations will be used only for the defense of their countries and the security of their peoples.

"The partnership between the nations of the North Atlantic Treaty is not for defense alone but of enduring progress. The

members of the Council look forward to the time when the main
energies of their association can be less concentrated on defense
and more fully devoted to cooperation in other fields, for the
well-being of their peoples and for the advancement of human
progress. . . ."

Among the countries which were members of the Atlantic
alliance, the decisions of their representatives at Lisbon called
forth a varied reaction. The essential achievement, perhaps,
was the one singled out by Mr. Eden on his return to London
—a definite improvement (or, at least, a confirmation) of the
prospect for collaboration among all the free countries of the
West, including Germany. As to the outlook for NATO's immediate military build-up in Europe, the optimism of Lisbon
was tempered by recognition of the heavy sacrifices that would
have to be made if the Council's targets were to be met. Within
four days of the Council's adjournment, the Western world was
jolted by the news that the new French cabinet headed by Edgar
Faure had been overthrown as a direct result of the Premier's
request for a 15 percent tax increase to meet France's obligations under the Lisbon program. "These discussions will raise
problems in many countries," said Secretary Acheson in his
radio report to the American people. "We have agreed on a
good and useful and possible year's work." But, he warned,
"the success of these measures will depend upon how vigorously they are followed up by further action." [12]

A somewhat similar appraisal was offered some weeks later
by General Eisenhower in his first annual report as Supreme
Allied Commander, Europe [13]—a document which not only provided the frankest and most comprehensive official analysis of
NATO problems ever to be made public, but which gained
added interest from the knowledge that its author would shortly
leave Europe to seek the Republican nomination to the presidency. "At this time," General Eisenhower wrote, "the forces
available to SHAPE are not of themselves sufficient to stay the
hand of an aggressor." They were not even sufficient, he said,

[12] Radio address, February 29, in *Department of State Bulletin*, XXVI, March
10, 1952, 363-366.
[13] *Documents on American Foreign Relations, 1952*, No. 13.

to enable the naval and strategic air forces of the alliance to exert their full effect. Compared to the situation twelve months earlier, however, the Supreme Commander saw a profound change—not only in morale, "the basic factor of all," but also in the combat readiness of the forces under his command:

"Already our active forces have increased to a point where they could give a vigorous account of themselves, should an attack be launched against us. In terms of army divisions, whether in service or quickly mobilizable, our forces in Western Europe have nearly doubled in numbers. . . . Readjustments in their deployment have enhanced their potential effectiveness against the threat from the East. Behind them is a steadily expanding supply system, and a command organization to plan and direct their coordinated efforts. Still far—disappointingly far—from sufficient for a determined defense, they nevertheless represent a fighting force in whose spirit and increasing fitness our nations can take considerable pride."

As to the future, General Eisenhower endeavored to put both Europeans and his own countrymen on guard against the tendency to delude themselves about each other's capabilities. "It would be fatuous," he told the Europeans, "for anyone to assume that the taxpayers of America will continue to pour money and resources into Europe unless encouraged by steady progress toward mutual cooperation and full effectiveness." And, at another point:

"The United States is currently making a tremendous effort to furnish a great portion of the capital outlay in military equipment. Without this, there could be no effective forces on the Continent within the next four or five years. But America cannot continue to be the primary source of munitions for the entire free world. To do so would be militarily unsound. Moreover, the United States cannot long continue such expenditures without endangering her own economic structure. The soundness of that structure is of vital concern to the entire free world, for its collapse would be a world-shaking tragedy."

But the experience of SHAPE had taught that similar considerations applied to the European economies as well. There, too, it was essential to maintain the economic and moral foundations without which defense was neither possible nor worth while:

"Everywhere we turned we ran into political and economic factors. One thing was clear—nothing would be gained and much lost through any substantial lowering of the already low standard of living in Europe. Our central problem was one of morale— the spirit of man. All human progress in the military or other fields has its source in the heart. No man will fight unless he feels he has something worth fighting for. Next, then, is the factor of the strength of the supporting economy. Unless the economy can safely carry the military establishment, whatever force of this nature a nation might create is worse than useless in a crisis. Since behind it there is nothing, it will only disintegrate."

The implication for American policy seemed clear. The direction of effort within NATO must continue to take into account not only the need for additional divisions but also the basic economic and psychological requirements of the countries that were undertaking to produce and sustain them.

"The tide has begun to flow our way and the situation of the free world is brighter than it was a year ago." Such was the conclusion that General Eisenhower drew from his twelve months at the center of NATO efforts. But, he emphasized, this was no time for relaxation:

"It would be disastrous if the favorable signs and developments recorded in this report were to put any mind at ease, or to create a sense of adequate security, for there is no real security yet achieved in Europe; there is only a beginning.

"Equally, it would be unfortunate if anyone were to find excuse for defeatism in the manifold difficulties and shortcomings of our joint effort to date. For we have made progress in all aspects of security. The momentum must be continued with renewed vigor, and since moral force is the genesis of all progress, especially progress toward security and peace, we must give primary attention to this vital element."

It was regrettable in some respects that the one man who, in the opinion of every qualified observer, had done most to inspire the peoples of Western Europe with a renewed sense of confidence and purpose was shortly to be removed from the

European scene. His basic mission at SHAPE was, no doubt, completed; but it would be difficult to find a successor with both the military competence and the personal qualities that had made the mission such a unique success.

That the new SACEUR would be an American was taken almost as a matter of course; and it was the British and French delegates to the new permanent Council who formally proposed, at its first meeting on April 28, that President Truman should be asked to designate another American officer to succeed the retiring Supreme Commander. General Eisenhower and others at SHAPE were known to favor the appointment of General Alfred M. Gruenther, whose experience as Chief of Staff to the Supreme Allied Commander had given him a familiarity with NATO problems that was felt to outweigh his comparative lack of seniority and field experience. Others had inclined to General Matthew B. Ridgway, who already had earned an international reputation as head of the United Nations Command in Korea. The solution adopted was one that would enable SHAPE to benefit from the qualities of both men. General Ridgway received the appointment as Supreme Allied Commander; General Gruenther remained as Chief of Staff; and Field Marshal Montgomery, the British Deputy Supreme Commander, promised to make his own knowledge and abilities available to the new team as long as they might be needed.

3. Germany: Integration or Neutralization?

General Ridgway's experience in the struggle with world Communism had thus far lain primarily on the military side; but his position in the Far East in connection with the occupation of Japan and the conduct of the Korean truce talks had enabled him to observe some other aspects of Communist operations, and he was destined to see still more before he took over his new command. In February, from his headquarters in Tokyo, he had witnessed an outbreak of serious rioting fomented by Japanese Communists in protest against measures

then being taken to draw Japan into the United States security
orbit. In early May, as he prepared to hand over his Far Eastern responsibilities to General Mark Clark, he was forced to
deal with a grave crisis involving the seizure of an American
brigadier general by the turbulent inmates of a Communist
prisoner-of-war compound on Koje Island off Korea. And when
he arrived in Paris to take up his new duties at the end of the
month, he was met by more Communist demonstrations of so
formidable a character that French authorities felt it necessary
to detain the acting head of the French Communist party and
talked openly of a plot against the security of the state. Similar
hostile manifestations greeted the new Supreme Commander
in Italy and other countries of Western Europe.

These occurrences, while not primarily aimed at completing
General Ridgway's political education, were nevertheless closely
linked in Soviet-Communist strategy. Scattered as they were,
each of them was a direct response to the general line of policy
being pursued by the United States and its associates in regard
to the reorientation of Japan, the repulse of aggression in
Korea, and the defense build-up in Europe. Thus they belonged
to the same over-all pattern as the Communist "peace" and
"hate America" campaigns, the groundless but vehement denunciations of alleged American bacteriological warfare tactics,
and the assault on United States economic policies at the Moscow economic conference. Even these activities, moreover, did
not complete the Soviet political warfare pattern. The missing
element—quite possibly the central element—in the Soviet design was a diplomatic offensive by which the Kremlin evidently
hoped to forestall the implementation of the broad program
which the NATO governments had accepted at Lisbon.

The heart of the Lisbon program had been the decision to go
forward with the rearmament of Western Germany in the
framework of a European Defense Community. And the most
dramatic response to this determination, which intimately involved the fate of fifteen Western governments, had come
neither from Bonn nor from any of the NATO capitals but
from a sixteenth government whose opinion had not been

sought and which, theoretically, had no concern in the decisions of the NATO partners. In Moscow, on March 10, Foreign Minister Vyshinsky sent for the diplomatic representatives of the United States, Great Britain, and France and handed them copies of an official note which was to be remembered as the principal Soviet diplomatic action of 1952. In contrast to most Soviet communications, it made no critical reference to the policy of the Western powers in Germany or to their relations with the Bonn government. Instead, it invited the three governments to join "urgently" with the U.S.S.R. in working out a peace settlement applicable to the whole of Germany and thus eliminating the "abnormal situation" which, it pointed out, still existed in that country almost seven years after the end of the war in Europe.[14]

Appended to the Soviet note was a suggested "basis" for a German peace treaty. Its conception differed radically from the ideas developed by Western diplomats and approved at Lisbon. The Western powers, convinced that the attitude of the U.S.S.R. would make it impossible to conclude a peace settlement with Germany as a whole in the foreseeable future, had resolved to make a separate "peace contract" with the government of West Germany alone. But now the U.S.S.R. proposed that "preparations of the peace treaty should be accomplished with the participation of . . . an all-German government." The Western allies had planned to maintain armed forces in Western Germany, the key area in the defense of Western Europe, for as long as might be necessary after the contractual agreements with the Federal Government at Bonn were signed and ratified. The Soviet proposals stipulated, on the contrary, that all armed forces of the various occupying powers should be withdrawn from Germany, and all foreign military bases on German territory should be liquidated, within one year after the suggested peace treaty came into effect. The West had contemplated the closest possible association of Western Germany with the system of security pacts which had been built up against the threat

[14] For the Soviet note of March 10 and subsequent correspondence see *Documents on American Foreign Relations, 1952,* No. 21.

of Soviet aggression; whereas the U.S.S.R. now proposed that the future unified Germany should be obligated "not to enter into any kind of coalition or military alliance directed against any power which took part with its armed forces in the war against Germany." The Western intention, finally, was to permit German rearmament only within a European army under international control; but now the U.S.S.R. suggested—in sharp contrast to earlier Soviet declarations—that a unified Germany should be permitted "to have its own national armed forces (land, air, and sea) which are necessary for the defense of the country," and to produce war materials and equipment to the extent required for these national forces.

Despite the novelty of some of its details, it seemed clear that this sudden proposal to establish a unified, rearmed, and neutral Germany was basically one more of those obstructive moves by which the Soviet Government had for years been endeavoring to frustrate the accomplishment of Allied purposes in the former Reich. But in proposing to reopen the discussion of a German peace settlement the U.S.S.R. was simultaneously reopening other fundamental issues which had been only partially submerged by the recent Western emphasis on completing the Peace Contract and the European Defense treaty. Any peace settlement with Germany as a whole, such as the Soviet Government now proposed, would involve much more than the liquidation of World War II. A unified German government, which alone would be capable of entering into final arrangements with regard to such matters as frontiers, reparations, and guarantees against future aggression, obviously could not be established unless a way was found to bridge the political, economic, and social chasm that had opened between the two parts of Germany since the war. Profound changes would first have to occur in the outlook and procedures of the Federal Republic, the Communist-controlled "German Democratic Republic," or both. And this in turn would require not only a modification of some of the arrangements made by the occupying powers but also a readjustment or redefinition of various interests which they themselves had always considered essential, both in relation to Germany and in relation to each other.

In its previous actions on the German question, the U.S.S.R. had seemed principally concerned to retain the territorial and other advantages it had seized in Germany for itself and its Polish satellite, and to remain in firm control of its zone of occupation in Eastern Germany under all circumstances. While posing as an advocate of German reunification and national restoration, the Kremlin had invariably accompanied its agitation along these lines with conditions which, if accepted, would have ensured continued Soviet control of Eastern Germany and favored the eventual extension of Communist control over the whole country.

The Allies, too, though in a different fashion, had subordinated all other considerations to the protection of their existing position in Germany and the incorporation of at least the Western part of the country into their own political, economic, and military system. Forced by Soviet noncooperation to embark on a separate policy in their zones of occupation, they had continued to call for German unity but in the meantime had geared their program of European recovery and defense to the revival of Western Germany as a separate entity and an essential element in a reviving Europe. In so doing, they had given the U.S.S.R. and its East German puppets an additional motive to pose as the real champions of the German people in their longing for national unity, peace, and independence. Such agitation, in the Soviet scheme of things, could be a most potent means of obstructing Allied plans by arousing contrary sentiment in Germany and elsewhere.

Soviet efforts along these lines had been especially noticeable ever since the fall of 1950, when NATO had approved the principle of West German rearmament and the Kremlin had responded by declaring that it would "not tolerate such measures aimed at reviving the German regular army in Western Germany." At the same time Moscow, in addition to denying the well-known fact that it was already engaged in building up a strong paramilitary force in Eastern Germany, had begun to agitate vigorously in favor of an early peace settlement with a unified but disarmed Germany. Despite the failure of the Paris conference of deputy foreign ministers, assembled on Soviet initiative in the spring of 1951, intensive discussion of German peace and unity problems had continued both internationally and within Germany. As negotiations for a separate peace settlement with the West neared completion, the Adenauer government and the West German Bundestag had found themselves simultaneously debating the conditions of an *all*-German peace settlement with the East German "People's Chamber" and its Communist bosses. At issue in this somewhat theoretical debate were the nature of the peace settlement that might be sought for Germany as a whole, the methods of achieving it, the type of government that might represent a unified Germany at a hypothetical peace table, and the character of the elections that would have to take place before any such all-German government could be formed.

Practically speaking, this discussion between democratic and Communist Germany had never got beyond the initial question of a suitable election procedure. With the backing of the Western Allies, the Bonn government had insisted that any all-German elections which might be held must be "free, general, equal, secret, and direct" and must take place under international control in order to prevent abuses. The East German authorities, presumably suspecting that any such procedure would be sure to result in a heavy Communist defeat, had shown marked resistance to the idea of "free" or "secret" elections; by early 1952, however, they had moderated their position to the extent of producing a draft electoral law that embodied a number of concessions to the Western point of view.[15]

But even if agreement on this point were reached, the question of international control of any all-German elections seemed likely to prove a stumbling block. The East Germans maintained that supervision of the elections was an internal German affair or, at most, a matter for the four occupying powers.

[15] Cf. Wolfgang Abendroth, "Die Diskussion über gesamtdeutsche Wahlen," *Europa-Archiv*, VII, March 20, 1952, 4781-4792.

The West Germans and the Allies, recalling the record of Soviet obstruction in German matters, insisted that this was not enough. As a first step toward a more acceptable election procedure, they had induced the United Nations General Assembly in the fall of 1951 to establish a commission to try to ascertain whether conditions in Germany were such as to make possible the holding of "genuinely free and secret elections" throughout the country. This move had been bitterly opposed by the U.S.S.R.; and the East German government, professing to regard the arrangement as an encroachment on the rights of the German people, had announced that it would neither cooperate with the commission nor admit United Nations representatives to those parts of Germany under its control. When the commission was established in February 1952, it quickly obtained assurances of full cooperation from the Allied and German authorities in Western Germany and West Berlin, but the corresponding authorities in Eastern Germany and East Berlin simply ignored its communications.[16]

All this agitation about German reunification and elections seemed a little unreal because none of the parties involved could be considered altogether in earnest. In leading the agitation for peace and unity, the U.S.S.R. and its East German agents were obviously more interested in making trouble for the Allies than in doing a service for the German people. In urging "genuinely free" all-German elections, the Allies had obviously not lost sight of more immediate objectives but were merely endeavoring to hold their own in the propaganda war and retain as much German support as possible for their own policy of integrating the Federal Republic with the West. Of the two parties, the Russians may have had the stronger reasons to press for real German unification, since to them it represented a definite alternative to the Allied integration policy and, presumably, the lesser of the two evils from the

[16] Cf. *The United States in World Affairs, 1951*, 391-394 and the commission's report in U.N. Document A/2122, May 5, 1952. Since the commission was instructed to make a simultaneous investigation in all parts of Germany, the noncooperation of the Eastern authorities prevented it from carrying out any part of its mission.

Soviet point of view. For the Allies, on the other hand, unification was at most a secondary objective. Integration, in the
Allied view, came first; once a democratic Western Germany
was safely linked with the rest of Western Europe, the country (so they reasoned) could be reunited by simply including
Eastern Germany in the institutions already set up to accom-
modate Western Germany. But there was to be no reunification
on terms that could prejudice either Germany's democratic
future or its assimilation into the West.

One may even speculate as to whether the Soviet pressure
on this issue did not actually result in speeding up the process
of West German integration instead of delaying it. The growing nationalist ferment in Germany, profoundly stimulated by
Soviet-Communist agitation, gave the Allies an additional incentive to hurry along the negotiation of the Peace Contract
and the E.D.C. while the Federal Republic was still in a comparatively amenable mood. For German opinion was by no
means uniformly behind the policies of the Adenauer government. The powerful Social Democratic opposition was dead
set against the Western program, which, it claimed, involved
the trading of fundamental German interests for an inferior
and insecure position in the Western camp. Not only Communists and Nazi sympathizers but many Germans of unimpeach-
able moderation and "respectability" deplored the existing
trend of Allied policy in Germany and were only too ready to
grasp at any plausible alternative held out to them from the
East.

Such, in essence, had been the status of the "German question" when Mr. Vyshinsky unfurled his note of March 10 [17]—
a document which was heavy with appeals to German national
sentiment and contained a special promise of equal rights for
ex-soldiers and ex-Nazis who were not actually serving court
sentences. This attempt to curry favor with conservative and

---

[17] The Soviet note had been foreshadowed by a communication from the East
German government (February 13) appealing to the four powers for a speedy
peace treaty which would end the division of Germany and establish Germany
as a "united, independent, democratic, and peace-loving state." (Text in *Europa-
Archiv*, VII, March 20, 1952, 4793.)

nationalist-minded Germans was nothing new; but in other respects the Soviet proposals differed markedly from past statements of the Soviet position toward Germany. Particularly striking was the intimation that the future unified German state, though forbidden to contract alliances against any of its late enemies, should be permitted to maintain the armed forces and war industry necessary for its own defense. For a government that had previously always insisted on Germany's complete demilitarization in accordance with the Potsdam Agreement of 1945, this was a revolutionary change of front. Moreover, the Soviet note was so phrased as to encourage a hope that the Kremlin's terms might be subject to still further modification in the event of a Big Four meeting such as Moscow was now proposing.

In conjunction with the recent limited concessions by the East German regime in the matter of free elections, it almost looked as though the U.S.S.R. were preparing to alter its whole approach to German matters. Presumably it had not abandoned its general aim of advancing Soviet-Communist interests in Europe and preventing the consolidation of the "imperialist camp," in which it included the West German republic. But the methods by which this aim was being pursued in the German arena seemed to grow more drastic as time went on. In its past moves for German peace and unification, the Kremlin had always stipulated that Germany must remain demilitarized and that unification must take place in a way that would give the Communists a better than even chance to capture control of the entire country. Now, in their eleventh-hour anxiety to block the integration process, they seemed to be hinting that these conditions might be reduced. To keep Germany away from the West, they might be willing not only to withdraw their support of the East German Communists but even to forego the demilitarization of the country, contenting themselves instead with its neutralization by suitable international agreements.

How genuine was the Soviet change of front? Was it a serious diplomatic initiative or merely a supreme "psychological" appeal, directed to German neutralists and, behind them, to the many Western opponents of the NATO program? The answer was not to be found in the vague terminology of the Soviet note. Only concrete negotiation would disclose what real concessions, if any, the Kremlin was prepared to make; and no such negotiations were destined to take place. Conceivably Moscow had been sufficiently impressed by the growing Western strength to consider a real readjustment of its German policy—which would not prevent it, of course, from continuing to exert pressure on future developments in Germany by other means. It is also possible that the Kremlin foresaw what actually occurred—that the Allies would decline to negotiate on the terms suggested, and that as a result there would be no need for the Soviet Government to specify the concessions it was prepared to make. Perhaps Moscow stood to gain some advantages in either case. If its proposals were accepted, Allied aims in Western Germany would automatically have to be abandoned; if, on the other hand, the Soviet proposals were rejected, the resultant wave of popular disillusionment in Germany and the West would make the accomplishment of Allied purposes that much more difficult.

Yet even the political strategists of the Kremlin could not formulate a proposal which would make a maximum impression west of the Iron Curtain and still satisfy their own minimum requirements. The appeal to German nationalism lost some of its force through the stipulation that Germany's permanent frontiers would be those "established" at Potsdam— i.e., that the U.S.S.R. and Poland would still retain the German territory they had annexed east of the Oder and Neisse rivers. The insistence on "democratic rights" for all Germans took on ominous overtones when read in conjunction with the standard Communist demand for "free activity of democratic parties and organizations" and the banning of organizations "inimical to democracy and to the maintenance of peace." The meaning which Communists attached to such phrases had been too often demonstrated in the postwar history of the Soviet satellite states. Nor was it reasonable to expect that the French and other

Western European peoples would welcome with much enthusiasm the prospect of a rearmed and reunited Germany—even
if neutralized—which guaranteed equal rights for former
Wehrmacht officers and former Nazis and which might some
day seek an alliance with the U.S.S.R. as Hitler's Germany had
done in 1939.

But with all its weaknesses, the Soviet note was bound to be
embarrassing to the Allies and to the Adenauer government
because it did offer a clear-cut alternative to the integration
policy, and one that had undeniable appeal not only to Germans but to many in the West who disliked the existing
plans for Germany and still hoped for a general alleviation
of the East-West tension. It was even conceivable that the reestablishment of Germany as a neutral power in the heart of
Europe—assuming that such a solution could be brought about
and maintained—might serve Allied interests as well as or
better than the existing policy. But the Allied governments
were frankly skeptical of Soviet motives, doubted the possibility of establishing Germany as a neutral buffer between themselves and the Russians, and desired above all to avoid further
delay in completing their arrangements with the Federal Republic. Any discussions they might enter into with the Soviet
Government were thus made subject to the condition that the
integration agreements must go through on schedule.

Despite their negative reaction, however, the Allies could
not afford to reject the Soviet overture out of hand. Public
opinion in France and Britain insisted that no chance for a conciliatory settlement of the German problem must be neglected.
As Clement R. Attlee, the leader of the British opposition,
remarked at a somewhat later stage of the proceedings:

"It is anybody's guess as to what this Russian approach means,
but we should not neglect any opportunity. After all, the overall
interest of the whole of us is to get a peaceful settlement in Europe
and to do away with the division of the world into two parts. Of
course, it may be that this is a manoeuvre merely to delay our
build-up. On the other hand, it may be that the Russians are beginning to realise that our strength is growing. . . . Therefore, I

say that on all counts we should take this matter up. We all hope that we shall get these talks." [18]

In France, where M. Schuman was again foreign minister in the new right-of-center cabinet of Antoine Pinay, the Russian overture not only excited the public but accentuated what seemed to be an incipient cleavage within the government itself. Those who were lukewarm toward the Schuman policy of reconciliation with Germany—including, it was said, the new Prime Minister himself—were eager to explore any alternative that might be offered. In Germany, naturally, the reaction was even more lively. Chancellor Adenauer remained firm in support of Allied views, but could not afford to appear neglectful of the possibilities seemingly opened up by the Soviet note. The still incomplete state of the contractual and E.D.C. negotiations, and the accompanying embitterment of Franco-German relations, made it imperative to avoid any course that would further alienate the great mass of West Germans from the policies of the governing coalition.

Torn between official skepticism and popular delusions, between reluctance to enter into fruitless discussion and public insistence on the desirability of negotiations, the Western governments declared themselves willing to exchange views with the Soviet Government but insisted at the same time that they would "not be deflected" [19] from their basic policy in Germany. In laboriously drafted notes delivered on March 25, they invited the U.S.S.R. to disclose its intentions in more detail, but pointed out that their own views apparently collided with those of the Soviet Government on at least two essential points: (1) the necessity of genuinely free all-German elections (unmentioned in the Soviet note) as an indispensable preliminary to the establishment of an all-German government and the conclusion of a peace treaty; and (2) their strong opposition to the proposal for a neutral, rearmed Germany. This latter expedient, they said, appeared inconsistent with their present plans for

[18] *Parliamentary Debates, Weekly Hansard,* House of Commons, May 14, 1952, 1480.
[19] Statement by Secretary Acheson, March 26, in *Department of State Bulletin,* XXVI, April 7, 1952, 530.

securing German participation in "a purely defensive European community"; thus they believed it "would be a step backwards and might jeopardize the emergence in Europe of a new era in which international relations would be based on cooperation and not on rivalry and distrust."

In essence, if not in form, the Western governments thus rejected the central feature of the new Soviet program. Further exchanges might serve to clarify Soviet views in some respects and, from Moscow's standpoint, would have the further desirable effect of heightening the agitation of European opinion. But they would hardly bring the Western powers into agreement with a government whose main purpose was to block the attainment of their own central policy objective. From an historical point of view, therefore, the interest of such further diplomatic notes as were exchanged during the next two months is somewhat academic. Both sides offered certain concessions in regard to electoral procedure,[20] thereby encouraging a quite unwarranted optimism in sections of the European public. But a slight narrowing of the differences on what was essentially a side issue could hardly lead to constructive results as long as both parties adhered to their basic position in more fundamental matters.

More noteworthy, perhaps, were the indications that if its diplomatic efforts miscarried the Kremlin might attempt to wreck the Bonn negotiations by other methods. As though foreseeing the failure of Moscow's diplomatic offensive, Soviet-Communist authorities in Germany were beginning to adopt what looked like tactics of intimidation. An attack by Soviet fighter planes on a French airliner en route to Berlin on April 29 might have been unpremeditated or accidental. But there was nothing unpremeditated about the bellicose statements

[20] In a note of April 9, the U.S.S.R. agreed to a four-power discussion of "free all-German elections" but reiterated its refusal to work with the U.N. Commission and, as an alternative, proposed a pre-election investigation by a four-power commission. Replying on May 13, the Western governments stressed their continued preference for the procedure sanctioned by the U.N. General Assembly, but expressed readiness to consider "any other practical and precise proposals for an impartial commission of investigation"—provided they were "likely to promote the early holding of free elections throughout Germany."

emanating from East German government quarters. Deputy Premier Walter Ulbricht was calling on the workers of Western Germany to resort to a general strike in order to prevent the fulfillment of Allied plans. President Wilhelm Pieck declared that if West German remilitarization became a fact, the "German Democratic Republic" would have to take measures for its own defense—in other words, to bring the secretly rearmed East German "security forces" into the open. If the West tried to drag Germany into a new war of aggression, said an East German official communiqué, "it would be preceded by a fratricidal civil war of Germans against Germans." Once again, ominous incidents began to occur on the highway that linked West Germany with the democratic outpost in West Berlin. "If the Americans turn Berlin into a bridgehead for their war of aggression," Herr Ulbricht threatened, "the Berliners will be the victims." [21]

Summing up its views in a new round of diplomatic notes on May 24, the Soviet Government declared that the delay in responding to its request for four-power talks was bound to strengthen the belief that the Western governments were interested "not in the unification of Germany and not in a peace treaty with Germany" but only in tying Western Germany more closely to "the aggressive North Atlantic bloc" and thus confronting the German people with a *fait accompli*—"the remilitarization of West Germany and the retention of Occupation troops in West Germany." While reasserting its own point of view on the substance of the future peace treaty, Moscow now proposed an end of note-writing and a commencement of four-power discussions without delay.

But this offer came too late; this particular engagement in the battle for Germany was already lost. The Soviet note found the Western Foreign Ministers already in Bonn, putting the finishing touches on the contractual agreements which they and Dr. Adenauer were to sign on May 26. One day later, in Paris, the necessary signatures would be affixed to the Treaty Constituting the European Defense Community and the accompany-

[21] Quoted in *Chronique de politique étrangère*, V, July 1952, 419-420, 430-431.

ing documents which, when ratified, would make Western
Germany a member of the Atlantic community in all but name.

4. Peace Contract and Defense Community

Although unable to forestall the signature of the various
treaties and agreements integrating Federal Germany with the
West, the Soviet maneuvers were not without influence on their
form and long-term prospects. By holding up to Western
opinion what looked like an alternative to the official Western
policy, Moscow had heightened the misgivings of those whose
attachment to the official policy had never been more than
lukewarm. Thus it had increased the pressure for further adjustments that would at least bring the treaties more nearly into
line with dissident opinion. German quarters, opposition and
governmental alike, had redoubled their insistence that the
terms of the settlement must not only be "equitable" in themselves but must in no way prejudice the chances of restoring
German unity. French circles, made apprehensive by the up-
surge of German nationalism, demanded more explicit guarantees that Great Britain and the United States would fully
support the new European community, not only against the
Russians but also against the Germans if the latter should
prove unruly. The last-minute modifications necessitated by
these and other demands sufficed to get the agreements signed,
but quite failed to satisfy opponents of the settlement. "Signing is not ratifying," as one Frenchman remarked; and the
atmosphere created by the Soviet notes was not propitious to
speedy ratification of the agreements in any of the major continental countries. The whole settlement, with all its implications for the European future, was thus burdened from the
outset with a weight of unpopularity that threatened to nullify
the vision and ingenuity of the statesmen who had devised it.

In examining the several elements of this diplomatic master-
piece,[22] it is useful to keep in mind the basic interests which

[22] For texts see *Convention on Relations with the Federal Republic of Germany:
Message from the President* (Senate Executives Q and R, 82nd Congress, 2nd
Session, Washington, June 2, 1952) and *Documents on American Foreign
Relations, 1952*, Nos. 19 and 20.

ran through the negotiations and whose interplay determined the character of the agreements ultimately arrived at. Fundamental to the entire undertaking, of course, had been the quest for an additional margin of security against a possible Soviet attack in Europe—a margin which, in the opinion of NATO authorities, could be achieved only by the inclusion of Western Germany in the over-all scheme of European defense. But the straightforward pursuit of this objective had been limited by other preoccupations which often conflicted with each other as well as with the main objective. Security against the U.S.S.R. and its satellites had to be combined with continuing security against Germany itself; and this aim, in turn, had to be reconciled with German insistence on equal rights in Europe, equal security against the U.S.S.R., and a continuing prospect of achieving the reunification of the German homeland.

The European army project, devised as a partial answer to these demands, had raised new issues in its turn. Each of the six participating countries had been obliged to determine how far, and under what conditions, it could entrust its own destiny to a supranational (and therefore foreign) authority which would henceforth control the principal instruments of its own defense. All of them, moreover, had recognized that no arrangement that was strictly limited to the six countries of the European Defense Community could possibly fulfill these varied requirements. Hence had arisen the universal demand that Britain and the United States—the two countries which, in reality, were still providing the backbone of continental defense—pledge to the new organization their lasting and efficacious support.

Although all parts of the proposed settlement were interdependent, the contractual agreements were signed before the European Army treaty; the liquidation of Germany's war against the West took precedence over the arrangements to associate the new Federal Republic directly with its European neighbors. In reality, of course, the relations between Federal Germany and the Western Allies of World War II had already been placed on a peacetime basis in most respects, and the state of war had been officially terminated by individual action of the Allied countries in 1951. Legally, however, German-Allied relations were still governed by an amended version of the Occupation Statute of 1949, under which the three Western powers not only continued to maintain occupation forces in Western Germany but also reserved to themselves the ultimate authority over all aspects of German public life. The hammering out of a new agreement to terminate the occupation and transfer most of this authority to the Federal Republic had been the principal task of the Allied and German experts who had been stubbornly negotiating the contractual agreements at the Petersberg outside Bonn since September 1951.

The complexity and difficulty of these negotiations can be inferred from the fact that the results were ultimately embodied in four conventions, seven annexes, four sets of clarifying letters, and a supplementary financial agreement—not to speak of other matters which were reserved for separate settlement.[23] But most of the disagreements revolved about one simple issue. What the Germans desired was to regain full "sovereignty" and authority to manage their affairs without interference. Yet even at this date the three Western powers contemplated no such blanket transfer of authority and re-

[23] One of the most important of these separate issues was dealt with by the London Conference on German External Debts (February 28-August 8, 1952), at which Germany agreed on terms of settlement for its prewar foreign indebtedness and thus cleared the way for partial cancellation of the Allied claims to reimbursement for postwar economic aid to the Federal Republic. (Cf. *Department of State Bulletin*, XXVI, 1952, 206-207, 397-398, 461-462, 473-477; XXVII, 1952, 252-260, 608-609; XXVIII, 1953, 329-330, 373-380; also *Report of the Conference on German External Debts, London, February-August 1952* [Department of State Publication 4746, Washington, 1952].) The problem of German assets in Switzerland was disposed of by a German-Swiss agreement (August 26) and an agreement between Switzerland and the U.S., U.K., and France (August 28) whereby German owners would pay Switzerland one-third of the value of their assets in that country and Switzerland would pay the Allies 121.5 million Swiss francs for distribution as German reparations (*Department of State Bulletin*, XXVII, September 8, 1952, 363-364). To provide partial indemnification for persecutions of Jews by the Nazi regime, the Federal Republic concluded agreements with the Government of Israel and the Conference on Jewish Material Claims Against Germany (Luxembourg, September 10) calling for payments in kind to a total value of DM 3.45 billion ($822 million) over a period of 12 to 14 years (*New York Times*, September 11, 1952 and *Europa-Archiv*, VIII, April 20, 1953, 5619-5636).

sponsibility. A definitive peace treaty, they pointed out, would have to await agreement with the Soviet Government; meanwhile, a part of the country was under Soviet occupation, and they themselves were obliged to garrison the remainder. This state of affairs, they said, compelled them, in the common interest, to retain certain special rights relating to the stationing and the security of their forces in Germany, the status of Berlin, and "questions concerning Germany as a whole"—which, naturally, would include the questions of German unity, of an eventual peace settlement, and of Germany's permanent frontiers. Furthermore, said the Allies, the fact that Germany had been the principal enemy state in the late war made it necessary to require certain assurances that the obligations assumed by the Federal Republic would be duly discharged and that there would be no repetition of the unfortunate events of the prewar period.

Although most inhabitants of the Federal Republic were not unwilling to leave responsibility for Berlin in Allied hands, there was strong resistance to other parts of the Allied program —the more so when it became evident that the Allies took a large view of what was required for "the security of their forces" in Germany and were even proposing to intervene directly in case of a future threat to public order or democratic government in Germany. To establish the exact rights and obligations of Allied and German authorities in matters of this kind required endless bargaining. Not less vexatious were the controversies that arose over such matters as the size of the future German financial contribution to European defense and the degree to which the Federal Republic must perpetuate Allied arrangements in regard to the deconcentration and decartellization of German industry and the sentencing of Nazi war criminals.

Agreement on the master convention regulating future Allied-German relations was achieved as early as November 1951 by simply leaving the most controversial issues to be dealt with in annexes and supplementary agreements. Additional points were settled during Dr. Adenauer's visit to Lon-

don on the eve of the Lisbon conference. Thereafter the negotiators continued to struggle forward from one roadblock to another. Repeatedly the fulminations of the Bundestag and the
sharp reaction of French political circles seemed likely to imperil
the entire venture. To add to the tension created by the Soviet
notes, the Franco-German controversy over the Saar had
entered an acute phase with the appointment of a French
ambassador to the Saar territory, a German complaint to the
Council of Europe against the banning of pro-German political
parties by the Saar government, the failure of an attempt by
Messrs. Schuman and Adenauer to relieve the situation by
direct talks, and the passage of a Bundestag resolution sharply
contesting the legality of French actions and recalling that the
Saar was technically still German territory.

One by one, however, the technical difficulties were
smoothed away, in a spirit which John J. McCloy, the American High Commissioner in Germany, described as one of "compromise and give-and-take on all sides." The Germans had
given way to the Allies in many instances, Mr. McCloy wrote;
but, he added:

"if the full truth is to be told it must be added that there were
at least as many cases in which the Allies gave way to German
requests. The final conventions bear little resemblance to those
which were originally proposed, and the differences are primarily
due to Allied concessions to the German negotiators and to Allied
recognition that in the new relationship the Federal Republic was
justified in demanding full equality." [24]

Of the three Allies, the French were slowest to accept this
principle. M. Schuman's hesitations persisted even after the
text of the accompanying E.D.C. treaty had been initialed in
Paris on May 7. In Bonn, on the very eve of the signature of
the contractual agreements, he insisted on a promise by his
American and British colleagues to secure additional guarantees
supplementing those already given or contemplated by their
respective governments.[25]

[24] Office of the U.S. High Commissioner for Germany, [11th] *Report on Germany*, September 21, 1949-July 31, 1952 (Cologne, 1952), 14.
[25] Cf. below, pp. 166-167.

The basic document signed at Bonn on May 26, entitled "Convention on Relations between the Three Powers and the Federal Republic of Germany," set forth in eleven brief articles the main principles which were to be spelled out in detail in the supplementary texts.[26] By its terms, the Federal Republic was to receive full authority over its internal and foreign affairs, with the exceptions already noted; the Occupation Statute would be abrogated, and the Allied High Commission replaced by Ambassadors of the three powers. Thereafter, the mission of the armed forces stationed on Federal territory would be the defense of the free world, of which the Federal Republic and Berlin were acknowledged to form a part; and the Federal Republic would itself contribute to this defense by participating in the European Defense Community. In case of an enemy attack, a threatened subversion of the "liberal democratic basic order," or other untoward development which the Federal Republic and the Defense Community could not handle and which menaced the security of Allied forces, the three powers could proclaim a state of emergency and, within certain defined limits, take all necessary measures to restore order and protect their forces. In this as in all other matters—including the exercise of their responsibilities in Berlin—they would work in close cooperation with and rely on the support of the Federal Republic. For its part, the Federal Republic agreed to conduct its policy in accordance with the principles of the United Nations and the Council of Europe and to "associate itself fully with the community of free nations."

The convention went on to reaffirm that all four governments aimed at the conclusion of a definitive peace for all Germany, which would include a settlement of frontier questions, and that they would continue to cooperate with a view to achieving by peaceful means their common aim of a unified Germany enjoying a liberal-democratic constitution and integrated within the European community. Such a unified Germany, said the convention, could join the European community

[26] *Documents on American Foreign Relations, 1952,* No. 19 (b).

on the same terms as the Federal Republic. In recognition of
the rapid changes that were taking place in the organization
of postwar Europe, provision was made for reconsidering the
contractual agreements in case of the reunification of Germany,
the establishment of a European federation, or any similar
fundamental development. Finally, it was stipulated that no
part of the agreement would become operative until (1) ratification was completed, and (2) the European Defense Community treaty entered into force.

No full account of the supplementary agreements designed
to put "teeth" in these undertakings is possible here.[27] Two
annexes to the basic convention defined (A) the obligations
of the Federal Republic in regard to the furnishing of material
aid to Berlin, and (B) the composition and functions of the
nine-man Arbitration Tribunal which would rule on disputes
arising under any of the various conventions. A separate convention setting forth the "Rights and Obligations of Foreign
Forces and their Members in the Federal Republic" obligated
the Federal Republic to provide whatever facilities were required by the Allied forces remaining in Germany and stipulated that criminal offenses by members of foreign forces would
be tried in military courts, other proceedings in German courts.
By a third convention, on "Finance," the Federal Republic
undertook to make an annual contribution to Western defense
on the same basis as the NATO countries; part of its contribution would go to the European Defense Community, and the
remainder to the support of other foreign (chiefly American
and British) forces in Germany. For the period up to June 30,
1953 the total German contribution (excluding certain domestic defense costs) was fixed at 850 million Deutsche Marks
($200 million) per month. Although NATO's three "Wise
Men" had pronounced this level of defense expenditure comparable to that of France, Great Britain, and other NATO
countries, the acceptance of their recommendation caused dis-

[27] Texts in *Convention on Relations Between the Three Powers and the Federal
Republic of Germany*, cited, 14-166; summary in *Documents on American Foreign Relations, 1952*, No. 19 (a).

appointment not only in Germany, where it was considered too high, but also in Britain, where it would necessitate supplementary arrangements for the financing of the British forces to be maintained in Germany.

Most difficult of all had been the issues dealt with—not always settled—in the "Convention on the Settlement of Matters Arising out of the War and the Occupation." In a formal sense, the purpose of this instrument was to provide for the dismantling of the occupation machinery and to regulate as far as possible the status of property rights, reparation obligations, and other matters that would normally be settled by a peace treaty. Beyond this, it undertook to determine the extent to which the Federal Republic would be bound to continue the political and economic policies introduced in Germany by the Allies. In practical effect, however, it signified the virtual abandonment of any further effort either to exact payment for Hitler's war or to "reform" Germany by external pressure— two undertakings that had proved incompatible with the role envisaged for Germany in the new Europe. The Allied surrender was decently masked by the establishment of new boards, commissions, and tribunals, by recognition of the rights of foreign bondholders and Allied nationals with property in Germany, and by expressions of good intentions on the part of the Bonn government. Henceforth, however, Bonn would be in the saddle. Among other things, it would have the right to nullify most Allied legislation (except certain laws of the four-power Allied Control Council) and would gain full control of civil aviation in its territory. Final settlement of the reparation problem was left for a future peace treaty, but the three powers undertook to refrain (as they had done in the past) from presenting any demand for reparations from the current production of the Federal Republic.

Like the Treaty of Peace with Japan concluded the year before, the German "peace contract" contained no provision concerning the limitation or control of armaments. Such stipulations, in the German view, would have been incompatible both with Germany's demand for "equal rights" and with effective German participation in Western defense. But the Allies, though they had already agreed that the remaining restrictions on German steel capacity and output should be lifted as soon as the Schuman Plan went into effect, were still quite unwilling to give the Federal Republic free license to reestablish an armaments industry in its territory. Apart from their lingering doubts about German reliability, there was an obvious danger that any defense industry situated in this strategically exposed area would quickly fall into Soviet hands in case of invasion.

To avoid the appearance of discrimination against Germany, the desired restrictions were incorporated not in the Peace Contract but in the European defense treaty, and made applicable—theoretically—not to Germany alone but to all members of the E.D.C. By the terms of the E.D.C. treaty, all defense production and related activities in the E.D.C. countries were placed under the authority of the European Defense Community itself, with the distinct understanding that the community would not authorize the production of atomic, chemical, or biological weapons, long-range missiles, heavy warships, or military aircraft in "strategically exposed areas." Chancellor Adenauer acknowledged that Germany was a strategically exposed area and promised, furthermore, that his government would tolerate no objectionable activities in the field of atomic energy.

The signature of the Treaty Constituting the European Defense Community, which was to link Western Germany in a peculiarly intimate association with France, Italy, Belgium, the Netherlands, and Luxembourg, took place in Paris on May 27. The number and bulk of the documents to be signed by the six foreign ministers (Dr. Adenauer appeared in his capacity as Minister of Foreign Affairs of the Federal Republic) exceeded even that of the contractual agreements concluded the day before. M. Schuman, who had contributed more to the preparation of this unique event than any other single individual, affixed his signature to at least twenty-one separate treaties, conventions, protocols, declarations, and letters. Dr.

Adenauer had occasion to write his name no fewer than nineteen times. Mr. Acheson, Mr. Eden, and representatives of the
other NATO countries looked on approvingly and intervened
on the comparatively few occasions when their own signatures
were required.

The most important of the documents thus approved were
(1) the Treaty Constituting the European Defense Community,
with annexes; (2) three protocols defining the relations between the E.D.C. and NATO; (3) a treaty of guarantee between the members of the E.D.C. and Great Britain; and (4)
a tripartite declaration by the Foreign Ministers of the United
States, the United Kingdom, and France. But the import of
this multifarious documentation is more readily appreciated if
attention is focused not on the individual texts but on the
principal fields in which agreement had at last been reached:
the character and institutions of the Defense Community, its
prospective role in the defense of Western Europe, and its
relationship to NATO and to Great Britain and the United
States.

The ambitious purpose of the new treaty [28] was defined in its
first article as the establishment of "a European Defense Community, supranational in character, consisting of common institutions, common armed Forces and a common budget." Its
exclusively defensive aims were to be realized through participation in the NATO system of European defense, integration
of the defense forces of the member states, and rational and
economic utilization of their resources. There would be no discrimination among member states. Any armed aggression
against a member state, or against the European Defense
Forces, would be considered an attack on all the member
states and resisted by them with all means in their power.

The European Defense Forces would consist of contingents,
either conscript or voluntary, placed at the disposal of the
Community by the member states. They would wear a common

[28] Text of treaty and related documents in *Convention on Relations Between
the Three Powers and the Federal Republic of Germany*, cited, 167-251; summary in *Documents on American Foreign Relations, 1952*, No. 20 (a).

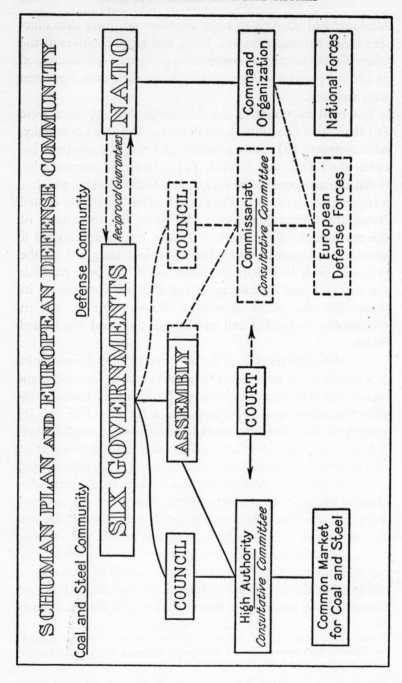

uniform and would be organized, equipped, and trained according to a common pattern and under the auspices of the appropriate NATO command. "National" military forces, as distinct from the integrated European Defense Forces, could be maintained only as required for such specified purposes as the defense of a member state's non-European territories, performance of approved international missions, and maintenance of internal order. Provision was made for the withdrawal of contingents from the European forces where necessary to meet a recognized emergency confronting one of the member states; but withdrawal for overseas service (e.g., in Indochina) would require the consent of the NATO command. The treaty was concluded for a period of fifty years, with provision for consultation in case the North Atlantic Treaty underwent a fundamental modification before the formation of a European federation or confederation.

The institutions of the E.D.C. would closely parallel and in some instances coincide with those of its elder sister, the European Coal and Steel Community.[29] Each of the two communities would operate through its own nine-man executive organ, made up of individuals chosen primarily for their general competence but with due regard for their national origins. The High Authority of the Schuman Plan would be charged with managing the common market for coal and steel, regulating production and distribution, overseeing investment, and ensuring the maintenance of free competition; the "Commissariat" of the European Defense Community would have comparable functions in the defense field. It would establish and carry out plans for the organization and deployment (though not the recruitment) of the European Defense Forces; prepare the common budget of the Community, and supervise the expenditure of the common funds; fix long-term armament, equipment, supply, and infrastructure programs, and have charge of procurement for the combined forces. In performing

[29] The Treaty Constituting the European Coal and Steel Community, which entered into force on July 25, 1952, appears in English translation in *Convention on Relations Between the Three Powers and the Federal Republic of Germany,* cited, 255-328.

its economic tasks it would be assisted by a Consultative Council including equal numbers of producers' and workers' representatives.

Again like the Schuman Plan High Authority, the E.D.C. Commissariat would not receive instructions from any single member government but would be responsible to all six governments collectively. Governmental authority would be brought to bear in each community by a similar device—a six-man Council of Ministers, comprising one member of each participating government. Tactfully described in terms of "harmonizing" executive action with government policy, the function of the respective Councils would actually be to issue directives and see to it that government views were followed in all important decisions. The E.D.C. Council would fix by unanimous vote the total budget of the Community and the contribution to be made by each individual state; by a two-thirds majority it would also determine how the money should be spent.[30] Voting procedures in the E.D.C. Council were so fixed as initially to give preponderant influence to France and Germany, as the states which were making the largest contribution to the Community, but would make it difficult for either country to impose a decision against the wishes of the other.

In addition to these separate institutions, the Coal and Steel Community and the Defense Community would have two institutions in common: (1) a Court of Justice, whose seven members would interpret the respective treaties and resolve the disputes to which they might give rise; and (2) a parliamentary Assembly, drawn from the six member countries, which would hold regular annual sessions and would have authority, among other things, to pass motions of censure requiring the resignation of the High Authority or the Commissariat. When sitting as the Coal and Steel Assembly, this body would have seventy-eight members—eighteen each from France, Germany, and Italy, ten each from Belgium and the

[30] Not less than 85 percent and not more than 115 percent of each state's contribution was to be spent within its own monetary zone.

Netherlands, and four from Luxembourg—drawn from the national parliaments or elected by universal suffrage. When functioning as the Assembly of the European Defense Community, the same body would be filled out by the addition of nine extra members—three Frenchmen, three Germans, and three Italians. In this latter capacity it could also modify or disapprove the budget prepared by the E.D.C. Commissariat.

So far as the E.D.C. was concerned, these institutional arrangements were to represent no more than an interim stage in the movement toward a broader European union. As one of its first tasks, the provisional E.D.C. Assembly was instructed by the treaty to submit plans for a definitive organization with a permanent assembly elected on a democratic basis. Further, the permanent organization was to be so conceived that it could constitute "one of the elements of an ultimate Federal or confederal structure, based upon the principle of the separation of powers and including, particularly, a bicameral representative system." The Assembly was also to study problems resulting from "the co-existence of different organizations for European cooperation, now in being or to be created in the future . . . in order to ensure that these organizations are coordinated within the framework of the federal or confederal structure." Its report was to be presented within six months; within three months after receiving it, the six governments were to call a conference to consider its recommendations. Thus the founders of the Defense Community announced a conviction that European unity in the defense field necessarily implied European political unity as well.

Provisions on the military role of the Defense Community were divided between the main treaty, a military protocol on organizational matters, and a secret annex defining plans for the actual build-up of the European Defense Forces. As had been expected, the six-power agreement in its final form provided for much less thorough "internationalization" of the European combat forces than had been envisaged in the original French proposal seventeen months earlier. Largely as a result of steady German pressure throughout the intervening period, it was now conceded that units of different nationalities would be combined or "integrated" not at the lowest organizational level but at the highest, that of the army corps. The basic national unit would be the equivalent of an infantry division and would have a peace strength of 13,000 and a war strength of 15,600 men. (For armored units the corresponding figures would be 12,700 and 14,600; for air units, comprising from thirty-six to seventy-five planes, they would be 1,300 and 2,000.) Basic units of different nationalities would be combined into army corps, whose command and general staff would be "integrated" from different nationalities. Logistical functions would also be performed on an integrated basis at the corps level so that individual divisions would not be able to operate autonomously. The naval forces responsible for protecting the sea approaches to the member states would likewise be organized into basic national units and given a European status. Pending the introduction of a uniform term of military service, the minimum period of service for conscripted soldiers in the Community would be eighteen months.

At the time of the Lisbon meeting it had been generally understood that the plans evolved by the European army conference envisaged the build-up of a European land force of forty-three divisions by the end of 1953. In May, more precise figures were issued. During the next three years, it was planned to develop an integrated force comprising altogether forty standing divisions or national units (fourteen French, twelve German, eleven Italian, and three Benelux) and fifteen reserve divisions. Binding commitments, however, had been entered into only in connection with the Lisbon program, which called for a total of twenty-five active NATO divisions (including British and American divisions) at the end of 1952; figures for the two following years were only estimates.

The close integration of the European Defense Forces with the larger NATO defense system was emphasized by a stipulation that forces of the Community might under certain circumstances be stationed outside the territory of the member states, where they would be available to aid in the defense of

NATO countries which were not themselves members of E.D.C. But assistance of this kind could be rendered only on the basis of clearly understood reciprocal obligations, binding on NATO as well as on the E.D.C. members. Definition of these reciprocal obligations, as they affected E.D.C.'s relationship with NATO in general and with the United States and Britain in particular, was an essential feature of the whole arrangement.

With the exception of Western Germany, all of the governments represented at the Paris ceremonies had of course already undertaken definite obligations toward one another through their common membership in NATO. Their problem, therefore, had been to include Germany in the same system of reciprocal obligations without actually making the Federal Republic a party to the Atlantic alliance. The solution, provisionally approved by the NATO Council at Lisbon, was to extend to the E.D.C. *as a whole* the guarantees and obligations that would under other circumstances have been extended to the Federal Republic as an individual NATO member. By this arrangement, all countries belonging to the E.D.C. undertook to regard any armed attack on one or more of the NATO countries in Europe or North America as an attack against themselves, and to react against it in the manner prescribed by the North Atlantic Treaty. Similarly, all of the NATO countries undertook to regard any armed attack on the territory of any E.D.C. member, or on the European Defense Forces, as an attack against themselves which would likewise bring the relevant treaty stipulations into effect. Provision was also made for close liaison between the appropriate technical bodies of E.D.C. and NATO and for mutual consultations and joint meetings between the Councils of the two organizations in appropriate circumstances.[31]

The demand for a special pledge of British support to the new community was met by a separate treaty between Great Britain and the six E.D.C. members. The parties to this arrange-

[31] Text of protocol to the North Atlantic Treaty in *Documents on American Foreign Relations, 1952*, No. 20 (b).

ment undertook to render "all military and other aid and assistance in their power" in case of an armed aggression in Europe against any E.D.C. member, against the European Defense Forces, or against the United Kingdom and its armed forces. This language, drawn from the five-power Brussels treaty of 1948, went further than the corresponding pledge incorporated in the North Atlantic Treaty, whereby each country undertook to assist the victim of aggression merely by "such action as it deems necessary, including the use of armed force." The net effect was to include West Germany (and Italy) in the close defensive alliance that already linked the British with their French and Benelux neighbors. Unlike the Brussels and E.D.C. treaties, however, the British guarantee did not run for a full fifty years but only for as long as Great Britain might remain a member of NATO. Theoretically, therefore, it might expire as early as 1970.

The United States had not been a party to the Brussels treaty and had not been willing, in any of the defensive treaties it had concluded since the war, to assume an automatic obligation to employ armed force in support of a victim of aggression. The only contractual obligation this country was assuming toward the E.D.C.—the only one that would require ratification by the Senate—was the above-mentioned protocol extending the relevant provisions of NATO to the members of the Defense Community. But this protocol by itself involved no commitment to contribute armed forces to the defense of Europe; and the six countries that were forming the E.D.C. would have been unwilling to take the plunge without some further assurance that the United States—and Britain—would continue to make their presence physically felt in the years ahead. This was essential, they insisted, not only because of the possibility of a Soviet attack but also because of their uncertainty about the ultimate direction of German policy. At Bonn, M. Schuman had refused to sign the contractual agreements unless his government received a specific guarantee against the possibility that the Federal Republic, after rearming itself under the auspices of the E.D.C., would break away and follow its own independent course.

Thus there was need for a final "tripartite declaration" in which Messrs. Acheson and Eden reaffirmed their governments' "abiding interest" in the success of the E.D.C. and gave the following pledge:

"Accordingly, if any action from whatever quarter threatens the integrity or unity of the Community, the two Governments will regard this as a threat to their own security. They will act in accordance with Article 4 of the North Atlantic Treaty [providing for consultation in case of a threat to the territorial integrity, political independence or security of any of the parties]. Moreover, they have each expressed their resolve to station such forces on the continent of Europe, including the Federal Republic of Germany, as they deem necessary and appropriate to contribute to the joint defense of the North Atlantic Treaty area, having regard to their obligations under the North Atlantic Treaty, their interest in the integrity of the European Defense Community, and their special responsibilities in Germany."

The ministers also reaffirmed the intention of all three powers to "maintain armed forces within the territory of Berlin as long as their responsibilities require it" and to "treat any attack against Berlin from any quarter as an attack upon their forces and themselves." [32]

Secretary Acheson, who had spent some uncomfortable hours while this statement was being put into a form that Congress might consider permissible, was entitled to an expansive comment when the last foreign minister had signed the last document.

"I wish to express my profound conviction," he said, "that what we have witnessed today may well prove to be one of the most important and most far-reaching events of our lifetime. . . . We have seen the beginning of the realization of an ancient dream —the unity of the free peoples of Western Europe." [33]

The accomplishment undoubtedly justified a sense of elation on the part of those who had labored so hard to bring it about.

[32] *Documents on American Foreign Relations, 1952*, No. 20 (c).
[33] *Department of State Bulletin*, XXVI, June 9, 1952, 895.

But only time could reveal how satisfactorily this elaborate construction would answer to the needs of the Western community and the mood of its peoples. None of the agreements would take effect until all of them had been approved by the constitutional processes of the various signatory states; and there was reason to apprehend considerable difficulty before the blueprints of Bonn and Paris could be converted into actuality.

The United States Senate was to show comparatively little hesitation in ratifying the Bonn convention and the protocol extending NATO's sphere of responsibility. The votes, taken on July 1, were 77-5 and 72-5 respectively.[34] British parliamentary approval was also granted promptly, though by a much smaller margin. But the continental legislative bodies, one or two of which were still completing action on the Schuman Plan, seemed unlikely to show great alacrity in accepting these new and more far-reaching commitments. It was in the nature of such laborious compromises that they could not fully satisfy any party; and some of the reactions, particularly in French and German opposition quarters, were far from reassuring. "Those who sign the contractual agreements will cease to be Germans" had been the warning of Kurt Schumacher, leader of the Social Democratic opposition in the Federal Republic. Now that the agreements were signed, the German opposition shifted its ground and demanded a court decision on the constitutionality of the E.D.C. treaty. This procedure would delay action on both parts of the settlement; and even if the treaty was ultimately found constitutional, there would remain a serious question as to the availability of a sufficient majority to ensure ratification by the Bundestag.

Apart from the instinctive tendency to cling to national independence as long as possible, the countries of Western

---

[34] Senate Executives Q and R, 82nd Congress, 2nd Session. Approval of the German peace contract was accompanied by an interpretation to the effect that any military implementation of its provisions (with the exception of the "reserve powers" retained by the Western governments) must be specifically authorized by Congress. See *Documents on American Foreign Relations, 1952,* No. 19 (c).

Europe still lay under the impression of the Soviet notes and had not forgotten the Kremlin's recent proposal for a radically different solution of the German problem. At the moment, Moscow seemed to have dropped its efforts in this direction. The Soviet counterpart of the ceremonies of May 26-27 was a tightening of the ring around Berlin, a reinforcement of the barriers between East and West Germany, and a series of Communist disorders in ostensible protest against the arrival of General Ridgway in Western Europe. But not a few Europeans continued to believe that all this might be changed if only the four powers would get together on the German question. Thus, while General Charles de Gaulle was denouncing his government for its "scandalous" plan to liquidate the French army, circles within the French Government itself were planning to defer action on the treaties until the possibility of a four-power conference had been further explored.[35]

Thus the outlook for the achievement of NATO's basic objective remained uncertain. The Russians had virtually admitted the defeat of their latest effort to block the consolidation of the West; but it remained to be seen whether the West, on its side, would know how to gather the fruits of its diplomatic victory. The next few months might well determine how far the Western peoples were capable, in General Eisenhower's phrase, of reconciling "the demands for association into larger groupings with the deep and spiritual ties to nationhood and sovereignty." The same period, too, might have decisive bearing on another side of NATO affairs which was sometimes overlooked in the general preoccupation with European matters. Of equal significance with the internal arrangements of the Atlantic community was the relationship of that community to the larger world outside—especially, perhaps, to the increasingly critical inhabitants of overseas areas which might well be destined to play a decisive role in the future strategy of war or peace.

[35] See especially the official statement reported in *New York Times,* June 12, 1952. Further Allied-Soviet exchanges on Germany are discussed below at pp. 283-284.

CHAPTER FOUR

SOME FAR EASTERN PERPLEXITIES

THE ATTEMPT to interpret mid-century world affairs in terms of a struggle between Eastern and Western governments or political concepts runs into difficulty as soon as attention is shifted to the Asiatic countries that skirt the Pacific and Indian oceans. Typically "Eastern" in their traditions and culture, these countries from the first had occupied a singularly elusive position in relation to the postwar conflict between the Soviet-Communist and other, nontotalitarian doctrines and ways of life. Their native outlook had as little in common with Stalinist Communism as with Western liberal democracy. If they were being gradually compelled to make a choice between these conflicting tendencies, it was as a result of pressure from outside rather than predilection for either of the principal competing ideologies.

For generations before World War II the existence of the Asian peoples had been fundamentally conditioned by the play of rival imperialisms, British, French, Dutch, Russian, Japanese. Growing political self-consciousness had found them eager to dispense with the apparatus of foreign control, but still largely dependent on the experience and technical resources of foreign mentors. Their natural preferences had seemed to point toward rapid and unconditional emancipation from foreign influence, as a step toward the self-regeneration of their ancient societies in an atmosphere untroubled by the rivalries or the cupidity of former imperialist nations. But the speedy emergence of such a group of independent, forward-looking Asian states had been hampered not only by their own social and technical backwardness and mutual rivalries but also by the reluctance of outside powers to renounce the positions of advantage they had secured in Asia in the past—particularly at a time when their own conflicts were sharpening in intensity and broadening in scope.

In the rapidly developing political struggle between the U.S.S.R. and the Western democracies, neither side could possibly have overlooked the importance of non-Soviet Asia as a factor in world politics and strategy. For the U.S.S.R., as we have seen, the intensification of the anticolonial movement in Asia was a primary method of attack against the "imperialist" states of the West; for the latter, continued command of Asia's potentialities was felt to be desirable in itself and indispensable if they were to face the struggle with Stalinist imperialism on equal terms. Placed between these intrusive forces, most of the Asian peoples revealed an unmistakable preference for neutrality. Where this was impossible, they tended to align themselves provisionally with whichever power or tendency seemed most likely to further what they considered to be their own interests as Asians. Certain elements, usually of a conservative social and political orientation, more or less unreservedly embraced the cause of France, Britain, or the United States. Possibly a larger number, in southeastern Asia and China at any rate, had found nothing unnatural in association with "progressive" and "nationalist" movements whose ultimate support, whether they realized it or not, lay in Moscow. Thus the postwar development in the Far East had acquired the character of a struggle between two outside forces for the allegiance and material resources of indigenous peoples whose own preoccupations were actually of a quite different order.

Unlike the situation in Europe, however, the political alignment in Asia was neither stable nor clear-cut. Geographic and ethnic diversity precluded the emergence of any simple political pattern. Even the Communist movements in this part of the world lacked the discipline and "monolithic" character that had generally prevailed among the European parties of the Cominform. The influence of Moscow seemed to become progressively more attenuated as it filtered downward through China to the more or less authentically Stalinist movements in Southeast Asia. There was no proof that the interests and ambitions of the Communist rulers in the U.S.S.R., China, North Korea, and Indochina conflicted in any fundamental way; yet the possibility of such conflicts could not realistically be ruled out, even if they did not appear as yet to have interfered with the pursuit of over-all Communist aims.

Within the Western, democratic camp the differences with respect to Asia were obvious to all the world. The United States, Great Britain, and France, which by the early 1950's had achieved such unprecedented unity of action in European affairs, had scarcely begun to harmonize their policies in the Far East. In principle, all three governments recognized a common interest in combating the march of Far Eastern Communism; in practice, each had felt free to carry on the struggle at its own pace and in its own way. The Communist victory in China, which had made the development of a common Western policy urgently desirable, had also rendered it even more difficult to achieve because of the inability of the Western governments—chiefly the United States and Great Britain—to agree upon a uniform attitude toward the new regime in Peking. Since Communist China quickly emerged as the strongest and most dynamic indigenous force in the Far East, disagreements over its status and prerogatives precluded a unified Western approach to any of the other Far Eastern issues in which the Peking government hastened to involve itself. The same circumstance had created a new obstacle to common understanding between the Western and the Asian peoples, since the latter tended in many cases to look with sympathy on the Chinese experiment and to confuse hostility toward the Chinese Communists with hostility toward Asian aspirations as such.

The disorganizing effect of such differences was aggravated by the circumstances of the Korean war. Although repercussions of the global Communist offensive were felt in every part of the Far East, their intensity varied with the distance from the main sources of Communist aggression. China itself, though a declared aggressor in Korea, had thus far been spared direct retaliation by the West because of the unwillingness of the United Nations (including the United States) to resort to any military action against it that might result in precipitating a general war. Within the boundaries of continental China, therefore, the struggle against "imperialism" and its native "lackeys" took the form of violent denunciation of the Western governments and peoples, elimination of Western commercial and missionary undertakings, brutal mistreatment of individual Westerners, and a ruthless campaign to eradicate the remaining traces of a "reactionary" or "bourgeois" mentality among the Chinese themselves.

Eastward and southward from China it was possible to distinguish two primary zones of conflict, in the first of which Communism generally held the initiative while in the second the vital decisions still remained with the West and its adherents.

The inner zone embraced Korea and those countries of Southeast Asia where actual fighting between Communist and anti-Communist forces was in progress. Theoretically, the United Nations "police action" in Korea was unrelated to the localized wars that the French in Indochina, the British in Malaya, and the new republican government in Burma had been forced to carry on year after year against native insurrectionary movements which, though somewhat heterogeneous in origin, undoubtedly benefited by Communist support and direction. Actually the connections were very close, as the British and French sometimes pointed out when taxed with their comparatively minor contributions to the Korean effort. Not only were all these aggressively revolutionary currents fed from the same Communist source, but strategically they represented concurrent demands on the attention and resources of the Communist world as well as the West. Many observers believed that the successful United Nations resistance in Korea had helped to prevent the mounting of any large-scale Communist offensive in Southeast Asia. Conversely, an armistice in Korea might enable the Chinese Communists to undertake new aggressions in the latter area—a possibility that Mr. Vyshinsky, among others, had presumably had in mind on January 3 when he undertook to alert the General Assembly against supposed American intrigues in Thailand and Burma.[1]

The outer zone of the Far East, in which Western (principally American) influence had gained clear preponderance, embraced practically the whole of the insular chain lying off Asia's Pacific coast. Often described as a "perimeter" essential to the postwar military security of the United States, its elements—the Aleutian Islands, Japan, the Ryukyus, the Philippines, and latterly Formosa—were geographically and politically heterogeneous in the extreme. There was little love lost among some of its peoples and governments. That they could be considered parts of a single whole at all resulted, on one side, from the determination of the United States to exclude Communist influence from areas deemed vital to its own security; and, on the other, from the recognition of the various governments concerned that their own security was irrevocably bound up with that of the United States.

This sense of mutual dependence had inspired the arrangements established in connection with the Japanese peace settlement, which were explicitly described as interim arrangements "pending the development of a more comprehensive system of regional security in the Pacific area." In these arrangements Australia and New Zealand had also joined, in the realization that their security, too, depended on the United States even more than on the British Commonwealth of Nations.[2] The further development of these reciprocal relationships, particularly as they involved the assimilation of Japan into the general structure of Pacific security, was one of the most important tasks confronting American diplomacy as it looked forward into 1952—a task that might eventually overshadow even the immediate preoccupations of the Korean war.

[1] Cf. above, pp. 26-27.
[2] *The United States in World Affairs, 1951,* 197-202.

1. A Few Clarifications

Although the interplay of political and military forces in the Far East reflected a situation of great instability, the pressure of events was constantly working to reduce it to a more coherent pattern. As the struggle with Communism in the Far East intensified and its demands on both sides became more evident, some of the illusions and reservations originally entertained by the major protagonists were gradually discarded. The Chinese Communists ceased seriously to pretend that their armies in Korea were true "volunteers" and virtually admitted that they were engaged in war not merely against "American interventionists" but against the organized body of the United Nations. The non-Communist powers little by little edged closer to recognizing that they had a vital interest not only in repelling aggression in Korea but also in strengthening each other's general security in the Pacific as well as in Europe. As a part of the same process, some governments which had originally been well disposed toward the Chinese Communists began to perceive that the actions of the Peking regime, no less than the sternly anti-Communist position of the United States, would necessitate a modification of their diplomatic attitude at least as long as hostilities in Korea continued.

Several developments at the beginning of 1952 illustrated this tendency toward a simplification of the broad pattern and a closer alignment among the nations resisting Communism in the Far East. The year had begun in an atmosphere of considerable anxiety, in which apprehension over the fate of the armistice negotiations in Korea had been aggravated by numerous portents of an impending crisis in Southeast Asia. If the Korean armistice talks broke down, it was asked, what was to be done next? Would the United States still adhere to the policy of limiting the conflict militarily to Korea, or would it insist on carrying the war to China in accordance with the recommendations put forward by General of the Army Douglas MacArthur and still favored by an influential section of American opinion?

In the latter case, would the United Nations, especially Great
Britain and the fourteen other countries with armed forces in
Korea, support or oppose the decisions of the Unified Command, now headed by General Ridgway? Supposing an armistice
was concluded in Korea, how were the principal United Nations members to get around their basic disagreement over the
demand of Communist China to supplant the Chinese Nationalist Government in the United Nations and on Formosa?
And meanwhile, armistice or no armistice, what would happen
if the 200,000 Chinese Communist troops who were reported
poised in China's southern provinces were to move against
Indochina, Burma, Thailand, or all three together? Each of
these questions recalled the fact that the Western powers had
no over-all plan of action for the Far East and might easily be
split apart in a crisis as a result of their differing opinions concerning the proper attitude to be maintained toward Communist
China itself.

A measure of reassurance with respect to the British position
on these matters was brought to Americans by Mr. Churchill
and Mr. Eden in the course of their January visit. The new
British government, it appeared, was more dubious about the
Chinese Communists than its predecessor had been, and did
not intend to jeopardize Anglo-American harmony by too doctrinaire an insistence on its own view concerning Peking's legal
status and claims. "We have discussed the many grave problems affecting our two countries in the Far East," said the joint
communiqué issued by the President and the Prime Minister
on January 9. "A broad harmony of view has emerged from
these discussions; for we recognize that the overriding need to
counter the Communist threat in that area transcends such divergencies as there are in our policies toward China." [3]

In his address to Congress on January 17, Mr. Churchill went
still further—much further, as it turned out, than some of his
own countrymen thought justified:

"You have rightly been resolute, Members of Congress, in confronting Chinese Communist aggression. We take our stand at

[3] *Department of State Bulletin*, XXVI, January 21, 1952, 84.

your side. We are grateful to the United States for bearing nine-tenths or more of the burden in Korea which the United Nations have morally assumed. I am very glad, but [that?] whatever diplomatic divergencies there may be from time to time about procedure, you do not allow the Chinese anti-Communists on Formosa to be invaded and massacred from the mainland. We welcome your patience in the armistice negotiations and our two countries are agreed that if the truce we seek is reached only to be broken, our response will be prompt, resolute, and effective. What I have learned over here convinces me that British and United States policy in the Far East will be marked by increasing harmony. . . .

"In the anxious and confused expanses of Southeast Asia, there is another sphere where our aims and interests and those of the French, who are fighting bravely at heavy cost to their strength in Europe, may find a fertile field for agreement. I feel sure that the conversations . . . between our two foreign Secretaries . . . will help to place the problems of Southeast Asia in their right setting.

"It would not be helpful to the common cause—for our evils all spring from one center—if an effective truce in Korea led only to a transference of Communist aggression to these other fields. Our problems will not be solved unless they are steadily viewed and acted upon as a whole in their integrity as a whole." [4]

Some progress toward viewing Far Eastern problems "as a whole" had meanwhile been achieved in Washington with the help of the American, British, and French Chiefs of Staff, who had conferred on January 9-14 and devoted much attention to the threat of an attack on Indochina by the Chinese Communists. Contrary to the hopes of the French, the United States, though it had been furnishing military equipment to France and the Indochinese states for the past two years, declined to undertake any definite commitment as to what it would do in a military way if the Chinese Communists actually launched an invasion. But it was at least agreed that all three powers would consider such action a matter which concerned the United Nations, as the agency ultimately responsible for international peace and security; and even this represented a more definite mutual commitment than they had assumed hitherto.

On January 28 one of the American delegates in Paris, John Sherman Cooper, announced the new policy to the General

[4] *Congressional Record,* Daily Edition, January 17, 1952, 280-281.

Assembly. Recalling Vyshinsky's ominous hints of a few weeks before, he declared:

"At this time I must, on instructions of my Government, state clearly that any such Communist aggression in Southeast Asia would, in the view of my Government, be a matter of direct and grave concern which would require the most urgent and earnest consideration by the United Nations." [5]

Similar statements were made by the British and French delegates—the former without qualification, the latter referring only to Indochina.

These declarations to the General Assembly were made in the course of debate on a relatively minor item of that body's agenda, the Chinese Nationalist charge that the Soviet Union had violated the treaty of friendship and alliance concluded between the two governments in 1945.[6] The important contemporaneous issues in the Far East—Communist China's political demands, and the situation in Korea—did not come before the Assembly officially, despite periodic efforts by the Russians to force them upon the Assembly's attention. In deference to American views, the question of Chinese representation in the General Assembly had been barred from the agenda at an early stage;[7] Korean matters, notwithstanding Vyshinsky's repeated overtures, were deferred for later consideration because the United States, together with Britain and France, was reluctant to open them up for general discussion until the prospects for a successful outcome of the armistice negotiations at Panmunjom had clarified. Ernest A. Gross of the American delegation was at pains to dispel any notion on the part of the Assembly that the United States was lacking in eagerness to end the Korean conflict.

"Precisely because we are anxious to go forward," he explained on February 2, "we desire to avoid premature political discussions which could postpone or complicate the conclusion of an armistice. It is the armistice which will open the way to constructive con-

[5] Statement to the First Committee, in *Documents on American Foreign Relations, 1952*, No. 24 (a).
[6] Cf. *ibid.*, No. 35 (b) and above, p. 26, n. 10.
[7] *The United States in World Affairs, 1951*, 384-385.

sideration of political issues. A lasting political solution to the Korean problem must rest on a sound and secure foundation. The successful conclusion of the negotiations at Panmunjon [*sic*] will provide that foundation." [8]

2. *Panmunjom Pandemonium*

To Vice Admiral Charles Turner Joy and the other American officers whose duty it was to attend the daily sessions in the armistice hut at Panmunjom, this forecast may have seemed unduly optimistic. The experience of more than six months had offered abundant proof that the authorities in Peking or Moscow had thus far been in no particular hurry to conclude an armistice, and suggested that their representatives might continue to drag out the talks for some time to come if, indeed, they did not eventually break them off altogether. From the enemy point of view, there was little need for haste. Since the commencement of negotiations in the summer of 1951, military operations on the ground in Korea had been confined to local and limited engagements along a stabilized battlefront. The drain of enemy casualties had been checked, and the Communists had thus gained a new advantage in addition to the one they already enjoyed thanks to the immunity accorded their bases and supply centers beyond the Yalu River in Manchuria. The respite had been employed in reordering, reinforcing, and reequipping the North Korean and Chinese forces, now estimated at over 700,000 ground troops in Korea itself and more than 1,200 aircraft, half of them jet planes of Soviet manufacture.[9] Backed by this formidable array of military power, and to the accompaniment of growing air battles over northern Korea, General Nam Il and his Chinese colleagues came regularly to Panmunjom to abuse, insult, and occasionally bargain with the United Nations.

[8] Statement to the First Committee and the Joint Second and Third Committees, in *Department of State Bulletin*, XXVI, February 18, 1952, 260. The Western proposal (text *ibid.*) was approved on February 5 as General Assembly Resolution 507 (VI) by a vote of 51-5-2.
[9] Hanson W. Baldwin in *New York Times*, January 6, 1952.

Since November 27, 1951, when the two delegations had agreed on a tentative cease-fire line and demilitarized zone which would separate the two armies in the event of an armistice, no final understanding had been reached on any part of the five-point armistice agenda originally adopted in the previous July.[10] Subcommittees had been at work on those sections of the agenda that dealt with enforcement of the armistice terms (Point 3) and with prisoners of war (Point 4); and early in February 1952 the Communists accepted a United Nations proposal to begin discussion of a final point (Point 5) which concerned the recommendations—presumably of a political nature—that were to be made by the armistice delegations "to the governments of the countries concerned on both sides." The reader who seeks to follow the details of these lengthy and envenomed discussions must be referred to other sources.[11] Here it is only possible to present the essence of the several controversies that marked this clash between incompatible aims and ideologies.

Point 3, enforcement of the armistice terms, had to do with the concrete arrangements for policing any armistice agreement that might be reached. This, obviously, was a matter of direct military significance, and one on which the Unified Command was unwilling to take any chances with an enemy whose record did not inspire confidence and who obviously hoped to remain in a strong military position even after an armistice was concluded. Both sides were agreed on the general principle that once an armistice was signed the forces in Korea should not be increased in strength, and that there should be "neutral" observers to check on alleged violations of the agreement. After

[10] For background cf. *The United States in World Affairs, 1951,* 141-151, 376-377, and 402.
[11] See especially the *Special Report of the Unified Command on the United Nations Action in Korea,* U.N. Document A/2228, October 18, 1952, reprinted in *Documents on American Foreign Relations, 1952,* No. 29; also Secretary Acheson's detailed review before the First Committee of the General Assembly on October 24, 1952 (excerpts in *Department of State Bulletin,* XXVII, November 3, 1952, 679-692 and November 10, 1952, 744-751); and the personal narrative of Admiral Joy, "My Battle Inside the Korea Truce Tent," *Collier's,* August 16, 1952, 36-42; August 23, 1952, 26-31; August 30, 1952, 70-72.

much haggling, it was further agreed that each side could rotate up to 35,000 of its military personnel each month while the armistice was in effect, and that there should be ten supervised ports of entry—five each in North and South Korea— for the replacement of men and matériel. But no agreement could be reached on two other points: (1) a United Nations demand that the enemy should refrain from reconstructing damaged airfields in North Korea—a proposal which the Communists indignantly rejected as an attempted intrusion on the internal affairs of the North Korean "People's Democratic Republic"; and (2) a belated Communist stipulation that the U.S.S.R., together with Poland and Czechoslovakia, must be included among the "neutral" nations which would supply the observation teams. The Unified Command, whose own "neutral" nominees were Sweden and Switzerland, was willing to agree to Polish and Czechoslovak observers. It balked at conceding a fictitious neutrality to the U.S.S.R., a power that not only supported the aggressors politically but was known to be furnishing much of their heavy equipment and practically all their aircraft.

Point 4, "arrangements relating to prisoners of war," concerned chiefly the mechanics of exchanging the prisoners held by the two sides as soon as the cease-fire entered into effect. A preliminary difficulty in this most ticklish phase of the negotiations concerned the number of prisoners actually in the possession of the belligerents. It had been commonly supposed that the Unified Command was holding roughly 170,000 prisoners, to some 65,000 held by the Communists; but when official lists were exchanged on December 18, 1951, it developed that the actual total held by the United Nations was only 132,474 (111,774 Koreans and 20,700 Chinese) whereas the enemy admitted to holding only 11,559 (7,142 South Koreans, 3,198 Americans, and 1,219 of other nationalities). In the case of the Unified Command, the discrepancy was accounted for by the omission of 37,500 South Korean civilians who had been impressed into Communist service but had escaped to the

United Nations lines and were now awaiting release.[12] As for the enemy list, United Nations quarters could only conclude that upward of 50,000 additional prisoners had either been massacred or (more probably in most instances) incorporated into the North Korean army.[13] This probability, combined with the uncertainty that surrounded the fate of some 600,000 displaced civilians on both sides of the lines, was scarcely calculated to get the negotiations off to an auspicious start.

But the principal stumbling block was the unforeseen discovery that a substantial portion of the prisoners held by the United Nations had no desire to be exchanged on conclusion of an armistice and, in fact, gave every indication that they would forcibly resist any attempt to effect their repatriation. The Unified Command, though hardly prepared for this development, promptly took the position that the repatriation of prisoners should be "voluntary" in all cases—that is, that no prisoner should be forced to return to Communist control against his own will, as freely expressed before an impartial authority. This concept, consistent though it was with Western humanitarian ideas, had not yet become established in the laws of war [14] and, unfortunately, proved wholly incompatible with the Communists' views. Every other disputed point in connection with prisoners was settled by the end of February; on this point the Communists refused to yield. To admit that there could be large numbers of Communists who actually did not

[12] The U.N. figure of 132,474 did include 16,000 South Koreans captured while actually fighting with the North Korean army. Subsequent release of an additional 11,000 South Koreans erroneously classified as prisoners of war reduced the total number of prisoners held by the U.N. to about 121,000. (See U.N. Document A/2228, October 18, 1952, 14.)

[13] A revised list submitted by the Communists in April increased their total from 11,559 to 12,100, including 7,700 South Koreans.

[14] The Geneva Convention Relative to the Treatment of Prisoners of War of August 12, 1949, to which the United States but not Communist China was a party, provides in Article 118 that "Prisoners of war shall be released and repatriated without delay after the cessation of active hostilities," but imposes no obligation on the detaining power to repatriate prisoners by force. For discussion of the legal aspects cf. the address of Secretary Acheson to the First Committee of the General Assembly, October 24, 1952; also Pitman B. Potter, "Repatriation of Prisoners of War," *American Journal of International Law,* XLVI, July 1952, 508-509.

want to return to their Communist homelands would have had embarrassing psychological repercussions throughout the world. Any likelihood that the enemy would accept such a humiliation for the sake of getting a Korean armistice was further reduced when the Unified Command announced the unflattering result of a preliminary screening of prisoners and internees held in United Nations camps. Despite considerable efforts to encourage prisoners to choose repatriation, Allied interrogators were obliged to conclude that only about 70,000 individuals—less than half the Koreans, and only a quarter of the Chinese—could be repatriated without the use of force.[15]

Apparently the Unified Command had detected a major flaw in the adversary's psychological armor. The Communists' embarrassment might be guessed from the violence of their propaganda denunciations of the United States on various speciously humanitarian grounds relating to prisoners and other matters. Unfortunately, however, the armistice negotiations had run into an obstacle that might not be susceptible of compromise, since it concerned not the technical details of an armistice arrangement but the strongest convictions of the two parties. The time might come when the uncertain fate of these prisoners for whose safety the United States had made itself responsible would threaten the entire armistice prospect and even—temporarily—the solidarity of this country with its allies.

Point 5, "Recommendations to the governments of the countries concerned on both sides," caused less difficulty than might have been expected in view of the fact that it necessarily involved most of the larger political aims for which the Chinese Communists professed to have entered the war. There already existed an understanding that once an armistice had been concluded, a high-level "political" conference should meet to dis-

[15] The 70,000 figure was subsequently admitted to be an estimate based on interrogations in those camps to which U.N. interrogators had access at the time. Completion of the screening process after the break-up of Communist-controlled compounds in June raised the total of prisoners who would not resist repatriation to 83,000, including 76,600 Koreans and 6,400 Chinese. Cf. U.N. Documents S/2700, S/2715, S/2789 (*Department of State Bulletin*, XXVII, August 11, 1952, 232; August 18, 1952, 272; November 17, 1952, 796) and U.N. Document A/2228, October 18, 1952, 17-18.

cuss the withdrawal of foreign forces from Korea and other questions involved in the peaceful settlement of the Korean question. Thus the most delicate issues would be reserved for later discussion. All that remained at this stage was to draw up terms of reference which would be acceptable both to the Unified Command, which wanted the conference strictly confined to Korean matters, and the Communists, who preferred a loose formula that would leave an opening for the discussion of broader Far Eastern issues such as Formosa and representation in the United Nations. Tentative agreement was quickly reached to recommend "to the governments of the countries concerned on both sides" the convocation, within three months after the armistice, of "a political conference of a higher level of both sides . . . to settle through negotiation the questions of the withdrawal of all foreign forces from Korea, the peaceful settlement of the Korean question, et cetera." The Unified Command stipulated that in its view "governments of the countries concerned" included the United Nations and the Republic of Korea; that "foreign forces" meant "non-Korean forces" (thus including Chinese); and that "et cetera" was not to be construed as referring to "matters outside of Korea." The Communists kept their own counsel.[16]

By the end of March, prolonged argument and a number of concessions by both sides had produced substantial agreement on all but three issues: (1) the construction and rehabilitation of military airfields, (2) the makeup of the "neutral" supervisory commission, and (3) repatriation of prisoners of war. Through the next four weeks these problems were further debated by staff officers and subcommittees, with no result except mutual exasperation. Then, on April 28, Admiral Joy presented to a closed meeting of the full armistice delegations a "final" proposal designed, he said, as "an over-all solution of the problems remaining to be solved." By its terms, the United Nations Command would waive any restrictions on the rehabilitation and construction of airfields provided the Communists, on their

[16] U.N. Command report, February 16-29 (U.N. Document S/2619, in *Department of State Bulletin*, XXVI, June 23, 1952, 999-1000).

side, would drop their demand for Soviet membership in the armistice commission and would also accept the principle of voluntary repatriation of prisoners.

The Unified Command looked on this concession as "a substantive matter of the first magnitude since it directly and substantially affects the military situation subsequent to an armistice." [17] But to the Communists the bargain was unacceptable. They were willing, they indicated, to drop their insistence that the U.S.S.R. be included in the neutral armistice commission. To the proposal that they renounce full repatriation of all their prisoners of war they would not agree, even though the United Nations Command offered to let them verify the results of the screening, to repatriate any prisoners who might change their minds, and to exclude those who refused repatriation from any further participation in the war. The Communists had no intention, they said, of acquiescing in what they described as a mere trick aimed at camouflaging the unlawful detention of 100,000 captives.

Thus ten months of negotiation had brought the parties to a complete impasse. Both sides claimed to have made their "last concession." The United Nations proposal, General Ridgway commented on May 7, not only represented "a fair and equitable reconciliation of the opposing points of view"; it embodied "the limit to which the United Nations can go" and was "not subject to substantive change." This stand was explicitly endorsed by President Truman, by the State and Defense departments, and by Foreign Secretary Eden in London. "To agree to forced repatriation," said the President, "would be unthinkable. It would be repugnant to the fundamental moral and humanitarian principles which underlie our action in Korea. . . . We will not buy an armistice by turning over human beings for slaughter or slavery." [18]

But with the rejection of the United Nations proposal of April 28, the Panmunjom armistice hut ceased to serve as a

[17] U.N. Command report, May 1-15 (U.N. Document S/2715, in *Department of State Bulletin*, XXVII, August 18, 1952, 272-273).
[18] *Ibid.*, XXVI, May 19, 1952, 786-788.

place of negotiation and was appropriated almost exclusively
to the purposes of Communist political warfare. Whether or
not the Communists had desired an armistice in the past, they
plainly were as unwilling as the United Nations to secure one
at the sacrifice of what they, too, seemed to consider a
fundamental principle. Their answer to the "firm, final, and
irrevocable" stand of the United Nations was a sharp intensification of their attempts to discredit the Unified Command by
"psychological" methods. Subsequent meetings of the armistice
delegations were "characterized by Communist tirades un-
equaled in their distortion of truth and in their ambiguity, insincerity and insulting language." [19] Within a few weeks Admiral Joy's successor as chief United Nations delegate [20] had
been forced to concentrate his efforts on limiting the frequency
of meetings as the only way of interrupting these floods of
invective.

Meanwhile Communist activities outside the armistice hut
were proving even more difficult to control. The germ warfare
propaganda campaign flared up violently again with the release of new Communist "evidence" featuring depositions
which allegedly had been obtained from two American air-
men shot down in January while dropping "germ bombs" in
North Korea. The familiar cycle was repeated once more:
American refutations,[21] Communist-sponsored "investigations"
(strictly confined, as always, to persons already committed to
the Communist line),[22] denunciations by Communist "peace"
bodies, and a new offensive by Mr. Malik in the United Nations.[23] These tactics kept the germ warfare issue alive through-

[19] U.N. Command report, May 1-15 (U.N. Document S/2715, in *Department
of State Bulletin*, XXVII, August 18, 1952, 273).
[20] Maj. Gen. William K. Harrison, Jr. succeeded Adm. Joy on May 23.
[21] See especially Secretary Acheson's statement of May 7 in *Department of State
Bulletin*, XXVI, May 19, 1952, 777.
[22] See especially the report of the French scientist Yves Farge, who was in
China and Korea from April 28 to June 16, in *Special Session of the World
Peace Council, Berlin, July 1-6, 1952: Report and Documents* (supplement to
New Times, No. 28, July 9, 1952), 22-29. A few weeks later the same charges
were endorsed by the Rev. Hewlett Johnson, "Red" Dean of Canterbury.
[23] The issue of bacteriological warfare was officially brought before the Security
Council by the U.S.S.R. on June 18. Cf. below, pp. 281-282.

out the spring and summer and provided a background for still more sensational developments which had meanwhile been brewing in United Nations prisoner of war camps in Korea.

Ever since the question of a prisoner exchange had first been taken up at Panmunjom in November 1951, the argument on both sides had been embittered by charges and countercharges concerning alleged mistreatment of prisoners and failure to observe accepted international standards of prisoner adminis- tration. Such tactics had been particularly rewarding to the Communists because they tended to divert attention from their own notorious shortcomings in regard to the treatment of prisoners and to becloud the issue created by their insistence on forced repatriation. Their efforts, moreover, were greatly facili- tated by conditions actually prevailing in the overcrowded and inadequately supervised prisoner compounds behind the United Nations lines. While the Unified Command was concentrating on more immediate problems, fanatical North Korean captives had been able in some instances to seize control, terrorize and even murder their anti-Communist fellow-prisoners. Directed from Communist headquarters, they operated as a virtual "fifth column" within the territory of the Korean Republic. In Febru- ary and March, rioting by Communist inmates of the huge United Nations prison camp on Koje Island, off the southeast coast of Korea, had been forcibly suppressed with heavy loss of life among the prisoners; subsequently the die-hard Com- munist complexion of the Koje compounds had been accentu- ated by the concentration there of most of the 70,000 individ- uals who claimed to desire repatriation to Communist territory.

As the impasse over the repatriation issue became clear, vio- lence among the 80,000 prisoners on Koje recurred on a larger scale. On May 7, the very day the "final" United Nations truce offer was publicized, Communist prisoners on Koje performed the unheard-of exploit of seizing the American camp com- mandant, Brigadier General Francis T. Dodd, and holding him as a hostage for three days while the whole world held its breath and United States Army quarters negotiated for his re- lease. The terms set by his captors clearly testified to a propa-

gandist motivation. Among them were "immediate ceasing of
the barbarous behavior, insults, torture, forcible protest with
blood writing, threatening confinement, mass murdering, gun
and machine gun shooting, poison gas, germ weapons, experiment of A-bomb by your command"; also, of course, abandonment of the principle of voluntary repatriation.[24] Most of these
demands were summarily turned down by the acting commandant; but the statement he eventually signed, "under great
duress," was nevertheless highly compromising from a psychological point of view and resulted in subsequent repudiation
by the Pentagon as well as disciplinary action against the signer.
Promising that prisoners on Koje could "expect humane treatment" in the future, it went on to imply, among other things,
that the screening of prisoners had been carried out by force—
something which, if it had been true, would have invalidated
the whole United Nations position in opposing forced repatriation.

While Communist propaganda made the most of this "admission" and world opinion looked on with unconcealed dis-
may at the bloody suppression of additional prisoner riots and
the forcible clean-up of the Koje situation, South Korean politics added their quota to what was fast coming to resemble a
morass of scandals. As the date for choosing a new chief executive for the embattled Korean Republic approached, the long-
standing constitutional struggle between President Syngman
Rhee and the National Assembly elected in 1950 had grown
more intense. The Assembly having refused to amend the constitution in order to permit popular election of the president,
Rhee and his supporters had undertaken to overawe it by mass
demonstrations, the arrest of a dozen deputies, and a proclama-

[24] *New York Times*, May 13, 1952. For additional details on the prisoner situ-
ation cf. Demaree Bess, "The Prisoners Stole the Show in Korea," *Saturday
Evening Post*, CXXV, November 1, 1952, 36-37 and 52-55; also the following
congressional documents (82nd Congress, 2nd Session, Washington, 1952):
General Ridgway: Hearings, Senate Armed Services Committee, May 21; *The
Prisoner of War Situation in Korea: Hearings*, House Appropriations Subcom-
mittee, June 9; House Report 2129 (on H. Res. 662), June 10. Concerning
Communist direction of the riots cf. *Department of State Bulletin*, XXVIII,
February 16, 1953, 273-275.

tion of martial law (ostensibly motivated by guerrilla activities) in the area of South Korea's temporary capital at Pusan. By early June these vigorous but hardly democratic tactics had prompted expressions of concern from United Nations civilian and military authorities in Korea, from Secretary-General Lie, and, according to report, from President Truman himself. They also strengthened the unfavorable reaction to Korean events which had been building up in various parts of the non-Communist world.

This reaction was especially marked in the United Kingdom, where Korean developments were watched with an interest corresponding to Britain's direct involvement in the United Nations action as well as its general stake in the East-West struggle. American conduct of the war in Korea had often provoked sharp criticism in British quarters, some of which had been highly irritated by the assurances of solidarity Mr. Churchill had conveyed to Congress in January. British reservations about the basic American attitude toward Communist China were not readily dispelled, even in the face of continuing Communist encroachment on the few remaining British interests in that country. Recent events in Korea—the failure to achieve an armistice, the continued build-up of the Communist armies, and now the troubles at Koje and Pusan—had intensified British misgivings and occasioned a number of intemperate speeches in the House of Commons. On June 11, Mr. Eden himself disclosed that President Rhee was being officially admonished to abide by the Korean Constitution and refrain from subverting the democratic principles which United Nations members with forces in Korea had been fighting to defend.[25]

But these preoccupations were subordinate in British minds to the larger question of what course the Korean war might take now that armistice negotiations had reached a dead end. Would the Communists renew the offensive? Current military

[25] The political effervescence in Korea was not brought under control until July 4, when the Assembly approved a compromise plan under which the president and vice-president would be elected by popular vote and the cabinet would be responsible to the lower chamber of a bicameral congress. President Rhee was reelected on August 5 by an overwhelming popular majority.

estimates, which credited them with close to a million men under arms, over 500 tanks and self-propelled guns, 1,000 jet planes and 800 other aircraft, left little doubt of their capacity to do so, even though the Unified Command appeared confident that its much smaller force could handle any situation the enemy might create.[26] This confidence was largely borne out by a special British "fact-finding" mission headed by Field Marshal Earl Alexander, the Minister of Defense, which visited Korea in June. The main result of the Alexander mission was a re-affirmation of confidence in American leadership of the Korean struggle and in the ability of the United Nations to cope with any renewal of offensive tactics. But this effect was marred by another of those inadvertences in official American quarters which seemed to outsiders to reflect insensitivity or indifference to the political implications of American action. Lord Alexander and his associates were treated with what seemed complete courtesy and frankness; but no one warned them that the United States was about to intensify its military action in Korea in a manner peculiarly trying to foreign nerves.

The failure of Admiral Joy's efforts at Panmunjom had left the Unified Command, now headed by General Mark Clark, with only one obvious means—short of a ground offensive of its own—to whittle down enemy strength and influence the Communists toward acceptance of its views. "Military pressure," Admiral Joy later wrote, "was the one argument that made sense to the Communists." The fixing of a de facto cease-fire line had made such pressure more difficult to apply: "We had lost the full use of our best argument, the magnificent Eighth Army." [27] In the air, however, the United Nations still retained the capability of inflicting severe punishment on enemy airfields, troop concentrations, and transport and supply centers. With other operations at a virtual stalemate, the Unified

---

[26] See especially Mr. Churchill's statement to the House of Commons on May 28 and the remarks of Gen. James A. Van Fleet, U.N. ground force commander, in *New York Times,* June 1, 1952. Total U.N. ground forces were estimated at around 450,000, including 250,000 from the U.S. and 150,000 South Koreans.
[27] *Collier's,* August 23, 1952, 30, 31.

Command was on the point of inaugurating a more vigorous air offensive against those installations which were helping to sustain the enemy effort. While still technically adhering to the policy of confining air operations to Korea, it was to interpret this policy with considerably more freedom than in the past.

The inauguration of this new phase came on June 23, the first anniversary of Mr. Malik's original armistice proposal, in what was described as the heaviest air attack of the almost two-year-old war. Five North Korean hydroelectric plants were bombed, without loss, by some 500 United Nations aircraft; among them was the important Supung (Suiho) plant on the Yalu River, which supplied large amounts of electric power to Manchuria as well as North Korea and for that reason had long been regarded in United Nations circles as an object of special delicacy. The military results of the raid were claimed to be highly satisfactory. Its political effects were quite the reverse. It brought no perceptible softening of the enemy attitude, but caused an immediate and strongly unfavorable reaction throughout much of the non-Communist world. The widespread fears of American "military irresponsibility" instantly revived, and with them the smoldering resentment over what was widely felt to be this country's excessive hostility to Communist China. The reaction of India's Prime Minister was characteristic. The Indian Government, Mr. Nehru said, was

"disturbed at the thought that the future of the United Nations and of war and peace might be decided without proper consultations, and might ultimately depend on the discretion of military commanders who would naturally think much more of local military objectives than of large questions affecting the world. . . . Any step taken to hinder a settlement [in Korea] was most unfortunate and regrettable." [28]

To the British the situation caused special chagrin because of the slight to Lord Alexander, who had arrived in Washington the day before the raid in company with the British Minister of State for Foreign Affairs. Secretary Acheson, in London

[28] Statement of June 28, in *Journal of the Parliaments of the Commonwealth*, XXXIII, July 1952, 554.

for discussions with his British and French colleagues, explained that the omission to inform them had been unintentional and was purely the result of "what in the United States is known as a 'snafu'." [29] Mr. Eden expressed official regret that Britain had been neither informed nor consulted, but said that the British Government fully supported its ally—in this particular instance. The Labor opposition, which forced a special debate on the matter, was less charitable and bitterly criticized the military reasoning which presumably had inspired the raid. "I think it is a profound mistake in psychology," said Mr. Attlee. " . . . I think it will lessen the chances of an armistice and may lead us dangerously nearer to a general conflagration in the East, and if that happens no one knows where it will stop." Aneurin Bevan, the left-wing Laborite whose influence threatened momentarily to eclipse Mr. Attlee's own, siezed the opportunity to demand a reversal of the whole American policy toward Communist China.

If one of the objectives of Communist strategy in the Far East was to create dissension among non-Communists and mobilize discontent against the United States, the Korean adventure was still paying dividends. It was true that the United Nations, under American leadership, had administered a series of sharp setbacks to Communist aims. South Korea was unconquered; Communist China was no nearer admission to the United Nations and control over Formosa; at the price of 1,683,545 casualties,[30] the enemy had not even managed to secure his minimum conditions for an armistice that would free his hands for new adventures elsewhere. By any conventional standard, Communist aggression in Korea had been a dismal failure.

[29] Statement of June 30, in *Department of State Bulletin*, XXVII, July 14, 1952, 60.
[30] Enemy losses through April 29 were listed by the U.S. as 1,176,195 battle casualties, 375,126 nonbattle casualties, and 132,224 military prisoners of war (*New York Times*, May 9, 1952). Total U.N. casualties were estimated in April at 419,456 and in August at 384,609, the decrease being explained by the reclassification of 63,000 South Koreans originally listed as missing (*ibid.*, August 31, 1952). U.S. casualties totaled 107,965 as of April 25 and 111,576 as of June 27, including 17,566 killed in action, 81,442 wounded, and 12,568 missing (*ibid.*, May 1 and July 10, 1952).

But these reverses were largely offset by the advantages the Communists still managed to extract from the peculiar conditions of the struggle and the incidental mistakes of their opponents. Much of the armed strength of the free world was being kept bottled up in the Korean peninsula; yet the accomplishments of the men who had been fighting the United Nations battle in Korea were seldom recognized either in America or abroad. American opinion focused almost entirely on the human costs of the adventure: 77,000 American casualties in the first year, 34,000 in the second; 17,566 Americans killed in action. Other United Nations members, on the contrary, seemed more concerned by the defects of American leadership than by the principles for which the war was being fought. Far from being a popular cause of the United Nations, Korea had become a running sore on the body of the free world. If large-scale fighting broke out again, the Communists were ready to face it on at least equal terms. Meanwhile the continuance of a state of war perpetuated a situation in which almost any move made by this country was likely to be condemned not only by Communists but by a large section of non-Communist world opinion.

3. Travail in Southeast Asia

If political and psychological factors played an important part in the anti-Communist struggle in Korea, their role was even more pervasive in other Far Eastern regions affected by Communist aggression. In Korea the really decisive factors were military. The armies, navies, and air forces of major world powers had engaged themselves on a scale that sometimes overshadowed both the interests of the local population and the wider political aims and principles at stake. In Southeast Asia, the predominance of military factors was less general and less strongly marked. The fighting that had been going on for several years in Burma, Malaya, the Philippines, and even in Indochina was smaller in scale and was still essentially concerned with local insurgent forces operating more or less independently of the major Communist powers. Despite Southeast Asia's obvious importance in the world balance of power, neither the U.S.S.R. nor China nor the United States had as yet assumed any irrevocable commitments there. Both sides had found it more convenient to leave immediate responsibility to local contestants, Asian and European, aided by such encouragement and material support as could be spared from more active theaters of conflict.

This limitation on the scope of military operations in Southeast Asia was not necessarily permanent, and those closest to the struggle did not underrate the significance of the comparatively small-scale warfare already in progress. General Jean de Lattre de Tassigny, whose vigorous leadership had averted a threatened military and psychological collapse in Indochina in 1950–1951, had put the matter strongly during a visit to Washington which had been devoted to pleading for more and faster American aid to the French and Vietnamese forces operating in northern Vietnam (Tongking):

"In this war, gentlemen, Indo-China is not the only stake. Southeast Asia, and even the whole of Asia is at stake. Tongking is the main redoubt, the keystone to the whole structure. The loss of Southeast Asia would mean that communism would have at its disposal essential strategic raw materials, that the Japanese economy would forever be unbalanced, and that the whole of Asia would be threatened. Once Tongking is lost, there is really no barrier before Suez. . . ." [31]

But conditions in Southeast Asia required a vastly different approach from the one adopted by the United States and the United Nations, under the spur of overt aggression, in the narrow territory of the Korean peninsula. The tensions and conflicts in Southeast Asia could not be looked upon as artificially generated disturbances caused by Communist trouble-makers. On the contrary, they were a reflection of deep-seated social and political maladjustments which had merely been seized upon by the Communists as a promising opportunity for ad-

[31] Address to the National Press Club, September 20, quoted in *New York Times*, September 21, 1951.

vancing their own cause. It was the acute demand for improved
conditions of existence—for release from poverty, hunger,
disease, exploitation, and the foreign control with which these
ills were popularly associated—that lent vitality to the Communist insurrectionary movements in Southeast Asia. Unless
the Western nations could find ways of meeting this demand
and helping the new nations in the area to establish themselves
on firm political and social foundations, it was doubtful
whether their anti-Communist efforts in the military field could
accomplish their long-run aim even if they succeeded in the
short run.

Southeast Asia, in short, was an area that demanded and
still offered scope for the long-range methods associated with
the Point Four concept and the endeavor to build "situations
of strength" in the free world. But the application of such
methods was made difficult by a variety of factors. The very
intensity of the "cold war" carried with it a heavy emphasis
on the military aspects of the struggle, in the thinking of the
Western nations and also in the allocation of their resources.
Many in the West were disinclined to promote radical reform
in Asia, whether from inertia, from skepticism about the ability
of the Asian peoples to manage their own affairs, or from
fear that any concessions made to the demand for change
would ultimately redound to the benefit of the Communists.
Any attempt to overcome the basic weaknesses of Southeast
Asia, moreover, would require joint effort on a large scale by
Asians and Westerners, and thus a considerably greater degree
of common understanding between them than had existed
hitherto. Western sources would hesitate to provide the necessary material and moral support unless convinced that the
Asians would not only reject Communism but align themselves
positively with the West. Asians, for their part, would hesitate
to accept Western support at all if it lessened their freedom
to choose their own political orientation. Left to themselves,
they were not over-eager to take sides in the global "East-
West" struggle. Any outside power—particularly any Western
power—that sought their collaboration would have to act with

considerable circumspection if their suspicions and nationalistic sensibilities were not to be unduly aroused.

American postwar policy toward Southeast Asia had shown awareness of these factors, and had been more or less consistently directed toward the support of national independence movements and the amelioration of economic and social conditions that made for instability in the area. But American action had been limited by concern for the interests of allied governments with possessions in Southeast Asia, by the heavy demands of the East-West struggle in other sectors, and latterly by a growing tendency to insist on an overtly anti-Communist orientation as the price of American support. This tendency, natural enough from the viewpoint of the United States, had aroused little sympathy in Asian quarters. It had engendered considerable ill-feeling between the United States and India, which had reached a high point in connection with the emergency food loan to that country in 1951.[32] Thereafter it continued to operate as a source of misunderstanding between the United States and some of the countries that were actually most in need of American assistance.

A vivid illustration was the controversy which developed early in 1952 over the question of United States aid to Indonesia, a nation whose remoteness from the threat of external aggression gave unusual scope to the peculiar psychological tendencies that prevailed in some degree throughout the region. Under the Mutual Security Act of 1951, all countries receiving military assistance from the United States were required to give an undertaking that they would fulfill their treaty obligations and make their due contribution to "the defensive strength of the free world"; those receiving economic assistance were asked for a more general pledge to join in promoting international understanding and good will.[33] Indonesia, hitherto a minor recipient of both military and economic aid, was asked to sign an agreement of the former type so that it might

---

[32] The United States in World Affairs, 1951, 256-257.
[33] Sec. 511, Public Law 165, 82nd Congress (Department of State Bulletin, XXVI, February 11, 1952, 238).

qualify for "equipment needed . . . for the maintenance of internal security." But the Indonesian Foreign Minister who ventured to comply with this request soon found himself bitterly attacked at home on the ground that he had abandoned Indonesia's "independent foreign policy" and steered his country into the "American orbit." The ensuing political storm brought down the entire Indonesian cabinet and left this country of 78 million inhabitants without a government for five and one-half weeks, from February 22 to April 1. The agreement with the United States had to be dropped, and with it any prospect that Indonesia would receive further military aid from this country. Not until late September was an understanding reached on an alternative aid program which would be strictly confined to economic and technical assistance and thus avoid further injury to the country's neutralist susceptibilities. The requisite agreement was eventually signed on January 12, 1953.

A similar attitude was evident in the mainland states of Southeast Asia, where the need for American aid was balanced by great reluctance to adopt policies which might be construed as anti-Communist and thus might prove irritating to a powerful neighbor like Communist China. Thailand, despite its uncomfortable position wedged between three countries in which hostilities against Communists were actually in progress, had been quite pro-American in its attitude, had sent a contingent of troops to Korea, and had still managed to escape any disturbance of its domestic tranquillity beyond an occasional reshuffle among the groups supporting Premier Pibul Songgram. The case of Burma was more difficult, and in some ways more characteristic. Burma's mildly socialistic government had the unenviable task of maintaining constant armed vigilance against three separate Communist or Communistic revolutionary movements, as well as trying to deal with a large-scale tribal insurrection and with the unsolicited presence of 10,000 or more Chinese Nationalist guerrillas who had been making themselves at home in the country ever since their expulsion from China in 1949.

Even though these Chinese forces were not supported by the United States, as had been claimed by Moscow and Peking, their activities created a delicate situation for a government which considered it vital to maintain "cordial" relations with Communist China. Late in March 1952, Burma's Premier U Nu announced that his government had decided to undertake military action against the unwelcome guests. At the same time he explained why Burma preferred not to act on the suggestion that the United Nations should be asked to investigate the situation. "If Communist China thought that [the inquiry] would be merely camouflage, then there would be difficulty," he pointed out. "No amount of clarification would satisfy Russia, Communist China and the United States." U Nu's further comments were even more illuminating, and helped to explain why his government had consistently fought shy of any political alignment with the United States despite the difficulty it was having in maintaining Burma's newly won independence.

"Nobody likes us," he said. "If we were to join the United States they would like us, and if we were to join the U.S.S.R. they would think we were fine fellows. We want to be liked, but we think our neutral policy is right and makes for world peace." [34]

Such an attitude, widespread as it was in Southeast Asia, might be a contribution to world peace or might prove in the long run to have been founded on a dangerous delusion. In any case it was one that could be fully indulged only by governments which had successfully asserted their independence of both the Communist and the Western camps. In Malaya and in the Associated States of Indochina, where British and French influence respectively was still paramount, the struggle with indigenous Communism was similar in origin but could not be so easily dissociated from the larger "East-West" conflict which was engaging the attention of the tutelary powers. "The struggle in Indochina," as American authorities were beginning to asseverate, "is an integral part of the world-wide resistance to Communist attempts at conquest and subversion." And as to Malaya, Secretary Acheson himself had

[34] *New York Times*, March 27, 1952.

declared that "The U.S. Government is fully cognizant . . . of the significance of the present struggle in Malaya as an integral part of the free world's common effort to halt Communist aggression." [35]

In the case of Malaya, where a British High Commissioner had been assassinated by Communist guerrillas as recently as October 1951, American interest had not been reflected in extensive military or economic assistance to the British authorities who were directing the fight against Communist terrorism. The energetic campaign launched early in 1952 by the new High Commissioner, General Sir Gerald Templer, remained a purely British-Malayan operation in which the United States confined itself to expressions of solidarity and good will. General Templer's responsibilities, according to an official British announcement, were not confined to the military sphere but would include the promotion of social and political readjustments; for it was the British intention that Malaya "should in due course become a fully self-governing nation" and, presumably, a member of the British Commonwealth. This declaration, which coincided with American views on the evolution of colonial peoples toward self-government, had been particularly welcomed by the State Department.[36] American interests, it was felt, would be well served if such a result could be brought about by the British through a combination of vigor and internal conciliation which did not require direct American action.

Unlike the Malayan Federation, the Indochinese states of Vietnam, Laos, and Cambodia already enjoyed the nominal status of independent members of the French Union and were recognized as such by the United States and more than thirty other governments. But in Indochina the United States had felt compelled to intervene directly at the side of France, and on a scale that dwarfed its anti-Communist efforts in other parts of Southeast Asia. There was still room for doubt about how

[35] Address by John M. Allison, Assistant Secretary of State for Far Eastern Affairs, July 1, in *Department of State Bulletin*, XXVII, July 21, 1952, 99; statement by Secretary Acheson, March 5, *ibid.*, XXVI, March 17, 1952, 427.
[36] Cf. *New York Times*, February 8, 1952 and *Department of State Bulletin*, XXVI, March 17, 1952, 427.

much real independence was enjoyed by the three Associated States; but there was no doubt about the critical nature of the anti-Communist struggle in Indochina, its crippling effect on the French military and economic position in Asia and Europe, and the necessity for continuing American support if the situation was to be kept under control. The cost of maintaining a French expeditionary force in Indochina annually absorbed a third or more of the French military budget. The six-year toll in officers and men killed and missing closely approximated the losses sustained by the United States in Korea.[37] There were recurrent demands in France, reminiscent of similar manifestations in the United States, that this "hemorrhage" be stopped by withdrawal from the conflict or by the equally unpromising course—especially unpromising in light of the experience at Panmunjom—of seeking a negotiated settlement under the auspices of the United Nations or the "interested" great powers.

Ever since the establishment of direct contact between the Chinese Communists and the Vietminh insurgents in Indochina in 1949, the cessation of the autumn rains had been followed by a renewal of insurgent military operations and a critical threat to the whole French-Vietnamese position in the Tongking delta area. The crisis of 1951–1952 was rendered unusually grave by the fears of imminent Chinese Communist intervention and by the depressing effect of the death of General de Lattre, the soul of French-Vietnamese resistance, in a Paris hospital. Once again, however, the critical months passed with nothing worse than the evacuation by the French of one important salient. The administrative vacuum caused by General de Lattre's death was eventually filled by sending Jean Letourneau, French Minister for the Associated States, to Indochina as High Commissioner. But the result of the winter's fighting was to emphasize more strongly than ever the degree to which continued resistance depended on large-scale shipments of American arms

---

[37] French Union killed and missing in Indochina through 1951 totaled 28,711; American dead and missing in Korea through January 3, 1952 aggregated 28,781.

and equipment, even if this country refused to assume any direct commitments of a military character.

The scale of American military assistance to France and the Indochinese States was already considerable and seemed destined to continue increasing. Despite the serious delays which had dogged the execution of the United States military aid programs in all parts of the world, deliveries of tanks, radio equipment, light and heavy arms, landing craft, aircraft and the like to Indochina had reached an estimated value of 80 billion francs ($228 million) by the end of January 1952. For 1952 the allocations were substantially larger; the total American contribution for the year was estimated in Paris at 175 billion francs ($500 million).[38] Before the end of May, the 150th shipload of American military matériel had been unloaded at Saigon. When M. Letourneau came to Washington in June it was announced that American aid now approximated one-third of the total cost of Indochina operations (estimated at over $1 billion annually) and would, moreover, be further expanded "within the limitations set by Congress." [39]

In extending material support to the anti-Communist effort in Indochina, the United States had not neglected the broad political aspects of the struggle. The French had been strongly encouraged to turn over more authority to the governments of the Associated States, in the interest of building up their strength and prestige and combating the nationalist appeal of the Vietminh. Particular stress had been laid on the development of the national armies of Vietnam, Laos, and Cambodia, in the hope that they could eventually take over the main responsibility for military operations in Indochina and enable France to concentrate more fully on its European military responsibilities. On the occasion of M. Letourneau's visit, the United States took the opportunity to stipulate that any additional American aid would be especially devoted to the furtherance of this project. American officials had noted with

[38] Chronology of International Events and Documents, VIII, March 6-19, 1952, 165.
[39] Communiqué, June 18, in Documents on American Foreign Relations, 1952, No. 24 (b).

satisfaction that the aggregate strength of the three Indochinese armies had meanwhile reached a level of fifty-two battalions, several of them commanded by native officers. Another evidence of increasing Indochinese participation in the war was the fact that 52 percent of the casualties during the early months of 1952 were sustained by Indochinese troops, as compared with only 9 percent in 1946.[40] Some observers hoped that the withdrawal of the French expeditionary force might begin as early as 1953.

All in all, the Indochinese situation seemed in Washington to justify considerably more optimism than would have been warranted a few months earlier. "The military situation appears to be developing favorably," said Secretary Acheson. ". . . There are increasing evidences of the growing vitality of the Associated States in handling their political, financial, and economic affairs. . . . The Communists have made a most determined effort in Indochina. Their aggression has been checked and recent indications warrant the view that the tide is now moving in our favor." [41] This estimate was at least partially borne out by the French commander on the spot, who had indicated that the Communists in the Tongking delta were not then capable of launching a serious offensive.

The difficulty with such evaluations was that they apparently took no account of the ever-present possibility of direct Chinese Communist intervention in Indochina. As in Korea in 1950, things appeared to be going reasonably well, provided there was no radical change in enemy tactics. The drain in casualties continued heavy; guerrilla raids and acts of terrorism kept the country from settling down; politically there remained a wide gap between the desires of Indochinese nationalists and the concessions France had been willing to make. Left to themselves, France and the Associated States no doubt could manage, with American aid, to hold the Communists more or less in check as they had done since 1946. But the prospect of indefinite continuation of hostilities was unpleasant in itself and doubly

[40] Department of State Bulletin, XXVII, July 21, 1952, 99.
[41] Statement of June 18, ibid., XXVI, June 30, 1952, 1010.

disheartening when it was remembered how easily the Chinese could at any time increase their clandestine aid to the Vietminh or even come openly to their assistance.

The recent tripartite warning that Chinese aggression in Southeast Asia would be a matter for action by the United Nations [42] would hardly suffice to deter a Chinese government that had shown so little deference to United Nations views in the past. That the United Nations would rally to the support of France and of Vietnam's Emperor Bao Dai was uncertain in itself in view of the widespread mistrust of French policy which prevailed among United Nations members, particularly in Asia. There was no indication that adequate plans had been developed by the West for meeting Chinese aggression against Indochina if it came. Nor did M. Letourneau's visit to Washington bring the Western governments much closer to a common front in Southeast Asia. Each of the free countries concerned, said the communiqué, had assumed primary responsibility for resistance "in the specific areas where Communism has resorted to force of arms"—the United States in Korea, France in Indochina, and Britain, presumably, in Malaya. The obligation "to help each other in their areas of primary responsibility" was expressly subordinated to this notion of a broad division of labor in the Far East. [43]

Behind the uncertainty which such a formula failed to allay were larger questions, affecting both the situation in Indochina and that of Southeast Asia as a whole. How adequate was the piecemeal approach officially favored by the Allies to the broad requirements of Southeast Asia's condition, political, economic, and social as well as military? The geographic and political diversity of the region undoubtedly militated against the development of common policies for all its component units, and went far to explain official Washington's coolness toward the popular idea of an all-embracing Pacific security pact. [44] But did it warrant the existing practice of dealing with each

[42] Cf. above, pp. 177-178.
[43] *Documents on American Foreign Relations, 1952*, No. 24 (b).
[44] Cf. the remarks of Mr. Allison in *Department of State Bulletin*, XXVII, September 29, 1952, 472.

situation on a local basis, without reference to the fundamental forces at work in all of them? Did it justify the attempt to solve emergent political and economic problems within the framework of local, short-term military necessity? Or did the situation call for a deeper and more comprehensive appraisal, one that would take into account both the long-term requirements of Southeast Asia's political evolution and the place of that evolution in the larger Asian picture? Was it possible that the key to Southeast Asian developments did not lie in Southeast Asia at all, but in another country which happened to be the concern of a different unit in the State Department?

Some observers suspected that the ultimate fate of Southeast Asia would be determined less by military developments in Tongking than by the political processes that were actually going forward in India, a country whose influence radiated throughout much of the Far East and whose experiment in nation-building could not fail to exert a profound effect on other countries with similar problems. India exhibited on the largest scale the typical characteristics of Asia in transition: immense poverty and want; keen preoccupation with national independence; sharp aversion for Western "imperialism" and "interference"; a marked preference for neutrality in the "cold war," tempered, however, by distaste for aggression and by consciousness of its own exposure to Communist pressures both from within and from beyond its frontiers. India, unlike China, had undertaken to try to solve its gigantic problems by democratic methods, and was thus holding up before the peoples of Asia an alternative to the methods of Communism. If the experiment failed, they would have that much less reason to resist the Communist seduction in their own countries.

Whether the Indian experiment would ultimately succeed or fail could not be clearly foreseen in 1952, when India's 360 million inhabitants celebrated their first general election by renewing the mandate of the dominant Congress party under Mr. Nehru but also elevated the Communists to the position of the second political force in the state. Yet no observer could fail to perceive that the future of democracy in India was bound up with the solution of grave economic problems, that the mere development of an adequate food supply for a nation of this size was a task of monumental proportions, and that the requisite effort could hardly be carried through without more generous assistance from abroad than was then in sight. Critics who pointed out that too much of India's own energies were tied up in its quarrel with Pakistan could not deny that outside help was indispensable if conditions in the subcontinent were to improve in any fundamental sense.

Some authorities took the view that the United States ought, in its own interest and that of Asia generally, to have made India the fulcrum of its Asian policy and should still give it the preference over a country like Japan, which was actually benefiting so heavily by American moral and material support.[45] But American strategic preoccupations in the Pacific had precluded any such choice. The possibility of large-scale American assistance to India, apart from private investment in Indian industrial development, had been restricted both by requirements elsewhere and by political differences between the American and Indian governments. Under the circumstances, the initiation by the two countries of a long-term community development project and various other undertakings under the Point Four program, with a first-year allocation of $50 million,[46] was a longer step forward in Indian-American economic cooperation than might otherwise have appeared. Such projects would not meet India's need for an estimated $1.25 billion in new foreign capital to carry out its five-year national development plan, but they would favorably affect the lives of some 12 million people and might set a pattern that could be expanded in the future.

The prospects for broadened activity in this general field were not enhanced by the actions of Congress on the Asian phase of the Mutual Security Program for the fiscal year 1952-53. Appropriations for direct military aid in Asia and the

[45] Cf. Maurice Zinkin, *Asia and the West* (New York, Institute of Pacific Relations, 1952), 205-207, 256-257, 292-293.
[46] *Department of State Bulletin*, XXVI, January 14, 1952, 47-48; June 30, 1952, 1015-1018.

Pacific totaled over $540 million; economic aid to be administered by the Mutual Security Agency, chiefly to Formosa and Indochina, came to nearly $203 million. These sums represented approximately 85 percent of the figures requested by the administration. But for Point Four aid to the area which included India, Pakistan, Burma, and Indonesia, Congress appropriated less than $68 million—under 40 percent of the administration's request, and only 8 percent of the total expenditure contemplated in the Asian-Pacific area.

"This is an exceedingly dangerous thing for the Congress to have done," said the President of the reduction in Point Four aid. "Take India, for example. India, the largest democratic nation in all Asia, is now engaged in a tremendous effort of her own to build up her economy and living standards—to show that democratic government and democratic methods can succeed in curing the poverty, the hunger and the misery that afflict so much of Asia. . . . Upon these efforts may well depend the whole future course of freedom and democracy on the continent of Asia. . . . The American people should carefully note the strange fact that prominent among the proponents of this cut were some of the very individuals who have shouted loudest that we are not doing enough in Asia." [47]

One broader undertaking that was based on a recognition of India's needs and of their underlying relationship to the whole Asian future was the six-year Colombo Plan for South and Southeast Asia, officially launched by the nations of the British Commonwealth in 1951. A collection of long-term national plans rather than a single all-encompassing development program, the Colombo Plan embraced India, Pakistan, Ceylon, Burma, the Indochinese States, and Nepal as well as the Pacific members of the Commonwealth. The United States, too, participated in the consultative committee of the Plan organization, but made no special financial contribution outside of the various bilateral aid programs it was carrying on in association with individual participating countries.

The total cost of carrying out the Colombo Plan had origi-

[47] Statement of July 15, in *Department of State Bulletin*, XXVII, August 4, 1952, 200.

nally been estimated at $5.2 billion, of which it had been hoped that as much as $2 billion might be obtained from the United States. Rising world prices had now rendered these estimates obsolete, as the Colombo Plan consultative committee frankly acknowledged when it met at Karachi in March 1952. No new global estimate was prepared, but the delegates concentrated in a spirit of "cautious optimism" on examining the national plans which most of the participants had submitted or were preparing. Some visible signs of progress were noted, and the belief was expressed that barring unforeseen developments the second-year program drawn up for 1952–1953 could be successfully carried out. The importance of the undertaking to the political as well as the economic future of Asia was fully recognized. No one, of course, could say whether the results of this long-term effort would show themselves soon enough, and in sufficient amplitude, to obviate the dangers which armed men of various nations were meanwhile holding at bay in the jungles and paddy fields of Southeast Asia.

4. The Island Chain

The conditions of the East-West struggle in the insular lands that fringed Asia's Pacific coast differed materially from those prevailing on the Asian continent. Immunity from attack or infiltration across land frontiers provided these countries with a measure of basic security which was denied to states in the exposed position of Burma, Indochina, or the Korean Republic. Further, their importance in American postwar strategic thinking assured them of this country's wholehearted interest and freed them from much of the uncertainty that occasionally surrounded American intentions in other areas. The extent of this American concern had often been demonstrated in the case of occupied Japan, the Ryukyus, and the Philippine Republic as well as the former Japanese-mandated islands, now governed by the United States as a strategic trust territory under the United Nations. In mid-1950 it had been strikingly evidenced once again by the decision not only to resist the Communist aggression in Korea but also to use American naval power to prevent any Communist attack on the island of Formosa, last stronghold of the Chinese Nationalist government and army under President Chiang Kai-shek.

Matching this unusual solicitude for the countries of the "offshore island chain" was the comparative benevolence toward the United States displayed by most of the island peoples and authorities. True, the people of Japan, Formosa, and the Philippines belonged to Asia by race and culture, were affected by many of the characteristic problems of Asian society, and displayed some of the typical attitudes to which Asian conditions in the twentieth century gave rise. But differing experience and circumstances, the comparatively generous tradition of American policy in the Far East, and a keen sense of present dependence on the United States had mitigated some of the negative features of the Asian outlook and made official cooperation with this country comparatively easy. Neutralism and anti-Americanism were relatively minor problems in most of the island countries. Conservative, anti-Communist governments were in control in Tokyo, Taipei, and Manila. Opinions differed about their qualifications to govern the peoples under their care, but there was not much doubt about their ability to maintain reasonable stability and provide the United States with such military facilities as it might require for the common defense.

Recognition of a common interest with this country did not, however, imply any great sense of mutual solidarity among the other peoples and governments concerned. The memory of Japan's imperialistic aggressions was too fresh, and the reviving power of the new Japan was potentially too formidable, to admit of much cordiality between the former lords of the Far East and their recent victims. The generous peace settlement concluded with Japan by most of the non-Communist world in 1951 had been brought about over strenuous protests from such countries as the Philippines and Indonesia and, moreover, without the participation of either India or China. India had refused to sign a treaty which, in its opinion, failed to restore Japan to complete independence and thus was offensive to the dignity of an Asian nation. Nationalist China, like Communist China, had been excluded from the peace conference because of the unwillingness of some of the Allied Powers to accept Chiang's government as the representative of the Chinese nation. A more thorough reconciliation between Japan and at least some of its late enemies in the Far East was one of the prerequisites for any general Pacific security pact that might be negotiated in the future. Meanwhile it was necessary to complete the rudimentary security structure which had been established by the Japanese Peace Treaty and the security treaties which the United States had simultaneously concluded with Japan, with the Philippines, and with Australia and New Zealand.

Because the nations concerned lacked any common point of departure except for their association with the United States, the problems of Pacific security had necessarily to be treated in an individual and somewhat fragmentary way. Each component of the island chain had its particular legal and political status, strategic function, and relation to the interests of other powers. The future status of American forces and installations in Japan was broadly regulated by the new American-Japanese Security Treaty. The Ryukyu Islands, including the important military base at Okinawa, were remaining directly under American control—subject, however, to a possible voluntary arrangement for placing them under a United Nations trusteeship at some future time. Formosa and the Pescadores Islands, renounced by Japan but not yet definitively assigned to any new claimant, seemed destined to continue under the de facto control of Nationalist China in accordance with policies for which its government and the United States assumed entire responsibility. The Philippines were already linked with the United States by reciprocal obligations which the new security treaty merely confirmed. Australia and New Zealand, under their separate security treaty with the United States, were broadly interested in these arrangements because each of the three signatory governments had recognized that its own peace and safety would be endangered by an armed attack on the territory, armed forces, public vessels or aircraft of either of the others anywhere in the Pacific area. [48]

In the Philippines and in Formosa, American missions were already engaged in helping to train and equip the local armed forces and strengthen the economies of the respective countries through various forms of economic and technical assistance. While the Philippine Congress deliberated over the Security Treaty and the Japanese Peace Treaty, American advisers continued to support the efforts being carried out under President Elpidio Quirino's government to reduce the national deficit and gradually curb the Communist-led Hukbalahap movement. In Formosa, American and Chinese energies were absorbed by the task of sustaining a heavily overburdened economy and bringing the Nationalist army of roughly 400,000 up to the standard that would be required for effective defense of the island. Long-range questions about the political future of Formosa, the possible use of Nationalist troops in Korea, or an eventual reinvasion of the Chinese mainland by Chiang Kai-shek's forces would be settled mainly by developments elsewhere. Immediate policy was determined by the compelling facts of Formosa's weakness and its position as a primary target of Chinese Communist ambitions.

In Japan, too, American policy was governed by acute awareness of the continuing Soviet-Communist interest in a country whose position and military and economic potential loomed constantly larger in the general Far Eastern balance of power. Japan's industrial strength, expanding population, and prospective political influence were such that its course over the next few years might well determine the whole future of Eastern Asia. Since the war, Japan proper (as distinguished from its insular dependencies, the Kurile Islands and Southern Sakhalin) had been protected by the United States occupation from the full weight of Soviet-Communist influence directed from

[48] For details cf. *The United States in World Affairs, 1951,* 186-190 and 197-202. The texts of the three security treaties appear in *Documents on American Foreign Relations, 1951,* 262 ff.

outside. The basic aim of the United States was to perpetuate this state of immunity, assimilate Japan politically and militarily into the non-Communist community of nations, and meanwhile retain the local military facilities necessary for the Korean operation and the general defense of the perimeter. In recent years these aims had been pursued more or less independently of the original Allied objective of preventing a resurgence of Japanese militarism. That particular danger was considered to have been eliminated by the reforms carried out during the postwar occupation of the country. Present United States plans involved the rearmament of a democratic, non-militarist Japan as an important factor in the military security of the free world.

As interpreted in Washington, Japan's assimilation into the non-Communist community involved three prime requirements. First, Japan must avoid political or economic contact with Communist China, both as a safeguard against Communist influence and as a proof of solidarity with the United States. Second, Japan must be prepared to assume responsibility for its own defense and, until ready to do so, must accept American defense collaboration which would be made available under special treaty arrangements drawn up in accordance with United Nations principles. Third, in its general economic and political evolution Japan must follow a course of development that would make it increasingly a positive influence for international harmony and thus a "sustaining member of the free world." Only thus, in the official American view, would Japan justify the magnanimity of the victorious non-Communist powers and contribute to a lasting solution of Far Eastern strategic and political problems. It was not too much to say that the future stability of the whole "defense perimeter" depended on the way in which these three interrelated requirements were fulfilled.

How fully Japan would respond to American expectations depended, in the last analysis, on the evolution of Japanese attitudes in the new situation that would be created as soon as the peace treaty went into effect. No final judgment on this point would be possible for some time to come. In the meanwhile, however, the Japanese Government had been compelled to take an immediate stand on the China issue in order to make sure that the peace treaty itself would be ratified by the United States Senate. The test of Japanese intentions was a provision in the Treaty of San Francisco which in effect called upon Japan to conclude a separate peace treaty with China, but failed to specify with which of the two Chinese governments the treaty was to be negotiated and at least theoretically left this point to the decision of the Japanese. Senatorial misgivings over this arrangement, heightened by awareness that many Japanese were eager to reestablish commercial and possibly even political connections with the China mainland, were dispelled at the beginning of 1952 when Premier Shigeru Yoshida gave the desired assurance that his government intended to opt for Nationalist rather than Communist China.[49] In fulfillment of this pledge, a Japanese diplomatic mission went to Formosa in February and, after a display of some obstinacy by both sides, a "Treaty of Peace between the Republic of China and Japan" was signed in Taipei on April 28.[50]

In its main provisions the Sino-Japanese peace treaty resembled the broader pact of San Francisco. Japan renounced all its claims to former Chinese territories, and to "all special rights and interests in China"; China, on its side, waived practically all claim to reparations from Japan "as a sign of magnanimity and goodwill toward the Japanese people." The principal difficulty stemmed not from the war that was being formally ended but from conflicting views about the present status and rights of the Chinese Republic at a time when it controlled no part of the Chinese mainland. The Chinese negotiators were anxious that their government should be recognized, at least tacitly, as the government having sovereignty over all of China; the Japanese were equally determined to

[49] *Documents on American Foreign Relations, 1952,* No. 25 (a); cf. *The United States in World Affairs, 1951,* 204.
[50] Text in *Free China Review,* II, No. 5, July 1952, 53-58. The treaty entered into effect on August 5, 1952.

avoid commitments which would tie their hands for the future and intensify the already virulent hostility of Communist China and the U.S.S.R., whose anti-Japanese alliance could always be invoked whenever they considered that Japan was guilty of an act of "aggression." Eventually the difficulty was got over by an exchange of notes specifying that the treaty applied to all territories "which are now, or which may hereafter be" under Nationalist control. By this means Japan carried out its side of the tacit understanding on which the United States Senate had meanwhile approved the main peace treaty together with the United States-Japanese security treaty. [51]

A further prerequisite to Senate action had been the completion of arrangements for the continuance of American forces in Japan during the period between the entrance into force of the peace treaty and the somewhat remote date when Japan would assume responsibility for its own defense. As in Germany, there was need for a special agreement, implementing the over-all security treaty, to regulate such matters as "the use of facilities and areas, the sharing of costs, the jurisdiction over persons, certain privileges and exemptions, and the method of continuous mutual consultation" which were deemed "necessary and appropriate for the United States Armed Forces to carry out effectively their security mission." To this end a United States-Japanese "administrative agreement" was negotiated by Dean Rusk, a special presidential envoy, and signed in Tokyo on February 28.[52] Like most such arrangements, it assured the United States forces of a privileged status which seemed excessive to some Japanese but no more than adequate to American military authorities. Its most noticeable shortcoming was the fact that it necessarily concerned only United States forces and made no provision for the forces of other United Nations which might find themselves in Japan in connection with the Korean campaign.

These formalities completed, the Allied occupation of Japan, and with it the Pacific phase of World War II, officially came

[51] Cf. above, pp. 60-61, 94.
[52] Text in *Department of State Bulletin*, XXVI, March 10, 1952, 382-390.

to an end on April 28, 1952. From then on, Japan and those
of its late enemies which had signed and ratified the Treaty
of San Francisco would be at peace.[53] Yet none of the statesmen who made official comments on the occasion ventured to
indulge in unqualified self-congratulation. President Truman,
Ambassador Dulles, and Premier Yoshida all emphasized the
difficulties ahead no less than the magnitude of what had been
accomplished. "We face a great test to human wisdom and
human courage," said the Japanese Prime Minister. His country, he seemed confident, had drawn the moral of its recent
experience:

"In making our new start today, our people know that no nation
can live unto itself, that no nation can draw dividends unless it
contributes to a common world effort and invests in the common
welfare of humanity. . . .

"Today, stimulated by a broader vision and understanding of
the principles of humanity, equality and justice, I can assure you
that our people will proceed forward drawing upon the fount of
our strength and unity. So rooted we can meet the challenge of
our times." [54]

What were the criteria for evaluating Japan's conversion to
a liberal and internationalist outlook? No more than a provisional inference could be drawn from the initial actions of the
Japanese Government and the apparent trend of public opinion
as the nation adjusted itself to the consciousness of independence. That trend, as far as outside observers could judge, stood
in about the same relation to Premier Yoshida's pronouncements as did contemporary tendencies in Germany to the democratic and pro-Western utterances of Chancellor Adenauer. In
each of these former enemy states the government of the day
seemed genuinely committed to solidarity with the democratic
world. But in each there was room for uncertainty as to how
far this solidarity would be carried in practice and, further-

[53] In accordance with Art. 23 of the Treaty of Peace, the treaty entered into
force on April 28 for all signatory states which had ratified it up to that time,
viz., Japan, Argentina, Australia, Canada, France, Mexico, New Zealand,
Pakistan, U.K., and U.S.
[54] *Department of State Bulletin*, XXVI, May 5, 1952, 689; see also the statements of President Truman and Ambassador Dulles, *ibid.*, 687-688, and the
evaluation of General Ridgway (May 22) *ibid.*, June 9, 1952, 926-927.

more, how far it corresponded to the subconscious tendencies that were at work in the population at large.

The events of 1952 would at least demonstrate that the Japanese Government and people were animated by no friendly sentiments toward the U.S.S.R., and that the internal Communist movement in Japan, though capable of creating major disturbances of public order, had lost whatever broad popular appeal it had threatened to acquire a few years earlier. A series of Communist-inspired disorders which had kept security forces on the alert throughout the spring culminated on May 1, three days after the end of the occupation, in an outbreak of mob violence that paralyzed Tokyo for several hours, causing hundreds of casualties and considerable property damage. Yet five months later, in the nationwide parliamentary elections held on October 1, the Communists were to poll little more than 2 percent of the total vote and would lose all of their twenty-two seats in the lower house of the Diet. Mistakes and internal divisions among the Communist leadership had seemingly completed the alienation caused by the hostile attitude of the Soviet Government, whose annoyance over the peace settlement had found vent in repeated seizures of Japanese fishing boats and their crews, continued detention of many thousands of Japanese prisoners of war, systematic flouting of Japanese governmental authority, and eventually, on September 10, in a veto of Japan's application for membership in the United Nations.[55]

But did Japan's repudiation of the U.S.S.R. and Communism signify attachment to the Western democratic cause? To this question neither the elections nor the performance of the government gave any clear answer—a fact which in itself was disconcerting to any who had looked on the peace settlement as the decisive stage in Japan's democratic redemption. Superficially the Yoshida government was evidently persevering in the policy of moderate conservatism at home and conciliation abroad which it had adopted under the occupation. Its main domestic accomplishment was the passage of a stringent sub-

[55] Cf. below, p. 287.

versives control bill which, though decidedly unpalatable to
the labor movement and to liberal Japanese opinion, was represented as necessary to combat the Communist menace. Possibly more significant than the government's position in this
matter was the growing prominence in Japanese life of persons
and tendencies associated with the country's nationalistic, antidemocratic past. "The one omnipresent phenomenon," wrote
one experienced American observer shortly after the elections,

"is the tide of resurgent nationalism now sweeping over all parts
of Japan and all sections of the population. . . . At present, it is
beginning to sweep members of the extreme right back into political prominence. And they are girding their loins for an all-out
struggle against liberalism and Americanism. . . ." [56]

But if the future of Japanese democracy was thus somewhat
problematical, it was already clear that America's most recent
ally was in no particular hurry to carry out some of the obligations it had assumed under the new treaties. Although the
Yoshida government negotiated a separate peace treaty with
India (June 9) [57] by which that country, too, waived all claim
to Japanese reparations, there was little progress toward negotiating reparation settlements with the Philippines and Indonesia as required by the San Francisco treaty. Meanwhile that
treaty remained unratified by the Philippine and Indonesian
legislative bodies.

Even more noticeable was Japanese inaction in the field of
national security. In promising to maintain armed forces in
and about Japan as a deterrent to possible aggression, the
United States had emphasized that it was acting "in the expectation . . . that Japan will increasingly assume responsibility
for its own defense." But Premier Yoshida had avoided precise
commitments on this score, and now that the treaties were in
effect he showed no eagerness to make a beginning. No preparations were made for a revision of the ban on national armed
forces in Japan's postwar constitution. The only important

[56] Robert A. Scalapino, "Japan and the General Elections," *Far Eastern Survey*,
XXI, October 29, 1952, 154.
[57] Text in *Contemporary Japan*, XXI, 1952, 325-328.

move toward the establishment of an adequate security force for this nation of 84 millions was an expansion of the occupation-inspired National Police Reserve from a total strength of 75,000 to 110,000 and its redesignation as a National Security Corps.[58] Throughout the election campaign, moreover, Premier Yoshida insisted that this step did not mean rearmament, and that he continued to oppose rearmament until a greater degree of economic reconstruction had been attained—possibly in about four years.[59]

In this somewhat evasive stand the Prime Minister was faithfully reflecting the hesitations of the Japanese public, a considerable section of which remained unreconciled to the prospect of direct rearmament and even to the basic concept of Japanese participation in the Western security system—including the concession of bases and other rights to the United States. Although some conservative-minded Japanese favored rearmament as a step toward full national "independence," neutralist sentiment and opposition to the American military program had considerable influence not only in Socialist and labor circles but even within the governing Liberal party. This factor undoubtedly contributed to the extent of the Communist-inspired disturbances during the spring, which took the form of a supposedly "spontaneous" popular protest against the policies of the Yoshida government and particularly its association with the United States. The same resentment over Japan's use by outsiders as a military base helped to explain the stubbornness of Japanese officials in a series of controversies respecting the jurisdiction of Japanese police and courts over personnel of the British and other armed forces participating in the United Nations action in Korea.

[58] In August a Security Board was established to coordinate the National Security Corps and the 7,500-man Maritime Safety Corps or coast guard, both of which were receiving substantial amounts of matériel on loan or lease from the U.S. (Cf. *New York Times,* August 2 and 5, September 4, October 16, and November 13, 1952.) The loan of U.S. naval vessels authorized by Congress through Public Law 467 was accepted by Japan in an agreement signed November 12 and approved by the Diet in December (*ibid.,* November 13, December 23 and 25, 1952).

[59] Scalapino, *loc. cit.,* 153.

Both in Japan and in the West it had been widely recognized that Japan's eventual orientation would be largely determined by its ability to find a formula ensuring its own economic survival in a politically divided world. Of central importance in this connection was the rebuilding of Japanese foreign trade, a process that admittedly would be made more difficult by the political objections to extensive Japanese trade with Communist countries. In this field, at least, there was no doubt about the readiness of the Japanese to exert their best efforts in the hope of regaining and extending their former world markets. The problem was rather one of overcoming the resistance of the outside world to a renewal of Japanese commercial competition. At the moment, Japan was benefiting heavily from the special circumstances of the Korean war and the various American aid programs in the Far East, which created an unusual demand for Japanese goods and services. Thus the country had been enabled to build up a comfortable surplus in its external balance of payments and even to resume service on its prewar bond issues in the United States and Britain. But a tremendous further expansion of Japanese exports would clearly be necessary if this adventitious prosperity was to be maintained; and there was plenty of evidence that as the range of Japanese commercial effort widened the opposition to it tended to solidify, both in directly competitive countries like Great Britain and even in certain sections of the American economy. If there was a satisfactory solution for this long-range problem, its outlines failed to emerge distinctly during 1952.

While the Japanese situation was slowly clarifying, other aspects of the many-sided Pacific security problem demanded American attention. The Tripartite Security Treaty between Australia, New Zealand, and the United States, informally known as the Anzus pact, had gone into effect on April 29, 1952, one day after the Japanese treaties. By its terms, the three signatory powers had provided for the establishment of a Council, consisting of Foreign Ministers or their deputies, to consider matters involved in the implementation of the treaty. The first meeting of this Council was held in Honolulu from

August 4 to August 7, with Secretary Acheson representing the United States and the Australian and New Zealand Ministers for External Affairs, Richard G. Casey and T. Clifton Webb, heading the delegations of their respective countries.

The chief purpose of the Honolulu meeting was to establish procedures and machinery for permanent liaison among the Anzus powers. It was decided that the full Council would meet once a year, alternately in the United States and in Australia or New Zealand, and that coordination during the intervals would be effected by deputies meeting in Washington—initially, the American Under-Secretary of State (David K. Bruce) and the Australian and New Zealand ambassadors to the United States. To provide the Council with military advice, each country undertook to designate a military representative; Admiral Arthur W. Radford, United States Commander-in-Chief, Pacific, was accredited to the Council as United States military representative. Arrangements were made for an early meeting of the military representatives "to work out details of the military machinery the general nature of which was agreed to." [60]

In addition to settling these details, the Ministers took the opportunity to "review matters affecting their common relationships in the Pacific area," including the situation in Korea, the resistance to Communist imperialism in Southeast Asia, and, more especially, the place of the Anzus Treaty in the general system of Pacific security that was coming into being. On this last point it could not be said that the views of the three allies were altogether in harmony. The United States, obviously, thought of Pacific security mainly in terms of a potential Communist military threat. But Australia and New Zealand were not greatly concerned over the possibility of direct Communist aggression in the Pacific; from their point of view the

[60] Communiqué, August 7, in *Documents on American Foreign Relations, 1952,* No. 26. For other material on the conference cf. *Department of State Bulletin,* XXVII, July 28, 1952, 141; August 11, 1952, 219-220; August 18, 1952, 243-244; August 25, 1952, 284-285. The military representatives met at Pearl Harbor in September and worked out "details of the military machinery required to advise the Council on the problems of military cooperation which may arise. . . ." (*New York Times,* September 26, 1952.)

treaty was actually more valuable as a protection against the new Japan than against land powers like the U.S.S.R. and Communist China. Without it, they would have been even more hesitant to acquiesce in the effort of the United States to build up Japan as a barrier against the Communist world. Even with the treaty in force, they were not entirely satisfied with the vague and noncommittal language in which the promises of American support were clothed; still less were they prepared to associate themselves directly with Japan in an over-all Pacific alliance of the kind toward which United States policy seemed gradually to be tending.

There were various other governments whose actual or potential relationship to the Anzus treaty was a source of disquiet. Great Britain had been noticeably unhappy over its exclusion from the pact, and had not concealed its desire to be included in any consultations among the Pacific powers. The exclusion of Great Britain carried with it some embarrassment for Australia and New Zealand, whose membership in the British Commonwealth implied reciprocal obligations toward the United Kingdom in both political and military matters. But if Britain were to be admitted to the Anzus association, its members—including the United States—could hardly avoid assuming some responsibility for the defense of British Far Eastern possessions like Hong Kong and Malaya. In that case, France and the Indochinese states would also have a claim to share the benefits of the alliance. Before long the original trio would become enmeshed in all the conflicting aims and aspirations of the Far East, including those of neutralist governments like Burma and Indonesia and politically controversial ones like Nationalist China and Syngman Rhee's Korean Republic. Thus, although the Anzus Council had authority to maintain a consultative relationship with other interested states and organizations in the Pacific area, it was scarcely surprising that the three ministers at Honolulu should decide that any attempt to do so immediately would be premature.

The Honolulu communiqué also dwelt on the loyalty of the Anzus powers to the United Nations Charter and emphasized

that no decisions had been reached nor any commitments undertaken "regarding matters of direct concern to our friends in
the Pacific area or elsewhere." This language was apparently
designed in part to allay the suspicions to which the meeting had given rise in Asian nationalist and neutralist circles.
For it was to be remembered that Australia, New Zealand, and
the United States all belonged to that exclusive community
of wealthy and well-established "Anglo-Saxon" democracies
which administered dependent territories and were suspected
by some outsiders of opposing the free exercise of the right of
self-determination and even of harboring feelings of racial
superiority toward their Asian brethren. In the United Nations,
they were often aligned with the Western European democracies in opposition to the sometimes intemperate claims of the
Asian-Arab, "anticolonial" states. Any signs of a similar alignment in the Pacific were bound to arouse mistrust in Asian
circles. Charges of "neo-colonialism" were heard even in the
Philippines, despite that country's privileged position in the
United States security orbit. In India it was suggested that the
embryo Pacific security system was threatening to degenerate
into "an organization of Imperialist Powers for the protection
of their interests." [61]

Such fears were closer to the unfounded allegations of
Soviet-Communist propaganda than they were to the real intentions of the Anzus governments. But, however groundless,
they emphasized once again the complex nature of the anti-
Communist defense problem in Eastern Asia and the Pacific.
Undoubtedly Communist aggression had to be vigorously resisted wherever it had appeared or might appear, in Korea, in
Southeast Asia, or on the islands of the "defense perimeter."
But this resistance had also to be organized and conducted in
a way that would earn the approval of the peoples concerned
rather than accentuating their distrust. Otherwise the scheme
of military defense that was being erected might prove in the
long run to be as ineffective as Hitler's Atlantic Wall. And,

[61] *Hindustan Times,* quoted in *Far Eastern Survey,* XXI, October 8, 1952, 141.

no matter how strongly the West denounced the evils of Communism, the mass of Asians would remain unconvinced unless the Western governments could prove, by their actions, that their cause was also the cause of a free Asia.

CHAPTER FIVE

CRACKS IN THE FREE WORLD

DIPLOMATIC MANEUVERS in Europe, military conflict in East
Asia, propaganda and political warfare in the United Nations
—these spectacular manifestations of the "cold war" were only
one phase of the global struggle between East and West. The
ultimate collapse of world "imperialism," according to Communist thinkers, would be brought about not so much by direct
action from without as by the internal weaknesses and "contradictions" of the imperialist system itself. Conflicts among and
within the imperialist nations, competition for new markets
and fields of investment, quarrels over the division of spoils,
and, above all, the ever-broadening struggle for independence
in the colonial and semicolonial countries could be relied upon
—so the apostles of world Communism affirmed—to weaken
the capitalist world to a point where its ability to resist the
onmarch of victorious "socialism" would be fatally impaired.

One need not be a Marxist in order to perceive that this view
of world developments contained some elements of realism in
spite of its dubious origins and frequent disregard for facts.
Although the term "imperialist" was more suitably applied
to the policies of the U.S.S.R. itself than to those of mid-century democracies like Great Britain, France, and the United
States, it was certainly true that the conflicting aims which
these governments still pursued to some extent in the period of
the cold war impaired their ability to take an adequate stand
against the Soviet-Communist challenge. It was also true that
events in what was loosely called the "colonial" world had for
some years been developing in a manner that was generally

unfavorable to Western interests and therefore quite consistent with the expectations of the Soviet rulers. This unfavorable trend was apparent not only in areas like Southeast Asia, where the anti-Communist policies of the Western powers lacked the full sympathy and support of the indigenous populations. It was even more evident in other parts of Asia and Africa where the Communist challenge had not yet been directly experienced, and where politically active groups felt less interest in resisting Communism than in completing the liquidation of the historical relationships which they lumped together under the name of Western "colonialism."

With certain obvious differences, a similar trend could also be distinguished among the republics of Latin America, where Western civilization, long-established political independence, and traditional friendship with the United States had not always produced wholehearted attachment to the Western democratic cause in world affairs. Despite strong historical and cultural ties with Western Europe and North America, much of Latin America had remained in a state of economic, social, and political development which recalled the impoverished countries of the other hemisphere rather than the comparatively wealthy nations of the Atlantic community and the British Commonwealth. Many Latin Americans shared the feeling, so prevalent in parts of Asia and Africa, of being "exploited" by a rich and powerful country—in this case the United States—which they suspected of trying to manipulate them in its own selfish interest. Hence there was no reason for astonishment if Latin-American governments occasionally showed sympathy for the anti-Western tendencies exhibited by Asian and African spokesmen and tended to adopt a parallel attitude on important international issues.

By any rational standard, of course, Soviet Communism represented as grave a long-term threat to the Asian, African, and Latin-American countries as it did to the leading nations of the West. Effective global defense against the Stalinist menace required their wholehearted participation, not simply in the interests of the Western powers but in their own ultimate interest as well. Yet many of these nations—including some, like Iran, which lay in the direct path of Soviet expansionism—had failed to react to this menace in accordance with Western expectations. It was not merely that their economic and military weaknesses precluded a major contribution to the defense of the free world. More fundamentally, it was beginning to appear that they lacked even the will to contribute. It is true that on certain critical occasions most of these countries had voted with the West in the United Nations and thus recorded their distaste for the aggressive practices of the Soviet Union. As a rule, however, it is not unfair to state that few of them showed great solicitude for the democratic cause as understood and interpreted by the Western powers. Only four nations in this group, for instance—Colombia, Ethiopia, the Philippines, and Thailand—were contributing significantly to the United Nations military effort in Korea. A larger number, having no real sense of solidarity with the West, tended to shut their eyes to the dangers of Communist imperialism and even attempted, on occasion, to exploit the circumstances of the East-West struggle as an opportunity to advance their own special interests at the expense of the Western nations.

It is difficult to attach a suitable label to this mentality, which was definitely not pro-Communist but which nevertheless was based on definite rejection of Western leadership and definite opposition to many aspects of Western policy. President Juan D. Perón of Argentina, the foremost challenger of United States influence in Latin America, advertised his movement of *"justicialismo"* as a "third way," equally distinct from capitalism and Communism. Indian publicists sometimes talked of an Asian "third force" which might some day hold the balance between the rival power blocs of East and West. Though these tendencies were supported by no formal organization in either hemisphere, Asian and African governments often practiced a coordinated type of diplomacy through the so-called Arab-Asian or Asian-African bloc of some thirteen nations in the United Nations General Assembly. With increasing frequency the twenty Latin-American governments, which formed their own bloc in the United Nations, found their policies developing in harmony with those of the Arab-Asian states. Together these two groups actually formed a majority in the sixty-nation Assembly. That their political outlook differed in some respects from that of the Western powers was evidenced not only by their lukewarm support of Western policies in relation to Korea but also by their constant agitation against all forms of "colonialism" and "exploitation"—concepts which they identified primarily with the West, and which they promoted in a way that not infrequently gained them the overt support of the Soviet bloc.

As a traditionally "anti-imperialist" power, the United States was no more unsympathetic toward the aspirations of such "anticolonial" governments than it was toward the political, economic, and military exigencies which governed the policies of its European allies. This country's natural course would have been to act as mediator and conciliator between its foremost allies, who were gradually liquidating their imperial commitments, and those of our friends who professed to find the pace too slow. Both groups, in the American view, shared the same fundamental interests in a world dominated by the Soviet menace. Yet conciliation of these opposite viewpoints had proved extraordinarily difficult. As time went on, the positions on each side had become increasingly rigid. The new nationalism of Asia had little of the spirit of compromise, and some of the "colonial" governments (which included Australia, New Zealand, and the Union of South Africa as well as several of the NATO powers) were strongly averse to yielding to the kind of pressure their critics chose to exert.

The United States itself, moreover, was widely distrusted as a power too thoroughly identified with the "imperialist" group to qualify for the role of impartial mediator. In the Western Hemisphere this country stood practically alone as the alleged embodiment of "imperialism." The Arab states, meanwhile, remained embittered by American support of Israel; India and the "neutral" governments of Southeast Asia insistently questioned the motives and aims of American policy in the Far East and deplored what seemed to them America's partiality for the European viewpoint in matters involving the status of dependent areas. European governments, on the other hand, frequently complained of insufficient American support on issues to which they themselves attached vital importance. This general dissatisfaction with American policy may have testified to the purity of this country's motives, but seriously handicapped its efforts to promote solidarity in the non-Communist world.

A few years earlier, the United States had announced a "bold new program" specifically designed to alleviate some of these problems through a gradual improvement in the living standards prevailing in economically underdeveloped areas, both colonial and independent, in Asia, Africa, and Latin America. But the beginnings of the Point Four program had been slow and uncertain; by 1951–1952, the series of anti-imperialist explosions that had occurred in Iran, Egypt, and French North Africa had shown that the beneficent results of purposeful economic development were not keeping pace with the mounting instability it had been designed to forestall. It was becoming doubtful, moreover, whether economic development in itself was really a sufficient answer to the problem. Leaders in the underdeveloped countries on the whole seemed less concerned with promoting higher living standards than with achieving independence from foreign control, whether political or economic, real or fancied. The drive against "Western imperialism" took many forms and was directed against a wide variety of specific targets. At bottom, however, it seemed to be the expression of a profound and universal psychological need—the need to develop a sense of individual worth, to count for something in one's own environment—that was equally characteristic of the Indian villager, the unemployed Arab intellectual, the African tribesman, and the South American peasant. To such a need, even the best-conducted program of economic and technical assistance could afford no more than a partial satisfaction.

Recognition of the deeper sources of the anti-Western movement did not lessen its significance as a factor in contemporary

world history. In the Moslem world, in Africa, even in Latin
America the situation had reached a stage that forebade complacency on the part of any Western government or statesman.
Behind the lines of the cold war, the Western powers had actually been placed on the defensive on three continents. The intensity of the attack differed from one area to another, but the
broad picture was one that might easily convince a Stalinist that
the "camp of imperialism" was about ready to break up.
Anti-Stalinists who looked about them could not deny that by
1952 the "free world" was exhibiting some formidable cracks.

1. Middle East Danger Spots

Among the countries in a state of more or less open rebellion
against the West, the group of Near and Middle Eastern nations that ringed the southern borders of the Soviet Union occupied a peculiarly delicate situation. "As far as sheer value
of territory is concerned," General Eisenhower had said of the
Middle East, "there is no more strategically important area in
the world." [1] President Truman had summarized the resultant
challenge to American statesmanship in his message on the
Mutual Security Program:

". . . The countries of these areas are of vital importance to the
security of the free world, but the problems of achieving constructive and orderly development are extremely difficult.

"Living standards are generally very low. Transportation and
land tenure systems are often archaic. Political and religious controversies simmer throughout the region. Nationalism is sometimes misdirected into fanatical outbursts which ignore the benefits to be gained from international cooperation. The Communists
are doing their best to stir up confusion and trouble."

These statements exaggerated neither the significance of the
Middle East to Western defense nor the influences which had
combined to make it one of the most critical zones of weakness
and disturbance on the entire globe. The pride of the Islamic
peoples in their long and glorious cultural traditions contrasted

[1] Quoted in Henry A. Byroade, "U.S. Foreign Policy in the Middle East,"
Department of State Bulletin, XXVII, December 15, 1952, 931-932.

pitifully with their inadequate, badly distributed resources and with the disorganization produced by their all too sudden exposure to the impact of modern Western civilization. Unable to cope with the political and social problems that flowed from this experience, the area was rent by acute tensions which set class against class, nation against nation, men of orthodox religion against the partisans of Western methods. An atmosphere of unrest and universal distrust, directed not only against the West but against neighboring groups within the same or nearby nations, hung over many parts of the Middle East and encouraged such outbreaks of primeval passion as had already occurred in Iran and Egypt and threatened at times to engulf the entire Moslem world.

Conscious of the area's direct exposure to Soviet attack and Communist penetration, the United States and Great Britain had shown a desire to remedy some of its more glaring weaknesses but had made little progress in face of the radical character of the difficulties, the lack of coordination between their own policies, and the unwillingness of many Middle Eastern governments to join hands with the West on realistic terms. Greece and Turkey, at least, which together constituted one anchor of the line of "containment" stretching through Iran and Afghanistan to Pakistan and India, had been preserved for the West by the policies which had eventually resulted in their voluntary accession to the North Atlantic Treaty. Israel, too, had been established as a nucleus of democratic and progressive tendencies in the Middle East, but only at the cost of what seemed the permanent alienation of the neighboring Arab states.

Elsewhere, the record and outlook were almost wholly negative. The proposal to establish a Middle East defense command which could potentially embrace all the nations between Turkey, the Red Sea, and the Persian Gulf had been blocked by Egypt's insistence on giving priority to its own program of unilaterally ousting the British from the Suez Canal Zone and the Sudan. Iran had chosen to prosecute its campaign against the Anglo-Iranian Oil Company and the British Government in a manner that debarred the West from assisting effectively toward the solution of its grave internal problems. Pakistan, at the eastern extremity of this zone of weakness, showed occasional signs of sympathy for the Western cause; but Pakistan's attention and resources were almost entirely absorbed by its standing quarrel with India over a variety of issues in which the question of Kashmir occupied the central place.

If the Soviet Union had demonstrated openly and consistently aggressive tendencies toward the Middle East, the besetting incoherence of Middle Eastern affairs might have been more easily overcome. It was the revelation of Soviet designs affecting Greece and Turkey that had placed those nations firmly within the Western camp; and students of Soviet affairs had no doubt whatever as to the continuing importance of the Middle East in Soviet political and strategic calculations. But since the withdrawal of Soviet forces from Iran in late 1946, the Kremlin had refrained from any move that could inspire Middle Eastern peoples with a sense of imminent peril or touch off a process of consolidation such as had occurred in Europe. By and large, Moscow had confined itself to assuring the Middle Eastern peoples of its own allegedly peaceful intentions, warning them of the dangerous consequences of association with the West, and encouraging their efforts to eradicate the last outposts of Western control in their own countries. This attitude assured full play to the many divisive tendencies within the area while leaving the Kremlin uncommitted until such time as more decisive intervention might seem profitable.

In 1951, as the revolt against the West gained strength and confidence, the situation in the Middle East had sharply deteriorated. In 1952 there were few signs of any reversal in the downward trend. The United States continued its somewhat perfunctory endeavors to develop the economic and social foundations of the area through the Point Four and related programs, setting aside some $51 million for "technical cooperation" in the Near East and Africa during the fiscal year 1952–53 as well as $130 million for assistance to refugees in Israel and the surrounding states. Small-scale military assistance to Iran was resumed after a temporary suspension necessitated by that country's refusal to comply with the terms of the Mutual Security Act. But few of the basic problems which kept this part of the world at odds with itself and with the West were brought appreciably nearer solution. The Kashmir controversy between India and Pakistan continued to defy the efforts of United Nations mediators; Iran rejected one proposal after another for the settlement of its dispute with Britain; Egypt and the other Arab states still refused accommodation with Israel or with the United Kingdom; new conflicts were precipitated by the impatience of nationalist elements in French North Africa and their championship by the governments of the Arab-Asian bloc. Only in Egypt were there new developments that might in time pave the way for a settlement of controversies which, thus far, had made a mockery of Western hopes for a coordinated defense of the Middle Eastern region.

The history of the Kashmir quarrel in 1952 amounted to a carbon copy—happily somewhat fainter than in previous years —of earlier efforts by the United Nations to establish conditions for a plebiscite in which the people of the disputed Kashmir state would indicate whether they desired to belong to India or to Pakistan. Ever since 1949 a succession of special representatives dispatched by the Security Council had been endeavoring to persuade the two countries to accept a sufficient degree of demilitarization in Kashmir to make possible the holding of a free plebiscite. Dr. Frank P. Graham, the latest of these emissaries, was as diligent and resourceful as his predecessors. In essentials, however, he was no more successful than they had been; for India insisted that Pakistan was in Kashmir as an aggressor, and on the strength of that contention refused to reduce its forces on the scale that both Pakistan and the United Nations representative thought necessary. The Security Council itself discussed the problem several times during the year, but in the end could think of nothing more promising than an admonition to both parties to get together on the basis of the mediator's recommendations.[2] Since India had rejected this advice before it was given, the year closed with no prospect for the healing of this permanent wound in the body of the non-Communist world.

The machinery of the United Nations had already proved inadequate to deal with the dispute between Iran and the United Kingdom over the nationalization of Iran's one big industrial enterprise, the British-owned Anglo-Iranian Oil Company, in April 1951. The Security Council had dodged a British complaint on the issue; the International Court of Justice was presently to disclaim any competence to rule on the merits of the case;[3] a mission of the International Bank for Reconstruction and Development had been able to find no formula acceptable to Prime Minister Dr. Mohammad Mosaddeq for putting the industry back in production and thus restoring the revenues the country had lost by seizing the industry and expelling the British technicians who had kept it in operation.

Meanwhile Iran's internal situation was steadily deteriorating, although less rapidly than most foreign observers had thought likely. Oil already held in storage could not readily be disposed of without the consent of the company, which claimed a proprietary interest. Most Iranians, living as they did in a subsistence economy, were not greatly affected by the loss of foreign exchange which had followed the stoppage of oil sales. For the moment the national treasury seemed able to meet immediate needs. Yet it was hardly to be expected that the situation could be maintained indefinitely. An economic crash, accompanied by political disturbances of unforeseeable scope, seemed all too probable unless the United States and Great Britain found some way of preventing it.

Although the British Government had accepted the fact of nationalization, it still insisted that substantial indemnification was due for the breach of the oil company's contract and the seizure of its properties. Pending the satisfaction of the com-

[2] U.N. Document S/2883, adopted December 23, 1952, in *Documents on American Foreign Relations, 1952,* No. 35 (i).
[3] For details cf. *American Journal of International Law,* XLVII, January 1953, 4-8.

pany's claims, it was disinclined to make any effort to help extricate the country from the economic morass into which Mosaddeq's policies had plunged it. British reluctance was all the greater because Mosaddeq obstinately refused to consider readmitting the British operatives who alone were capable of restoring oil operations in an orderly manner. The United States, despite uneasiness over the growing social and political unrest in Iran and the possibility of a Communist coup, was likewise unwilling to satisfy Iran's demands for emergency financial assistance under circumstances that would in effect underwrite Dr. Mosaddeq's refusal to consider a reasonable settlement.[4] Yet the Iranian Government, unable to operate the oil industry itself but with its confidence in ultimate rescue apparently undiminished, continued to insist that it would consent to no scheme which could involve restoring the least British foothold in the country.

In July a sharp internal crisis in Iran resulted in a strengthening of Mosaddeq's internal position and gave the Western powers a disagreeable taste of what might happen if the country was allowed to degenerate into complete anarchy. Precipitating a showdown with moderate elements in the palace and parliament who desired a conciliatory settlement of the oil problem, the aged premier demanded an extension of his authority and, when this was refused, yielded his post to the veteran politician Ahmad Qavam es Sultaneh, a patriot of the old school who took office with the expressed intention of reaching an adjustment with the British. But Qavam and the Shah had reckoned without the mobs and religious fanatics who formed the basis of Mosaddeq's power. Violent protest demonstrations flared in the streets and bazaars of Tehran and other Iranian centers; ominously, the Communist Tudeh party entered the fray in open support of Mosaddeq's National Front. Within five turbulent days, Qavam was fleeing for his life and Mosaddeq was back in power, stronger than ever. His first major act, after curbing the zeal of his uninvited but useful

[4] State Department announcement, March 20, in *Documents on American Foreign Relations, 1952,* No. 23 (a).

Communist supporters, was to secure a parliamentary grant of dictatorial powers for a period of six months.

These disorders had taken an outspokenly anti-Western form which spelled a further impairment of United States popularity and prestige in Iran. In Washington the time seemed ripe for a more vigorous effort to enlist British cooperation in the search for an oil settlement. The result was a joint proposal, put forward in the name of President Truman and Prime Minister Churchill on August 30, whereby Iran was offered substantial inducements to settle its accounts with the oil company. Iranian and company representatives, it was suggested, should confer with a view to arranging for "the flow of oil from Iran to world markets"; claims and counterclaims arising out of the nationalization of the company's properties in Iran should be referred to the International Court. If Iran accepted these proposals, said the two statesmen, the company would also attack the problem of purchase and shipment of oil already stored in Iran; the British Government would relax the measures it had taken against Iran by way of economic reprisals; and the United States would come to the rescue of Iran's budget with an immediate grant of $10 million.[5]

This offer, Secretary Acheson emphasized, was considered "fair and reasonable and had no strings attached." From Dr. Mosaddeq's viewpoint, however, the inducements it held out were overshadowed by the immitigable distrust with which he regarded the aims of the British Government and the oil company. His objective was to secure Iran's reentry into international oil operations under auspices in which the British company would have absolutely no part; and his confidence in being able to do so was heightened by the presence in Iran just at this time of an American oil executive who was visiting the country in a private capacity and obviously felt no particular solicitude for the rights of the British concern. Mosaddeq, therefore, not only rejected the Anglo-American offer—he had at first declined to receive it at all—but put forward new de-

---

[5] *Documents on American Foreign Relations, 1952*, No. 23 (b). Excerpts from later correspondence appear *ibid.*, Nos. 23 (c)-23 (f).

mands of his own of a character so intransigent that he could not have thought their acceptance likely. Rehearsing the Iranian viewpoint in a long and contentious message on September 24, he asserted that as a preliminary to any settlement the sum of £49 million ($137.2 million) allegedly due to his government from the oil company must be paid "in advance and on account" and numerous other conditions accepted in their entirety within ten days. Otherwise, he announced, Iran would sever diplomatic relations with both the United Kingdom and the United States.

Subsequent correspondence having failed to bring the parties appreciably nearer agreement, Iran did break off relations with the United Kingdom—though not with the United States—on October 22. Although this was not to be the end of attempts to find an oil settlement, it did suggest that while a man of Mosaddeq's temperament remained in control there would be scant possibility of a settlement that the British Government would feel able to accept. If Iran was to sell its oil at all, it would have to find purchasers who were willing and able to invade the British company's preserve, run the risk of capture by British vessels on the high seas, and submit to litigation in foreign courts. Some weeks later, on December 6, the State Department announced that it would not stand in the way of any Americans who chose to assume such risks. Since Washington admittedly did not believe that small-scale operations along these lines would solve Iran's problem, its stand caused irritation in Britain but gained little appreciation in Iran.

Meanwhile the United States showed no disposition to depart from its policy of denying Iran economic aid (other than Point Four aid) so long as the latter refused to avail itself of the opportunity to dispose of its oil through British channels. Some observers dissented from this policy and held that it was vitally necessary to help Iran keep afloat, independently of its stand in the oil controversy. True, the popular passions which had thus far sustained Dr. Mosaddeq in his battle with the oil company did not appear to offer a very firm basis for Iranian cooperation with the West in other respects. It was doubtful

that the situation would be greatly ameliorated by such internal
expedients, however desirable in themselves, as the agrarian
reform program which Dr. Mosaddeq had initiated in the intervals of his quarrel with Britain. While the oil issue remained
unsettled, Iranian pride would rule out any genuine collaboration with the West and the country would remain an area of
concentrated misery and instability, a tempting object of Communist exploitation, and a dangerous breach in the defense of
the free world.

Unfortunately the same was true of Egypt and other countries of the Arab world where the growth of comparable tendencies in recent years had raised a possibility that local and
Western interests might be as difficult to reconcile as they had
proved to be in Iran. The situation in the Arab countries was
more complex but fundamentally not dissimilar. A social and
economic system profoundly inadequate to contemporary needs
had produced a set of governments which saw their best means
of gaining and holding power in cultivating the latent anti-
foreign tendencies which were widespread in the Arab populations. These tendencies had been mobilized in more or less
equal measure against the new state of Israel, against Great
Britain, and against the United States, which not only supported Israel's claim to exist as a Middle Eastern nation but
seemed ready to uphold Britain's treaty rights in the Suez Canal
Zone and the Sudan until such time as suitable alternative arrangements might be devised.

Egypt, as the wealthiest and most influential of the Arab
states, had served as the fountainhead of anti-Western tendencies in the Arab world; and Egyptian policy, under the nationalist government which had come to power in 1950 and
unilaterally denounced the British treaties in 1951, had by now
precipitated a situation at least as grave as that produced by
Dr. Mosaddeq and his Iranian supporters. Through the late fall
and winter of 1951, a full-scale guerrilla war had been carried
on against the reinforced British garrison in the Canal Zone.
Early in the new year, a series of ugly incidents had led up to
a frightening climax on January 26, a day of carnage when

frenzied mobs had surged through Cairo, pillaging and wrecking British, American, and French establishments and causing the deaths of seventeen Europeans. The government of Mustafa al-Nahhas Pasha and his nationalist Wafd party, it appeared, had succeeded in unchaining a monster it could not control. Fortunately, however, there were still cool heads in Egypt. King Faruq abruptly dismissed the Nahhas cabinet and substituted a moderate regime. Once the situation had been brought under control, the new government resumed the attempt to persuade the British to honor Egypt's "national aspirations" by withdrawing voluntarily from both the Canal Zone and the Sudan.

These aspirations, championed by all Egyptian governments, were not in themselves impossible of fulfillment. The British had long since indicated that they were ready to relinquish their bases in the Canal Zone as soon as satisfactory alternative arrangements for Middle Eastern defense could be put into effect. Their only absolute stipulation regarding the Sudan was that the Sudanese people must be given an adequate opportunity to decide their own future. The diplomatic difficulty lay in reconciling these principles with the desire of the Egyptians to secure immediate control of both areas, irrespective of the realistic requirements of defense or the true preferences of the Sudanese. But there was also a further difficulty connected with the instability of Egyptian affairs and the uncertain tenure of Egyptian governments. The very moderation of the new Egyptian leaders disqualified them, in the eyes of many of their countrymen, as spokesmen for the national cause. Internal conditions in Egypt, moreover, were far from satisfactory. Revelations of corruption in court, political, and army circles had led to widespread condemnation of the whole parliamentary system and helped to sustain the popular unrest which had broken out so dangerously in January.

Thus in July there was a second political overturn, this time of a more drastic character, A sudden *coup d'état* led by a relatively obscure soldier, General Mohammad Nagib Bey, was followed by the abdication and precipitate departure of King

Faruq himself and the commencement of a thoroughgoing purge of political and public life. Week by week, as Nagib penetrated deeper into the morass of official corruption, he found it necessary to extend his powers. On September 7, after arresting fifty-one prominent figures associated with the former regime, he personally assumed the premiership. In October the power of the Wafd, the largest group in the country, was curtailed under a rigorous program for the reorganization of political parties. Before the end of the year, all political parties had been suppressed and the constitution had been abrogated in preparation for the drafting of a new constitution "acceptable to the nation." Meanwhile this energetic and obviously well-intentioned dictator had embarked on a bold scheme of land reform and showed every intention of pressing the first serious attack ever attempted on his country's monumental social and economic problems.

Nagib's advent was symptomatic of a phenomenon that was occurring on a rather wide scale in the Arab world as the incapacity of the old-style parliamentary regimes exhausted the patience of ambitious army officers. Eight months earlier, in November 1951, a similar coup in Syria had brought to power a similar figure, Colonel Adib al-Shishakli. In Lebanon, military pressure initiated a change of regime in September-October 1952 which was followed by a grant of decree powers to the new civilian government. In Iraq another military man, General Nur-al-Din Mahmud, was to step directly from the post of army chief of staff into that of prime minister on November 23, after disturbances in which a Baghdad mob had attacked police stations, the British Embassy, and the offices of the United States Information Service.[6]

The example of General Nagib in Egypt would be largely instrumental in determining whether military regimes of this type could repair some of the damage inflicted on the Middle East and on Arab-Western relations under more orthodox

---

[6] In Jordan a more peaceful change of government occurred on August 11 with the deposition of the mentally incompetent King Talal I and the accession of his 17-year-old son Hussayn I under a Council of Regency.

political leadership. That Nagib had a shrewder appreciation of the realities than some of his predecessors had shown was evident from the first. A patriot but not a fanatic—such was the impression created by his early performance. With his advent, hope revived for a settlement of the Anglo-Egyptian controversy and, thereafter, of the broader problem of a Middle East defense arrangement which would include the Arab states and possibly Israel as well. Even toward Israel, Nagib had not displayed the blind animosity that possessed so many Arab statesmen. Conceivably, his rise to power might signify the beginning of better days. Anglo-Egyptian discussions, limited for the time being to the Sudan question, recommenced in the autumn under more favorable auguries than for some time past.

Thanks to the quiet abandonment of Egypt's demand for unconditional annexation of the Sudan, the two governments arrived without undue difficulty at a considerable measure of agreement. The British had already moved to confer self-government on the Sudan at an accelerated pace. Thereafter, it was agreed, there would be a transitional period under suitable international supervision, followed by a "free" choice by the Sudanese of their future political status. But the Egyptians obviously still intended that these arrangements should result in the Sudan's accession to Egypt; the British, on the contrary, still strove to hold open the door to complete Sudanese independence or, if the Sudanese preferred, to membership in the British Commonwealth. Several times during the autumn Nagib made public statements demanding the "freedom of the Nile Valley" and the "complete evacuation of Egypt" in tones which ominously recalled earlier Wafdist declarations and, if taken literally, would practically preclude agreement with the British and thus destroy the tenuous basis for Egyptian cooperation with the West. Were these Nagib's real sentiments, or was he fighting to maintain a popularity threatened by deteriorating economic conditions and the mercurial temper of the Egyptian masses? In the best of cases, popular feeling undoubtedly would set strict limits on Nagib's freedom of action, as it did on that of similar leaders in other Middle East countries.

Even if the problem of Britain's position in Egypt (and in Iraq and Jordan) eventually proved capable of solution, the unsolved Palestine problem would remain a formidable obstacle to Middle Eastern pacification and consolidation. As yet there was no evidence that opinion in the Arab countries would tolerate so much as a formal settlement of their 1948–1949 war with Israel, still less the participation of Israel in a regional defense arrangement. The Palestine Conciliation Commission, reconstituted in January by the United Nations General Assembly,[7] reported in October that the atmosphere for an overall Palestine settlement simply did not exist and that the group had been forced to limit its mediatory efforts to the subsidiary issue of blocked Arab bank accounts in Israel.[8] The essential barrier to a settlement—the refusal of the Arab governments to recognize the existence of Israel within its de facto frontiers, and to drop their demand for the return to Israel of more than 800,000 Arab refugees still under the temporary care of the United Nations—seemingly was as insurmountable as ever. While this condition persisted, there would remain a serious threat to the internal peace of the Middle East and the chances of overcoming the area's economic, political, and military weaknesses would be seriously if not fatally prejudiced.

Through most of 1952, both the United States and the Soviet Union avoided direct interposition in the conflicts that tortured this segment of the Middle East. The Kremlin, while evincing hostility to the Middle East Command scheme and sympathy with the "anti-imperialist" trend in Egypt and elsewhere, was evidently content to bide its time and await developments. Not until the end of the year did it show signs of what might be a more determined effort to win Arab favor with the commence-

[7] General Assembly Resolution 512 (VI), January 26, 1952, in *Documents on American Foreign Relations, 1952*, No. 35 (a). By Resolution 513 (VI), adopted the same day, the Assembly had approved a $250 million, three-year budget for relief and "reintegration" of Arab refugees from Israel under the auspices of the U.N. Relief and Works Agency for Palestine Refugees in the Near East. An appropriation of $60 million for this purpose was included in the U.S. Mutual Security legislation for 1952–53.
[8] Twelfth Progress Report of the United Nations Conciliation Commission for Palestine, May 1-October 7, 1952 (U.N. Document A/2216, October 8, 1952). For further action by the Assembly cf. below, pp. 366-368.

ment of an openly anti-Semitic policy in its own domain and the dropping of all pretense of friendship for Israel. The United States, on the other hand, concealed neither its benevolent feelings toward the government of Israel nor its partiality for the Middle East Command project; but at the same time it endeavored to spare Arab susceptibilities by avoiding any overly close association with British policy. A suggestion by Mr. Churchill early in the year that "token forces" of the United States, France, and Turkey should be sent to the Suez Canal Zone, thus symbolizing the "unity of purpose" of the countries sponsoring the Middle East Command project, evoked a wholly unfavorable response in Washington. The Middle East might be an area of common concern, most Americans reasoned, but the immediate responsibility was better left to the country directly involved.

United States attempts to remain in the background were more successful here than in French North Africa, the third great center of conflict between an established European position and the aspirations of indigenous Moslem peoples. Here, too, a system of imperial control built up through many decades was now being vigorously challenged, both by self-appointed leaders of the peoples affected and by Arab and Asian governments which were making it their business to oppose Western "colonialism" in all its forms. But since Tunisia and Morocco were French protectorates rather than independent states, the controversy took a different form from the attack on British rights and interests in Iran and Egypt. The French-controlled Tunisian and Moroccan governments had no way of bringing their grievances to international notice except through the action of other interested governments in the United Nations; and there the merits of the controversy were obscured by disagreement as to whether it was a proper subject for international discussion at all.

From the American point of view the immediate interest of French North Africa lay primarily in its strategic potentialities in relation to the East-West conflict, and only secondarily in its bearing on the French world position and the solidarity of the non-Communist nations.[9] Frenchmen and Moslems looked at the matter from an opposite standpoint. To the former, North Africa was a living testimonial to the French colonizing genius and a vital element in France's position as a great power. To the latter, it was a last crumbling stronghold of the European colonialism which had been successfully routed in every other section of the Mediterranean; thus it represented an intolerable anachronism in an age when even a much less advanced territory like neighboring Libya had been judged ready for independence.

The problem might have been simpler if the populations of the French North African territories had been more nearly homogeneous and if French policy in earlier decades had been directed toward preparing them for ultimate self-government and independence. Their actual development, demographic, political, and economic, had been so closely involved with that of the "mother country" that no clean-cut separation could be imagined that would not inflict serious damage on both French and indigenous interests. No serious difficulties had developed in Algeria, conquered in the 1830's, which had been virtually assimilated into the French Republic with the general acquiescence of its million French and 8 million Moslem inhabitants. Tunisia and Morocco, on the other hand, had been brought into the French political system on terms that precluded either full integration or full independence. Under the Tunisian treaty of 1881 and the Moroccan treaty of 1912, both theoretically remained autonomous protectorates, ruled by native sovereigns under French guardianship. In fact, both had been governed directly by France, primarily in the French interest; both had been extensively settled by French colonists, who enjoyed a privileged status in their new homes and would strongly resist any attempt to curtail their rights; both had been included

[9] The special problem of American treaty rights in Morocco (*The United States in World Affairs, 1951*, 290 n.) was resolved in a manner generally favorable to the U.S. in a decision rendered by the International Court of Justice on August 27 (cf. *Department of State Bulletin*, XXVII, October 20, 1952, 620-623 and *American Journal of International Law*, XLVII, January 1953, 8-15 and 136-145).

within the postwar French Union under conditions which confirmed the exclusion of the indigenous majority from any real
voice in public affairs.

These conditions had led to passionate and growing protest
in the two North African protectorates long before the rioting
which focused world attention on the problem in 1951–1952.
The nationalist movement in Tunisia, the smaller but by far
the more highly developed of the two countries, had been a
vital force for at least two decades and had aligned the overwhelming majority of Tunisia's 3 million indigenous inhabitants behind its demand for full independence in some form of
military and economic alliance with France. Unsatisfied by the
slender concessions obtained for them by Foreign Minister
Schuman in 1950–1951, the leaders of the Neo-Destour (New
Constitution) or nationalist party had intensified their agitation in Tunisia and also in Paris and in the United Nations.
When the French had abruptly rejected their basic demands in
December 1951, they had embarked on a deliberate policy of
creating violent incidents with the aim of arousing the sympathy of world opinion.

The resultant wave of disorders, which were aggravated by
the arrest of the Neo-Destour leader, Habib Bourgiba, required
the dispatch of reinforcements from France and Algeria. On
March 26, 1952, the French Resident-General, Jean de Haute-
clocque, proclaimed martial law throughout the protectorate
and arrested the Tunisian premier (Mohammed Chenik) and
three of his ministers. This show of force, though bitterly criticized abroad and by some elements in France, checked the violence and terrorism in Tunisia itself and cleared the way for a
fresh attempt at pacification. A new program of reforms, providing for a considerable extension of Tunisian autonomy in
internal matters, was presented in June to the French National
Assembly and to the Bey of Tunis, Sidi Mohammed al-Amin
Pasha. But the times were unfavorable to compromise. In Paris,
Right and Left joined forces to defeat the measure—the Right
because it went too far, the Left because it did not go far
enough. In Tunis, the Bey evaded French pressure and took the

unexpected step of assembling an advisory council of native leaders which, after studying the French proposals for two months, unanimously rejected them as inadequate.

Nationalist demands in Morocco were treated with less deference by French authorities. Conditions there were more primitive, and the opposition movement headed by the Istiqlal (Independence) party was less broadly based and influential than its Tunisian counterpart. French administration in Morocco had been primarily military in character; cultural and economic differences among the 8 million Arab and Berber inhabitants of the protectorate had favored a policy of strict authority and "divide and rule." Thus in 1950, when Sultan Sidi Mohammed ben Youssef had unexpectedly requested a revision of the protectorate treaty, his demands had been met not by concessions but by intensified pressure on the part of General Alphonse Juin and his successor as Resident-General, General Augustin Guillaume. Compelled at first to dissociate himself from the Istiqlal, the Sultan nevertheless withdrew his condemnation at the earliest opportunity and in March 1952 renewed his appeal to the French President for a revision of the 1912 treaty and an extension of Moroccan home rule. For six months this appeal went unanswered. Not until September, when agitation by the Arab-Asian bloc had ensured that the matter would come before the United Nations General Assembly, did France reply. Then it enumerated a series of conditions which, though represented as essential to protect the rights of French citizens, were wholly unsatisfactory to the Sultan and his advisers.

Attempts to interest the United Nations in the situation of the two protectorates had figured prominently in the tactics adopted by the North African nationalist leaders and their Arab-Asian supporters. Agitation in and around the Paris session of the General Assembly in 1951–1952 undoubtedly contributed to the tension which was steadily building up in both protectorates. But to secure formal consideration of the North African problem by the United Nations was not an easy matter in view of the exclusive nature of France's treaty relationship with the two protectorates and the reluctance of many governments, including the United States, to antagonize France and subject the world organization to additional strain. Thus the efforts of Egypt, Pakistan, and others to place the Moroccan situation on the Assembly's 1951 agenda were eventually defeated, though only by the close vote of 28 to 23 with seven abstentions.[10] Attempts by Tunisian representatives in Paris to interest the Assembly in their case were likewise unsuccessful.

But the foes of "colonialism" were disinclined to let the matter rest, and the arrest of the Tunisian government leaders on March 26 gave them a new opportunity. The Assembly having adjourned, eleven Arab and Asian governments demanded on April 2 that the Security Council itself give prompt attention to the Tunisian situation, which, according to them, seriously endangered the maintenance of international peace and security. Just how the situation in Tunisia affected peace and security outside the protectorate was not altogether apparent, since no one suggested that the Arab-Asian states intended to go to war about it. Whether or not the submission to the Security Council was justified by the facts, however, there was no doubt that the position taken by the members of that body would have profound repercussions both in France and in the Arab-Asian countries. Agreement to consider the Arab-Asian charges would be a direct rebuff to France, which contended that the complaint was unjustified in law and in fact and, moreover, could do nothing but harm at a time when France was endeavoring to promote negotiation and agreement with responsible Tunisian authorities. Yet refusal to entertain the complaint would be just as bitterly resented by a dozen or more governments whose enthusiasm for Western policies and for the United Nations itself was by no means excessive.

Many of these governments had blamed the United States for the failure of their effort to secure a hearing in the General Assembly. In the Security Council, the American position would almost certainly be decisive. Seven votes were needed to put the matter on the agenda. Five countries, including the U.S.S.R., were definitely in favor of discussion; only two, France and

[10] *The United States in World Affairs, 1951*, 410.

Great Britain, were definitely opposed. If the United States adhered to its usual policy of promoting full discussion of all issues brought before the United Nations, at least one of the doubtful governments would certainly follow its lead. But this was a lead that the United States was most reluctant to give. Apart from the legal and political questions involved, to do so might well offend France to a degree that would prejudice its future role not only in the United Nations but also in the North Atlantic Treaty Organization and the still pending European Defense Community. Thus the United States decided to abstain from voting. "It is the belief of my Government," Ambassador Ernest A. Gross told the Security Council on April 10, "that at this moment it is more useful to concentrate on the problem of facilitating negotiations between the French and the Tunisians than to engage in debate at this table." [11] Three delegates abstained with him when the vote was taken on April 14, and the Arab-Asian motion was lost.

"Naturally," Secretary Acheson commented, "if our hope concerning the prospects for the resumption of negotiations prove [sic] illusory, any U.N. member is free to bring up the case again." [12] French-Tunisian negotiations in fact were not resumed—thanks to the refusal of the Tunisian leaders to negotiate—and on June 20 the entire bloc of thirteen Arab-Asian countries moved again. This time they requested that the General Assembly be convened in special session to consider the deteriorating Tunisian situation. Twenty-three United Nations governments supported this request; twenty-seven, including the United States, opposed it. All else having failed, the Arab-Asian delegations thereupon announced that they would take steps to place the question on the agenda of the regular session of the Assembly when it convened in the autumn. Early in August the same governments gave notice that they would also renew their attempt to obtain an Assembly debate on Morocco. Thus they made certain that agitation in the pro-

[11] *Department of State Bulletin*, XXVI, April 28, 1952, 679.
[12] *Ibid.*, May 19, 1952, 799.

tectorates would continue through the autumn while the Assembly prepared to debate their case.[13]

2. The Discovery of Africa

Even before the critical events of 1951–1952, the problems of the Mediterranean basin and Northern Africa had been

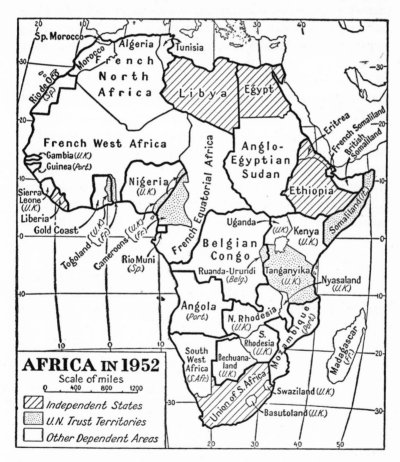

AFRICA IN 1952
Scale of miles
0   400   800   1200

- ▨ Independent States
- ▦ U.N. Trust Territories
- ☐ Other Dependent Areas

moderately familiar to those Americans who took a regular interest in world affairs. Much less was known, except to a narrow circle of specialists, about the contemporary state of Africa

[13] Cf. below, pp. 359-363.

south of the Sahara. It was not until 1952, indeed, that the African continent as a whole thrust itself decisively upon the American consciousness. A series of remarkable motion pictures focused attention on the grandeur of the African landscape, the variety of its animal life, its picturesque tribal customs and social and racial problems. Economists and businessmen began to display unwonted interest in Africa's developmental possibilities. Military authorities expatiated on its importance as a source of strategic materials, a means of access to the oil of the Middle East, and a staging area for large-scale operations in any East-West conflict. Publications on all phases of African affairs began to appear in a steady stream. John Gunther prepared to write a book which would be called *Inside Africa*.

It was not surprising that few Americans had previous knowledge of a continent which thus far had played a rather subordinate role in world history. Remote from the centers of higher civilization, difficult of access, even more difficult to develop, Africa proper had remained on the sidelines of international politics. Not until World War II and its aftermath had decisively weakened the position of the European colonial powers in Asia had the status of their African possessions moved more definitely into the foreground of public attention. The late 1940's and early 1950's had witnessed a profusion of grandiose African development schemes, inspired primarily by the hope of creating a substitute for the lost wealth of Asia. Simultaneously the rise of nationalist and anti-European agitation in the Middle East had spurred plans for a reconcentration of military strength on Africa soil.

The initiators of these far-reaching projects did not always take adequate account of factors that tended to limit Africa's potentialities as a basis for Europe's postwar reconstruction. A little experience revealed that the undeveloped wealth of the continent was significant but neither as inexhaustible nor as readily exploited as some had imagined. The most accessible agricultural lands were often poor and depleted; climatic influences and the prevalence of disease in both animals and humans severely restricted the possibilities of agricultural development. Exploitation of Africa's undoubted mineral wealth—gold, diamonds, and uranium in South Africa, copper and uranium in the Belgian Congo, copper in Northern Rhodesia, chrome in Southern Rhodesia, tin in Nigeria, manganese in the Gold Coast, iron in Sierra Leone—opened broader prospects. But here, too, there were limitations, occasioned not only by difficulties of access and development but more especially by the deficiencies, both quantitative and qualitative, of the available labor force.

For the basic problems of Africa were human problems relating to the characteristics of the peoples who inhabited the continent and their relations to their natural environment, to each other, and to the governments which had assumed responsibility for their welfare and control. And the basic fact about mid-century Africa was a growing restlessness among its indigenous peoples, which had already reached such proportions as to make it doubtful how far they would cooperate in the further development of the continent as part of the European political and economic system.

By and large, the indigenous peoples of Africa had been even less well prepared than other "backward" populations to face the situation created by European penetration of their homelands. Their tribal structures and primitive civilizations had lacked the toughness and elasticity which were needed to sustain the impact of white rule and Western technology. The experience of European tutelage had produced a thorough-going disorganization of native life without creating an adequate basis on which Europeans and Africans could coexist and collaborate under the new circumstances of the advancing twentieth century. All over Africa in the 1940's and 1950's, old forms were dissolving and novel pressures were developing with explosive force. To some observers events seemed to be moving with catastrophic violence toward an outcome that eluded human foresight.

A theoretical goal for an awakening Africa had been established in those portions of the United Nations Charter which stressed the principle of "equal rights and self-determination of peoples" and implied that foreign rule over dependent peoples like those of Africa must find its ultimate justification and fulfillment in the emergence of the latter into full self-government. But this concept, though nominally endorsed by practically the entire membership of the United Nations and strongly pressed by the governments of the "anticolonial" bloc, could have meaning only in reference to a more or less distant future. Its emphasis on long-range political and ideological objectives offered little guidance in dealing with the immediate social and economic problems which confronted those powers with direct interests and responsibilities in Africa. Yet the notions of equal rights and self-determination had become so thoroughly embedded in the international outlook of the mid-twentieth century as to constitute not only the principal standard for evaluating African developments but one of the most powerful influences on those developments themselves.

The background of African controversies in the 1950's is most readily grasped by making a rough geographical distinction between (1) the area often referred to as "Atlantic" or "tropical" Africa, comprising the African west coast, the Congo basin, and Portuguese Angola; and (2) the more easterly belt of territories running from the Union of South Africa northward through the Rhodesias, Tanganyika, and Kenya and up to the sources of the Nile. In the former area political evolution had been comparatively tranquil; it was primarily in the latter region that situations of a more dangerous character had been developing.

The favored position of Atlantic or "Black" Africa, as it was sometimes significantly called, reflected both its relative unsuitability for white settlement and the unusually favorable conditions it afforded for the production of certain minerals and highly priced tropical commodities like cocoa and palm oil. The first circumstance prevented any acute struggle between natives and white settlers for possession of the land; the second made possible a considerable degree of native prosperity and, in some areas, an unusually rapid spread of education. These features were strongly marked both in the Belgian Congo and in the British West African possessions, particularly Nigeria and the Gold Coast. Belgian policy had emphasized the economic and technical advancement of the native population and as yet had encountered little agitation for political rights; British policy had been directed with fair consistency toward the preservation and development of the native culture and the gradual delegation of administrative functions to native authorities.

In the Gold Coast, the most advanced of the British West African colonies, this policy had of late years been carried to quite remarkable lengths, largely in response to native pressure which had occasioned disorders throughout the colony in 1948. A special committe of inquiry had recommended the establishment of a native legislative assembly based on a universal franchise. In 1951 the colony held its first general elections, the first responsible native government was set up, and the upper levels of the civil service were thrown open to qualified natives.

The initial success of the Gold Coast experiment was calculated to strengthen the belief that the African situation did not lack favorable potentialities. Unfortunately, however, it was largely overshadowed by the ominous trend of affairs in other parts of Africa where the meeting of diverse civilizations had taken place under less favorable conditions and given rise to bitter racial and social antagonisms. In contrast to the relatively homogeneous populations of the African west coast, the Union of South Africa and its northern neighbors were areas of multiracial settlement. Greater accessibility, the lure of diamonds and gold, and the attraction of suitable farm lands had led to the establishment in the midst of the native masses of large and permanent white settlements, numbering some 2.6 million in the Union of South Africa, 120,000 in Southern Rhodesia, 40,000 in Northern Rhodesia, 35,000 in Kenya. Important Asian groups, Arab and especially Indian, were a further complicating element. The conjunction of extreme racial differences with extreme discrepancies in economic and cultural status made for a situation of acute tension. The aspirations of the non-European masses for living space and development, and the agitation of their leaders for political rights, collided head-on with the determination of the white minorities to maintain their identity and privileged position.

The racial antipathies which clouded every economic, social, and political relationship in this section of Africa were aggravated by the absence of any impartial authority which could effectively mediate between the non-European masses and the dominant but insecure white element. That element held absolute authority in the Union of South Africa, and de facto control in the self-governing colony of Southern Rhodesia; in the other territories its influence generally dominated both the local administrations and the policy of the British Colonial Office. Its tendency had everywhere been to appropriate the best of the available lands for its own use, reducing the natives to a precarious tenant status as "squatters" or "resident native laborers" or pushing them back into inadequate "reserves." The more moderate elements among the white settlers, especially in the British crown colonies, did not exclude the possibility of a gradual improvement in the status of the nonwhites, but insisted that white political domination must be maintained at least for the foreseeable future.

It was in the Union of South Africa that the repressive tendencies of white rule had reached their most extreme development. There the dominant element among the whites—descendants of the original Dutch settlers—had frankly rejected any idea of compromise between the races and set out to establish the permanent supremacy of the white population. Under Afrikander leadership—and, thus far, with the general assent of the English-speaking minority in the white population—South African policy had for decades been directed toward ensuring the complete political and economic subservience of the native Africans. Since 1948 the Nationalist party government headed by Dr. Daniel F. Malan had undertaken to carry the process a step further by segregating the Union's non-white population geographically as well as economically and socially. Under the policy of *apartheid,* which found its legislative expression in the so-called Group Areas Act adopted in 1950, native Africans who had flowed into urban areas in response to the Union's growing industrialization were to be pushed back into their overcrowded and depleted reserves; similar separate areas were also to be established for Indians and "Coloreds" or persons of mixed blood. Nationalist aims, moreover, did not appear to stop even here. The long-run objective of Malan's policy, which inevitably recalled that of Adolf Hitler in its open espousal of racist doctrine, seemed to involve the setting up of an authoritarian Boer republic in which not only people of nonwhite races but also those of British descent and culture would be relegated to an inferior status.

Aside from its doubtful compatibility with continued membership in the British Commonwealth, such a prospect was bound to arouse resistance even within that section of the English-speaking community whose fear of the African majority had hitherto induced it to follow the Nationalist lead. A major crisis arose in June 1951 as the result of Malan's disregard for constitutional limitations which stood in the way of his continuing attack on the rights of non-Europeans. By an ordinary act of parliament, Colored voters in the Cape Colony were removed from the general electoral register and given four separate European representatives in the lower house of parliament. But under South Africa's basic law (the South Africa Act adopted by the British Parliament in 1909), the political rights of the Cape Colored could legally be altered only by a two-thirds majority of both houses of parliament meeting together. Such a majority had been beyond the reach of the Malan government, and the act was accordingly invalidated by the South African Supreme Court in March 1952. But Malan and his supporters, nothing daunted, replied with another law (June 3) declaring Parliament itself a "High Court" with power to overrule even the Supreme Court on constitutional matters. This legislation in its turn was unanimously rejected by the Supreme Court's Appeal Division on November 13.

These maneuvers disturbed Malan's English-speaking critics not only because the disenfranchisement of Colored voters threatened the electoral prospects of the opposition United party, but more fundamentally because the whole position of the British element in South Africa was bound up with continued observance of the South Africa Act and the constitutional safeguards based upon it. Beyond this, a good many South Africans were gravely disturbed by the way in which Malan's government was slamming the doors on any possibility of interracial conciliation. Thus the introduction of the Separate Representation of Voters Act had been the signal for widespread protest demonstrations and had even led to a temporary fusion of such normally antagonistic racial elements as the Indian National Congress, the African National Congress (the principal vehicle of articulate African opinion) and, among the whites, the United party, the small Labor party, and a new war veterans' organization known as the Torch Commando. The predominantly English-speaking province of Natal even threatened to secede from the Union. But effective resistance was difficult in an atmosphere already poisoned by interracial fear and hatred, and against a government that displayed few scruples about its means of repressing dissent. A rigorous "Suppression of Communism Act" proved useful in attacking the opposition at its weakest point, the trade-unions. The most effective trade-union leader (E. S. Sachs) was arrested and imprisoned and most of his associates were effectually muzzled.

The opportunity provided by this struggle between the Malan government and the white opposition was fully exploited by non-European inhabitants of the Union, both African and Indian. In June 1952 both groups embarked on a passive resistance campaign which involved widespread and deliberate violation of the segregation laws affecting native areas, post offices, and railroad stations. Centering in relatively liberal urban areas in the Cape Colony, the campaign had led to over 2,000 arrests within the first five weeks without departing from the nonviolent lines intended by its organizers. As tension mounted, however, it began to verge more and more toward violent demonstrations, and finally exploded in October in a series of bloody riots in Port Elizabeth and at various places in the interior.

Spokesmen for the Malan government, using the narrowly nationalistic phraseology in vogue in so many parts of the world, strenuously insisted that the *apartheid* policy and the methods of implementing it were a purely domestic, South African matter. In taking this stand, however, they ignored both the concern aroused by their actions in liberal circles throughout the world, and the influence that developments within the Union were exerting in other parts of Africa. For the policy of *apartheid*, far from being confined to the Union, had shown a strong tendency to spread northward into the British crown colonies. Already Southern Rhodesia boasted a system of segregation somewhat milder but no less resolute than that of South Africa. A further extension of the principle seemed quite likely to result from the proposed union of Southern Rhodesia, Northern Rhodesia, and Nyasaland in a Central African Federation, as recommended by the Southern Rhodesia government and approved by British authorities in London. Principally for that reason, the federation scheme was bitterly opposed by spokesmen for the native majorities in Northern Rhodesia and Nyasaland, who professed to place little reliance on the assurances of the British Government that native interests would be adequately protected. Not a single African representative from Northern Rhodesia or Nyasaland could be persuaded to attend the conference held in London in April-May 1952 at which a federal constitution for the three territories was worked out.

Even more acute and ominous were the contemporaneous developments in Kenya, scene of the gruesome atrocities perpetrated by the secret Mau Mau society in its campaign to drive the white "intruders" from the land. This long dormant conspiracy, which reflected the growing difficulties of the Kikuyu tribe in supporting its increasing numbers on the lands allotted to it, suddenly reawakened at the beginning of 1952 with burnings of white farms and crops and the murders of some white people. From August onward—a period roughly coinciding with the defiance campaign in the Union—its activities rapidly increased in scope and violence. Opponents among the Kikuyu leaders were brutally eliminated; in October one senior chief was murdered in broad daylight and a second hacked to pieces with his police escort while attempting to disperse a Mau Mau assembly. The arrival of British reinforcements and a systematic effort to isolate the Mau Mau failed to stem the tide of outrages. Despite the admitted risk of uniting the whole tribe behind the rebels, British authorities fell back on a policy of wholesale removals and reprisals that recalled the unsuccessful policies employed in Malaya before the arrival of General Templer.

These outbursts gave some inkling of the political, social, and economic tensions developing throughout Eastern Africa and of the deeper, irrational forces which threatened to take control of the situation. Driven from his land and confined to insufficient and deteriorating native reserves, his tribal system and social framework broken by contact with the superior civilization of the West, the African native lacked any adequate means of social or spiritual support. The Christian churches had failed to fill the void. Leaders of the Dutch Reformed Church in the Union were among the outspoken protagonists of the *apartheid* policy; the other white churches failed to inspire African confidence and were suffering an exodus into African-Christian sects which served as breeding grounds of racial passion and emphasized the breach of confidence between the races.

It is scarcely necessary to point out that such conditions were well suited to promote the aims of international Communism, even if Communists had played no great part in creating them and had thus far done little to impart a specific direction to the prevalent unrest. At the moment, direct Communist influence in most parts of Africa did not appear very great. Communism had undoubtedly gained enough adherents in the industrialized society of the Union to afford an additional pretext—though hardly a justification—for the repressive policies of the Malan government. Some observers thought they detected the long

arm of Moscow behind the spectacular rise of Kwame Nkrumah, the new Prime Minister of the Gold Coast, as well as in
the Mau Mau agitation. There was, without doubt, a possibility
that Communist agitators might rapidly extend their influence
in a situation so filled with explosive potentialities. Meanwhile, conditions in Africa were already offering indirect but
considerable benefit to the Communist cause, thanks to the fear
and distrust that racked the people of the continent and the
reflected bitterness that permeated much of the non-Communist
world whenever African issues came under international observation.

Almost since the beginning of the United Nations, conditions in Africa had been an object of special concern to the
governments of the "anticolonial" bloc and therefore a source
of friction between them and the governments with administrative responsibilities in Africa. Here again, there was a fundamental rift between wealthy, powerful, "white" nations like
Great Britain, France, Belgium, and the South African Union,
and the newer constellation which revolved mainly around
India, Pakistan, Egypt, and other Arab countries. Repeatedly
the agitation of this latter group for a radically new approach
toward African problems had exasperated their opponents to
a point which threatened both the effective operation of the
United Nations and the harmony of international relations in
the non-Communist world.

The anticolonial attack on African conditions was directed
along two main lines, one aimed at all countries which administered non-self-governing territories, the other aimed specifically at the Union of South Africa as the seat of the most
objectionable tendencies in African administration. In the
Trusteeship Council and in the various organs of the General
Assembly, the anticolonial governments kept up a running fire
of criticism against the administering powers for the alleged
shortcomings of their administrative practices and their failure
to accelerate the development of self-government, both in the
trust territories they administered in behalf of the United
Nations and in the other non-self-governing territories where

they retained ultimate political responsibility. Although many of these embittered exchanges ostensibly turned on rather intricate technical issues, the anticolonial bloc made no secret of the fact that its final objective was the liquidation of every kind of colonial or pseudocolonial relationship, in Africa and throughout the world. This aim emerged very clearly at the Paris session of the Assembly in 1951–1952 when the anticolonial bloc insisted, against bitter opposition by the bloc of administering states, on a formal declaration by the Assembly to the effect that "all peoples shall have the right of self-determination" and that "States having responsibility for the administration of Non-Self-Governing Territories should promote the realization of that right in relation to the peoples of such Territories." [14]

South Africa had incurred the particular reprobation of the anticolonial bloc—and, indeed, of most of the United Nations —for its own practices as administrator of a dependent area as well as for its own internal policies. Both problems interlocked, for it was through the virtual annexation of the former League of Nations mandated territory of South West Africa that the Malan government had obtained the parliamentary majority it needed to give effect to its *apartheid* policy at home. But the Union's consistent refusal to place South West Africa under the United Nations trusteeship system had occasioned intense bitterness and led to increasing noncooperation between South Africa and the world organization. By 1951–1952 the South African delegate was beginning to absent himself from discussions of the problem in the Assembly and Dr. Malan was making open threats of withdrawal from the United Nations if the agitation continued.

Certainly not less explosive were the attacks in the United Nations on the Union government's own internal policies. As in the case of Tunisia and Morocco, these attacks more than

[14] General Assembly Resolution 545 (VI), adopted February 5, 1952. This language, according to the resolution, was to be included in one or both of the international covenants on human rights being drawn up in accordance with the Assembly's instructions. For further discussion cf. *The United States in World Affairs, 1949,* 366-382; *1951,* 414-415; and below, pp. 365-366.

made up in vehemence for any weakness in their legal foundation under the United Nations Charter. The Charter, of course, forbade the United Nations "to intervene in matters which are essentially within the domestic jurisdiction of any state"; but it also required all members of the world organization to cooperate in achieving "universal respect for, and observance of, human rights and fundamental freedoms for all without distinction as to race, sex, language, or religion"—objectives which seemed as remote from the actual policies of the South African Government as they were from that of the Soviet Union and its satellites.

For six years the General Assembly had been dealing intermittently with the problem of South African racial policies as the result of complaints by India against the numerous restrictions imposed on the 300,000 persons of Indian origin who for generations had made their homes in the Union. Repeated efforts to induce the Union to work out a conciliatory solution in consultation with India and Pakistan had resulted only in mutual embitterment. No negotiations had been held, and the situation in areas of Indian settlement had grown steadily worse. At its last two sessions the Assembly, in recommending a new attempt at negotiation, had sharply but vainly condemned the *apartheid* policy as "necessarily based on doctrines of racial discrimination" and had urged the Union to suspend the operation of the Group Areas Act until negotiations could be completed.[15] In September 1952, as a result of the further deterioration of conditions in the Union, India and its twelve Arab-Asian associates requested the General Assembly to take up at its forthcoming session the whole question of race conflict in South Africa as it resulted from the Union's *apartheid* policies—which, they said, were contrary "not only to the basic premises of the United Nations and to its specific and repeated recommendations, but also to the trend of opinion all over the world." [16]

[15] General Assembly Resolutions 395 (V), adopted December 2, 1950, and 511 (VI), adopted January 12, 1952.
[16] U.N. Document A/2183, September 12, 1952.

On these as on so many other world problems, the United States had been torn between conflicting policy considerations which thus far had prevented it from developing a firm line of action. South Africa, with all its shortcomings, was an important buttress of the non-Communist world—a member of the British Commonwealth, a participant in the United Nations action in Korea, a co-sponsor of the proposed Middle East Command. It would have an indispensable role to play in any future arrangements for the military defense of Africa; its mineral and industrial resources had recently taken on extraordinary importance with the realization that the South African gold mines might well become the world's most abundant source of uranium, the material used in the release of atomic energy. These advantages might be largely nullified if external criticism provoked the Union government into withdrawing from cooperation with the free world. But they would also be nullified if the deteriorating racial situation in South Africa was allowed to get out of hand; and meanwhile conditions there were exerting an unhealthy influence throughout the non-Communist world. South Africa was a test case, Mr. Nehru had said:

"In the eyes of the great majority of Asians and Africans, the South African Union represents Western civilization. . . . If the discriminatory policy of the Union is allowed to develop without being condemned by the Western democracies, the Asian and African peoples will hardly be able to place their confidence in the declared desire of the West to unite in order to maintain peace and achieve collective security based on respect for human rights and fundamental freedoms." [17]

Though anxious to act as a moderating influence in this clash of viewpoints, the United States had met with little success in its efforts to reduce the bitterness of South African controversies. Nor had it been much more successful in promoting conciliation on a broader plane between the anticolonial governments and those of its own allies who administered African territories. General professions in favor of African self-

[17] Quoted in *Chronique de politique étrangère*, V, May 1952, 359.

government and independence, a friendly attitude toward independent African countries like Liberia, Ethiopia, and the new state of Libya, were not enough to allay the suspicions of the anticolonial bloc. Nor was this country's resistance to United Nations interposition in the affairs of non-self-governing territories sufficiently firm to win the gratitude of those governments which the ardor of the anticolonial bloc had forced onto the defensive. There was every indication that the anticolonial governments planned to precipitate a showdown on African matters at the next session of the General Assembly. Some observers wondered whether the United States could continue to balance between the two camps or would at length be forced to make a definite choice for one or the other.

3. Good Neighbors Adrift

A discussion of Latin American affairs in this chapter on "Cracks in the Free World" may seem a trifle anomalous to those who think of the inter-American "system" as a guarantee of solidarity among the nations of the Western Hemisphere. It is true that the tradition of inter-American friendship and cooperation limited the disruptive tendencies in this part of the world and helped, even amid sharp mutual irritations, to maintain an underlying sense of community which was wholly lacking in Asia and Africa. The Latin-American governments, though broadly sympathetic to the "anticolonial" trend in world affairs, did not as a rule associate themselves with the more extreme agitation of the Arab-Asian bloc. Nor was the United States confronted in Latin America with quite the passionate antagonism that faced its allies in various parts of the world and not infrequently extended to this country as well.

Yet when due allowance was made for the tempering effects of geography and historical tradition, conditions in Latin America bore sufficient underlying resemblance to those in Asia and Africa to warrant serious misgivings. "Please do not underestimate the gravity of the Latin American situation," said one particularly critical observer not long after the close of 1952.

"Never, in more than three decades of intimate association with that part of the world, have I seen our relations at so low an ebb as now. As we permitted the Red Dust to settle over China, so, by similar ineptitude, we are losing this hemisphere. The loudly-proclaimed affection of war-days for our good neighbors to the South has been forgotten or relegated to obscurity by the top Washington authorities. This about-face—which I do not believe accurately interprets popular sentiment in this country—has lost us both friends and influence. Meanwhile, and even more serious, the Communists have been expanding their control over the Guatemalan government and Congress. . . . Under orders from Moscow, Communists are attempting to infiltrate everywhere in Latin America. Perhaps even more dangerous than their direct penetration in these countries is that where they cannot get in on their own, they are using the parallel and overlapping 'Hate the United States' totalitarianism known as Peronism." [18]

Not all authorities took quite so dark a view; yet it was indisputable that the United States Government, preoccupied as it was with pressing business elsewhere, had tended to let Latin-American affairs take care of themselves and that the results had not been entirely consistent with this country's declared interests. Since the meeting of American Foreign Ministers in Washington in the spring of 1951, there had been no visible effort to maintain the solidarity of the American nations as a group in the political and economic tasks of the cold war. The Latin-American side of the $6 billion Mutual Security Program for 1952–1953, involving an appropriation of $51.7 million for military aid and $20.3 million for technical cooperation, was handled in more or less routine fashion by both the executive and Congress. Almost equally routine were the compliments scattered by Secretary Acheson early in July when he paid an official visit to Brazil at the conclusion of a trip which had also taken him to London, Berlin, Vienna, and Dakar.[19]

Although Mr. Acheson professed on that occasion to be greatly struck by "the warmth, the cordiality, the friendliness"

[18] Address by the Honorable Spruille Braden before the Foreign Policy Association, New Orleans, January 28, 1953.
[19] Department of State Bulletin, XXVII, July 14, 1952, 47-50; July 21, 1952, 87-91; July 28, 1952, 132-134.

of his reception by the Brazilian people, he undoubtedly realized that such sentiments were not fully typical of current Latin-American attitudes toward the United States. While their close economic ties with this country ensured a measure of continuing collaboration independent of the surface tides of politics, opinion in the Latin-American republics tended to concentrate more on the shortcomings than on the mutual benefits of this relationship. Those Latin Americans who found satisfaction or advantage in repeating outmoded slogans about the "North American colossus" and *"Yanqui"* imperialism complained in one breath that this country was discriminating against its closest neighbors by channeling the bulk of its economic aid to Europe and Asia; in the next they asserted that Latin America was being "exploited" or even "strangled" by United States capital. A steady growth in "anti-imperialist" agitation, in this case directed almost exclusively against the United States and against enterprises owned or controlled by United States citizens, was the most noteworthy development on the Latin American scene in 1952 and formed the chief link with related trends in other parts of the free world. Developments in Latin America offered more than one parallel to the agitation against the British oil company in Iran and the Arab revulsion against defense cooperation with the West.

Among the sharpest indications of anti-United States feeling, both as a popular force and as an influence upon the policies of Latin-American governments, was the widespread resistance stirred up by this country's plans for closer military cooperation with individual Latin-American countries in the defense of the Western Hemisphere. Although the importance of Hemisphere defense had been emphasized in numerous inter-American declarations, it had not hitherto figured very prominently in the postwar military policy of the United States. The Pentagon, however, was anxious not to have to assume major defense responsibilities in Latin America in case of war, and for that reason was desirous of helping selected Latin-American countries toward a position in which they would be better able to protect their own territory and maintain "common lines of communication and base installations." Thus it was proposed to furnish certain Latin-American nations with a limited amount of military assistance on a grant basis, over and above the more substantial assistance in equipment and training which Latin-American governments were receiving from this country for payment. Appropriations of $38.2 million for 1951–52 and $62.4 million (later cut to $51.7 million) for 1952–53 were expected to suffice for the rehabilitation of obsolescent matériel and complete the "capital equipment" of the most important Latin-American forces designated for the defense of the Hemisphere.[20]

Eight Latin-American countries had been tentatively selected by the Joint Chiefs of Staff as the most suitable participants in this program; but action could not begin until they had fulfilled certain special requirements laid down by Congress. Under the terms of the Mutual Security Act of 1951, military aid to Latin American countries could be furnished on a grant basis only in accordance with approved defense plans which required the recipient country "to participate in missions important to the defense of the Western Hemisphere"; further, each recipient of aid was required to sign an agreement "designed to assure that the assistance will be used to promote the defense of the Western Hemisphere." [21] This requirement was interpreted by the executive branch as covering various forms of cooperation with the United States in which Congress was particularly interested and which, moreover, had been emphasized in resolutions adopted by the consultative meeting of American Foreign Ministers in 1951. Thus the draft agreements prepared for discussion with potential beneficiaries provided that each recipient government should facilitate United States access to strategic materials, cooperate in limiting trade

---

[20] *Mutual Security Act of 1952: Hearings*, Senate Foreign Relations Committee, 82nd Congress, 2nd Session (Washington, 1952), 25, 727-731. Military equipment provided under this program was to consist of "specialized items for air and marine antisubmarine patrol; for defense of coastal regions against naval, air, and submarine attack; and for the protection of strategic installations." (*Department of State Bulletin*, XXVIII, March 30, 1953, 464.) For further details cf. *Documents on American Foreign Relations, 1952*, No. 30.

[21] Section 401, Public Law 165, 82nd Congress, approved October 10, 1951.

with the Communist bloc, fulfill its military obligations under existing treaties, and "make, consistent with its own political and economic stability, the full contribution permitted by its manpower, resources, facilities, and general economic conditions to the development and maintenance of its own defensive strength and the defensive strength of the free world." [22]

Logical though such stipulations might be from the standpoint of the United States, in Latin America they were widely interpreted as encroachments on the "sovereignty" of the prospective recipient countries. In some instances they occasioned a response hardly less violent than that of Indonesia and Iran when confronted with similar requests. No great difficulty was encountered in negotiating satisfactory agreements with Ecuador (February 20), Peru (February 22), Cuba (March 7), and Colombia (April 17). Opposition centered primarily in Mexico, Brazil, Chile, and Uruguay—countries that happened to be among the most democratically governed in Latin America and which might therefore have been expected to respond most readily to suggestions from the United States. Moreover, although the Communists in each of these countries were among the most vigorous opponents of the agreements, the reaction against them was obviously much wider in character. Apparently they formed a convenient target for the discharge of negative feelings toward the United States which had been building up for some time past.

Initially the most serious difficulty developed in Mexico, where both Communists and conservatives raised such a hue and cry that the government felt constrained to discontinue negotiations with this country before any agreement could be concluded. Considerably greater success attended the United States negotiators in Brazil (March 15), Chile (April 9), and Uruguay (June 30); but here, too, there had been such signs of opposition from non-Communist as well as Communist quarters that ratification by the respective legislatures threatened to be extremely difficult. In Chile, ratification was not com-

[22] Agreement with Ecuador, February 20, in *Documents on American Foreign Relations, 1952*, No. 31.

pleted until July 3, after stormy scenes which necessitated the protection of the legislators by a police cordon. In Brazil and Uruguay the agreements were strenuously debated during the autumn but the chambers adjourned for the year without taking any final action.

The most striking feature of this development was not the fact that Latin-American Communists saw fit to oppose the agreements just as violently as their European counterparts had opposed the Atlantic Pact and the European military aid program. More significant was the fact that here the Communists were able, in certain instances, to paralyze governmental action as they had seldom if ever been able to do in Western Europe. The reason, obviously, was not that the Communists were stronger in Latin America than in France or Italy, but that their agitation against United States policies exactly coincided with tendencies that were also dominant in important non-Communist quarters. It was the combined attack from Left and Right that had blocked three of the eight military assistance agreements and seriously threatened a fourth.[23] This convergence of Communist agitation with other tendencies which may properly be called Rightist or even neo-Fascist in character —and which, moreover, were not less strenuously opposed to the United States than Communism itself—was the phenomenon that gave Latin American politics in the early 1950's their peculiar quality and justified the particular concern of many United States observers.

It is true that opinion in this country, in so far as it was alerted to possible political dangers within the hemisphere, still reserved its chief misgivings for the various evidences of direct Communist penetration in Latin America. Thus attention in the United States tended to focus primarily on countries like Guatemala, where Communists had undoubtedly gained a remarkable ascendency over the government of President Jacobo Arbenz Guzmán, and Brazil, where they appeared to exercise a wholly undesirable influence in the armed forces as well as

[23] Negotiations with a ninth country, the Dominican Republic, were commenced in September and resulted in the signature of an agreement on March 6, 1953.

in parliamentary circles. What sometimes escaped United States observers was the degree to which a handful of genuine Communists were magnifying their normal influence by associating themselves with a much broader movement of Latin American opinion. In fact, the Communists in Latin America were riding a wave of nationalism which they had not produced but were finding it just as profitable to encourage as did the Tudeh party amid the not wholly dissimilar conditions of Dr. Mosaddeq's Iran. Communist agitation in Latin America, dangerous as it undoubtedly was, was only one manifestation of deeply rooted social and political maladjustments which seemed to be producing a gradual but profound transformation in Latin-American political relationships.

Closely linked with the popular reaction against the United States, and possibly even more fundamental in character, was a reaction against the democratic processes of government which had been considered normal in the inter-American family even when neglected in practice. In parts of Latin America, democracy had never been strong; yet seldom had it seemed so widely in retreat as in the period since World War II. Within the preceding four or five years, a whole series of Latin-American countries had succumbed to military dictatorships or embraced authoritarian regimes of one kind or another. In 1952 the pace was accelerated, with revolutionary *coups d'état* in Cuba and Bolivia, perpetuation of the military dictatorship in Venezuela, and the installation of a potentially authoritarian government by popular vote in Chile.

It would be incorrect to suggest that all antidemocratic movements in Latin America were necessarily hostile toward the United States. Military dictatorships established with little or no semblance of popular consent, such as those in Peru and Venezuela, sometimes looked more benevolently on this country than did the authoritarian or semiauthoritarian regimes installed by popular majority like that of President Perón in Argentina. This fact in itself was an indication that anti-United States feeling in Latin America was a widespread psychological tendency, not the monopoly of any political movement. None the less disconcerting, however, was the growing prevalence in Latin America of radical, demagogic, anti-United States tendencies of the type which President Perón had made familiar during the past seven years. If the trend toward nationalistic self-assertion, suppression of democratic liberties, and agitation against the United States had any common source or inspiration, it undoubtedly lay in Buenos Aires rather than in Moscow. The years of Perón's fascist-type rule had made the Argentine capital the principal seat of authoritarian and anti-United States tendencies in South America, but with an influence that radiated far beyond Argentina's frontiers.

Since Perón's triumphant reelection in November 1951, the United States had apparently concluded that no favors this country could grant would divert Argentina from the hostile course to which its strong-armed president had committed it. Thus no new United States loan was offered to stabilize the inflated Argentine currency; no suggestion was made that Argentina be included in the new military aid program; no "tycoon-diplomat," but an ordinary career Foreign Service officer, was sent to represent the United States in the Argentine capital. But neither Washington's displeasure nor a disastrous decline in agricultural production, the restlessness of his own military and "shirtless" supporters, and the death of his wife and political ally were to curb Perón's ambitions. Backed by a still extensive popular following in which, for the moment, even the Communists had openly joined, he seemed more determined than ever to extend his influence by a combination of subterraneous intrigue and open baiting of the United States. His newspaper bitterly denounced the military aid agreements as an "imperialist" device by which the United States allegedly sought "cannon fodder" for its wars in Latin America. His government-controlled labor movement sponsored a new Latin-American labor confederation openly aimed at contesting the leadership of Latin-American workers. His bureaucracy exerted a most unneighborly pressure against adjoining Uruguay in the endeavor to limit that country's role as a haven for Argentine political refugees and a source of unbiased information for the Argentine people.

Most important, Perón openly took sides in the politics of other Latin-American countries and found abundant cause for satisfaction in the placing of men of similar outlook in positions of power. Of the major political reversals which took place in Latin America during 1952, only the *coup d'état* of March 10 in distant Cuba was wholly free of Perónist overtones. There, the return of General Fulgencio Batista, Cuba's long-time "strong man," had all the trappings of the conventional Latin-American revolution. Batista's predecessor, President Carlos Prío Soccarás, fled the country with his associates and the democratic Cuban constitution of 1940 was suspended. But the new dictatorship gave evidence of a strong anti-Soviet bias, and the United States military aid program was able to go forward without interruption.

Quite different tendencies were at work in Bolivia and other South American countries. On April 9-11 Bolivia's National Revolutionary Movement (M.N.R.), a coalition of extreme Rightist and Leftist forces which had kept the country on edge since 1946, expelled the ruling military junta and cleared a path to the presidency for its exiled leader, Víctor Paz Estenssoro, who had won a plurality in the presidential election of 1951. The new president, a friend and admirer of Perón, had followed developments from the quiet of a Buenos Aires apartment. Although he denied that the coup had been carried out with Argentine assistance, the nationalist and anticapitalist emphasis of his program was clearly in consonance with Perónist ideas and just as clearly at variance with those of the United States. As their first order of business Bolivia's new rulers undertook to "regain control of the country's resources" by nationalizing its major foreign-owned industry, the tin mines on which the United States would be entirely dependent if its access to tin sources in Southeast Asia were cut off. No particular attention was paid to the problem of compensating the foreign owners. To fill the vacuum to be made by the expulsion of United States capital, monopolistic privileges were conferred on an Argentine group which was called in to construct a tin smelter and other industrial projects avowedly designed to begin the country's industrialization and lessen its economic dependence on the United States.

When the people of Ecuador went quietly to the polls on June 1 to select as their next president a twice-deposed former chief executive, José M. Velasco Ibarra, they appeared relatively untroubled by suggestions that there was a Perónist taint among the candidate's supporters. But when Chile's presidential election took place on September 4, there was little doubt in anyone's mind that the Nationalist candidate, General Carlos Ibañez, was a devotee of Perón's way of thinking if not an actual political ally. General Ibañez had ruled Chile with a heavy hand from 1927 to 1931; the announcement of his candidacy had followed a conference with Perón; his platform combined nationalism with appeals to proletarian sentiment and half-promises to nationalize Chile's basic, largely foreign-owned industries. Three days before the election he warned his followers, many of them former supporters of the Nazi-Fascist Axis, to be ready to "act in the streets" if necessary. But Chileans were tired of the indecisive, inflationary, democratic regime of President Gabriel Gonzáles Videla, and undisturbed by these ominous portents. They gave to General Ibañez almost as many votes as were cast for his two nearest rivals combined —more than eight times the vote polled by the Communist-supported candidate.

"A rebellion against imperialism and exploitation," was the comment of an Argentine newspaper on Chile's election. The Ibañez victory, it said, was attributable to the "same reactions that determined the verdict of popular will in our own country —a victory of revolutionary Perónism." "This is a people's movement of a clearly anti-imperialist character," said one of Ibañez' own supporters:

". . . This is a phenomenon that, at this moment, affects many countries, especially those that like ours, are essentially producers of raw materials. . . . Without any doubt they represent the desire of the peoples to claim their national sovereignty and attain economic independence. Bolivia is a case like ours."

Quite similar was the appraisal of the *New York Times* correspondent:

"There is no doubt that [Ibañez'] victory means one more country won to the chauvinistic tendencies typified by President Perón of Argentina, by the new regime of Víctor Paz Estenssoro in Bolivia, to some extent by President José Maria Velasco Ibarra in Ecuador and, in its early stages, by the present Brazilian Government, through Congress rather than through the administration." [24]

General Ibañez himself disavowed any Nazi or Perónist tendencies and denied reports that he was planning to denounce the new United States military aid agreement, reestablish diplomatic relations with the U.S.S.R., or embark on a hasty nationalization policy. But, he added,

"It will be very difficult, if not impossible, to maintain a cordial and friendly attitude with any powers that believe that Chile, because she is a little country, should renounce her rights and sovereignty and submit herself to their influence and leadership in international affairs."

Before long it was reported that the new Chilean regime was planning to sound out Argentina and other "nonimperialist" countries with regard to possible investment and other economic ties which would be free from United States influence.[25]

One further election took place in Latin America in 1952, but this time the outcome contrasted sharply with the apparent wishes of the electorate. On November 30, the three-man military junta which had governed Venezuela since 1948 fulfilled its long-standing promise to restore democratic processes by permitting popular election of a "congress" or, rather, a constituent assembly. Unwisely counting on its own supposed popularity, the junta made little or no attempt to influence the vote, with the unlooked-for result that its ticket was presently found to be running well behind that of a left-of-center opposition

[24] Cf. *New York Times,* September 6 and 7, 1952.
[25] *Ibid.,* September 10, October 12, and December 25, 1952.

group. Censorship was hastily imposed; then came the unconvincing announcement that the junta, despite early indications to the contrary, had actually won a decisive victory. Anticipating what was cynically described as the popular will, the army thereupon elevated Colonel Marcos Pérez Jiménez, the leading figure in the junta, to the provisional presidency. Venezuela's ruling class, its brief democratic interlude over, settled back to enjoy the income from an oil industry which, though foreign-owned, was too profitable to them to think seriously of nationalizing.

The impression created in the United States by all this turbulence was, on the whole, one of rather helpless dissatisfaction. The State Department, which as recently as 1949 had sharply reproved the violent overturns and undemocratic practices which were becoming common in Latin America,[26] had apparently decided not to offer further resistance to a trend which more often than not could claim a good deal of popular support. Public opinion in this country appeared somewhat divided. One rather articulate group, focusing its attention mainly on the Communist threat, was equally critical of Communist agitation and State Department "weakness" and tended to welcome the spread of authoritarian government in Latin America as the best available security against Communism. Others were more impressed by the fact that Communism in Latin America had been most successful when it managed to associate itself with the same indigenous nationalist movement by which Perón and others had also profited. The main purpose of Communist infiltration, according to Serafino Romualdi of the American Federation of Labor, was "to steer these nationalist and neo-Fascist movements along the path of anti-Americanism and bitter opposition to the free labor movement."[27]

To most of those who viewed the problem with detachment it seemed probable that the antidemocratic, anti-United States trend in Latin America had reached its present disquieting

[26] *The United States in World Affairs, 1949*, 477-478.
[27] *New York Times*, September 19, 1952.

proportions largely because neither the indigenous regimes nor the United States, with all its paraphernalia of technical co-operation programs and Export-Import Bank loans, had really succeeded in getting at the deeper sources of Latin American unrest. Such movements as the drive for nationalization of for-eign-owned enterprises that was sweeping Latin America might be unrealistic in inspiration and irritating in their effects, but testified to a deep-seated discontent with existing conditions— a discontent that was aggravated by the economic strains of the rearmament period and could not fail to produce continu-ing unrest and instability. In recent years the United States had been too preoccupied with more active cold war fronts to real-ize what an important phase of the world struggle was actually taking place on its own doorstep. Even if it decided to occupy itself more actively with Latin-American affairs in the future, it faced a difficult situation in which too much helpfulness would be denounced as interference while too little would be resented as neglect.

There was no other country with which the United States could share responsibility for straightening out its relationship to its southern neighbors. In this respect the Latin-American situation differed essentially from that of other "anti-imperi-alist" centers like North Africa, the Middle East, and Southeast Asia, where decisive responsibility still rested with France or Great Britain no matter how far this country might urge them to adopt the American viewpoint. In some ways conditions in the Western Hemisphere were easier to deal with, being re-mote from East-West battlefronts and still governed by the amicable conventions of the inter-American system. Yet no ob-server of world politics could fail to be struck by the similarity of the basic "anti-imperialist" trend which had come to prevail among the comparatively underprivileged peoples of the West-ern as well as the Eastern Hemisphere. World developments in the second half of 1952 were to lay still further emphasis on the importance of this trend, as an essential factor in the life of the free world and in the struggle of the free nations against Soviet Communism.

CHAPTER SIX

POLITICS EAST AND WEST

HISTORIANS OF the cold war may detect a peculiar seasonal rhythm in the advances and retreats of Soviet policy and the answering moves of the United States and its partners. The key developments in the East-West struggle tended to occur in the spring or early summer of the year; the late summer and autumn months were more likely to be a period of readjustment to new conditions than one of significant innovation. Thus the Communist aggression in Korea, occurring on June 25, 1950, gave the impetus from which developed most of the great events of the ensuing twelve months, including the successful resistance of the United Nations, the intervention of the Chinese Communists, and the commencement of large-scale rearmament by the United States and its allies. Almost exactly a year later, on June 23, 1951, Moscow's intimation that it was ready to consider a cease-fire and an armistice transformed the international situation once again and prepared the atmosphere for a year of exhausting but never quite hopeless negotiations in Korea and of growing doubt and uncertainty in many affairs of the free world.

Although June 1952 witnessed no single event of comparable magnitude, that month may also be regarded as an important turning point in international affairs, the prelude to still another phase of the continuing East-West struggle. As in mid-1951, the processes set in motion by earlier Soviet maneuvers had practically run down. The refusal of the Communist negotiators to agree to the "voluntary" repatriation of prisoners had brought the armistice talks in Korea to a dead end. The signature of the German Peace Contract and the Treaty Constituting the European Defense Community had spelled defeat, for the moment at least, of the Soviet diplomatic campaign in favor of a unified and neutral Germany. On a dozen minor cold-war fronts, East and West remained completely deadlocked. Signs of renewed unrest in Iran and other "anti-imperialist" countries suggested that the next major challenge to the Western position might well come from that quarter rather than from the U.S.S.R. or Communist China. In both camps, a moment had come which called for stocktaking and readjustment in anticipation of the next major phase in world developments.

Such a process of stocktaking and readjustment on the part of both main contenders in the cold war was actually to focus world attention from July onward, placing a characteristic imprint on all phases of international affairs throughout the second half of the year. The United States, responding to the normal rhythm of American political life, was about to enter on the complex process of deciding what leaders and what policies were to guide it during the next four years. This supreme operation of the American system would absorb most of the nation's attention until November 4 or even until the new administration took office in January 1953. Meanwhile the Soviet Union, too, was preparing to place its political institutions on public view in a manner that would carry important implications for the future policy and leadership of the Soviet state. On August 20 it was revealed that delegates of the All-Union Communist Party of the U.S.S.R. had been summoned to meet in Moscow on October 5 in a general congress—the nineteenth since the party's foundation, and the first since before World War II. This assembly, it was announced, would carry out a far-reaching reorganization of the party structure, approve a new five-year economic plan for the U.S.S.R., and hear a comprehensive report which would be delivered not, as was customary, by the seventy-two-year-old Premier Stalin but by Deputy Premier Georgi M. Malenkov, a leading Politburo member who had been widely mentioned as Stalin's probable successor.

As a study in comparative politics, the concurrence of these two events was highly suggestive. The contrast between the free-swinging, undisciplined, but essentially democratic character of America's presidential campaign and the somber, mechanical performance of the party functionaries in Moscow was full of significance both for the philosophic student of human institutions and for the specialist in international affairs. From the standpoint of world opinion, there can be no question that the personalities and behavior of the two American candidates, their broad humanity and responsiveness to the currents of popular feeling, evoked a more sympathetic response abroad than did the dogmatism and sectarian hatred that inspired the utterances of the Soviet bosses and their obedient claque. This undoubtedly was true even among those foreigners who had still to make up their minds concerning the ultimate merits of the two systems, and who may have resented the fact that their own destinies were so largely governed by the internal politics of other countries. In terms of "psychological strategy," this concrete exhibition of the way American democracy actually functioned was more effective than any amount of synthetic "propaganda."

In other respects, however, the advantages in this unscheduled competition were not all on the side of the United States. The one-party system and strict control which prevailed in the U.S.S.R. enabled its leaders to conduct a major operation of domestic politics such as the party congress without disturbing the normal processes of government and foreign policy. Like every other public event in the Soviet Union, the congress itself was an act of official state policy, carried out as an organized demonstration of support for the general aims of the Soviet Government. While party delegates cheered the latest exposition of the Soviet "line," Soviet officials were already basing their words and actions on it.

American political processes were less favorable to the continuity of world policy in a "political" year. The price of the two-party system was a temporary division of the nation into sharply opposed camps, and a virtual paralysis of official action not only in the United States itself but throughout the entire

area of American world relationships. American political leaders were less free than their Soviet counterparts to concentrate
on the great problems of the East-West struggle. The quest for
electoral victory at home was a prior claim on their energy and
intellectual resources. Their shrewdest blows had to be reserved
not for the national adversary but for their own political com-
petitors, a circumstance which inevitably encouraged negative
criticism and not infrequently made for oversimplified judg-
ments on external problems. It was only natural, moreover,
that the possibility of a change of political leadership in the
United States should cause uncertainty in foreign quarters,
where the aims of the Truman administration were well understood but where the party of Senator Taft and General Eisenhower was still something of an unknown quantity. Despite the
evidence of agreement between the two presidential candidates
on the most vital foreign policy matters, no one, in Washington
or abroad, was in a hurry to make important decisions until
the outlook was clarified. Thus the presidential campaign, far
from serving as a support of a continuing national policy, occasioned a virtual hiatus in policy at the very time when the
Soviet Union was preparing to press forward on the basis of
a new and publicly unquestioned appraisal of the entire world
situation.

The months of campaign confusion did serve to emphasize
some aspects of the American outlook which would be influential in future policy making. The choice of General Eisenhower as the Republican standard-bearer made it certain almost
from the outset that whoever won the election, the United
States would continue to pursue an active role in world affairs.
Despite considerable differences between the two parties and
their leaders, it was actually the similarity of their basic assumptions in foreign policy matters that stood out most sharply
when the campaign was viewed in its world setting.

Still more noteworthy, perhaps, was the fact that these assumptions coincided to a considerable degree with those that
evidently guided this country's bitterest enemies. Although the
United States and the U.S.S.R. approached the problems of

international life from opposite standpoints, the preeminent role of international policy in the modern world, and the supreme importance of relations between the Soviet and non-Soviet nations, seemed to be recognized with equal clarity on both sides of the Iron Curtain. Authoritative spokesmen of both camps insisted, with equal fervor if not with equal sincerity, that "peace" was their supreme objective and that it was threatened solely by the warlike actions of the other party. On neither side, however, did there seem to be much expectation that the antagonism between them could be resolved by direct contact. Each, therefore, proposed to pursue its aims by means of a global policy directed, in the last analysis, at the moral and physical disablement of the other.

Neither in the United States nor in the U.S.S.R. did this program explicitly involve the use of military force against the centers of the adversary's power. Initially, at least, the leaders on each side appeared to be thinking mainly of other types of action, aligned with those deeper historical forces which were felt by each to be working irrevocably for the other's destruction. The Russians, without relaxing their military preparations, obviously meant to continue their efforts at splitting the Atlantic alliance and encouraging the revolutionary movement in the colonial and underdeveloped countries; thus they demonstrated an unshaken faith in those internal "contradictions" of capitalist society on which they still counted to bring about the collapse of the free world. Americans would prefer to concentrate on more tangible aspects of the East-West relationship, beginning with the war in Korea; but they, too, would place their reliance not in arms alone, but also in those "moral and spiritual" forces which they knew to be inherent in their type of society and which, they were assured, could effectively contribute to the ultimate demolition of the Soviet tyranny.

Here, obviously, were two parallel but mutually incompatible approaches to the problem of East-West relations—incompatible not only in an ethical sense but also because the success of either implied the total frustration of the other. Not more than one of the two strategies, Soviet and American, could succeed, and neither party was to make clear what it would do if its calculations should prove to have been incorrect and its own position should come to be seriously endangered by the operations of its adversary. In the meantime, however, both would continue to remind each other in the day-to-day conduct of their relations that their aims and outlook in both small and large matters were totally opposed.

1. Diplomatic Dead End

There was little direct interaction between the American election campaign and developments in connection with the Soviet party congress. The nomination of General Eisenhower on July 11 apparently convinced the Soviet leaders, if they had entertained any doubts on the matter, that there would be no radical change in American foreign policy whatever the outcome of the voting. Far from displaying a preference as between the Republican and Democratic nominees, Soviet organs embraced both candidates in their "Hate America" campaign on a completely equal footing, assuring whoever would listen that both were equally subservient to the "warlike" plans of American "monopolists" and "aggressive circles." Throughout the summer and autumn, while Americans were acquainting themselves with the actual differences between the two candidates, the world-wide mobilization of hatred against this country went steadily forward by every means within reach of the Soviet Government and the Communist apparatus.

Few could appraise this virulent campaign against the United States and all it stood for with such authority as George F. Kennan, one of the most experienced officers of the American Foreign Service and one of the first who had drawn America's attention to the menacing trend of Soviet postwar foreign policy. In 1952 such warnings were no longer necessary. The pendulum of American opinion had swung to the opposite extreme, and American-Soviet relations had deteriorated to a degree that was causing acute concern to many serious students of world affairs. Some alleviation of the prevailing antagonism, if it could be brought about, seemed to be in the clear interest of the United States and all other countries. Thus when Mr. Kennan was sworn in as United States Ambassador to the U.S.S.R. in April 1952, he had expressed a hope of being able "to make a contribution to the reduction of existing tensions and the improvement of the international atmosphere."

But even so well-informed an authority had failed to measure the depth of hostility toward this country prevailing in official Moscow and throughout its area of influence. No words of conciliation could penetrate the steady roar of anti-American propaganda. Within a few months of his appointment, the new ambassador had felt constrained to compare his situation in the U.S.S.R. with his wartime internment in Nazi Germany. His remark, made in the course of a brief visit outside the country, immediately came to the knowledge of Soviet authorities and provoked the most drastic response. On October 3 Mr. Kennan was declared *persona non grata*. Although the United States rejected the demand for his formal recall, he could not return to his post. With his mission terminated the hope for any improvement, however slight, in American-Soviet relations.[1]

The animosity that Ambassador Kennan had experienced in concentrated form in Moscow was encountered in different degrees by American representatives throughout the world whose duties brought them in contact with Soviet diplomats or with local mouthpieces of the Soviet-Communist propaganda line. The "Hate America" campaign was world-wide in scope. Nowhere did it flourish more vigorously during the spring and summer of 1952 than in the various organs of the United Nations—especially those which, though nominally concerned with plans for world disarmament, were actually being misused by Soviet representatives as a means of spreading falsehoods about the United States and its alleged use of bacteriological warfare in the Far East.

The early frustration of the United Nations Disarmament

[1] Cf. *Department of State Bulletin*, XXVI, April 21, 1952, 643; XXVII, October 13, 1952, 557 and October 20, 1952, 603; also *New York Times*, July 27 and September 20, 1952.

Commission by tactics of this kind has already been described. Despite the U.S.S.R.'s evident unwillingness to modify its basic position on disarmament, however, the Western representatives to that body had continued to treat it as a forum for the serious discussion of armament problems. In April the United States had submitted a working paper containing elaborate "Proposals for Progressive and Continuing Disclosure and Verification of Armed Forces and Armaments"; in May it had joined with Britain and France in suggesting actual numerical ceilings on national armed forces.[2] But these proposals had not been taken seriously by the Soviet delegate. Although Mr. Malik spent some time in demonstrating what he called the "hypocrisy" of the Western approach and reiterating the time-worn Soviet demand for an immediate prohibition of atomic weapons and a one-third cut in the armed forces of the major powers, his main interest lay elsewhere. Most of his energy was devoted to keeping international attention focused on the subject of bacteriological warfare, both by repeating the familiar charges against the United States forces in Korea and by encouraging the false impression that the United States opposed *all* measures aimed at eliminating bacteriological weapons by international agreement.

On June 18, moreover, the U.S.S.R. proceeded to transfer this effort from the Disarmament Commission to the more august forum of the Security Council. As chairman of the month, Mr. Malik offered a proposal that all states which had not yet done so be officially urged by the Security Council to ratify the Geneva Protocol of 1925, which prohibited the use of bacteriological weapons. The obvious target of this maneuver was the United States, which had originally advocated the Geneva agreement but had never ratified it and, since it contained no provisions for enforcement, now considered it wholly unsuited to modern requirements.

[2] The proposed ceilings were 1,000,000 to 1,500,000 for the U.S., the U.S.S.R., and China; 700,000 to 800,000 for the U.K. and France; and proportionately lower limits for other countries. Cf. *Documents on American Foreign Relations, 1952*, No. 34 (a) and (b).

Perceiving that the Soviet proposal was mainly a device to gain further circulation of the charges relating to germ warfare in Korea, the American delegate in the Security Council (Ernest A. Gross) countered by renewing this country's demand for an impartial, on-the-spot investigation of these allegations by the International Committee of the Red Cross. Every government represented on the Security Council, except the Soviet Union, supported this proposal. On June 26 the motion regarding the Geneva Protocol was rejected by the abstention of all delegates except Mr. Malik; on July 3, the same ten delegates voted in favor of the United States resolution, but Mr. Malik cast the forty-ninth Soviet veto to defeat it. The United States then introduced a new resolution rejecting the Communist germ warfare accusations and condemning "the practice of fabricating and disseminating such false charges." This proposal in turn was supported by a majority of the Council (with Pakistan abstaining) but was defeated by another Soviet veto—the fiftieth—on July 9.

At a later stage the United States offered the Disarmament Commission a full explanation of its views on the Geneva Protocol and also a set of proposals for the elimination of bacteriological weapons and facilities as part of a comprehensive disarmament program with adequate safeguards against evasion.[3] Meanwhile, however, the germ warfare campaign continued to rage with unabated force outside United Nations headquarters. Communist delegates made it the principal feature of a special session of the Communist-dominated World Peace Council, held in Berlin on July 1-6, and contrived to give the charges still wider circulation at the eighteenth International Red Cross Conference which began in Toronto on July 22. In Peking, the most ambitious effort yet undertaken in this field was brought to completion in August when a group of Western scientists, invited by the World Peace Council, signed a report professing to present final, scientific proof of

[3] Cf. *Department of State Bulletin*, XXVII, August 25, 1952, 294-297; also U.N. Document DC/15, September 4, 1952 (*ibid.*, October 27, 1952, 671-672).

charges which more impartial authorities were still prevented from investigating.[4]

It was in this atmosphere of lies and bitter recrimination that Moscow and Washington meanwhile continued their permanent diplomatic duel over Europe, the Far East, and the lesser matters that arose in the course of their direct bilateral relations.[5] In Europe the tension was further aggravated by constant friction with the various Communist satellite authorities. Czechoslovakia still turned a deaf ear to all appeals in behalf of William Oatis, the American newspaper correspondent who had been sentenced to ten years' imprisonment on espionage charges in July 1951. Berlin was a scene of constant Communist pressure which culminated on July 8, 1952 in the abduction of Dr. Walter Linse, a prominent West Berlin jurist and anti-Communist, from in front of his home in the American sector. Soviet authorities offered as little satisfaction in the Linse case as they did on the frequent occasions when Western authorities in Berlin were compelled to protest against interference with their freedom of access to the city.[6]

Since the failure of its diplomatic campaign directed against Western Germany's inclusion in the Western treaty system, the Soviet Government appeared to have lost most of its immediate interest in German unification; indeed, it had established a virtual "no man's land" along the borders of the Western zones and was actively engaged in degrading the puppet East German republic to the lowly status of its other Eastern European satel-

---

[4] "Materials on the Work of the International Scientific Commission for Investigation of the Facts Concerning Bacteriological Warfare in Korea and China," U.N. Document S/2802, October 8, 1952.

[5] The most durable of these bilateral controversies arose from the continued refusal of the U.S.S.R. to return 670 naval and merchant vessels and agree on partial payment for certain other items delivered under wartime lend-lease. In June 1952 the U.S.S.R. expressed readiness to return 186 naval craft, but refused to make practical arrangements to that end and reiterated its opposition to other aspects of the settlement proposals made by the U.S. See the Soviet note of June 16 and the U.S. reply of November 5 in *Department of State Bulletin,* XXVII, November 24, 1952, 819-821.

[6] Details of the "harassment campaign" against Allied interests in and around Berlin will be found *ibid.,* XXVI, May 26, 1952, 820; June 9, 1952, 902; XXVII, September 1, 1952, 311-320; November 24, 1952, 823-824; XXVIII, January 5, 1953, 12-13.

lites. Thus the diplomatic notes on Germany which continued to pass back and forth between Moscow and the Western capitals rang even hollower than before.[7] On July 10 the United States, Britain, and France resumed the debate over Germany by proposing an early four-power meeting to arrange the first steps toward holding all-German elections—to be conducted, they insisted, in accordance with principles already laid down by them and rejected by the Soviet Government. Moscow replied on August 23 that the Allied proposals were "an insult to the German nation" and that any four-power meeting would have to discuss all sides of the German question, including the preparation of a peace treaty and "the date of withdrawal from Germany of Occupation troops." To this the Allies replied on September 23 with an uncompromising restatement of their own view. Meanwhile the United Nations commission on Germany, having quite failed to gain access to the Soviet zone and East Berlin, concluded that the outlook for an impartial survey of electoral conditions throughout the country was hopeless and adjourned *sine die*.

Germany, however, was not the only country whose national life was crippled by great-power disagreements. Austria, too, was still under four-power military occupation for lack of the state treaty which the four powers had been discussing since 1947 but which Soviet obstruction had thoroughly blocked since 1949. Early in 1952, the Western powers had adopted a new tack in hopes of circumventing the few remaining points of disagreement and, incidentally, relieving Austria of some of the onerous financial and economic provisions already agreed upon with the Soviet Government. On March 13 they laid before the U.S.S.R. a new, abbreviated draft Austrian treaty in eight articles, admittedly limited to bare essentials, which merely called for the restoration of Austria's independence, forbade its political or economic union with Germany, provided for the withdrawal of occupation forces, and exempted the country from reparation obligations. To the suggestion that this short treaty should now be substituted for the much longer

[7] *Documents on American Foreign Relations, 1952,* No. 21.

draft previously under discussion, the U.S.S.R. made no reply for five months. Not until August 14, after two follow-up notes from the West, did it respond by bluntly refusing to discuss the new draft on the alleged ground that it failed, among other things, to "guarantee democratic rights and freedoms to the Austrian people" (!) or to specify Austria's right to maintain national armed forces. In addition, the Kremlin expressed sharp irritation over the fact that the Austrian Government had meanwhile announced its intention of laying the country's unhappy situation before the United Nations.[8]

Rather than resume the endless bickering over the older draft, the West offered to meet these objections by incorporating four of its fifty-nine articles—dealing with human rights, democratic institutions, dissolution of Nazi organizations, and limitation of Austrian armed forces—into the new short-form treaty. These articles, already agreed to by the U.S.S.R., would have explicitly required Austria to oppose any revival of Nazi or militarist activity and would have limited its defense forces to an army of 53,000 and an air force of 5,000 with ninety planes. But the U.S.S.R. would have none of this procedure. Instead of accepting the invitation to a new meeting of the four-power treaty deputies, it presented another note on September 27 in which it insisted that the Western recommendations were basically improper and unacceptable.[9]

One of the principal grounds cited by the Kremlin for its obstruction of the Austrian treaty was the nonobservance by the Western Allies of certain wholly unrelated provisions of the Peace Treaty with Italy. That part of the Italian Peace Treaty which concerned the establishment of the Free Territory of Trieste had, of course, never been fully carried out because of disagreements between the U.S.S.R. and the Western powers; the latter, in fact, had long since concluded that the relevant

[8] U.S. note (March 13) and Soviet reply (August 14) in *Documents on American Foreign Relations, 1952*, No. 22. For further details cf. *Department of State Bulletin*, XXVI, February 4, 1952, 160; March 3, 1952, 326-327; March 10, 1952, 379-380; May 19, 1952, 778; August 25, 1952, 283-284; September 1, 1952, 321-322.

[9] U.S. note (September 5) and Soviet note (September 27) in *Documents on American Foreign Relations, 1952*, No. 22.

treaty provisions were unworkable, and a part of Trieste consequently remained under Anglo-American military occupation pending a settlement of the rival claims to the territory put forward by Yugoslavia and Italy. Against this arrangement the U.S.S.R. had repeatedly protested, just as it had protested against the Western decision in the fall of 1951 to relieve Italy of the military restrictions included in the same peace treaty.[10] But the Soviet Government showed less concern about that part of the Italian treaty in which it had undertaken to support Italy's application for membership in the United Nations. In fact, the Soviet delegate had vetoed Italy's application for United Nations membership every time it had come before the Security Council—twice in 1947, once in 1948, and once again in 1949. On February 6, 1952, despite a special plea adopted by an overwhelming majority of the General Assembly, he had vetoed Italian membership in the world organization for the fifth time.[11]

The Soviet refusal to countenance Italy's admission to the United Nations was not based on any serious denial of that country's qualifications for membership. It was part of a larger Soviet policy aimed at forcing the United Nations to admit five applicants for membership from among the U.S.S.R.'s own satellites. Soviet representatives had repeatedly made known that as soon as the Security Council endorsed the applications of Albania, Bulgaria, Hungary, Outer Mongolia, and Rumania, the U.S.S.R. would withdraw its objections to the admission of eight Western-supported candidates—Austria, Ceylon, Finland, Ireland, Italy, Jordan, Nepal, and Portugal. This Soviet plan for the *en bloc* admission of thirteen new members actually enjoyed considerable non-Communist support, but was firmly opposed by the United States and, less strenuously, by certain other governments which agreed that the five Soviet-supported candidates did not measure up to the standards for member-

---

[10] Soviet note (June 24) and U.S. reply (September 20) in *Department of State Bulletin*, XXVII, October 6, 1952, 521-522. On the revision of the military clauses of the Italian treaty cf. *The United States in World Affairs, 1951*, 342-344.

[11] For background cf. *The United States in World Affairs, 1951*, 395.

ship established by the Charter. At the Paris session of the
General Assembly, an advisory resolution proposed by the
Soviet Union and urging the admission of thirteen states had
narrowly failed of adoption despite this country's opposition;
the final vote, on February 1, was 22 in favor, 21 opposed, and
16 abstaining.

In the Security Council, which had decisive authority over
the admission of new members, a similar plan put forward by
the Soviet Union was defeated on February 6 and again on
September 8. The "package deal" rejected by the Security Council differed from that considered by the Assembly only in that
an application from the new state of Libya had meanwhile increased the total number of candidates under consideration to
fourteen. But neither Libya nor any of the older candidates
could gain admittance so long as the West continued to oppose admission of the five Soviet satellites. Security Council
resolutions recommending the admission of the various Western-supported candidates on an individual basis had already
been vetoed by the U.S.S.R., and on September 16 a similar
motion on behalf of Libya was defeated by the fifty-first Soviet
veto. Thus the membership of the United Nations remained
frozen at a total of sixty.

Although the U.S.S.R. had made clear its willingness to settle
this particular issue through diplomatic bargaining, there were
certain other applicants for United Nations membership whose
admission it was apparently not prepared to countenance under
any circumstances. One of these was the Republic of Korea,
whose candidacy it had opposed for several years. In 1952 four
other Far Eastern states were included on the Soviet black list.
On September 18, Mr. Malik cast the fifty-second Soviet veto
to block the admission of Japan, whose membership was
favored by all other members of the Council but declared unacceptable by the Soviet spokesman at a time when, according
to him, Japan was still suffering under foreign "occupation"
and had not concluded normal peace treaties with the U.S.S.R.
and Communist China. Next day, September 19, Mr. Malik
cast three more vetoes to prevent the admission to membership

of the Indochinese states of Vietnam, Laos, and Cambodia. Ten members of the Council had supported these applications; the same ten combined to vote down Mr. Malik's proposal to admit the Communist "Democratic Republic of Vietnam."

The denial of Japan's aspirations for United Nations membership was a reminder that the Soviet Government still remained wholly unreconciled to the Western orientation that country had assumed under the San Francisco peace treaty and the United States-Japanese security treaty. In denouncing those arrangements, moreover, Moscow spoke not only for itself but also for its most powerful ally, Communist China. The latter had no voice in the United Nations but, of course, remained a factor in the East-West conflict and fully seconded the U.S.S.R.'s objections to the Japanese settlement as well as to all other aspects of American policy in the Far East. Western observers were not sure that Peking and Moscow always saw eye to eye on ideological questions, on economic relations, or even on the conduct of the Korean war and the armistice negotiations. But there was no doubt that they had a strong bond of union in their common aversion to the policies which had brought about Japan's emergence as a strongly anti-Communist power and an integral part of the American "defensive perimeter" in the Pacific.

A significant demonstration of Soviet-Chinese Communist solidarity in Japanese matters had occurred in mid-September, on the conclusion of month-long negotiations carried on in the Soviet capital by a high-level Chinese Communist delegation under Prime Minister Chou En-lai. The communiqué which marked the formal close of the talks on September 16 [12] was nothing if not laconic, stating merely that "important political and economic questions" had been discussed "in an atmosphere of friendly mutual understanding and sincerity." The lack of precise detail, coupled with Moscow's ostentatious demonstrations of respect for the visiting Chinese, left Western commentators free to speculate that the Kremlin had not felt able to fulfill all its ally's hopes for economic and military aid. The

[12] *Documents on American Foreign Relations, 1952,* No. 27.

Peking government, undeterred by the strains of the Korean war, was about to embark on a five-year industrialization plan whose implementation would require far more assistance than the five-year, $300 million credit the Soviet Union had promised it in 1950.

Only two specific agreements were made public in connection with the Soviet-Chinese talks, both of them relating to the execution of the Soviet-Chinese agreement of February 14, 1950 which had provided for the liquidation of Soviet rights in Manchuria. In accordance with that agreement, it was announced, complete control of the jointly operated Chinese Changchun Railway would be handed over to the Chinese by the end of 1952. But previous arrangements relating to the important naval base of Port Arthur were now significantly modified. Under the 1950 agreement, Soviet troops were to have been withdrawn from Port Arthur not later than the end of 1952. Now, however, it was decided—ostensibly on the request of the Chinese—that the Soviet troops would remain until such time as both parties had concluded peace treaties with Japan. The reason given was that Japan's conclusion of "a separate treaty with the United States and several other countries" had created "conditions . . . dangerous for peace and favorable for a repetition of Japanese aggression." In reality, of course, it was not likely that the two governments could seriously fear aggression at any early date by a country which had proved highly reluctant even to begin rearming for its own self-defense. But the reference to Japan might make it easier for Chinese opinion to accept an arrangement which was evidently dictated by both governments' unwillingness to be caught unprepared in case of a spread of hostilities in the Far East.

The likeliest source from which such hostilities might spread was still, of course, the Korean conflict. Here, too, relations between East and West—or, in this case, between the Communist aggressors and the United Nations—remained in a condition of virtual stalemate on both the military and political levels. Militarily, the two armies maintained their lines throughout the summer with no significant change; the more vigorous use of United Nations air power which had been initiated with the Yalu raids in June caused considerable damage to the enemy, and some misgivings in United Nations quarters, but offered no prospect of forcing a solution if hostilities were to remain confined to the Korean peninsula.

In the deadlocked cease-fire negotiations at Panmunjom, there had been a flicker of hope early in July when the Communists hinted that they might not insist on the repatriation of every single prisoner held by the United Nations but would accept a "reasonable total" of 110,000—provided, however, that all of the Chinese prisoners were included. But when the Unified Command announced that further investigation revealed only 83,000 out of the 121,000 prisoners in its possession who would accept repatriation, the enemy raised his terms once again [13] and both sides relapsed into the repetition of well-worn arguments. While staff officers of both sides worked out a draft of those provisions of the armistice agreement which had already been agreed upon, the Unified Command managed to limit the enemy's use of invective only by holding down the number of plenary sessions.

As the date of the new meeting of the General Assembly approached, United Nations negotiators at Panmunjom made a last effort to break the deadlock on prisoner repatriation. On September 28 they suggested several alternative methods of ensuring that each prisoner would really be completely free to choose for or against repatriation without pressure from either side. When these proposals in turn were rejected on October 8, the United Nations chief negotiator announced that his delegation would not continue coming to Panmunjom "merely to listen to abuse and false propaganda." He was not breaking off the talks, he emphasized, but he was calling a recess until such time as the Communists were ready either "to accept one of our proposals or to make a constructive proposal of your own in writing which could lead to an honorable armistice." [14]

[13] U.N. Document S/2835, November 4, 1952 (*Department of State Bulletin*, XXVII, December 15, 1952, 958).
[14] *Department of State Bulletin*, XXVII, October 6, 1952, 549-550; October 20, 1952, 601-602. In rejecting the U.N. proposals, the Communists suggested a

As the echoes at Panmunjom died down, military action along the Korean front began to increase in intensity. But the suspension of armistice talks did not leave the Communists without a propaganda forum for Korean affairs. When the General Assembly met in New York on October 14, Mr. Vyshinsky was ready to resume where North Korean General Nam Il had left off. Meanwhile in Peking the same effort was being carried forward at an "Asian and Pacific Peace Conference" (October 2-12) where over 360 delegates from thirty-seven countries—all, of course, either Communists or sympathetic to the Communist interpretation of world affairs—heard speeches and passed resolutions demanding that the Korean war be ended on a "just and reasonable basis" through the unconditional repatriation of all prisoners of war. The same gathering reaffirmed the Communist position on American "germ warfare" and "indiscriminate bombing" in Korea, the resurgence of Japanese "militarism," and the alleged need for a five-power "peace pact" and the prohibition of atomic and other weapons of mass destruction. "The decisions adopted at Peking," commented the Moscow publication *New Times*, "will go a long way towards further strengthening the unity of the peoples in the sacred battle for peace." [15]

To many Americans the deadlocked and embittered state of East-West relations and the constant vilification of their own country that accompanied it were a source of profound irritation. Their concern could only be intensified by the realization that each month brought a further increase in the stock of weapons that both sides were amassing against the possibility of a head-on collision. There was a widespread feeling in the United States that, for better or worse, some means must speedily be found to break the stalemate and clear the atmosphere. Such reactions, moreover, were not necessarily limited to Americans. Those who possessed an insight into the workings of

---

new procedure of their own which, however, was completely unacceptable to the U.N. since it still involved the involuntary delivery to them of all Chinese and North Korean prisoners. (*Ibid.*, November 10, 1952, 751-754.)

[15] M. Markov, "The Asian and Pacific Peace Congress," *New Times*, No. 42, October 15, 1952, 9.

the Soviet system were fairly sure that some of the Soviet leaders, too, had their doubts about the wisdom of letting the existing state of affairs continue and might be favorably inclined toward either a "breathing spell" or a "showdown" of some kind in East-West relations.

That Stalin himself was not dissatisfied with the effects of the prevailing tension was, however, strongly suggested by the report of an interview he accorded in July to Pietro Nenni, leader of the left-wing Italian Socialist party. According to an unauthorized account of this conversation which appeared in a British weekly, Signor Nenni found the Soviet Premier surprisingly confident—he was even represented as deriving "a jovial pleasure from his teasing diplomacy"—and quite unwilling to regard the rearmament of the Atlantic allies as a serious military threat. While admitting the terrible destructiveness of strategic bombing—"It is of course possible for the Americans to destroy Moscow and for the Russians to destroy New York"—he appeared doubtful that air power was a decisive weapon and seemed more impressed by the fact that the United States and its allies were as yet in no position to wage land warfare against the Communist states on any considerable scale. "It was quite clear from the conversation," the report continued, "that Stalin and his colleagues are ready to face ten or fifteen years of cold war in the confident anticipation that the Eastern bloc will stand the economic strain better than the Western world. And since they feel this confidence, they do not feel the least inclined to make any concessions for the sake of an early peace settlement." [16]

This attitude obviously did not exclude the use of conciliatory tactics to confuse and divide the Western powers. Certain diplomatic moves in the course of the summer, notably the withdrawal of Mr. Malik as Soviet representative at the United Nations and the appointment of Andrei A. Gromyko as Soviet Ambassador to Great Britain, encouraged a belief in some quar-

[16] R. H. S. Crossman, "Nenni and Stalin," *New Statesman and Nation,* XLIV, September 20, 1952, 308. For Nenni's not very convincing disavowal of the article cf. *New York Times,* September 20, 1952.

ters that the Kremlin might after all be interested in promoting some relaxation of the tension. But it was characteristic of Soviet cold war tactics that whenever Moscow seemed on the point of adopting a more conciliatory tone, some incident occurred to send the tension mounting up again. By early autumn the manifestations of Soviet truculence were once more beginning to multiply. There was the summary demand for the recall of Ambassador Kennan. Denmark received a blunt warning against allowing the establishment of NATO bases on its territory. Two Soviet jet fighters fired shots at an American hospital plane en route to Berlin, recalling earlier Soviet attacks on a French airliner over Germany and on two Swedish aircraft in the Baltic. On October 7, an American B-29 Superfort with its crew of eight disappeared off northern Japan, after being approached by an unidentified aircraft from the direction of the Soviet-occupied Kurile Islands.[17] By such means the delegates to the Communist party congress in Moscow could be assured that their leaders were vigilantly defending the interests of the "country of socialism."

2. The Communist Party Congress

Observers of Soviet affairs in the period of the Nineteenth Party Congress, which met in Moscow from October 5 to October 14, found themselves in much the position of a theater patron who enjoys a good view of the stage but finds that the play is being given in an unfamiliar language. The external features of the performance can be observed and analyzed; experience and imagination permit some inferences as to the relations of the characters and the motives of their behavior; but the essential significance of the drama is likely to escape him because it depends on matters that lie entirely beyond his observation. Thus his impressions may be accurate as far as they go, but can never fully illuminate the intentions of the dramatist or the success of the performance.

[17] As usual in such cases, the U.S.S.R. claimed that the plane had violated its "state frontier." Cf. *Department of State Bulletin*, XXVII, October 27, 1952, 649-650 and XXVIII, January 5, 1953, 11-12.

Interpretation of the Soviet congress and related developments suffers from very similar handicaps. Although in this case the actual text of the play was immediately made available to the outside world, the stage directions were carefully withheld and the actors' real thoughts remained too well hidden to admit of any but the most tentative analysis. Only the performers themselves, together with those spectators who enjoyed access behind the scenes, could be sure they knew the meaning of what was taking place. Outsiders had no better recourse than to scrutinize each fragment of evidence by the light of historical precedent and current conditions and thus try to reconstruct, so far as possible, the thinking of the Soviet leaders.

This process, though it left many vital questions unanswered, at least yielded a good many indications that the congress marked no fundamental change in the Soviet world outlook or in Soviet world policy. Communist leaders from the U.S.S.R. and fifty foreign countries had been assembled not for an announcement of major innovations but rather for a reaffirmation of existing lines of action. The underlying theme was one of self-congratulation on the successes of the past few years and of rededication to the principles which were claimed to have received such brilliant vindication under Stalin's leadership. The principal concern, aside from the general stimulation of Communist fervor and the virtual deification of Stalin himself, was evidently to bring about such minor readjustments as were considered desirable in order to maintain a basic continuity in party and state affairs, economic planning, and international policy.

Events since the announcement of Stalin's death on March 5, 1953 have strengthened the impression that one of the main purposes of the congress was to initiate a transfer of power into the hands of a successor who would enjoy the personal and public blessing of the aging Soviet dictator. Although there is no evidence that Stalin was contemplating early or complete retirement from the Soviet scene, the choice of Malenkov to deliver the principal report to the congress on behalf of the

Central Committee of the Communist party was bound to strengthen his claim on other functions of the Soviet leader which might be vacated in the future. The subordinate role assigned to other potential contenders like V. M. Molotov and L. P. Beria could hardly be construed otherwise than as an intimation that they stood lower in Stalin's estimation than the fifty-year-old Deputy Premier who already wielded primary responsibility for managing the vast apparatus of the Soviet Communist party.

The changes in party organization adopted by the congress were generally of a nature to fortify Malenkov's grasp on the levers by which the Soviet state and society were manipulated. More significant than the change in the party's name from "All-Union Communist Party (Bolsheviks)" to "Communist Party of the Soviet Union" was the replacement of its inner directorate, the famous Politburo of the Central Committee, by a Presidium whose functions would be similar but whose enlarged membership (twenty-five members and eleven alternates) left room for elevation to the top level of several party operators in charge of important Soviet ministries, republics, and regions.[18] The designation of new members to the Presidium and to the party's much larger Central Committee gave prominence to younger men whose party background would presumably mark them as "Malenkov men." Many observers who recalled how Stalin had exploited his party influence in the struggle for power in the 1920's felt that Malenkov would enjoy a similar advantage in any future competition for leadership of the Soviet state and party.

It is even possible to interpret certain contemporaneous developments in the satellite countries of Eastern Europe as part of the broad movement which seemed to be carrying Malenkov toward the top position in the Soviet world. The tragedy of

[18] On March 6, 1953 this Presidium (not to be confused with the Presidium of the Council of Ministers [cabinet] or the Presidium of the Supreme Soviet [parliament]) was reduced to ten members and four alternates. The party statutes as approved by the congress appear in *Current Soviet Policies: The Documentary Record of the 19th Communist Party Congress and the Reorganization After Stalin's Death,* edited by Leo Gruliow (New York, Praeger, 1953), 28-33.

these hapless countries, whose fate was to figure largely in American thinking during the election campaign, comprised two distinct elements. For their peoples, the outstanding feature of existence behind the Iron Curtain was the progressive "sovietization" of economic and social life, with its accompaniments of ruthless regimentation, police terror, deportations, and forced labor. For their Communist leaders, it was the continuing cycle of purges which were gradually eliminating all those who displayed any trace of individuality or local patriotism and replacing them by men whom Moscow deemed efficient and reliable rather than imaginative. The two processes were interrelated in that failure to maintain a satisfactory pace of sovietization—usually described as "sabotage" in collusion with the "imperialist West"—was a sure road to liquidation. But the frequent leadership changes in the "people's democracies" also had elements of a factional power struggle whose ramifications appeared to extend beyond their boundaries and in some instances to involve the Kremlin itself.

The great wave of purge trials which had swept over Eastern Europe in 1949 had aimed primarily at isolating and discrediting the rebellious Tito government in Yugoslavia and eliminating men like Laszlo Rajk in Hungary and Traicho Kostov in Bulgaria who could be suspected of similar "national Communist" leanings. With the dismissal and incarceration of Czechoslovakia's Foreign Minister, Vladimir Clementis, in 1951 it had seemed that this process was virtually complete, and that Moscow could henceforth rely on the loyalty of such "internationalist" Communist figures as Boleslaw Bierut in Poland, Rudolf Slansky in Czechoslovakia, Matyas Rakosi in Hungary, and Ana Pauker in Rumania. Yet the purges and the accusations of conspiracy with the West did not cease. In November 1951, Slansky was arrested and indicted on espionage charges which allegedly involved links with Clementis and other prominent Czechoslovaks in a plot to assassinate President Klement Gottwald. Six months later, Mme. Pauker was dropped from the Rumanian Politburo in a shake-up ostensibly directed against "deviations and conciliatory attitudes"; before long she, too, had been shorn of all her honors and relegated to the darkness in which fallen Communists awaited the day of reckoning.

The realignments of the Eastern European governments which accompanied these moves were doubtless designed to strengthen the Soviet grip on the countries concerned. But it was also remarked that Slansky, Mme. Pauker, and several of their Communist co-victims had risen to prominence at a time when the Eastern European parties were supposed to be developing largely under the guidance of the late Andrei Zhdanov, Malenkov's old rival in the Soviet Politburo. Now that Zhdanov was dead and the reins of power would soon be slipping from Stalin's grasp, it was natural to ask whether men who aspired to leadership in the U.S.S.R. were not also concerned to install their own trusted agents in positions of power in Eastern Europe. The fact that the deposed Slansky and Pauker were Jews while Malenkov had the reputation of an anti-Semite was hardly conclusive at a time when Rakosi, another Jew, seemed to be maintaining and even strengthening his position in Hungary; yet it is surely no coincidence that Slansky's trial in November 1952 was to initiate a wave of scarcely concealed anti-Semitism both in Eastern Europe (including Hungary) and in the U.S.S.R. itself.

That Malenkov's growing influence in Soviet affairs could entail a basic relaxation in the aims of Soviet world policy seemed most unlikely. His activities to date had given no reason to suppose him a friend to the West. But even if it was true that his feet were already planted on the road to power, there was no certainty that Malenkov would gain undisputed authority in the Soviet realm for some time to come. Whether Stalin lived or died, the direction of the Soviet state would remain a corporate rather than an individual enterprise; responsibility would be shared with other leaders who were also Stalin's trusted disciples. And meanwhile Stalin himself remained very much in the picture. His personality dominated the party congress just as it had dominated every public action in the U.S.S.R. for a quarter of a century. His views would determine the outlines of future policy, even if the detailed execution had to be left to others. It was his newest literary effort—a 25,000-word memorandum on "Economic Problems of Socialism in the U.S.S.R.," published in the magazine *Bolshevik* two days before the congress and immediately hailed as Stalin's crowning contribution to socialist theory—that gave the congress its theme song and laid down the basic principles which presumably would guide the future development of the Soviet state.[19]

This document, which purported to rank with and even to supersede in part the theoretical writings of Marx, Engels, and Lenin, was not a comprehensive analysis of the world situation. It was a series of disconnected observations, dating from the early part of 1952, on a draft textbook on political economy which was being prepared under the auspices of the Central Committee of the Communist party. Accordingly, it could not be read as an exhaustive statement of Stalin's views on either domestic or foreign affairs. But in addition to enunciating various new dogmas regarding the course of economic development in the U.S.S.R. and the eventual transition from "socialism" to "communism" (an event which, incidentally, seemed to recede farther into the distance as the years of Soviet rule wore on), it offered a number of insights into Soviet attitudes and expectations in international matters. Read by itself, it could be taken to reflect rather far-reaching changes in the Soviet outlook on world affairs. Its implications seemed rather less novel when it was studied in connection with other expressions of Soviet policy, including the directives for the new Five-Year Plan and the report submitted by Malenkov on behalf of the Central Committee.

To those who sought a clear indication as to whether or not the Soviet Government was contemplating early war with the West, the Fifth Five-Year Plan, establishing targets for the expansion of the Soviet economy during the years 1951–1955,

[19] *Bolshevik*, No. 18, September 1952; English text in *Current Soviet Policies*, cited, 1-20 and (in part) in *Documents on American Foreign Relations, 1952*, No. 10.

was disappointingly ambiguous.[20] Described as "a plan of peaceful economic and cultural development" and "a big step forward in the development from Socialism to Communism," it was plainly designed not only to demonstrate "the radical superiority of the socialist economic system over the capitalist" but also to promote and further accelerate the tremendous expansion of the U.S.S.R.'s industrial base—and hence of its war potential—which had been in progress ever since World War II. Industrial output was slated to increase by 70 percent during the five-year period, with continued emphasis on capital formation at the expense of consumers' goods. Steel production, which had stood at 18.3 million metric tons in 1940 and 27.5 million tons in 1950, was scheduled to attain 44.2 million tons in 1955. Other targets for that year included 33.9 million tons of pig iron, 377.5 million tons of coal, 69.5 million tons of petroleum, and 168 million kilowatt hours of electric generating capacity.

Impressive as these figures were by Soviet or any other standards, their probable attainment would leave the Soviet Union still lagging far behind the United States in industrial power. So long as this inferiority persisted, moreover, any Soviet regime would have at least one strong incentive to avoid or postpone a military conflict with the West. On the other hand, the pace of industrial development in the U.S.S.R. and its satellites was such that the hope of some day overtaking and even surpassing the West in industrial production could no longer seem wholly unwarranted. Given time to outproduce the West and shift the balance of economic forces in their favor, the Soviet leaders might well feel justified in looking forward to the eventual realization of what they liked to call the "final victory" of socialism. Meanwhile each year would find them that much better prepared to face the eventuality of military conflict with the West if circumstances should so dictate—the more so since a much larger proportion of their

[20] The text of the plan as approved by the party congress appears in *Current Soviet Policies,* cited, 21-28.

total output could be devoted to military ends than was true in the West.

Confidence in the soundness of Soviet economic policies and in the ultimate triumph of the Soviet cause sounded through every line of Stalin's theses on the "Economic Problems of Socialism," just as it had sounded through the published version of his July interview with Nenni. On that occasion, Stalin had given the impression that the U.S.S.R. was "ready to face ten or fifteen years of cold war in the confident anticipation that the Eastern bloc will stand the economic strain better than the Western world." In the "theses" he expounded the same idea at greater length, adding a reproof for those comrades who had, he said, been guilty of underestimating the inherent disabilities besetting the U.S.S.R.'s capitalist adversaries. "The camp of socialism," he declared, was being continually strengthened through economic cooperation and mutual assistance between the U.S.S.R. and the "people's democracies"; and meanwhile the "general crisis in the world capitalist system" had been intensified in a manner that was bound to produce dissension—and even war—between countries of the capitalist camp. Now as in the past, Stalin insisted, the "contradictions" among the capitalist countries were even stronger than those between the camps of capitalism and socialism.

For the student of world affairs this was the essential kernel of Stalin's pronouncement. He made no definite prediction as to the future relations between East and West, or between the "socialist" and "capitalist" camps. What he did say was that those relations would be enormously influenced by conflicts of interest—particularly economic interest—among the capitalist states themselves. For Stalin, the trade problems which had been causing such concern to the Western governments were actually the rock on which the Western coalition would break up. The passage of China and the Eastern European "people's democracies" from the capitalist into the socialist camp, he asserted, had resulted in the disintegration of the single, universal world market and the establishment in its place of "two parallel world markets . . . counterposed to one another." The

shrinkage of the capitalist world market meant "that the sphere
of exploitation of world resources by the major capitalist
countries . . . will not expand, but contract, that the world
market conditions will deteriorate for these countries, and that
the number of enterprises operating at less than capacity will
multiply in these countries." Their efforts to offset these difficulties with "the Marshall Plan, the war in Korea, the armaments race and militarization of industry" looked to Stalin
"very much like a drowning man who clutches at a straw."

The inevitable result of this situation, Stalin implied, would
be an open revolt of Great Britain, France, Western Germany,
and Japan against what he pictured as the economic hegemony
and "oppression" of the United States.

"Is it to be assumed that [Britain and France] will endlessly
tolerate the present state of affairs, in which the Americans, using
the stratagem of Marshall Plan aid, are penetrating the economy
of Britain and France, seeking to turn them into appendages of
the U.S. economy, in which American capital is seizing the raw
material sources and export markets in the Anglo-French colonies
and thereby preparing a catastrophe for the high profits of Anglo-
French capitalists? Would it not be more correct to say that first
capitalist Britain and then capitalist France will ultimately be
forced to wrest themselves from the embraces of the U.S.A. in
order to assure themselves an independent position and of course
high profits?"

As to the future course of Western Germany and Japan,
which were now "leading a sorry existence under the heel of
American imperialism," Stalin professed to have no doubts. "To
think that these countries will not attempt to rise to their feet
again, smash the U.S. 'regime' and break away on a path of
independent development is to believe in miracles."

"But it follows from this," Stalin insisted, "that the inevitability of wars among the capitalist countries remains." The
most that could be expected from "the present movement for
peace" was the prevention or postponement of "a *particular*
war," the temporary preservation of a *"particular"* peace, "the
resignation of a bellicose government and its replacement by
another government, ready to preserve peace for the time be-

ing." But this would not eliminate the inevitability of wars among capitalist countries. "In order to eliminate the inevitability of wars imperialism must be destroyed."

Did Stalin really believe what he said about the inevitability of wars among capitalist countries—and this at a time when the entire free world lived under the shadow of Soviet armed might and its principal members had committed themselves to an unprecedented degree of mutual support? Perhaps not. Perhaps his assurance that the "capitalist" world could not unify itself was no more than a reminder to Communists everywhere that conflicts among the free nations were important to the U.S.S.R.'s world strategy, and should be encouraged by all available means. Perhaps, on the other hand, his theoretical training, plus his observation of the real difficulties under which the Western coalition was laboring, had convinced him that the "capitalist" nations would really resume in due course the efforts at mutual extermination from which they had desisted as recently as 1945. At all events, he was making it clear that cleavages in the non-Communist world would continue to play a larger role in Soviet thinking than they had as yet done in Washington and the other Western capitals.

Dated February 1, 1952, Stalin's remarks had been composed without reference to particular developments in the free world's economic and political life. He could not have known, for instance, that the first half of 1952 would actually see a considerable slump in production and trade in both Europe and Asia, and a consequent tightening in the economic predicament of Great Britain and other Atlantic nations. He had not been aware that a prolonged steel strike in the United States would cost this country well over one-tenth of its potential 1952 production and aggravate the strain on the combined resources of the Atlantic alliance. He could not have foreseen that 1952 would bring no move toward United States customs simplification or any of the other measures which economists thought necessary if the free world was to adjust its trade relationships to the situation created by the East-West split. Stalin was looking, he said, not at "external appearances which glitter on the surface" but at "those profound forces which, though at present operating imperceptibly, will nevertheless determine the course of events." His confidence in those forces might help to explain his equanimity in face of the existing East-West stalemate, the ever-present political tension, and the growing military strength of the Western bloc.

At one point in his argument Stalin even seemed to discount the likelihood of an all-out military clash between East and West. The "capitalist" countries, he said, knew that war with the U.S.S.R. would be even more dangerous than war among themselves, since it would call in question not merely "the supremacy of certain capitalist countries over other capitalist countries" but "the existence of capitalism itself." Furthermore, they were aware of the Soviet Union's "peaceful" policy and knew that it "will not itself attack the capitalist countries." In some Western quarters these remarks encouraged a belief that now at last the Kremlin was really in a mood to seek at least temporarily improved relations with the West. Even Secretary of State Acheson, to whom it had become virtually second nature to warn against any peaceful protestations emanating from the Kremlin, ventured the opinion "that the Communist world is being forced to adjust its tactics to the new situation created by the growing strength of the free world." [21] But the scope of this hypothetical readjustment was sharply narrowed by the declarations of Malenkov and other Soviet leaders, including Stalin himself, at the party congress. Though largely based on Stalin's paper, these dealt more directly with immediate East-West relations and made clear that there was to be no letdown whatever, on the verbal level at least, in the continuing onslaught against the United States and its allies.

Malenkov's report on behalf of the Central Committee, delivered on October 5,[22] typified the utterances at the congress in tone and content. What Stalin had presented as dry, abstract

[21] Pittsburgh speech, October 6, in *Department of State Bulletin,* XXVII, October 20, 1952, 596.
[22] English text in *Current Soviet Policies,* cited, 99-124; reprinted in part in *Documents on American Foreign Relations, 1952,* No. 11 (a).

dogma was now repeated, elaborated, and rounded out into a comprehensive restatement of the whole Soviet position on world affairs. Stalin, with pretended scientific objectivity, had talked of the "camps of capitalism and socialism." For Malenkov's purpose these became "the aggressive, antidemocratic camp headed by the U.S.A., and the peace-loving, democratic camp." The United States was depicted as the "new center of reaction and agression" from which came "the fundamental threat to the cause of peace, to the cause of the freedom and national independence of peoples," and which was "strenuously spurring the other capitalist countries on to war," dictating "the aims of the war, its plan of action and the forces which are to take part in it," deciding "other questions of the preparation for the war, dictating their will," and acting not merely as an aggressor but also as "an international gendarme trying to stamp out freedom wherever it can and to install fascism."

But against this menace, according to Malenkov, "the peace-loving forces" in all countries had "risen to determined battle in defense of peace and the national independence of their countries." For the first time in history there was "a powerful and united camp of peace-loving states." At its center, of course, was the Soviet Union, which, Malenkov asserted, continued to stand for "peace and the strengthening of business relations with all countries" and still believed in the possibility of peaceful coexistence between capitalism and Communism —provided, of course, that there was "a mutual desire to cooperate, readiness to carry out commitments undertaken, and observance of the principle of equality and noninterference in the internal affairs of other states."

Notwithstanding what he described as an unshakable devotion to these peaceful principles, Malenkov emphasized that the U.S.S.R. did not fail to take account of "the menace of new aggression on the part of the berserk warmongers." It was strengthening its defense capacity, he said, and would continue to do so. It was "not frightened by threats from the warmongers." The Soviet people had thrashed aggressors in the Civil War and in the Second World War; "and they will thrash them again if they dare attack our homeland." Given the increasingly precarious state of the capitalist world, moreover, he asserted that there was "every reason to believe that a third world war would cause the collapse of the world capitalist system." Under such circumstances, the party's tasks in the sphere of foreign policy were to promote the struggle for "peace," continue the policy of "international cooperation and promotion of business relations with all countries," strengthen relations with the other Communist governments, and "tirelessly . . . strengthen the defense power of the Soviet state and increase preparedness to deal any aggressors a crushing rebuff."

"The Soviet state is no longer a solitary island surrounded by capitalist countries," Malenkov boasted as he neared the conclusion of his lengthy address:

". . . There is no force in the world that can halt the onward movement of Soviet society. Our cause is invincible. We must keep a firm hand on the helm and go our own course, yielding neither to provocation nor to intimidation. Under the banner of the immortal Lenin, under the wise leadership of the great Stalin, forward to the triumph of communism!"

The speeches of Molotov and other Soviet worthies could add little to this presentation, the tone of which was one of such unlimited self-assurance as almost to suggest that the Soviet leaders would face the prospect of war or peace with equal confidence. Speaker after speaker assured the cheering delegates that the "peace-loving" Soviet Union was ready for any eventuality; no one offered a reliable clue as to how far it would exert itself, if at all, to avoid war if a major crisis arose. The emphasis was all on peace and "socialist construction"; but, as Marshal Nikolai Bulganin pointed out, it was no secret that the Soviet economy could, if necessary, be shifted to war production "in a maximally short time." Though there was no reference to Lenin's thesis that war with the capitalist world was inevitable, there was equally little indication that the U.S.S.R. planned any constructive move to mitigate the tension of international affairs.

One important source of friction with non-Communist nations that the Kremlin evinced every intention of maintaining in full vigor was the quasi-treasonable agitation of the Communist parties in France, Italy, and other "capitalist" countries. In recent years, direct Communist political activity—as distinguished from the Communist-supported "peace" movement—had actually achieved no great success in most parts of the world. Membership rolls had dwindled; the French Communists had suffered severely at the hands of the government following their abortive manifestations against General Ridgway a few months earlier; Communism in Japan had just sustained a crushing setback in the elections of October 1. But one of the highlights of the Soviet congress was an ostentatious reaffirmation of solidarity between the Soviet party and its foreign auxiliaries. Communist leaders from abroad reiterated the pledge that the peoples of their countries would never fight against the Soviet Union. Stalin himself took the rostrum on October 14 to assure the foreign parties of Moscow's full support and of its confidence in their "successes and triumph . . . in the countries where capital holds sway." [23]

"Naturally," Stalin said, "our Party cannot remain indebted to the fraternal parties [for their support] and must in its turn afford support to them and likewise to their peoples in their struggle for liberation, in their struggle for the preservation of peace. As is known, that is exactly what it is doing." The task of the foreign "Communist, democratic or workers' and peasants' parties," he said, was the easier because victory had already been achieved in one part of the world and, furthermore, because their chief enemy, the bourgeoisie, had changed its character, fallen a prey to reaction, lost its popular ties, and dropped all pretense of upholding "bourgeois democratic freedoms" and "national independence and national sovereignty." It was up to the "Communist and democratic parties," Stalin intimated, to raise the fallen banners of liberal-

[23] *Current Soviet Policies,* cited, 235-236; *Documents on American Foreign Relations, 1952,* No. 11 (b).

ism and nationalism and thus gather around themselves the majority of the people in each nation.

To many observers this sounded like an invitation to foreign Communists to renew the "popular front" tactics of the 1930's. There were, in fact, some indications that the European Communist parties, especially in France, were casting about for ways of broadening their mass support in what they still found it profitable to call the struggle for "peace." At all events, Stalin's final word to the international Communist movement was unmistakable evidence that Communist policy throughout the world would continue to aim at widening and exploiting the cleavages within as well as among the non-Communist nations.

The Communist world, too, had its internal cleavages, notwithstanding the display of unity that characterized the party congress. One of these was soon to be high-lighted by the spectacular trial of Slansky, Clementis, and a dozen other prominent Czechoslovak Communists who were dragged into court and, on November 27, found guilty of fantastically improbable acts of treason, espionage, and sabotage allegedly committed on behalf of the West. But Moscow had a faculty of turning even its weaknesses to account in the pursuit of its over-all aims. The Prague trial seemed to herald the inauguration of a more or less openly anti-Semitic policy—a development which might shock some who had believed in Moscow's propaganda about the equality of peoples, but which could be useful to the Kremlin in eliminating persons whose loyalty was considered doubtful, solidifying domestic support in the U.S.S.R. and its satellites, and promoting Soviet influence in such areas as the Middle East.

Thus, although the development of the Slansky trial had not been generally foreseen at the time of the Moscow congress and might reflect an internal struggle for power in the Soviet Union rather than a calculated act of foreign policy, it was not necessarily inconsistent with the general strategy which the congress had reaffirmed. That strategy, it seemed, still consisted in being prepared for war but in placing primary re-

liance on the "internal contradictions" which limited the reviving strength of the West and—if Soviet theory was right—
must one day disintegrate it entirely. Whether this expectation
would be confirmed in any degree by events, or whether it was
the Soviet empire itself that was doomed to eventual disintegration, would be determined not only by Soviet actions but
also, and primarily, by the actions of the Western nations and
most particularly the United States.

3. The Great Crusade

There was a remarkable if superficial parallel between the
basic idea of Soviet world strategy as elaborated at the Moscow
congress and an idea which was to contribute significantly to
the Republican victory in the American election. The aim of
Soviet policy, clearly, was the disintegration of the free world;
the aim of American policy, according to the official Republican doctrine of 1952, should be the disintegration of the Soviet
empire. There was also, to be sure, a vital difference between
the two concepts, not only in their ethical basis but also in the
method of operation they implied. In keeping with the ma-
terialistic outlook of Marxism-Leninism, the Soviet leaders
counted primarily on the clash of material interests to destroy
the solidarity of their non-Communist opponents; Republican
theorists preferred to rely primarily on "nonmaterial" forces
to accomplish the downfall of a system which, they pointed
out, rested on the systematic violation of moral principle.

The idea that the Soviet tyranny could eventually be brought
to ruin as a result of its own "inner contradictions" and the
yearning for freedom on the part of its victims was not entirely
new in American political thinking. Some efforts inspired by
this theory were already being carried on by private groups
such as the National Committee for a Free Europe and the
Committee for Free Asia. The impulse to "make some trouble
for Joe Stalin in his own back yard" had given rise to an important provision of the Mutual Security Act of 1951, which had
already occasioned numerous official protests by the U.S.S.R.

and some of its satellites.[24] But it had remained for John
Foster Dulles, the leading Republican expert on foreign affairs
and a frequent contributor to the foreign policy efforts of
the Truman administration, to develop a systematic doctrine in
which the "liberation" of peoples enslaved by Soviet tyranny
was presented as a clear-cut alternative to the more cautious,
established philosophy of "containment." This task Mr. Dulles
performed in an article published in *Life* magazine in May
1952, a few weeks after the ratification of the Japanese and
Pacific security treaties had rounded out his period of service in
the State Department.[25]

The new doctrine was well attuned to the mood of impatience which had come to possess so many Americans amid the
frustrations of the cold war and the restraints inseparable from
the containment policy. Although it would be an exaggeration
to say that Mr. Dulles' ideas swung the election in favor of the
Republican party, they went far to establish the atmosphere of
the Republican campaign and embodied the major new commitment in foreign affairs which was to be assumed by the
new Republican administration. "Our present negative policies," Mr. Dulles wrote, "will never end the type of sustained
offensive which Soviet Communism is mounting; they will
never end the peril nor bring relief from the exertions which
devour our economic, political and moral vitals. Ours are treadmill policies which, at best, might perhaps keep us in the same
place until we drop exhausted . . . even the present lines will
not hold unless our purpose goes beyond confining Soviet
Communism within its present orbit."

There were three truths, Mr. Dulles said, that needed to be
remembered in such times:

"1) The dynamic prevails over the static; the active over the
passive. . . .

"2) Nonmaterial forces are more powerful than those that are
merely material. . . .

[24] Cf. *The United States in World Affairs, 1951,* 131-132, 396-401; *Department of State Bulletin,* XXVII, December 1, 1952, 850-852 and 862-863.
[25] John Foster Dulles, "A Policy of Boldness," *Life,* XXXII, No. 20, May 19,
1952, 146-160.

"3) There is a moral or natural law not made by man which determines right and wrong and in the long run only those who conform to that law will escape disaster. This law has been trampled by the Soviet rulers, and for that violation they can and should be made to pay. This will happen when we ourselves keep faith with that law in our practical decisions of policy. . . ."

The logical conclusion from these premises, Mr. Dulles implied, was the abandonment of the "negative" policy of containment and the adoption of new policies leading to the liberation of the "captive peoples" dominated by the U.S.S.R. in both Europe and Asia. But this desirable end, he emphasized, must and could be achieved by nonviolent methods:

"We do not want a series of bloody uprisings and reprisals. There can be peaceful separation from Moscow, as Tito showed, and enslavement can be made so unprofitable that the master will let go his grip. Such results will not come to pass overnight. But we can know, for history proves, that the spirit of patriotism burns unquenched in Poles, Czechs, Hungarians, Romanians, Bulgarians, Chinese and others, and we can be confident that within two, five or 10 years substantial parts of the present captive world can peacefully regain national independence. That will mark the beginning of the end of Soviet despotism's attempt at world conquest."

It was hardly surprising that a program which promised early action, far-reaching accomplishments, and no specified risks should have commended itself to other Republican leaders whose hope of victory in November depended on convincing the public that they could succeed in a world where Democrats supposedly had failed. When Mr. Dulles undertook to draft for the Republican campaign platform a foreign policy plank which should be equally acceptable to the Taft and Eisenhower wings of the party, its dominant idea turned out to be the very one which had already been set forth in the *Life* article.

A Republican victory, the platform adopted at Chicago asserted, would "mark the end of the negative, futile and immoral policy of 'containment' which abandons countless human beings to a despotism and Godless terrorism which in turn enables the rulers to forge the captives into a weapon for our destruction." It would enable the United States to resume its historic role as "the dynamic, moral and spiritual force which was the despair of despots and the hope of the oppressed." Included in the platform was this specific assurance:

"The policies we espouse will revive the contagious, liberating influences which are inherent in freedom. They will inevitably set up strains and stresses within the captive world which will make the rulers impotent to continue in their monstrous ways and mark the beginning of their end." [26]

The choice of General Eisenhower to head the Republican ticket (after a bitter preliminary battle with the Taft forces, the General was overwhelmingly nominated on the first ballot on July 11) made it certain that the "liberation" idea would continue to be taken seriously by the party leadership. General Eisenhower announced that his campaign would be conducted as "a great crusade—for freedom in America and freedom in the world." The "liberation" theme was obviously congenial to him and, indeed, inspired some of his most noteworthy campaign utterances. In an address to the American Legion convention in New York on August 26, he even seemed to imply that liberation of the captive peoples was a *sine qua non* of peaceful relations between the United States and the U.S.S.R.:

"We can never rest—and we must so inform all the world, including the Kremlin—that until the enslaved nations of the world have in the fullness of freedom the right to choose their own path, that then, and then only, can we say that there is a possible way of living peacefully and permanently with communism in the world."

It must be confessed that the reaction to this declaration was not universally favorable, either at home or abroad. In their subsequent development of the theme, both General Eisenhower and Mr. Dulles were at pains to emphasize that the liberation of the captive peoples must take place exclusively by peaceful means. "There are countless peaceful ways," said Mr. Dulles on September 3, "by which the tasks of the Russian despots can be made so unbearably difficult that they will

[26] Excerpt from Republican party platform, adopted July 10, in *Documents on American Foreign Relations, 1952*, No. 7 (a).

renounce their rule." Expounding his views on political warfare in San Francisco on October 8, General Eisenhower declared:

"The first objective is to render unreliable in the mind of the Kremlin rulers the hundreds of millions enslaved in the occupied and satellite nations. Peace will then have her triumph no less than war. . . .

"In spirit and resolve we should see in this 'cold war' a chance to gain a victory without casualties, to win a contest that can quite literally save peace."

Those who remembered that it had taken a world war to dissolve the decrepit Hapsburg and Ottoman empires of the early twentieth century continued to wonder whether these expectations might not be oversanguine. Yet it was to be noted that the major Republican campaign theme, for all its apparent novelty, was not in any fundamental sense inconsistent with the previous development of American foreign policy. The importance of "moral and spiritual" force had not been overlooked in Democratic foreign policy pronouncements; and the antithesis between "containment" and "liberation" was not really so complete as it was made to appear for campaign purposes. Even the containment policy had not been without its positive aspect, though this had centered in the endeavor to build "situations of strength" in the free world rather than in thoughts of a counteroffensive against the Soviet tyranny. Yet the Democratic administration had not failed to consider the possibility that American interests might be furthered by eventual "processes of disintegration" behind the Iron Curtain. President Truman had even assured a group of Rumanian political exiles that "if I can continue our program which I have inaugurated, you are going to be a free country again, before you pass on to the next world." [27]

The really outstanding feature of the national debate of 1952, then, was not the varying emphasis on different features of the established national policy but the consistent recognition, by Republicans and Democrats alike, that foreign affairs had actually become the decisive factor in the national destiny and

[27] *New York Times*, May 29, 1952.

that the world situation was one which, in reality, admitted of only minor differences in interpretation and approach. Not only the two presidential candidates but nearly all Americans apparently had come to feel that supreme values like peace and freedom were attainable only through an active world policy that recognized both the hostility of the U.S.S.R. and the need for close association with like-minded peoples. General Eisenhower himself took note of this development on several occasions, notably in a speech at Detroit on October 24. The debate between "isolationism and internationalism," he said, was "a debate of the dead past."

"The vast majority of Americans of both parties know that to keep their own nation free, they bear a majestic responsibility for freedom throughout the world. As practical people, Americans also know the critical necessity of unimpaired access to raw materials on other continents for our own economic and military strength."

This clarification of the national outlook, which marked a considerable advance even over the "great" debates of 1951, had two main aspects. One was the virtual disappearance of those dissenters who in 1948 had still condemned the containment policy as unjustified provocation of the Soviet Union and had cast more than a million votes for the Progressive party candidacy of Henry A. Wallace. By 1952, very few Americans retained any illusions regarding the possible benevolence of the U.S.S.R. Even the idea of trying to relieve the tension by direct negotiations with Stalin seemed to arouse no particular interest. Although both candidates underlined their readiness to meet with the Russians under suitable conditions, the mood of this campaign was not one to encourage such gestures as President Truman's abortive 1948 move to send a personal emissary to Moscow. Weeks before his nomination, General Eisenhower had voiced what appeared to be a national sentiment when he expressed the view that the basic issues of the cold war stemmed from "a direct clash of two ideals" and thus were in essence "not negotiable." [28]

[28] *New York Times*, June 8, 1952.

Much more remarkable was the fact that both parties took the field with candidates who not only recognized the fundamental nature of Soviet hostility but also insisted that only cooperative action on a world scale offered a reasonable chance of meeting and eventually transcending it. That this would be the position of any Democratic candidate had, of course, never been in doubt, though few had realized with what skill and persuasiveness it would be expounded by Governor Adlai E. Stevenson of Illinois, the eventual choice of the Democratic nominating convention. In the Republican party, on the other hand, these internationalist doctrines were less firmly established. It was among the Republicans in Congress that there had been most resistance to foreign aid, NATO, and participation in the defense of Western Europe; among their numbers were the principal advocates of reduced defense spending, high tariffs, and unilateral action of various kinds in the Far East. Republicans of this turn of mind had been largely successful in setting the tone of the Chicago convention, and had not concealed their hope that a quick nomination of Senator Taft would lead to the espousal of their views by the party as a whole.

The fact that General Eisenhower's supporters at the convention were able to overcome this determined opposition could not in itself be construed as a repudiation of the party's so-called isolationist wing, since it was evident that the General had been selected rather for his vote-getting appeal than for his internationalist views. Yet the outcome of the convention balloting ensured that in the ensuing campaign the electorate would not be required to choose between a global policy and attempted isolation; its choice would lie between methods of implementing a world-wide responsibility explicitly recognized by both principal candidates as well as by their most active supporters.

"An impressive double demonstration of political sagacity," was the characteristic verdict of the London *Economist* on the choices of the two nominating conventions.[29] Americans who

[29] *Economist*, CLXIV, August 2, 1952, 265.

found time to watch the sinister maneuvers of Messrs. Molotov, Malenkov, and the rest had every reason to congratulate themselves that their own destinies could be entrusted to men of the caliber of Dwight D. Eisenhower and Adlai E. Stevenson. In this nonpartisan record it would be invidious and, indeed, wholly misleading to concentrate all attention on the Republican party and its nominee. Fairness as well as historical truth require that due recognition be accorded the merits of the losing candidate. Not a few Americans felt that it was actually Governor Stevenson who revealed the surer grasp of the world situation and a capacity for grappling with it by no means inferior to that of his opponent. After the voting was over and the statistics of the Eisenhower landslide had been tabulated, Governor Stevenson's campaign speeches would still retain their value as a lucid and inspiring commentary on America's mid-century adventure in world affairs.

Yet it was the Eisenhower campaign that would go into history as the stronger influence on the national destiny, not only because it turned out in the end to have been spectacularly successful but because it did represent a break, of significant though undetermined proportions, with the recent tradition of American foreign policy. Governor Stevenson did not pretend that his views on international matters differed in any substantial way from those of President Truman and Secretary Acheson. The Democratic outlook was settled, homogeneous, and well known; if it was endorsed by the voters, the world would know in general terms what to expect. Republican attitudes, on the other hand, were by no means fully crystalized; under an umbrella of broad principles, they continued to develop throughout the campaign and afterward. That was why the machinery of international affairs came to a virtual standstill during the months of the campaign, and failed to regain momentum even after the voters had declared themselves. International business could not resume fully until it was seen how these new principles would be applied in practice.

The uncertainty that surrounded Republican intentions in the international field was a reflection of the widely differing views that continued to prevail in different sections of the Republican party. All Republicans, needless to say, shared fully in the national antipathy toward the U.S.S.R. and international Communism, and it was but natural that this transcendent fact should form the starting point of their campaign strategy. At the very outset, however, they had been confronted with a familiar difficulty: for the party in power also claimed to have been aware of the Soviet-Communist threat, and in fact had been engaged for years in carrying out policies explicitly designed to meet it. The basic aim of the Republicans, therefore, had been to differentiate their position on the East-West struggle from that of the administration by convincing the voters (1) that the Democrats in reality had shown insufficient awareness of the Communist peril, and (2) that the Republicans would fight this menace with superior insight and with techniques which were both better and more economical. These two contentions made up the substance of the party platform and of all subsequent campaign declarations.

In repudiating the administration's past conduct of the national affairs, Republican spokesmen were limited neither by lack of ammunition, by differences among themselves, nor by the bipartisan restraints which had narrowed the scope of opposition criticism on foreign policy matters in recent campaigns. The utter incompetence of the administration, its criminal neglect of the Far East, and even its susceptibility to Communist influence had become articles of faith on which all Republicans felt able to agree. For years they had been denouncing the entire administration record in terms which necessarily raised a question in some minds as to how much, if any, of the existing foreign policy would actually survive a Republican victory at the polls.

To develop a positive Republican foreign policy program was naturally more difficult. No single idea, but a combination of ideas was required to enlist the support of such widely diverse elements as the Taft "isolationists," the Eisenhower "internationalists," and the many independent voters who would be needed for victory in November. The answer was found in a marriage of Mr. Dulles' ideas on "dynamism" with Senator Taft's ideas on economy. In the eyes of many Republicans, the two concepts went hand in hand; the "dynamic" approach was not only desirable in itself but promised to be the most economical as well. Senator Taft himself had spoken out for propaganda and infiltration of the Iron Curtain countries in the same preconvention speech in which he called for the termination of economic aid to Europe and the abandonment of "organized charity" to other nations.[30]

To judge by the campaign platform, moreover, a Republican administration would be economical with its sentiments as well as its dollars. "Enlightened self-interest" would be the guide of all its actions. Though it would display a particular solicitude for the peoples of Eastern Europe and Eastern Asia, it would not "try to buy good will," nor did it seem likely to pay as much heed to foreign opinion as the Truman administration had done. It would press hard for the unification of Europe, but its support of NATO, and of the United Nations, would be somewhat temperate. In seeking "the expansion of mutually advantageous world trade," it would emphasize exports rather than imports. In its military policy it would pay deference to the principles of collective security, but its main emphasis would be devoted to the enhancement of national striking power. Specifically, it would seek:

"to develop with utmost speed a force in being, as distinguished from paper plans, of such power as to deter sudden attack or promptly and decisively defeat it. This defense against sudden attack requires the quickest possible development of appropriate and completely adequate air power and the simultaneous readiness of co-ordinated air, land, and sea forces, with all necessary installation, bases, supplies and munitions, including atomic energy weapons in abundance."

As reflected in the party platform, in short, the Republican outlook had much in common with that of the majority in the 82nd Congress—that majority which, as we have seen, had stopped far short of the administration concept of international

[30] *New York Times,* June 28, 1952.

obligation and had clipped and curtailed the administration program in many important aspects. The very emphasis on the phrase "enlightened self-interest" implied a belief that American interests were more readily separable from those of the world community than the Truman administration had appeared to think possible. If the Republicans under General Eisenhower's leadership were entering the electoral arena as internationalists, they would still be internationalists with a considerable difference. How far would the difference be lessened by General Eisenhower's personal influence and experience of world affairs? Or, conversely, how far would he himself think proper to defer to the views of his erstwhile opponents within the Republican party?

Contrary to expectations, the course of the campaign produced no final answer to these questions. In general, however, the Republican nominee seemed to accomodate himself without difficulty to the campaign strategy of the party experts. He joined with obvious zest in the denunciations of the incumbent administration. He convinced Senator Taft that in foreign policy matters they differed only in degree, not in purpose. He gave assurances that national expenditure could be reduced by one-fourth within three or four years. He promised to rout the "pinks" as well as the Communists from government, and made no exception in his endorsement of other Republican candidates for public office. He said little about the matters which had preoccupied him during his recent service in Western Europe, but fully embraced the Republican contention that the Far East was at least equally deserving of American interest and support. His statements on foreign aid and trade problems maintained a meticulous balance between conflicting doctrines in his own party. If his personal preference seemed always to incline in an "internationalist" direction, his pronouncements were formulated with too nice an appreciation of opposing views to indicate the precise course that American policy would take under his leadership.

As the campaign proceeded it became evident that no issue related to the over-all East-West struggle—unless it might be

the alleged Communist infiltration of the national government
—so interested the public as the Korean war with its accompaniment of high taxes, casualties, and the draft. This, moreover, was an area in which the debating advantage lay almost
entirely with the opposition. However creditable the motives
behind American policy in Korea, and whatever calamities this
country's intervention might have forestalled, no one could
pretend that the over-all results had been particularly satisfactory. It was on the responsibilities, the conduct, and the
possible termination of the Korean war that General Eisenhower was to deliver his most effective campaign pronouncements.

Unlike Senator Taft and some other Republicans, General
Eisenhower never questioned that the administration had acted
properly in intervening, through the United Nations, to check
the Communist aggression in Korea in 1950. But that aggression, he insisted, had been the direct result of the administration's own incompetence and vacillation. Repeatedly he recalled
the speech of January 1950 in which Secretary Acheson had
defined an American "defense perimeter" in the Pacific and
had said that nations outside this line would have to rely for
their defense on their own efforts—backed, however (as Republicans sometimes forgot to add) by "the commitments of
the entire civilized world" under the United Nations Charter.
That speech, General Eisenhower held, had been as good as
an open invitation to the Communists to attack. Furthermore,
he said, the original error had been compounded in the subsequent conduct of hostilities. And in agreeing to open cease-
fire negotiations in the summer of 1951, the United States had
walked into a wide-open Soviet trap: "For 15 months now, free
world diplomacy had been trying to climb the walls of a bear
pit . . ." [31]

So far as the conduct and eventual termination of hostilities
were concerned, General Eisenhower had always avoided endorsement of the MacArthur plan for achieving "victory" by
carrying the war to Communist China. On June 5, some weeks

[31] *New York Times,* October 9, 1952.

before his nomination, he had expressed strong doubt "that in the present situation there is any clear-cut answer to bringing the Korean war to a successful conclusion." But as the campaign progressed and the emotional importance of the issue became more apparent, these doubts tended to disappear. Although the candidate refrained from explicitly endorsing the MacArthur program, he indicated at least qualified support for the proposal to extend the range of strategic bombardment beyond the Yalu River.

General Eisenhower's principal recommendation, however, concerned the progressive replacement of American by South Korean troops—a process that actually was already under way but which, according to the administration, could not be very rapid in view of the South Koreans' deficiencies in equipment, training, and especially officer personnel. One of the most widely quoted, if not the most felicitous, of General Eisenhower's campaign statements was made in a speech at Champaign, Illinois on October 2:

"There is no sense in the United Nations, with America bearing the brunt of the thing, being constantly compelled to man those front lines. That is a job for the Koreans. We do not want Asia to feel that the white man of the West is his enemy. If there must be a war there, let it be Asians against Asians, with our support on the side of freedom."

While controversy still raged around these and similar statements, the campaign reached its climax in a speech in Detroit on October 24 in which the Republican candidate appeared to take personal responsibility for finding a way out of the Korean impasse.

"The first task of a new Administration," he said, "will be to review and re-examine every course of action open to us with one goal in view: To bring the Korean war to an early and honorable end. That is my pledge to the American people. . . .

"Where will a new Administration begin?

"It will begin with its President taking a simple, firm resolution. That resolution will be: To forego the diversions of politics and to concentrate on the job of ending the Korean war—until that job is honorably done.

"That job requires a personal trip to Korea.

"I shall make that trip. Only in that way could I learn how best to serve the American people in the cause of peace.

"I shall go to Korea."

The sensation caused by this announcement was such that few noticed the qualifications which General Eisenhower introduced in subsequent speeches. Other aspects of the campaign —the "liberation" theory, the tax cuts, the promised repudiation of wartime secret agreements, the long-awaited denunciation of the McCarran-Walter Immigration Act, even the pledge to clean up "the mess in Washington"—paled into relative insignificance. Those who had been swept off their feet by this personal declaration were hardly to be influenced by Governor Stevenson's assertion that the key to the Korean situation lay in Moscow rather than in Korea. In retrospect it seems probable that the outcome of the election, in so far as it was not already wrapped up in such formulas as "I like Ike" and "It's time for a change," was finally decided by the words "I shall go to Korea."

Among the 61,547,861 Americans who flocked to the polls on November 4, the supporters of General Eisenhower and his running mate, Senator Richard M. Nixon of California, outnumbered Democratic voters in all but nine of the forty-eight states. Eisenhower and Nixon carried thirty-nine states with 442 electoral votes; Stevenson and the Democratic vice-presidential candidate, Senator John Sparkman of Alabama, carried nine Southern states with 89 electoral votes. The division in the popular vote was in the closer proportion of five to four— 33,927,549 votes for Eisenhower, 27,311,316 for Stevenson, plus an insignificant 308,996 for all minor parties combined.[32] Swept into office with the presidential nominee, though often by far smaller majorities, were enough Republican congressional aspirants to provide a narrow Republican majority in the House of Representatives. In the Senate, the Republicans were sure of forty-eight seats; in addition, it was likely that the next President would be able to count on a good deal of Democratic

[32] *New York Times,* December 13, 1952.

support for policies inspired by what seemed to be his basically internationalist position. If the outlook was clouded by the return of some few Republican legislators who normally opposed many of the things for which the General had appeared to stand, the dimensions of his personal victory suggested that he could exercise a considerably greater ascendancy within his own party than President Truman had been able to do in recent years.

How did this prospect fit in with the expectations that had recently been voiced in Moscow, where both candidates had been dismissed as tools of a doomed capitalist order? Soviet quarters neither commended nor deprecated the choice of the American voters; American publications, by and large, made equally little attempt to relate the outcome of the election to the current version of the Soviet "line." In Europe, on the other hand, voices were raised here and there which suggested that the matter was not without interest from the standpoint of long-range Soviet strategy. It was somewhat disconcerting, for instance, to find the French neutralist organ Le Monde predicting that the election would actually result in "an aggravation of those 'contradictions of the capitalist system' on which Lenin and Stalin have always based their best hopes." Even more remarkable was the opinion of the generally pro-American Economist that "In Soviet ruling circles . . . the Eisenhower victory will not have been entirely unwelcome, the argument being that tensions between European and American foreign policies, particularly with respect to Asia, will be aggravated by a Republican State Department and a more aggressive Pentagon." [33] These views are cited here to indicate a divergence in American and European understanding and approach which became accentuated as time went on.

At a time when Soviet Communists were gloating over the impending breakup of the free world, it was perhaps not unworthy of note that the victorious party had shown more preoccupation with its own projects for the discomfiture of the

[33] Le Monde, November 6, 1952, quoted in Chronique de politique étrangère, VI, January 1953, 101; Economist, CLXV, November 15, 1952, 462.

Kremlin than with questions relating to the solidarity of the non-Communist nations. "Why was it," Walter Lippmann asked a week after the election, "that by common consent there was in the campaign no discussion of, hardly so much as an allusion to, the serious problems of foreign policy which now demand our attention?" [34] True, General Eisenhower had frequently stressed this country's need of allies, its support of the United Nations, and its devotion to world freedom and prosperity. He had recognized and expressed acute concern over the lukewarm attachment to American purposes which prevailed in so many parts of the world—a phenomenon which, naturally, he had attributed exclusively to the shortcomings of the administration in power. A new administration, he had promised, would help these nations to "develop the will and readiness to defend freedom for its own sake, and our security will thereby be strengthened." [35]

Yet it could not be said that such a prospect had been viewed with universal enthusiasm in other non-Communist countries. Although General Eisenhower's nomination had been generally welcomed in the free world, it had been recognized that party considerations would henceforth weigh heavily in his outlook; and the tone of the Republican campaign had seemed, if anything, to suggest a reinforcement of those tendencies in American policy which had thus far failed to win general support abroad. In dissociating themselves from the traditionally internationalist position of the party in power, some Republicans had leaned rather noticeably in the other direction. Amid various professions of regard for other peoples, especially in Asia, there had been a conspicuous vagueness about the degree to which foreign needs and attitudes would actually be taken into account in the framing of future policy.

Various groups had found cause for misgiving in specific features of the campaign. The substitution of "liberation" for "containment" as the declared aim of American policy had

[34] *New York Herald Tribune,* November 11, 1952.
[35] *New York Times,* September 5, 1952.

stirred old fears lest some imprudent action by this country plunge the world into war. According to the *Economist,* it had sent "shivers down every European spine and seemed to confirm the insidious propaganda that paints the clumsy Americans as the chief threat to peace." [36] Europeans had also been disturbed by what looked like a reversal of emphasis in favor of the Far East; some Asians, on the other hand, had detected a note of patronage in the partiality displayed toward them, and responded somewhat doubtfully to the promise of a more active policy in their part of the world. United Nations quarters had felt that they sensed a good deal of Republican hostility toward the world organization; those who were preoccupied by world trade problems had feared the Republicans were too wedded to protectionism to undertake the major readjustment of tariff and customs barriers which seemed indispensable if trade and payments relationships were to be reconstructed on a sound basis.

Repeatedly such apprehensions had been charmed away by General Eisenhower's forthright campaign declarations, only to revive once again as he turned to reassure his own less internationally-minded supporters. Nor had foreign observers been unimpressed by the insistence of Governor Stevenson, President Truman, and other Democratic leaders that such misgivings were in fact only too well founded. Whatever General Eisenhower's personal inclinations, Democratic speakers had warned, as President he would be fatally handicapped by the "isolationists" of the Republican "Old Guard" in Congress. Thus in Europe, where the campaign was followed with particular attention, not a few who had prayed for General Eisenhower's nomination had presently found themselves devoutly wishing success to his opponent. News of the overwhelming Eisenhower victory brought expressions of polite gratification from virtually all non-Communist quarters abroad. Real jubilation, however, seemed to reign only in countries like Nationalist China, Spain, Iran, and some of the Arab states which felt they

[36] *Economist,* CLXV, October 18, 1952, 137.

had special grounds for dissatisfaction with the Truman administration and much to gain from a radical change in American policy.[37]

"I am aware of the fact that General Eisenhower's victory may be disturbing to some of our friends abroad who will fear lest our foreign policies change," said Mr. Dulles the day after the election. "This may be heightened by the fact that many of his views were distorted during the campaign. But all friendly people throughout the world can rejoice in the assurance that he will be a man of peace, vision, and understanding. These qualities will mold his foreign policy." Such qualities would clearly be needed if the solidarity of the free world was to be reestablished and the Communist reliance on "internal contradictions" in the "camp of capitalism" disappointed. It was high time for a reaffirmation of basic American intentions which would allay these doubts and instill new life into the faltering machinery of NATO and the United Nations. The business of those institutions had come virtually to a halt as the world awaited the judgment of the American electorate; it could not resume with any assurance until the consequences of the national choice had been more clearly defined.

In the meantime, there was ground for encouragement in the degree to which the outcome of the contest had been determined by considerations of world importance. Americans, clearly, were beginning to get the habit of looking at their problems in a global setting. At least one authority was to find the greatest historical significance of the 1952 campaign in "the fact that so many persons clearly put foreign affairs above their domestic concerns, even to voting consciously against what they considered their pocketbook interest. In this respect," he wrote, "the election may have been a remarkable vindication of the American political system." The completeness of the vindication, as well as the destiny of the free world, obviously rested with the citizens of both political persuasions who had

[37] This analysis is based principally on dispatches published in the *New York Times*, which supported Eisenhower editorially throughout the campaign.

now to close ranks and, in the same writer's words, "make the voice of American unity heard above the clamor of the dividing dissensions of the past." [38]

[38] Samuel Lubell, "Who Elected Eisenhower?" *Saturday Evening Post*, CCXXV, No. 28, January 10, 1953, 78.

CHAPTER SEVEN

TOWN MEETING OF THE WORLD

THE WORLD-WIDE impact of American political processes could nowhere be better observed than in the General Assembly of the United Nations, whose annual sessions invariably coincided with the political campaign season in the United States. The last presidential campaign, in 1948, had found the Assembly meeting in Paris, where the winds of American politics had been tempered both by distance and by the reassuring presence of Mr. Dulles, the authorized spokesman of the then Republican nominee, as second in command and later acting head of the United States delegation. In 1952 both these advantages were lacking. The Assembly was meeting for the first time in the permanent United Nations headquarters in New York; and the American delegation included neither Mr. Dulles nor anyone else with authority to speak for General Eisenhower. There had been, moreover, a strong possibility that the United Nations itself might figure as a campaign issue in view of its close relation to the Korean war and to an outlook on international affairs with which some influential Republicans were not in sympathy.

In recognition of the difficulties this situation might easily create for the work of the Assembly, the opening of the Seventh Regular Session had been postponed—not, however, until after the election but only until October 14, a date when political turmoil in the United States was actually at its height. A number of important delegates, headed by Mr. Eden and M. Schuman, had announced that they personally would not appear in New York until after November 4, by which time it was hoped that the atmosphere would have cleared sufficiently to allow the Assembly to transact serious business. As things turned out, however, even this expectation proved unduly optimistic. Although work began promptly on the Assembly's most important agenda item, the problem of Korea, the Assembly was to find itself hampered even after the election by its almost total ignorance concerning the views of the President-designate. Not without discomfort, delegates were to realize that the hiatus in American policy would hardly terminate before the new administration was formally installed on January 20, 1953.

The experience of the 1952 Assembly in trying to promote a solution of the Korean conflict was typical in some degree of a new trend that was meanwhile becoming evident in the life of this sixty-nation body which Mr. Dulles had once called the "town meeting of the world." The dominant feature of all Assembly sessions, the opposition of East and West and the contempt of the Soviet Union for the opinion of fifty-five non-Communist nations, remained as pronounced as ever; Mr. Vyshinsky, by his blunt rejection of a Korean peace plan endorsed by an overwhelming majority of the Assembly, was actually to break his own world's record for tactless intransigence. Within the non-Communist majority, however, there was reason to ask whether the functions of leadership were not tending to some extent to elude the grasp of the United States and its close allies. Characteristically, perhaps, it was not an American plan for Korea which Mr. Vyshinsky rejected, but a compromise proposal put forward by India—one for which the United States itself had shown little enthusiasm until it became evident that a prolonged process of amendment had made it satisfactory to substantially everyone except the Soviet bloc.

A somewhat similar tendency could be observed in the Assembly's handling of other items on its agenda, particularly those that were not directly related to the problems of "international peace and security." In general, United States views no longer seemed to command as much deference as at previous sessions; increasingly the initiative, and the preponderance of voting power, seemed to lie with other non-Communist delegations which were neither wedded to the American viewpoint nor directly amenable to American influence. This trend in the Assembly's operations might be considered either healthy or dangerous, according to one's individual view of the United Nations and of its relation to United States interests. In either case, it was a phenomenon that could not be accounted for solely by the slackening of American leadership during the election period. More fundamentally, it reflected a new assertiveness on the part of governments which were not closely associated with the United States or its NATO partners but were highly conscious of their own importance and did not consider their interests by any means identical with those of the North Atlantic allies.

The source of these new tendencies, in brief, lay in the very countries which have already been identified as a major dissentient element in the free world—in countries like India, Pakistan, Burma, Indonesia, the Arab states, and, last but not always least, the twenty republics of Latin America. Admittedly, the issues on which these countries chose to assert themselves most vigorously were those to which the United States attached a rather subordinate importance, because they were not directly connected with the maintenance of peace and security in a world dominated by the Soviet threat. Nevertheless such issues, especially those concerned with the status of dependent peoples and with the progress of underdeveloped areas, were coming to play an increasingly prominent role in the business of the Assembly and in the politics of the free world. This in itself was partly the result of pressure from "anticolonial" or "neutral" governments, whose collective weight was such that when they worked together they could exert a decisive influence not only on specific decisions of the Assembly but even on the scope and emphasis of the Assembly's deliberations.

Previous sessions of the Assembly had been dominated without exception by the issues of the cold war between East and West; and, as Secretary-General Trygve Lie pointed out in his annual report to the 1952 Assembly, it was still true that "tensions and conflicts between the Western Powers and their supporters on the one hand and the Soviet Union and its allies on the other hand persist with undiminished intensity inside and outside the United Nations." But apart from the Korean problem, the 1952 Assembly was to show rather less concern with the East-West conflict than with another broad problem which Mr. Lie considered "of equal gravity for our times . . . the problem of political, economic and social adjustments between the more advanced, industrialized nations on the one hand and the under-developed nations on the other hand." This problem, the Secretary-General pointed out,

"is especially acute in parts of Asia, the Middle East and Northern Africa, but it is present also in the rest of Africa and in Latin America. The rise of nationalism and the demand for greater equality of rights, freedom and economic opportunity among all these peoples are facts of our times as significant as the 'East-West' conflict. These are historic forces that will not be denied. They constitute one of the greatest challenges to contemporary civilization. The question is whether, by enlisting moderation and realism on all sides, we can find effective ways to answer this challenge by peaceful and evolutionary means rapidly enough to prevent the violent upheavals and widespread chaos that are likely if we do not." [1]

This, surely, was a question deserving the most serious and responsible attention on the part of the world's principal representative body, although the extent to which "moderation and realism" would characterize its discussion of matters like Tunisia, Morocco, and race conflict in South Africa was to remain a matter of opinion. These explosive issues, brought before the Assembly on the initiative of the Arab-Asian bloc, did not directly involve the United States, but claimed its anxious attention because of their direct bearing on the strength and solidarity of the non-Communist world. But there was also a series of related questions, primarily concerned with economic and social standards in underdeveloped countries, in which the United States was beginning to emerge as a definite opponent

[1] *Annual Report of the Secretary General on the Work of the Organization, 1 July 1951 to 30 June 1952* (General Assembly *Official Records, Seventh Session*, Supplement 1), Introduction (reprinted in *Documents on American Foreign Relations, 1952*, No. 32).

of the tendencies and doctrines that were gaining ground in Asia, Africa, and Latin America.

Finally, the 1952 Assembly was to witness the maturing of a new issue which threatened to set the United States in opposition to what seemed the prevailing philosophy of the United Nations as a whole. The Seventh Assembly session coincided with a widely publicized inquiry into the loyalty of American employees of the United Nations by a subcommittee of the Senate Internal Security Committee. Sensational charges given currency as a result of these hearings were to give a new impetus to anti-United Nations feeling in this country, and would cast a veil of uncertainty over the future relationship between the United Nations and the very country which had done most to bring it into being.

1. Action on Korea

Despite the growing emphasis on the problems of colonial and underdeveloped areas, it was not to be expected that the Assembly would meet in an atmosphere untroubled by signs and portents of the ever-dangerous struggle between East and West. The fortnight preceding its convocation on October 14 had been especially rich in danger signals—the blunt Soviet demand for the recall of Ambassador Kennan, Malenkov's report to the Communist party congress, the shooting down of an American airplane off northern Japan, the suspension of the Korean armistice negotiations, and the renewal of heavy fighting along the Korean front. Indochina, too, had returned to the headlines with the cessation of the summer rains and the commencement of determined, possibly dangerous Communist operations in northwestern Vietnam and in the Red River delta around Hanoi.

To snatch the initiative at another point, Czechoslovakia had chosen this moment to renew the Soviet bloc's familiar complaint against the United States for allegedly organizing subversion and espionage against the U.S.S.R. and the "People's Democracies" under a provision of the Mutual Security Act of

1951.[2] Poland now seized the first opportunity to propose to the Assembly a comprehensive program of "Measures to Avert the Threat of a New War"—a new edition of the familiar Soviet propaganda anthology, with its time-honored demand for settlement of the Korean war in accordance with Communist views, a one-third reduction in the armed forces of the Big Five, unconditional prohibition of bacteriological and atomic weapons, condemnation of NATO, and a "pact of peace" among the great powers.[3] Vyshinsky's prompt endorsement of the Polish plan indicated that its provisions would form the basis of Soviet propaganda strategy in this as in past assemblies.

The Western powers, however, were not to be outdone in any contest for the Assembly's attention. The agenda was already studded with controversial items relating to disarmament, collective security, the admission of new members, the nonrepatriation of Greek children and prisoners held behind the Iron Curtain, the unfulfilled pledge to restore Austria's sovereignty and independence. As the Assembly opened, the United States moved to include on the agenda an additional proposal, already vetoed by the U.S.S.R. in the Security Council, for an impartial investigation of the Communist charges relating to alleged use of bacteriological warfare by the United Nations forces in Korea.

Not many of these items were to be reached by the time the Assembly recessed for the Christmas holidays. But one prompt rebuff was administered to the Soviet bloc on October 25 when the Assembly decided, under urging by the United States, to defer until a later session any consideration of the stock Soviet demand for the ouster of Nationalist China from the Assembly and its replacement by Communist China.[4] Two days later the

[2] Czechoslovakia complained directly to the U.S. as well as to the U.N.; see *Department of State Bulletin*, XXVII, December 1, 1952, 850-852.
[3] U.N. Document A/2229, October 18, 1952.
[4] The vote of 42-7-11 (42 in favor, 7 opposed, and 11 abstentions) suggested that Peking's continuance in the role of an aggressor against the U.N. was not improving its chances of gaining recognition by the Assembly. The year before, a similar decision had been adopted by the narrower margin of 37-11-4; in 1950, before the Chinese intervention in Korea, a motion to seat a Chinese Communist delegation immediately had been defeated by only 33-16, with 10 abstentions.

West scored up another minor victory with the election of Yugoslavia (in preference to Czechoslovakia, the Soviet-supported candidate) to fill a vacancy on the eighteen-member Economic and Social Council.

In minor housekeeping matters of this kind the Assembly could act according to its own best judgment, assured that there was no way its decision could be invalidated by the dissenting governments of the Soviet bloc. The same was unfortunately not true of more vital matters which were either subject to the Soviet veto in the Security Council or required active Soviet cooperation if the Assembly's purposes were to be accomplished. Examples in the former category were the Assembly's repeated recommendations regarding the admission of new members to the United Nations, all of which had perforce been rejected by the Security Council because of the Soviet veto. Conspicuous in the latter group had been the effort to assist in bringing about free elections as a preliminary to the reunification of Germany, which had been nullified by Moscow's refusal to countenance the admission of a commission of inquiry to the parts of Germany in which it exercised control.

That the Assembly would continue to be dogged by such difficulties could be foreseen from the beginning of the Seventh Session. Its deliberations on most East-West issues would be marked by the exchange of oratorical invective rather than by practical accomplishment. The majority decision on the question of United Nations membership would take the usual form— individual endorsement of new candidates recommended by the West (Japan, Vietnam, Cambodia, Laos, Libya, and Jordan); rejection of the usual "package deal" advocated by the Soviet bloc; and a decision to explore once again the possibility of somehow circumventing the blockade against new admissions maintained by the U.S.S.R. in the Security Council.[5] With equally good intentions, and with equally little prospect that its words would be heeded in Moscow, the Assembly addressed an "earnest appeal" to the Big Four powers "to make a re-

[5] General Assembly Resolution 620 (VII), adopted December 21, 1952, in *Documents on American Foreign Relations, 1952*, No. 33 (b).

newed and urgent effort to reach agreement on the terms of an Austrian treaty"[6] and condemned the failure of the Soviet satellite states to emulate Yugoslavia's good example in facilitating the repatriation of Greek children removed from their homeland during the guerrilla fighting in 1946–1949.[7]

Korea was obviously another area where the Assembly had no way of enforcing its recommendations if, as was all too probable, the Communist governments chose to ignore them. Its ability to influence the situation in Korea was no greater than the military capabilities of the United Nations Command, which, moreover, was nominally responsible to the Security Council rather than the Assembly and actually received its instructions not from the United Nations but from the Defense Department in Washington. In the fall of 1950, the Assembly had acquiesced in the intention of the Unified Command to carry the fight across the 38th parallel and try to unify Korea by force of arms. That attempt, however, had gravely miscarried. In 1952, the establishment of "a unified, independent and democratic Government in the sovereign State of Korea" still stood as the declared political objective of the United Nations; but, as Secretary Acheson had pointed out, no one had "undertaken the obligation to unify Korea by force,"[8] and neither the United States nor any other member government was prepared to undertake the military effort that would be needed to drive the Communist aggressors out of North Korea. For more than a year the interest of the United Nations had been focused on the more limited objective of securing an armistice along the existing battle line. Even this goal had thus far eluded the United Nations negotiators at Panmunjom.

Knowing the obstacles to effective action by the Assembly in matters of this kind, and recognizing the unwillingness of most United Nations members to provide any additional sup-

[6] Resolution 613 (VII), adopted December 20, 1952, in *Documents on American Foreign Relations, 1952*, No. 35 (h). The Soviet bloc maintained that Austria was none of the Assembly's business and refused to participate in the discussion or vote.
[7] Resolution 618 (VII), adopted December 17, 1952.
[8] *The United States in World Affairs, 1951*, 112.

port for the military effort in Korea,[9] the United States delegation had gathered in New York with very modest expectations. Even if there had been a chance that Peking and Moscow would heed the Assembly more readily than they had heeded the United Nations armistice delegation, it seemed unlikely that the Assembly would be any more successful in finding a way around the fundamental disagreement as to the exchange of unwilling prisoners of war. If anything, there was a danger that too much helpfulness on the part of the Assembly would make the situation more difficult by casting doubt on the merits of this country's position in regard to prisoner repatriation. The United States was satisfied that there was no alternative to its insistence that no North Korean or Chinese prisoner should be repatriated against his will. Every reasonable method of giving effect to this principle, Washington felt, had been fully developed at Panmunjom, only to meet with uncompromising rejection by the Communist negotiators. The most the Assembly could realistically be expected to do, in the American view, was to endorse this country's conduct of the armistice negotiations and give its moral support to the position taken by the United Nations negotiators on instructions from Washington.

To this end the United States went out of its way to furnish the Assembly with full details of its conduct of the armistice negotiations. A special report from the Unified Command reviewed the entire record since the date of the first Soviet "peace" move on June 23, 1951.[10] Secretary Acheson, in a personal appearance before the Assembly's Political and Security Committee on October 24, analyzed the situation in great detail and reminded the fifty-nine other delegations that, great as was the general yearning for peace, "we must not and we cannot buy peace at the price of honor." No act of the Assembly,

[9] As of October 18 the Unified Command listed 16 U.N. members with forces actually engaged in Korea: Australia, Belgium, Canada, Colombia, Ethiopia, France, Greece, Luxembourg, Netherlands, New Zealand, Philippines, Thailand, Turkey, Union of South Africa (air forces only), U.K., and U.S. (U.N. Document A/2228, October 18, 1952).

[10] *Special Report of the Unified Command on the United Nations Action in Korea*, U.N. Document A/2228, October 18, 1952 (*Documents on American Foreign Relations, 1952*, No. 29).

Mr. Acheson insisted, must "weaken or destroy the noble purpose" of the sacrifices made by men of the United Nations in
Korea.[11] Thus the draft resolution on Korea which he introduced on behalf of the United States and twenty other governments merely "noted with approval" the conduct of the armistice negotiations to date and called upon Communist China
and North Korea to avert further bloodshed by accepting the
principle of nonforcible repatriation of prisoners.[12]

This proposal was obviously closer to the Assembly's views
than the alternative plans submitted on behalf of the Soviet
bloc, which purported to be based on "new" proposals advanced by the Communists at Panmunjom but seemed nevertheless to insist on the total repatriation of prisoners under all
circumstances.[13] Nevertheless the Assembly as a whole was not
in a mood to accept the American recommendations without
careful scrutiny. Too much uncertainty prevailed on several
material points. A good many delegates were asking themselves whether the next administration in the United States
would adhere as steadfastly to the principle of nonforcible repatriation as the Truman administration had done. Even among
the sponsors of the twenty-one-power draft resolution, there
were some who thought they glimpsed a possibility of compromise in Vyshinsky's calculated vagueness on some aspects of
the Panmunjom deadlock. Other delegates had come to New
York with original plans for resolving the prisoner issue which
they were anxious to ventilate before resigning themselves to

[11] Department of State Bulletin, XXVII, November 3, 1952, 679-692 and November 10, 1952, 744-751.
[12] U.N. Document A/C.1/725, October 24, 1952 (Department of State Bulletin, XXVII, November 3, 1952, 680), sponsored by all the governments listed
in note 9 above except South Africa and also by Denmark, Honduras, Iceland,
Nicaragua, Norway, and Uruguay.
[13] The Polish proposal presented on October 17 and endorsed by Vyshinsky the
next day called for (1) immediate cessation of hostilities; (2) repatriation of all
prisoners; (3) withdrawal of all foreign (including Chinese) armed forces
within two to three months; and (4) unification of Korea by Koreans under the
supervision of an international commission. A series of essentially similar plans
was introduced by Vyshinsky in the First Committee. (Cf. U.N. Documents
A/2229, October 18, and A/C.1/729 and Revisions, October 29 and November
10, 1952.) On the Panmunjom proposals cf. above, pp. 290-291.

a condition of stalemate such as seemed to be implied in the American proposal.

Thus American hopes for a quick passage of the twenty-one-power resolution were disappointed. While awaiting the outcome of the election and a statement by the successful candidate, the Assembly's First Committee undertook to make its own canvass of possible compromise solutions. Mexico had already suggested that prisoners who refused repatriation might be granted asylum in the territory of other United Nations members until normal conditions were reestablished in the Far East. Peru now proposed that unwilling prisoners be turned over to a special United Nations commission, which would be responsible for protecting their interests and might facilitate their permanent resettlement in other countries or in United Nations trust territories. Canada, Brazil, and Egypt stressed various ways of clarifying the procedures for prisoner exchange developed by the Unified Command. But Mr. Vyshinsky threw cold water on all these projects when he reminded the committee on November 10 that they all maintained the principle of nonforcible repatriation and thus ran counter to his government's insistence that *all* prisoners must be repatriated in accordance with the Soviet reading of international law.

But the major effort to find common ground between the American and Soviet positions was still to come. On November 17, while the delegates were considering additional suggestions made by Pakistan and Israel and anxiously awaiting an expression of General Eisenhower's views,[14] the representative of India circulated a lengthy draft resolution which had been worked out after exhaustive consultation with Arab-Asian delegations and other interested parties. Its central aim, like those of all other proposals from non-Communist quarters, was to establish a face-saving procedure which might be accepted by the Communists even though it left unwilling prisoners free to reject repatriation. The particular device proposed by India

[14] Republican Senator Alexander Wiley of the U.S. delegation announced on November 19, after conferring with General Eisenhower, that the latter emphatically agreed with "the principle of no forcible repatriation of Communist prisoners." (*New York Times*, November 20, 1952.)

was a four-power Repatriation Commission which would take charge of all prisoners on their release from military control, and would consist of two small powers nominated by each side (e.g., Czechoslovakia, Poland, Sweden, and Switzerland) plus an umpire who would be responsible for resolving deadlocks. Prisoners desiring to return to their homelands would be free to do so as soon as they had been registered and classified. The status of any prisoners who had *not* been returned home at the end of ninety days would be referred to the post-armistice "political conference" which was already provided for in another section of the draft armistice agreement.[15]

This ingenious proposal likewise failed to commend itself to the Kremlin. Quite unintentionally, however, it very nearly played into Moscow's hands by causing an open split among the principal non-Communist governments. As India's first full-dress contribution to the Korean debate since the rebuff administered to its mediation efforts in 1950,[16] the plan was one that obviously involved the prestige of the New Delhi government as well as its invincible faith in its peacemaking abilities. Recent messages from the Indian representative in Peking had created an impression in New Delhi that the Chinese Communists genuinely wanted an armistice; India had gone to great pains to try to remove the only obstacle that seemed to stand in the way. To dismiss this effort would be risking a serious affront to the Nehru government, irrespective of the merits of its plan for resolving the prisoner issue.

Yet the Indian draft resolution was not one that the United States felt able to support without substantial changes. Although it explicitly provided that "force shall not be used against prisoners of war to prevent or effect their return to their homelands," it seemed to the American delegation to fall considerably short of guaranteeing fair treatment to those prisoners who did not wish to be repatriated. The proposed Repatriation Commission did not look like a body that could function

---

[15] U.N. Document A/C.1/734, November 17, 1952 (text in *New York Times,* November 18, 1952).
[16] *The United States in World Affairs, 1950,* 225-229.

smoothly or protect the prisoners' interests effectively. Furthermore, the resolution was decidedly vague about what would ultimately happen to those prisoners who opted against repatriation. To hold them for future disposition by a hypothetical "political conference," American quarters felt, was equivalent to threatening them with permanent captivity and thus amounted to a form of pressure to accept repatriation.

These American misgivings were not fully shared by other non-Communist delegations, some of which not only felt that the Indian plan could be made workable but were much more reluctant to offend the Indian Government. British Foreign Secretary Eden, addressing the Political Committee on November 20, called the Indian proposal "timely and constructive" and agreed with the opinion expressed by the Indian delegate that it would be a mistake "to examine too legalistically every word and every phrase." Great Britain, Mr. Eden indicated, would support the plan if it could be amended in just two particulars: (1) in the interests of effective and impartial operation, the "umpire" should be made a full member and president of the Repatriation Commission; and (2) more explicit provision should be made for the welfare of nonrepatriated prisoners, whom the Indian plan tended to leave in a state of "suspended animation" but who were properly the responsibility of the United Nations.

Although these proposed modifications were in the direction favored by the United States, they still did not go far enough to meet the views of the American delegation. They still left open the possibility that the prisoner issue would merely be postponed for ninety days and then come up again at the post-armistice "political conference"; and, to the United States, that prospect was peculiarly repellent. The political conference was likely to face disagreements enough without being saddled with responsibility for tens of thousands of turbulent expatriates. As a minimum requirement, therefore, the United States was disposed to insist that referral to the political conference be ruled out, whether or not the Indian delegation consented to amend its resolution in that sense. Great Britain, on the other hand, was unwilling to insist on such modifications unless India was willing to accept them. On November 22 it was revealed that the United States and Great Britain were in open disagreement on the matter. American representatives, on direct instructions from Secretary Acheson, declared that they could not accept India's plan unless its "loopholes" were definitely plugged. Mr. Eden remained extremely reluctant to go along with the extensive changes on which this country insisted. Canada, France, and various other governments openly leaned toward the British position.

The consequences of this difference might have been more far-reaching had not succor appeared from an unexpected quarter. While the United States was laboring to hold the sponsors of the original twenty-one-power resolution in line and considering how far it must hold out for further modifications of the Indian draft, Mr. Vyshinsky had been awaiting instructions from Moscow as to the attitude he should adopt toward New Delhi's plan. Despite certain ominous portents in the Soviet press, many delegates had believed the Soviet reaction might be favorable. India had reported a positive, or at least noncommittal, reaction from Communist China: "There is nothing definite from China. Nothing definite means something good," Nehru had said on November 23.[17] The U.S.S.R., presumably, would not set itself directly against the wishes of its Chinese ally—especially when confronted with such a tempting opportunity to widen the incipient split among the non-Communist governments.

What was the general surprise, therefore, when Vyshinsky in his statement to the Political Committee on November 24 not only declined to endorse the Indian resolution but went out of his way to disparage it and insult the Indian delegate, V. K. Krishna Menon, and his government. "The draft resolution of the Indian delegation," he averred, "is designed not to put an end to the war but to perpetuate it . . . the Indian draft resolution is unsatisfactory and consequently unacceptable." Next day the New Delhi government received word from

[17] New York Times, November 24, 1952.

China that its proposal could not be accepted by the Peking authorities.[18]

This brusque rejection, though it apparently destroyed the last hope of an early truce in Korea, had the beneficial effect of healing the breach among the non-Communist delegations. The Indian delegate, though still hopeful of better news from China, had yielded to pleas from Britain and Canada in favor of a strengthened Repatriation Commission and a more adequate provision for unrepatriated prisoners; the United States, satisfied that its minimum conditions were being met, had decided to hold out no longer. In its final form the Indian resolution still provided that the status of any prisoners remaining unrepatriated at the end of ninety days would be referred to the political conference. If, however, the political conference failed to reach a decision within a further thirty days, responsibility for the care, maintenance, and subsequent disposition of any prisoners whose future was still unprovided for would rest with the United Nations, which would act "strictly in accordance with international law" in all matters relating to them. The twenty-one-power resolution having been quietly dropped, this text was overwhelmingly approved by the Political Committee on December 1. Two days later the full Assembly approved the modified Indian draft by a vote of 54-5, with only the Soviet bloc opposed and only Nationalist China abstaining;[19] it also rejected, by a smaller majority, the Polish-Soviet armistice plan still advocated by Mr. Vyshinsky.

The text of the Indian resolution was promptly cabled to Peking and Pyongyang, accompanied by a personal plea from the Assembly president, Lester B. Pearson of Canada. But with the U.S.S.R. flatly and publicly opposed, the chances of its acceptance by the Communists could hardly be considered bright. Already Peking had intimated through various channels that it stood by the Soviet Union and considered the Indian plan unacceptable. On December 14, Premier Chou En-lai publicly

[18] *New York Times*, November 25, 1952; *Journal of the Parliaments of the Commonwealth*, XXXIV, January 1953, 128.
[19] Resolution 610 (VII), adopted December 3, 1952, in *Documents on American Foreign Relations, 1952*, No. 35 (c).

reaffirmed this stand at great length in an official reply which termed the Indian resolution "illegal" and "unreasonable" and declared that it "runs counter to the conscience of man, completely violates humanitarian principles, international practice as well as the provisions of the Geneva Convention and the draft-armistice agreement." With the receipt of a similar reply from North Korea a few days later, the hopes that had inspired the Indian effort were at least temporarily laid to rest.[20]

Although these developments clearly did not improve the chances for an early peace in Korea, some observers were inclined to interpret the Assembly's overwhelming vote in favor of the Indian resolution as a diplomatic victory for the United States. India, it was pointed out, had received a rough but valuable lesson in the ways of Communist diplomacy; furthermore, for the first time in the Korean war, the entire bloc of Arab and Asian states had voted solidly on the same side as this country. In other respects, however, the United States had narrowly avoided a major diplomatic reverse. True, the Indian resolution had eventually been brought into conformity with the basic United States position. But the Arab-Asian states which voted for it had been displaying their solidarity with India, not with the United States. The Indian initiative had not only obliged this country to shelve its original (twenty-one power) plan but had threatened for some days to separate it from its closest allies. That this mishap was avoided could be attributed partly to Vyshinsky's rude intervention, which rendered the whole question somewhat academic; partly to the efforts of the British and Canadians to effect a compromise between the Indian and American viewpoints; and, of course, partly to the realism which induced the United States to go along with the majority as soon as it was satisfied that the Indian plan involved no departure from the basic principle of nonforcible repatriation.

Whether the Indian proposal had ever had a chance of ac-

[20] Mr. Pearson's report of the correspondence is U.N. Document A/2355, December 23, 1952; salient portions are reprinted in *Department of State Bulletin*, XXVIII, January 12, 1953, 74-78.

ceptance by the enemy depended on factors which were effectually hidden from the outside world. There had undoubtedly been indications from time to time that the Chinese and North Koreans, if not the Russians, would welcome any proposals that would enable them to liquidate the war without undue loss of "face." War weariness was thought to be rife in North Korea; a few months earlier, Premier Kim Il Sung had even been heard to suggest the desirability of an armistice that would leave neither victors nor vanquished.[21] On that occasion Peking had hastened to reaffirm its own intention to fight on to "final victory"; but in New Delhi, at any rate, it was believed that even the Chinese would not necessarily be deaf to offers that took account of their political position and aims. Nehru later revealed that an effort had been made to acquaint the Peking authorities in advance with the main provisions of the Indian resolution, but that no reply had been received.[22] Such an attitude seemed to admit of only two interpretations: either the Chinese Communist leaders found the American position on the prisoner issue (and on the other issues which would doubtless come up at the political conference) basically unacceptable; or they still felt compelled to subordinate their own interests to a larger Communist strategy directed from Moscow.

The attitude of the U.S.S.R. was likewise one that could only be guessed from somewhat fragmentary evidence. The tenacity with which Vyshinsky had fought the principle of "voluntary repatriation" suggested to some observers that the Kremlin was concerned with much more than the fate of a few thousand Chinese and Koreans. Moscow may have sympathized with Peking's fear that the Chinese prisoners, if not repatriated, might ultimately find their way into the armies of Chiang Kai-shek. Beyond that, moreover, it can hardly have wished to set a precedent that might encourage the defection of many thousands of its own troops in case of war with the West.

[21] *New York Times,* August 15, 1952.
[22] Statement to the House of the People, December 15, in *Journal of the Parliaments of the Commonwealth,* XXXIV, January 1953, 127.

Quite apart from its stand on the prisoner controversy, however, the Kremlin evidently continued to look on the Korean war as an enterprise that cost comparatively little in a material sense but still yielded considerable rewards. Soviet-made jet aircraft and other equipment were still being expended at a fairly liberal rate; but the men who were dying every day on "White Horse Hill," "Triangle Hill," and "Sniper Ridge" were Chinese and Koreans, not Russians. If there was little likelihood that the United Nations could be ousted from the peninsula, they could still be made to pay heavily for the position they maintained there. By December, total casualties sustained by the United Nations forces since the beginning of the war were estimated at 364,370 (including South Koreans), compared with 306,070 a year previously. United States battle casualties had climbed from 116,655 at the end of August to 128,238 at the end of December, and included 22,556 dead, 92,933 wounded, and 11,356 captured or missing.[23] Meanwhile the continuance of heavy fighting and occasional prisoner riots provided abundant material for anti-American propaganda and ensured that Korea would continue to be a sore spot in the politics of the free world.

This, of course, was the situation which had helped to make the Korean war a decisive issue in the American election, and which General Eisenhower had pledged his best efforts to remedy. While the United Nations Assembly was adopting the amended Indian resolution, the President-designate had been spending three crowded days in Korea in fulfillment of his campaign pledge to explore every possibility of bringing the war to an honorable end. His conclusion may have disappointed some voters who had placed exaggerated reliance on the magic of the General's personality; but it was reassuring to others who had feared lest he underestimate the complexity of the issue. "We have no panaceas, no trick ways of settling any

[23] The December 31 total for U.S. casualties included 1,393 previously missing but returned to military service. Total enemy casualties were estimated at 1,764,-940 as of December 13; enemy battle casualties were listed by the Defense Department as 1,299,961 as of December 1. (*New York Times*, September 4, 1952 and January 1 and 3, 1953.)

problems," he said at the conclusion of his Korean survey. "How difficult it seems to be in a war of this kind to work out a plan that would bring a positive and definite victory without possibly running the grave risk of enlarging the war." The impression that the next administration would endeavor to avoid this last eventuality—even though it might authorize more vigorous military action on various Far Eastern fronts—was strengthened a few days later when General Eisenhower, emerging from a conference with General MacArthur on the latter's personal plan for ending the war, emphasized once again the thesis that peace in Korea was not an isolated problem but was intimately related to peace in the world at large.[24]

Amid the general preoccupation with the military action in Korea and the unsuccessful diplomatic efforts at Panmunjom and in the United Nations, it was sometimes forgotten that there still remained one theoretical approach toward a Korean armistice which had not been and, presumably, would not be explored by either the old or the new administration. The disagreement over the exchange of prisoners had loomed so large in recent months that it was generally regarded as the essential barrier to an armistice. Few stopped to recall how closely Communist China's original intervention in the Korean conflict had been linked with its wider political demands, especially for representation in the United Nations and for the discontinuance of American support of Chiang Kai-shek. If the United States had been prepared to modify its basic position relative to the two Chinese governments, it was at least conceivable that it would have found Peking more amenable to a satisfactory disposition of the prisoner issue.

This possibility had not been overlooked in British Laborite circles, which often took a rather facile view of the political and ethical problems involved. "The war in Korea would be brought to an end in a few weeks," Aneurin Bevan had said, "if the great American people could be brought to see that they must recognize the Chinese Revolution as an accomplished

[24] *Ibid.,* December 6 and 18, 1952.

fact." [25] Even in the United States, so eminent a citizen as Supreme Court Justice William O. Douglas still advocated an attempt to reach "a political settlement with Red China" as "the only *peaceful* way of getting the Chinese Army out of Korea and of unifying that nation." [26] Justice Douglas emphasized, however, that the price of a settlement would be too high if it involved the delivery of Formosa to the Communists, an act which, he said, would make the West "accomplice to the murder of millions of people."

No such political settlement was likely to be sought in any case, since any political concessions to Communist China would run directly counter to the current American concept of appeasement. Far from being delivered to the Communists, Formosa and the Nationalist Government seemed likely to play an increasingly prominent role in future American policy for the Far East; President Chiang Kai-shek was already beginning to intimate that in another year his forces would be ready to reinvade the Chinese mainland. Continued support of the Nationalist Government had been a deliberate choice of the United States, in which the majority of Americans apparently concurred. Yet it would have been unrealistic not to recognize that this preference, fully justified though it might be, played an identifiable part in the difficulties with which the United States was struggling in Korea and throughout the Far East.

The burden the United States had assumed in the Far East was undeniably a heavy one, in political as well as military terms. Before the General Assembly recessed on December 22, the Soviet Union had contrived once again to place this country in the dock and force it, under the most painful conditions, to justify its actions in Korea before the entire United Nations. On December 14, the very day when Communist China formally rejected the Indian resolution, violence had flared on a large scale among the inmates of a United Nations internment camp on Pongam Island off Korea's south coast. Confronted

[25] *Ibid.*, November 24, 1952.
[26] William O. Douglas, "The Choice in Korea: Recognize or Crush Red China," *Look*, XVI, No. 27, December 30, 1952, 14.

with what looked like a mass break-out attempt by some 3,600 captives—mainly Korean guerrillas and Communist civilians— American and South Korean guards opened fire, killing eighty-two and wounding 120, five of whom later died. Such occurrences, even though deliberately staged on orders from Communist higher authority, inevitably created a bad impression throughout the world. But the sharp criticisms immediately voiced in Britain and other non-Communist countries were as nothing to the violence with which the Russians chose to exploit the issue in the closing hours of the General Assembly.

Having completed a substantial portion of its scheduled business, the Assembly had planned to recess on December 21 and continue the session after the Eisenhower administration took office. Vyshinsky and other delegates had already departed. But in the middle of the night of December 20-21, United Nations authorities received an urgent communication from Andrei Gromyko demanding that the Assembly immediately consider an additional agenda item—"The mass murder of Korean and Chinese prisoners of war by United States armed forces on the island of Pongam." This "shabby midnight propaganda stunt," as United States delegate Ernest A. Gross called it, was to keep the Assembly in session until 4:45 a.m. on December 22, a fact which naturally caused irritation among homeward-bound delegates. Their annoyance, moreover, was not directed exclusively against the Soviet Union, the government directly responsible for the inconvenience. As on similar occasions in the past, there was also evidence of some dissatisfaction with the United States as the country whose management of affairs in Korea had once again exposed the United Nations to a political tornado.

The draft resolution on the affair which Gromyko offered for the Assembly's consideration—a text reeking with expressions like "inhuman brutalities" and "systematic extermination" —obviously had no chance of passage. When the voting took place toward dawn on the 22nd, it mustered only the five affirmative votes of the Soviet bloc. But the significance of the

Soviet maneuver lay not in its foreseeable outcome but in the mere fact that the United States was once again being placed on the defensive in circumstances which, unfortunately, could not possibly add to its prestige or moral standing. Whatever credit this country had gained by its humanitarian stand in the matter of prisoner repatriation threatened to be offset by the discredit the U.S.S.R. was once again heaping upon its whole record of prisoner administration.

The explanations of the Pongam incident presented by the American delegates were factual and should have been entirely convincing. They showed fairly clearly that the riot, synchronized with Peking's rebuff to the governments which had voted for the Indian resolution, "was part of a conspiracy and a design which was undoubtedly related to the actions taken by the Assembly." [27] But nothing the United States delegates might say could restore life to the eighty-two slain rioters. Such loss of life in itself was a "grave matter," the British spokesman remarked; and others among the forty-five delegates who opposed the Soviet resolution evinced considerable unhappiness about the merits of the case and urged that the matter be fully investigated.

Most noteworthy, perhaps, was the attitude of India and other Asian-Arab states, which had endorsed the United States position in the resolution of December 3 but now reverted to their normal aloofness. "We do not believe that our unity can be broken or undermined by acts of lying desperation such as those we have witnessed here," Ambassador Gross had said. Yet despite the violence of the Soviet resolution and of Mr. Gromyko's supporting comments, ten Arab-Asian delegates declined to vote in defense of the United States. By abstaining on the Soviet resolution these countries—Afghanistan, Burma, Egypt, India, Indonesia, Iran, Pakistan, Saudi Arabia, Syria, and Yemen—emphasized once more the independent position they had established and maintained in all the business of the Assembly.

[27] *Department of State Bulletin*, XXVIII, January 5, 1953, 16-20.

2. Continents on the March

To the Asian diplomats who refused to censure Gromyko's "knock on the door at midnight," Korean matters had not necessarily been the most vital part of the Assembly's business. The ten states which they represented were the sturdiest adherents of that group of some dozen or fifteen nations, commonly referred to as the Arab-Asian or Asian-African bloc,[28] whose members were distinguished by their independent slant on various matters beside the East-West conflict. Most of these governments tended to build their foreign policies around two broad aims quite distinct from those of the Western powers: first, the maintenance of an independent international status in which they would not be adjuncts of either of the two leading power blocs, but would be free to act in a way that might tend to mitigate the existing division of the world into two camps; second, continuing, active prosecution of the battle against "colonialism" and Western "imperialism," which they had substantially won in their own lands but professedly intended to go on fighting until it was liquidated throughout the world.

The foreign policy of India, to which other members of the group normally looked for leadership, was based on a clear and self-conscious formulation of these aims. Other Arab-Asian states tended to act on the same principles even though their philosophic basis had been less fully thought out. The former of the two aims had quite obviously inspired the Indian resolution on Korea, with which all regular members of the Arab-Asian group had quickly associated themselves. The second just as clearly underlay what many of these states considered the main business of the Assembly's session, the attack on "colonialism," racial discrimination, and other practices which

[28] The 12 states which most commonly voted together as an "Arab-Asian bloc" were Afghanistan, Burma, Egypt, India, Indonesia, Iran, Iraq, Lebanon, Pakistan, Saudi Arabia, Syria, and Yemen, occasionally joined by the Philippines and Thailand. The term "Asian-African bloc" designates all or most of these states plus Ethiopia and Liberia.

they associated with white rule in dependent areas and in the Union of South Africa. Some observers believed that the problems of South Africa, French North Africa, and "colonialism" generally had so dominated the outlook of Asian and African governments in this Assembly that their attitude on Korea had been largely governed by their success, or the lack of it, in promoting what they considered the rights of dependent and colored peoples. If this was true, the vote on Gromyko's resolution might reflect some dissatisfaction with the stand taken by the Western powers, including the United States, in these other matters which Asians and Africans took even more closely to heart.

The emergence within the General Assembly of a group of non-Communist governments which were held together largely by their disagreement with important phases of Western policy was a phenomenon which had thus far been regarded with comparative equanimity by the United States delegation, yet which seemed to justify real concern on the part of the United States and those of its partners who attached importance to the principle of solidarity among the non-Communist nations. This was all the more true because it had occurred at a time when American policy had been consciously directed toward building up the General Assembly as the most dependable organ of the United Nations. Opposition by the Arab-Asian nations could sharply reduce the effectiveness of American moves in the Assembly, the more so because the Arab-Asian position frequently evoked a certain sympathy on the part of other small countries in Africa and even in Latin America. Experience had shown that a combination of Asian, African, and Latin American states, together with the five votes of the Soviet bloc, could actually deprive this country of a working majority in the Assembly.

Aside from such parliamentary inconveniences, the situation was disquieting because it reflected conditions of very real and bitter conflict in many parts of the non-Communist world—conditions which, of course, were looked upon in Moscow as once important factor in what it hoped was the coming downfall of the West. Violent words in the General Assembly were directly related to violent deeds in Tunisia, Morocco, and South and East Africa. The deepening crisis in Kenya Colony, which had caused the British authorities to declare a state of general emergency and resort to mass arrests of suspected Mau Mau terrorists, added to the embitterment of debates in the Assembly's Fourth (Trusteeship) Committee; the assassination of a Tunisian Nationalist leader on December 5 helped to inflame still further the zeal of France's critics in the North African discussion. The growing irritation of the "anti-colonial" section of world opinion spelled danger not only for the orderly functioning of the United Nations but also for the world position of the Western powers as trustees of Western civilization. Braced against the Communist threat in Europe and Asia, the Western nations also faced what amounted to a full-scale, if largely nonviolent, revolt in areas where their supremacy had once been virtually unquestioned. Whether or not these two revolutionary forces—the Communist and the non-Communist—eventually coalesced, the combined attack from both sides of the Iron Curtain undoubtedly had placed the Western powers in a situation of exceptional difficulty.

Convinced that no compromise was possible with the antagonist behind the Iron Curtain, the United States had refused to take an equally pessimistic view of the conflict between its allies and the countries of the anticolonial bloc. Instead, this country had urged both parties to reconcile their differences peaceably and expeditiously so that all non-Communist peoples could join hands against the common Soviet peril. But this outlook was not fully shared either by the anticolonial group or by "colonial" governments like those of Great Britain, France, Belgium, and South Africa. The former insisted that the liquidation of "colonialism" must remain their first order of business. The latter maintained that it would be disastrous to give in to such demands by prematurely relinquishing their own responsibilities. Their own position, the colonial powers maintained, was legally and morally sound and must be upheld, as a matter of right and an essential element of their political and military strength.

Although controversies of this kind were finding their way into the United Nations with increasing frequency, the world organization was not ideally equipped to deal with them in spite of its avowed concern for the welfare and progress of dependent peoples. The primary function of the United Nations, in the eyes of its founders, had been the adjustment of disputes among individual states, not the accommodation of a quasi-revolutionary movement which in fact was sweeping over half a world and respected neither political boundaries nor legal and administrative forms. The powers of the Trusteeship Council and the General Assembly were too limited to deal effectively with such a movement; the Charter itself was so framed as to leave it very doubtful whether some of these matters were proper subjects of United Nations concern at all. Thus the insistence of the Arab-Asian nations on securing a hearing for their grievances raised basic questions of legality and policy. Was it permissible, and, if permissible, was it wise to involve the United Nations in such matters as the internal policies of the South African Government, the administration of France's North African dependencies, and the standards and practices prevailing in non-self-governing territories generally?

Many delegates, by no means confined to the Arab-Asian bloc, considered it both permissible and wise. The mere proposal of such items for the Assembly's 1952 agenda, said Hernán Santa Cruz, the representative of Chile, revealed the existence of "a veritable world revolution" whose causes and repercussions had never yet been thoroughly examined by the United Nations. The Assembly, he said, had an obligation to look into this phenomenon more closely if it did not wish to lag behind the march of events and, moreover, to let this "revolution" develop in a direction that might lead "to conflicts and war among nations as well as to social conflicts and strife within nations." "This is an irresistible avalanche," Mr. Santa Cruz emphasized:

"the more quickly we take cognizance of these conditions the sooner shall we be in a position to adopt the only logical course to cope with them, which is to give these movements a peaceful character by satisfying legitimate demands and ensuring collaboration for the common good and general progress." [29]

The United States took a more hesitant position, one that showed the influence of its concern for legality and its desire to avoid unnecessary offense to the governments of either group. Admitting the interest of the United Nations in "encouraging and assisting peaceful and orderly transition toward self-government," Secretary Acheson warned the Assembly against forgetting that the primary responsibility still belonged to France, Britain, and the other powers directly concerned. The role of the General Assembly, he said,

"should in most situations of this kind be one of accommodation. These are not cases in which it is the function of the General Assembly to impose settlements upon the parties involved. Here it is rather the primary function of the United Nations to create an atmosphere favorable to settlements which accord with Charter principles but which should be worked out by the parties directly involved." [30]

It could hardly be maintained, however, that such an atmosphere had usually resulted from Assembly intervention in these matters—or that France, Great Britain, and other governments which were accustomed to hearing their policies attacked in most unconciliatory terms had any reason to desire the Assembly's assistance in adjusting relations with their dependent peoples. On the contrary, they took their stand directly on the letter of the United Nations Charter—particularly Article 2 (7), which forbade the United Nations "to intervene in matters which are essentially within the domestic jurisdiction of any state"—and insisted that the Assembly was overstepping its proper limits when it tried to interfere in the relations between governments and governed. South Africa's position in this respect had become well known through its walkouts and

[29] U.N. Document A/PV.379, October 16, 1952, 22.
[30] Address to the plenary session, October 16, in *Department of State Bulletin,* XXVII, October 27, 1952, 642.

similar tactics at previous Assembly sessions, and no one was surprised at its delegate's bitter, one-man fight against the proposals to censure his government's discriminatory policies within the Union. But Mr. Eden and M. Schuman, when they reached New York early in November, proved equally firm even if more diplomatic.

Great Britain, Mr. Eden assured the Assembly, was "very well aware of the wide desire for self-government in Asia and Africa."

"We have always respected these aspirations and we always shall. But we consider it a duty to protect the peoples of certain territories from becoming the sport of international politics. Their standard of life is rising steadily, and is already in some cases higher than that of some countries which most bitterly criticize the colonial Powers. . . . We are asked by some here to give up this work. Let me make our position clear: nothing will induce us to do so. . . .

". . . If we attempt to stretch the meaning of the Charter and extend the areas in which the United Nations has jurisdiction, we run grave risks—unless we can carry all our fellow Members with us—of weakening the very structure of the United Nations. . . . The object of our Organization is to promote general international co-operation and good feeling. It was never intended to be an agency for controlling the domestic policies of its various Members or for intervening between them and the territories for which they are internationally responsible." [31]

France's position, as defined by M. Schuman—with whom Mr. Eden said he fully agreed—was even plainer. It merited special attention, moreover, because it reflected so clearly the state of mind of a great power whose world position of late had been undermined from many directions. French convictions in the matter of Tunisia and Morocco were obviously no less strong than those of France's Arab-Asian critics. Weeks earlier, the French cabinet had unanimously decided that it must resist United Nations intervention to the limit, even to the point of denying recognition to any United Nations commission that might be set up to investigate conditions in the North African protectorates. Marshal Juin, former Resident-General in Mo-

[31] U.N. Document A/PV.393, November 11, 1952, 210.

rocco and now commander of the NATO land forces in Central Europe, had been quoted as recommending that France actually withdraw from the United Nations if the latter tried to interfere.[32] When the United States voted early in the Assembly's session to give the Moroccan and Tunisian items a favored spot on the agenda, French quarters had made no attempt to conceal the intensity of their dissatisfaction. The strain imposed on the relations between the United States and France was not the least of the untoward effects which the North African situation was exerting in world politics.

When M. Schuman came before the Assembly on November 10, he presented a good many facts and figures designed to illustrate the constructive role which France had played and, he said, intended to continue playing in the North African protectorates. It would be "a serious and unpardonable mistake," he declared, "if territories still imperfectly developed, for which [France] is now responsible in varying degrees, set themselves up as independent states before they were able to meet the heavy responsibilities which that would imply." Furthermore, he warned, intervention by the Assembly could have grave repercussions both outside and within the United Nations:

"The more I think of it, the more I am convinced that what is involved in this matter is not only North Africa, not only the interests of France—vital interests which France is entitled to protect and will protect with all its strength—but also a sound conception of the United Nations itself. The Organization is threatened by a distortion which would be pernicious to itself, to the Member States and to the cause of peace. . . .

". . . My Government declares itself compelled in all conscience to warn the Assembly against the consequences of an interference to which in no case and under no conditions could it consent. Consequently my Government can agree to discuss neither the principle nor the manner of such interference."

If the Assembly made the "fatal mistake" of trying to interfere in the North African situation, it would do so without France's participation or consent.[33]

[32] *New York Times*, October 18, 1952.
[33] U.N. Document A/PV.392, November 10, 1952, 198-199.

In certain important respects the position of the colonial powers and South Africa in these matters invited comparison with that of the Soviet Union on various "cold war" issues to which allusion has already been made. In resisting pressure to change their policies, they could base their position not only on a literal interpretation of the Charter but also on the fact that they still retained actual control of the territories under their jurisdiction. Led by the Asian-African bloc, the Assembly might exhort or condemn—provided the necessary votes were available. Its actions might even serve to encourage unrest in the territories in question, as France claimed they were doing in North Africa. But the Assembly could not directly alter the situation unless an accused government should voluntarily accept its advice. And, since the advice offered was generally of a kind that no accused government found it possible to accept, the immediate effect of the Assembly's actions in this field was not, after all, so very great.

Over a period of years or decades, however, the pressure of anticolonial sentiment seemed likely to result in revolutionary changes in many parts of the world. The General Assembly session of 1952, though only a minor incident in this broad process, was highly instructive in its revelation of clashing viewpoints and of the varying results achieved by the Asian-African bloc on different sectors of the anticolonial front. Where the Asian-African states were united among themselves and gained the support of Latin-American sympathizers, they seemed irresistible. Where these conditions did not obtain, they still were unable to impose their views on the Assembly as a whole, let alone on the colonial powers.

During the first eight weeks of the Assembly session— through the week of December 1, which began with a committee vote in favor of the Indian plan for Korea and ended with the adoption of two resolutions condemning South African racial policies—the Asian-African crusade appeared to be carrying everything before it. A coalition of Asian-African and Latin-American delegates, often supported by the Soviet bloc, virtually dominated the Assembly's Trusteeship Committee;

in the Ad Hoc Political Committee, a similar combination had been working over the South African situation with scant regard for the sensibilities of the South African delegate or for the appeals to moderation voiced by the United States and various European delegations.

Two resolutions on the South African situation were approved by the committee and adopted by the Assembly on December 5. The first, sponsored by fifteen Asian-African states, recalled South Africa's noncompliance with the Assembly's earlier admonitions concerning its treatment of persons of Indian origin in the Union and provided for the setting up of a new Good Offices Committee to facilitate a settlement of the problem by direct negotiation among South Africa, India, and Pakistan. Despite the South African delegate's warning that his government would not cooperate in this procedure any more than it had done on earlier occasions, the resolution was adopted in plenary session by a vote of 41-1, with 15 abstentions. South Africa cast the lone dissenting vote; both the United States and the Soviet bloc voted with the majority, while Britain, France, and the other colonial powers abstained in token of their disapproval.[34]

The proposal to examine the whole question of South African racial policies, as an alleged threat to international peace and a violation of the principles of human rights, had even broader backing—four Latin-American states were included among the eighteen sponsors—but gained fewer supporters in the Assembly. The United States, which had not opposed a fresh approach to the problem of Indians in South Africa, was among the numerous governments which recoiled from the proposal to establish a three-man commission "to study the racial situation in the Union of South Africa in the light of the purposes and principles of the Charter." While disagreeing with the South African contention that the whole matter was outside the jurisdiction of the United Nations, this country was nevertheless opposed to any attempt at direct intervention.

[34] Resolution 615 (VII), adopted December 5, 1952, in *Documents on American Foreign Relations, 1952*, No. 35 (d).

It favored instead a compromise plan, broached by the four Scandinavian countries, whereby the Assembly would have contented itself with a general statement in favor of racial equality. But despite the abstention of the United States, Britain, and twenty-one other countries, the resolution to set up a study commission passed the Assembly by a majority of 35-1.[35] Again South Africa's dissenting vote emphasized the prospect that it would refuse to cooperate in the procedure prescribed by the Assembly.

These two votes on South Africa, neither of which seemed likely to lead to an improvement in the actual situation in the Union, marked the high tide of Arab-Asian success at this session of the Assembly. Delegates of the Arab-Asian-African bloc had some reason to congratulate themselves over their record of accomplishment thus far and the prospects which seemingly still lay before them. "Africa and Asia are on the march," declared Mme. Vijaya Lakshmi Pandit, the head of the Indian delegation, "and they will no longer accept the indignities imposed on them in the name of a white civilization." [36] In a broad sense, this was doubtless true; but Mme. Pandit may nevertheless have overestimated the ability of the Asian-African group to impress its views on the rest of the Assembly. During the important two weeks that remained before the midwinter recess, it would be on more difficult ground where failures would be at least as frequent as successes.

The exuberance of the Arab-Asian states was momentarily checked by a meeting of the Security Council on the Kashmir problem (December 8) at which Mme. Pandit found herself denouncing the policies of another Asian government, Pakistan, as vigorously as she had denounced those of the Malan regime in South Africa. Another reminder of differences within the

[35] Resolution 616 (VII), adopted December 5, 1952, in *Documents on American Foreign Relations, 1952*, No. 35 (e). The Scandinavian text was approved as part B of the same resolution by the smaller vote of 24-1-34. Consideration of a third South African problem, the status of South West Africa, was later postponed to the Eighth Session of the Assembly.
[36] U.N. Document A/PV.401, December 5, 1952, 336.

anticolonial bloc was the commencement of discussions on Palestine, an issue on which only the Moslem states formed a reasonably cohesive group. More important was the evaporation of some of the outside support which had been available to the Asian-African bloc while South Africa was under chastisement. Some of the coming issues, including those of French North Africa, were open to wider variations of opinion; and France, though it had refused to take part in the Assembly's debate on the North African items, had seized the opportunity to do some effective lobbying among the Latin-American governments. Experience in the North African case was to show that without substantial Latin-American support the Asian-African group still tended to find itself seriously outnumbered.

The unfavorable impression caused in New York by France's determination to boycott the Assembly's debates on Tunisia and Morocco had not been lessened by news of conditions in the protectorates. French proposals envisaging different degrees of home rule had already been rejected by the native rulers in both Tunisia and Morocco; and the effervescence in both areas had increased as the moment for debate in the Assembly approached. On December 5, one day after the Political Committee began consideration of the Tunisian item, the bullet-riddled corpse of the one important Tunisian nationalist leader who was not already in prison was discovered on a Tunisian highway. An immediate general strike by Tunisian workers ensued, but prompt action by the French averted major disturbances, and the most serious repercussions were actually felt not in Tunisia but in Morocco. There, rioting flared in Casablanca and rapidly assumed dangerous proportions; on December 8, a regular pitched battle resulted in anywhere from fifty to over 100 deaths. Within a week of the first outbreaks, the French army and police forces had rounded up well over 1,200 Moroccan suspects, arresting both Communist and nationalist leaders in what seemed a rather transparent, though unsuccessful, attempt to suggest that the disturbances were largely of Communist origin.

These tragic events cannot be said to have dampened the

ardor of the Asian-African representatives in New York, but may have helped to convince some other delegations that so explosive a situation required delicate handling. The case against French rule in Tunisia was vigorously presented by Sir Mohammed Zafrullah Khan of Pakistan and others; but on December 10 the Asian-Africans encountered an important setback when the Political Committee rejected Pakistan's request that the Bey of Tunis be invited to send a representative to take part in the debate. This proposal was strongly resisted by the United States, among others, as being incompatible with the Bey's treaty obligations and quite unlikely to contribute to a peaceful settlement of the problem. In the American view, Philip C. Jessup reminded the committee, the Assembly's task was not to dictate the course of events but merely "to try to create an atmosphere in which negotiations between France and Tunisia can proceed in a calm and forward-looking manner." [37] Twenty-six delegates, including those of the colonial powers and many Latin-American states, indicated by their votes that they shared this view; the Pakistani proposal garnered only the twenty-four votes cast by the delegates of the Asian-African bloc, the Soviet bloc, Bolivia, Chile, Guatemala, Yugoslavia, and Nationalist China.

A somewhat similar alignment determined the fate of the two substantive proposals on North Africa which the Arab-Asian bloc had introduced. The thirteen-nation draft resolution on Tunisia sharply criticized the situation existing in the protectorate and urged France not only to reestablish normal conditions but also to resume negotiations with "the true representatives of the Tunisian people" (i.e., the nationalists) in order to implement their "right of self-determination" and fulfill their "national aspirations." Discounting the announced attitude of the French Government, the draft resolution further provided for a United Nations Good Offices Committee which would be charged with the task of assisting negotiations and

[37] Statement of December 10, 1952, in *Department of State Bulletin*, XXVIII, January 5, 1953, 34-35.

reporting back to the Assembly.[38] But only twenty-four delegates were willing to support this far-reaching motion—the
Asian-Africans, the Soviet bloc, Guatemala, Yugoslavia, and
again Nationalist China. After the resolution had been defeated in committee on December 12, most of its supporters
(except the Soviet bloc) rallied to a milder alternative which
had meanwhile been suggested by eleven Latin-American states.
This text offered no direct criticism of France but expressed
confidence that that country, "in pursuance of its proclaimed
policies," would "endeavor to further the effective development
of the free institutions of the Tunisian people"; further, it
voiced the hope for continued negotiations "on an urgent basis
with a view to bringing about self-government for Tunisians." [39] In the final vote on December 17, the Latin-American
draft was adopted by 44-3, with eight abstentions. Of the
colonial and North Atlantic powers, six, including the United
States, voted favorably; three opposed the resolution on principle; three abstained, together with the Soviet bloc. France
did not participate.

Two days later the Assembly approved a similar compromise
resolution on Morocco, sponsored by the same eleven Latin-
American states, by an almost identical majority. The previous
history of the Moroccan resolution had also been similar except
that the Arab-Asians, foreseeing the defeat of their own draft
resolution (which called for an early peaceful settlement in
accordance with "the sovereignty of Morocco, the aspirations
of her people and the Charter of the United Nations"),[40] had
narrowly failed to amend the Latin-American draft in accordance with their own ideas. Originally the Latin-American resolution had made no allusion to self-government but referred
only to "the fundamental liberties" and "free political institutions" of the people of Morocco and to "legitimate rights and
interests under the established norms and practices of the law

[38] U.N. Document A/C.1/736, December 2, 1952.
[39] Resolution 611 (VII), adopted December 17, 1952, in *Documents on American Foreign Relations, 1952*, No. 35 (f).
[40] U.N. Document A/C.1/L.12, December 15, rejected by Committee I on December 17, 1952.

of nations"; but in the course of committee debate the Arab-Asians managed to include an amendment submitted by Pakistan which categorically demanded "self-government for Moroccans." [41] In the plenary session the United States and the other advocates of moderation succeeded in restoring the resolution to its original form. [42]

Both the Tunisian and Moroccan resolutions also appealed to the parties to settle their disputes in accordance with the spirit of the Charter and refrain from "any acts or measures likely to aggravate the present tension." The French, for their part, were equally anxious to see the disputes settled, though not necessarily in the manner envisaged by their critics in the Assembly. In Paris, the defeat of the Arab-Asian program was rightly interpreted as a defeat for the nationalist movement within the protectorates, and thus as an opportunity for the vigorous reassertion of French control. The Istiqlal in Morocco had already been crippled as a result of the Casablanca riots; most of the Tunisian leaders were also in confinement, and it was safe to assume that the Bey, too, would have been considerably shaken by the disappointment of his hopes for stronger United Nations action. On December 18, accordingly, Paris seized the opportunity to send the Bey a peremptory note, widely described as an ultimatum, insisting that he institute immediately certain of the internal reforms which he had hitherto rejected as inadequate. Faced with the alternatives of compliance or possible removal, the Bey capitulated and on December 20 signed two decrees providing for elections to the hitherto appointive municipal and district assemblies in the protectorate. This diplomatic victory for France would not solve the underlying problems of French rule in North Africa, but promised at least to hold back for a few weeks or months

---

[41] U.N. Document A/C.1/L.13, December 16, as amended by A/C.1/L.14, December 16, and adopted by the committee by 40-5-11 on December 17, 1952. The vote on the Pakistani amendment was 28-23-4.

[42] Resolution 612 (VII), adopted December 19, 1952, in *Documents on American Foreign Relations, 1952,* No. 35 (g). The vote on the key paragraph was 29-8-22; the resolution as a whole was adopted by 45-3-11.

the movement which some delegates to the Assembly were describing as an "irresistible avalanche."

If France and South Africa had borne the brunt of the Asian-African attack in the Assembly's two political committees, in the Fourth or Trusteeship Committee they shared the dock with Belgium, Australia, New Zealand, the United Kingdom, and to some extent the United States. It was this committee that annually reviewed the record of all governments which administered dependent territories, whether under the United Nations trusteeship system or on their own responsibility; and neither the energy of the prosecution nor the stubborness of the defense was lessened by the fact that in 1952 other aspects of the case against colonialism were being tried in other courtrooms.

The doctrine that animated the anticolonial group in all these matters had been succinctly stated by Sir Zafrullah Khan in the debate on North Africa: Even good government, he had remarked, was no substitute for self-government. The prevailing view in his part of the world seemed to be that the existing governments in dependent areas were not good and could not be too rapidly supplanted through the exercise of the "right of self-determination" by their inhabitants. The tendency to take a dark view of existing conditions was strengthened by the accounts of spokesmen for various native African organizations who were invited to appear before the committee and encouraged to expound their grievances against the administering authorities.

But here, too, the Asian-African states and their sympathizers from Latin America failed to put across their entire program, despite the fact that they usually received the support of the five Soviet-bloc delegations. Too many governments found themselves in the same position as the United States—sympathetic to the theory of colonial self-government, but realistically aware of the unpreparedness of many dependent peoples to govern themselves; anxious to retain the good will of the anticolonial countries, but bound by ties of interest and loyalty to the countries that were actually struggling with the responsibilities of colonial administration. In this dilemma, the United States and a number of European and Latin-American governments refrained from voting consistently with either bloc but endeavored to judge each issue on what seemed to be its realistic merits. The result was a record that testified largely to the dissatisfaction of the anticolonial bloc but revealed that the administering states, too, had both staying power and a case which was not entirely unrecognized by the Assembly.

Few of the fourteen resolutions eventually adopted by the Assembly on the reports of the Fourth Committee [43] require detailed comment in this broad survey. Their general tendency was to encourage maximum educational, economic, and social progress in trust and other non-self-governing territories and to give the indigenous inhabitants a chance to participate directly in measures taken for their benefit. Two or three of them were adopted, largely at the instance of the United States, in a form that fell considerably short of the aims of the anticolonial states. Among the initiatives which this country helped to oppose were (1) a motion to censure Great Britain for removing certain tribesmen from their lands in the Tanganyika trust territory, and (2) a demand for the unification of British and French Togoland under a single trusteeship administration in accordance with the wishes expressed by spokesmen for the Ewe people, whose territory the existing frontier bisected. On the other hand, American opposition failed to prevent the adoption of a resolution by which the Assembly appeared to claim a voice in determining whether or not particular territories were to be considered non-self-governing at all.[44]

Possibly the most significant argument in this general field concerned the future of the Assembly's Committee on Information from Non-Self-Governing Territories, which had become the principal instrument for the expression of United Nations interest in those dependent areas that were not included in the trusteeship system and thus were not directly subject to United

[43] Resolutions 643 (VII)-656 (VII), adopted December 10, 20, and 21, 1952.
[44] Resolution 648 (VII), adopted December 10, 1952 by 36-15-7.

Nations supervision. First set up in 1946 and reestablished for a three-year term in 1949, this committee was nominally concerned only with reviewing information submitted by governments, but had been viewed with high hopes by the anticolonial group—and with consistent misgivings by the administering states—as an entering wedge for the assertion of real international authority over all non-self-governing territories. In pursuance of this concept, the Fourth Committee decided on November 8 to recommend that the Committee on Information be established virtually on a permanent basis—i.e., for three years and automatically thereafter (unless the Assembly decided otherwise) "for as long as there exist Territories whose peoples have not yet attained a full measure of self-government." [45] But on this issue the administering powers decided to make a firm stand. When the matter came before the plenary session on December 10, France, Belgium, and Great Britain reminded the Assembly that their governments did not share the prevailing view concerning United Nations responsibility in this field. If the Committee were extended for more than three years at this time, they warned, their governments would be unable to participate in its work. Faced with an ultimatum which would have reduced the committee to complete futility, twenty-nine delegates changed their minds. The committee was extended for another three years, with provision for a reexamination of the whole question in 1955.[46]

But the anticolonial group had still another means of bringing its views to world attention. As an outgrowth of the debate on human rights in the last Assembly and in the Commission on Human Rights, a resolution on "The Right of Peoples and Nations to Self-Determination" had been in preparation in another of the Assembly's committees. As submitted to the plenary session on December 16, it included a categorical demand that all members of the United Nations should "recognize and promote" the exercise of the right of self-determina-

[45] U.N. Document A/2296, Resolution IV, approved by a committee vote of 40-12-2. The vote on the key paragraph was 23-16-15.
[46] Resolution 646 (VII), adopted December 10, 1952 by 53-2-3. The plenary vote in favor of indefinite continuance of the committee was 11-18-30.

tion in non-self-governing and trust territories, and should ascertain the wishes of the peoples concerned "through plebiscites and other recognized democratic means, preferably under the auspices of the United Nations." This again seemed to the administering powers, including the United States, as an unwarranted intrusion on their field of responsibility. But here they were unable to sway the majority. The offending text was adopted by a vote of 40-14, with six abstentions; among the majority were seventeen of the twenty Latin-American states.[47]

The dependence of the Asian-African bloc on Latin-American support came out even more clearly in the debate on the Palestine problem, which was also regarded, by the Arab governments at least, as a phase of their battle against Western "imperialism." The annual discussion of Palestine affairs, though it regularly generated intense heat in the Assembly, had as regularly failed to produce any visible improvement in the tense situation that still surrounded Israel, its Arab neighbors, and the 800,000-odd Arab refugees uprooted by the fighting in 1948–1949. Early in the Seventh Session, the Assembly had agreed without difficulty that the reestablishment of the refugees in the economic life of the Near East was going to take longer than had been hoped, and would require a reallocation of the funds budgeted for relief and long-term "reintegration." [48] On the political problems of a Palestine peace, however, the Assembly was faced with a discouraging report from its own Palestine Conciliation Commission and could find few grounds for optimism in more recent reports from the area.

Amid a bewildering variety of resolutions and a whirlwind of charges and countercharges by the Arab and Israeli delegations, the main questions before the Seventh Assembly appeared to be (1) how it could best encourage a commencement

[47] Resolution 637 (VII), adopted December 16, 1952, in *Documents on American Foreign Relations, 1952,* No. 36 (a). Section B of this resolution, asking administering states to make progress reports on self-determination to the United Nations, was approved by 39-12-5, again with the U.S. opposed.
[48] Resolution 614 (VII), adopted November 6, 1952. For background cf. above, p. 240.

of direct peace negotiations between the Arab states and Israel, and (2) how far it should insist on the fulfillment of recommendations approved at earlier sessions which had called, among other things, for the assignment of the larger part of Palestine to the Arabs, the repatriation and resettlement of the Palestine refugees who had fled from Israel, and the establishment of a permanent international regime for Jerusalem and the Holy Places.[49] Israel, having disregarded these recommendations and succeeded in establishing itself as an ethnically homogeneous state whose provisional frontiers included the modern city of Jerusalem, took the position that the Assembly's past resolutions were obsolete and that peace negotiations should start from the situation that now existed. The Arab states, on the other hand, insisted that they would negotiate only on the basis of previous Assembly resolutions, which they, too, had often disregarded in the past but now supported because they were much less favorable to Israel than the existing situation.

In conformity with this preference, the Arab delegations supported a proposal introduced by four Asian states which called in effect for a reorganization and continuation of the Palestine Conciliation Commission and the encouragement of negotiations on the basis of past resolutions.[50] In view of Israel's strong de facto position, however, most delegates had come to believe that there was no real prospect of a settlement being effected along these lines. Many of them felt that the important thing was to get the two sides together for direct negotiations without insisting too much on the unenforceable decisions of the past. This was the main objective of an eight-power draft resolution, introduced by Norway on behalf of a variety of NATO and Latin-American states, which merely "recalled" earlier resolutions without explicitly reaffirming

[49] Especially Resolutions 181 (II), adopted November 29, 1947; 194 (III), adopted December 11, 1948; and 303 (IV), adopted December 9, 1949; for background cf. especially *The United States in World Affairs, 1949*, 405-410.
[50] U.N. Document A/AC.61/L.25, December 3, sponsored by Afghanistan, Indonesia, Iran, and Pakistan but disapproved by the Ad Hoc Committee on December 11, 1952 by a vote of 14-27-13.

them and which, after various amendments, received committee approval on December 13.[51] Once again, it seemed, the Arab-Asians were about to be thwarted by a combination which included the United States, most of the NATO and "colonial" powers, and a majority of the Latin-American states.

But once again the Arab-Asian bloc rallied—aided, this time, by a newspaper report which strengthened the impression that Israel was disinclined to make major concessions in any of the matters in dispute.[52] In the plenary session on December 18, eight delegates who had supported the resolution in committee changed their position and the resolution received only 24 affirmative votes, to 21 opposed and 15 abstentions. This was far less than the two-thirds majority required for adoption; and it was evident that one decisive factor had been a switch by several Latin-American delegates who were especially concerned for Catholic interests in the Jerusalem area. Their change of heart not only prevented the Assembly from taking any stand on the troubled Palestine issue but emphasized once again the influential position which the Latin-American states were acquiring as arbiters between the Arab-Asian and the NATO-colonial powers.

3. The Burdens of Hospitality

Most of the Latin-American delegations had thus far refrained from committing themselves to an all-out "anti-imperialist" or "anti-Western" position on the problems of Asia, the Near East, and Africa. But there were other matters of interest to the Assembly in which their opposition to the orthodox Western approach was more clear-cut. This was conspicuously true of questions in the economic and social field, especially those concerned with the extension of basic human rights and the status of economically underdeveloped territories. In matters of this kind, moreover, the United States was unable to stand on the sidelines as it still did to some extent in the debate

[51] U.N. Document A/2310, December 15, 1952, approved by 32-13-13.
[52] Dispatch by C. L. Sulzberger, in *New York Times*, December 15, 1952.

on colonial issues. It was an ironic fact that the position of this country, which had been a prime leader in the human rights movement and the originator of the Point Four program, had actually become a source of loudly voiced dissatisfaction among non-Communists as well as Communists on three continents.

The more controversial phases of United Nations discussion on economic development problems had hitherto centered around (1) the admitted need of the underdeveloped countries for large amounts of new investment capital, and (2) the insistence of the United States that the way to obtain it was not by setting up new agencies for the distribution of American public funds but by creating a "climate" which would be more attractive to *private* investors, both American and foreign.[53] This position was realistically attuned to the views of the American business community and to the fiscal position of the United States Government, which plainly was not able to provide really substantial funds for investment in underdeveloped countries in addition to its obligations for defense and military aid. Unfortunately, however, the emphasis on the role of private capital, coupled with the insistence on creating improved conditions for foreign private enterprise in the underdeveloped countries, ran directly athwart the dominant "anti-imperialist" trend in these countries themselves. There the tendency was not to increase but to limit the role of private foreign capital, as part of the general movement to shake off "imperialist" influence and gain direct control of national resources. Iran's treatment of the Anglo-American Oil Company and Bolivia's nationalization of its American-owned tin mines reflected an attitude that was actually becoming more and more prevalent in the underdeveloped countries of both hemispheres.

This attitude found strong expression during the first half

[53] This view was authoritatively restated in *Guidelines for Point 4: Recommendations of the International Development Advisory Board*, June 5, 1952, in *Documents on American Foreign Relations, 1952*, No. 3 (c). Cf. also the speech of Isador Lubin to the Assembly's Second (Economic) Committee (October 30) in *Department of State Bulletin*, XXVII, November 17, 1952, 779-785.

of the Assembly session in resolutions sponsored by under-developed countries with the object of reaffirming their desire for public financing of economic development and, in addition, striking another blow in what many of them considered their long-term battle against foreign private enterprise. The major resolution on financing economic development specifically re-affirmed the Assembly's interest in two projects toward which the United States, as the only prospective source of develop-ment capital on a large scale, was lukewarm at most. One was a special international development fund "for grants-in-aid and for low interest, long-term loans to under-developed coun-tries for the purpose of helping them, at their request, to accelerate their economic development and to finance non-self-liquidating projects which are basic to their economic develop-ment." The other was an "international finance corporation" to contribute to economic development through "the financing of productive private enterprise in underdeveloped countries"—in other words, by providing foreign capital without foreign control.[54] This resolution was not directly opposed by the United States. The American delegate, after citing the consider-able accomplishments already achieved through foreign pri-vate investment in recent years, confined himself to a reminder that this method of stimulating the flow of investment was not viewed with favor by the one country that might theoretically have been capable of implementing it.

The second resolution, though couched in general terms, could be interpreted as directly critical of the United States as well as neglectful of justice and legality. First introduced by Uruguay and sharpened by a Bolivian amendment, its original text asserted that members of the United Nations not only should recognize the right of each country to nationalize and freely exploit its national wealth as an essential factor of economic independence, but should also refrain from using their governmental and administrative agencies "as instruments of coercion or political or economic intervention"—which sounded like a rebuke to the United States Reconstruction

[54] Resolution 622 (VII), parts A and B, adopted December 21, 1952 by 52-0-5.

Finance Corporation for its insistence on setting a low import price on Bolivian tin. No suggestion was made, on the other hand, that countries which desired to nationalize their resources had any obligation to abide by international law and agreements or respect the foreign rights and interests involved; and an amendment in this sense proposed by the United States was rejected by the heavy vote of 28-17, with five abstentions.

On this occasion India chose to exercise its conciliatory talents to narrow the differences within the non-Communist group. The resolution was softened into a recommendation to member states to "refrain from acts, direct or indirect, designed to impede the exercise of the sovereignty of any State over its natural resources"; in this form it passed the relevant committee by a vote of 31-1, with the United States still opposed and nineteen delegations abstaining. In the plenary session the Assembly approved a further amendment by India, citing "the need for maintaining the flow of capital in conditions of security, mutual confidence and economic co-operation among nations." The final vote was 36 in favor (15 Asian-African, 15 Latin-American, and 6 Communist states); 4 opposed (United States, United Kingdom, New Zealand, and South Africa); and 16 abstentions (including 10 NATO members and 5 Latin Americans).[55]

In the field of human rights, the Seventh Assembly witnessed no direct conflict between Western and majority views. The contentious issue of the draft covenants on political-civil and economic-social rights was bottled up for the moment in the Human Rights Commission; and no delegate ventured to oppose the Assembly's approval of a draft convention on the Political Rights of Women which aimed at ensuring equal political rights for the softer sex in all countries that chose to ratify it.[56] In the allied field of freedom of information, how-

[55] Resolution 626 (VII), adopted December 21, 1952, in *Documents on American Foreign Relations, 1952,* No. 36 (c). Also adopted against the advice of the U.S. was Resolution 623 (VII), December 21, 1952, originally proposed by Argentina, which recommended various types of official action aimed at ensuring better terms of trade for raw material-producing countries. The vote was 35-15-9.

[56] Resolution 640 (VII), adopted December 20, 1952 by a vote of 46-0-11.

ever, the United States continued to fare badly at the hands of
a coalition—chiefly made up of underdeveloped and "anticolonial" countries, though headed, rather paradoxically, by
France—which frankly did not share this country's interest in
promoting the free circulation of news and ideas in the present
stage of the world's affairs.

American hopes of securing agreement on a positive convention on freedom of information had already been abandoned in view of the insistence of these governments on encumbering it with reservations and restrictions of various kinds.
The efforts of the American delegation at the 1952 session
were aimed primarily at discouraging the Assembly from taking any further action in this field until some "new approach"
had been discovered. But by this time the restrictionist bloc
had gone over to the offensive. Thus American admonitions
failed to prevent them from disinterring and opening for signature the old Convention on the International Right of Correction, which had thus far been successfully opposed by the
English-speaking countries because of its many bureaucratic
limitations on the freedom of journalistic enterprise.[57]

In case this selective record should seem to overemphasize
the occasions when United States views were disregarded by
the Assembly and to ignore the more numerous instances in
which the American position coincided with that of the majority, it must be remembered that it was generally the points
of disagreement within the non-Communist world that loomed
largest in the thinking of the Soviet rulers, the non-Communist
governments, and, not least, the American public. And the
over-all record of the Seventh Assembly in its deliberations on
political, economic, and social matters was not one to reassure
those Americans who sensed that world opinion as reflected in
the United Nations was tending to move in unfamiliar and

[57] Resolution 630 (VII), adopted December 16, 1952 by a vote of 25-22-10.
The Soviet bloc also voted against this effort, which involved the establishment
of a procedure for the correction of false and distorted news reports. For the
U.S. position cf. the speech by Charles A. Sprague (October 24) in *Department of State Bulletin*, XXVII, November 17, 1952, 789-792.

possibly unwholesome directions. The United States, as one conservative Senator was to remark a few months later, found itself in a "new and revolutionary era." [58] The instinctive reaction of many Americans was to try to protect their country against these revolutionary tendencies by adopting a more defensive attitude toward the institution in which they found their clearest expression.

Even those Americans who viewed the stirrings and strivings of the outside world without alarm could cite grounds for dissatisfaction with the way the United Nations organization was functioning. Far from having fulfilled what was to have been its primary function of maintaining international peace and security, it had neither prevented the aggression in Korea nor compelled the aggressors to desist; many Americans felt that it had actually hampered this country in the conduct of hostilities in the Far East, without providing the material and moral support which might have justified its interference. Meanwhile the attempt begun in 1950 to develop the potentialities of the General Assembly as the primary agency of collective security seemed to have become largely enmeshed in the slow-moving procedures of the Collective Measures Committee: even the 1951 resolution calling for an embargo on the shipment of strategic goods to Communist China was not being carried out to entire satisfaction.

To be sure, the United States had at least managed to prevent Communist China from gaining representation in the United Nations; but it had found no acceptable way to secure the admission to membership of thirteen of its own friends which were excluded by the Soviet veto. And meanwhile the presence of the U.S.S.R. and its four satellite delegations was a source of continuing frustration and subjected the United States to endless abuse which was immediately disseminated to the world by New York's unrivaled publicity media. As Mrs. Eleanor Roosevelt of the United States delegation remarked concerning Soviet misrepresentations of economic and social conditions in this country:

[58] Senator Everett M. Dirksen, quoted in *New York Times*, April 8, 1953.

"This is the seventh year in which I have heard these same old, stale charges hurled against the United States. On several previous occasions I have replied to these charges, point by point, with the true facts. But, after all, no one ever expects replies to Soviet slanders to have any effect whatsoever on their representatives. Each year I present the facts about the situation in the United States; and then the next year these representatives offer up the same old distortions of fact." [59]

Not a few Americans found it peculiarly galling that an organization in which their country suffered such open disrespect was actually situated on American soil and, moreover, largely supported by the American taxpayer. Dissatisfaction with the general role of the United Nations had played a part in the recent congressional decision to insist that there be no further delay in reducing this country's financial contribution to a maximum of 33⅓ percent of the United Nations budget, as compared with 38.9 percent in 1951 and 36.9 percent in 1952. But the attempt of Senator Alexander Wiley of the United States delegation to secure international concurrence in this decision did not increase the harmony of debate in the Assembly's Administrative and Budgetary Committee. The scale of assessments was fixed by the Assembly, not by the member governments, and was determined not by the sentiments of national legislatures but by ability to pay as established by an expert committee. The most that Senator Wiley could obtain, thanks to the friendly intervention of a Canadian delegate, was a reduction of the United States share to 35.12 percent in 1953 and a promise that thereafter no member would be asked to contribute more than one-third of the total.[60] In a 1953 operating budget of $48,327,700, the United States would thus be assessed for slightly less than $17 million; the shares of the U.S.S.R. and Great Britain, assessed respectively at 12.28 percent and 10.30 percent, would be in the neighborhood of $6 million and $5 million respectively.[61]

59 *Department of State Bulletin,* January 19, 1953, 116.
60 Resolution 665 (VII), adopted December 5, 1952 by a vote of 44-6-2 with the U.S.S.R. opposed and the U.S. abstaining.
61 These assessments were independent of the budgets of the U.N. Specialized Agencies and the special U.N. programs for technical assistance, Palestine

Friction over United Nations operating costs frequently merged with the friction generated by other aspects of United Nations endeavor. The feeling of irritation that permeated the New York Headquarters in late 1952 was aggravated by reports from Paris, where the UNESCO organization, best known of the United Nations Specialized Agencies, was holding its Seventh General Conference from November 12 to December 11. Noteworthy developments of the UNESCO session included the admission of Spain to membership, the withdrawal of Poland, and the resignation of Director-General Jaime Torres Bodet in protest against an economy budget ($18 million for two years) adopted on the insistence of the United States and Great Britain. The budget controversy had produced a familiar alignment: "It was a case of the United States, Britain and her Commonwealth lands and most of the European countries against the smaller nations of Asia, Africa and Latin America." [62] But news that UNESCO was in difficulties could only confirm the misgivings of such Americans as considered that agency to be the instrument of a sinister and un-American world conspiracy.

Those Americans who believed that the United Nations, with all its shortcomings, was a necessary and on the whole a useful institution were not remiss in calling attention to its virtues and answering the stock arguments against it. During the autumn President Truman, Secretary Acheson, General Eisenhower, Governor Stevenson, and many lesser figures made speeches or issued statements which emphasized their continued belief in the organization despite the evidence of disillusionment and hostility prevailing in a considerable section of the public.[63] Figures were compiled which showed that the annual per capita cost of the United Nations and its Specialized Agen-

refugees, and Korean reconstruction. According to figures released by the U.S. Mission to the U.N., contributions by the U.S. from fiscal year 1952 funds came to about $9.2 million for the Specialized Agencies and $72 million for special programs.
[62] *New York Times*, November 22, 1952.
[63] Cf. *Department of State Bulletin*, XXVII, 1952, *passim* and *New York Times*, October 25, 1952.

cies to the people of the United States was only 16 cents, that of its special programs only 46 cents. But such efforts did not altogether succeed in stemming the tide of reaction against the United Nations. For a development had meanwhile occurred which touched the American people in a peculiarly sensitive spot. The United Nations, they had learned, was tainted with the same evil that many believed to have seriously infected their own government. Some of its officials, it appeared—and not only Russians, Czechoslovaks, and Poles, but also Americans—were actually to be regarded as instruments of the international Communist conspiracy.

Proper evaluation of this discovery requires more attention to the technicalities of United Nations organization and procedure than most citizens were able to give at the time. Students of international organization are aware that the function of the United Nations staff, or Secretariat, is to provide the many technical and administrative services involved in operating an organization of sixty governments representing every part of the earth and every type of political and social philosophy. Its members are not normally called upon to engage in confidential negotiations or to handle confidential documents of individual governments. As Secretary-General Trygve Lie later pointed out, the Secretariat

"works in a glass house, not only physically, but in every respect. It is not a profitable place for spies and saboteurs. Almost all meetings and documentation of the United Nations are open for all to see and hear. No military secrets are ever handled by the Secretariat." [64]

Directives on the conduct of the Korean war, for example, were sent directly from the Pentagon Building in Washington to General Clark in Tokyo; the Secretariat handled only the unclassified communiqués and reports of operations sent back by the Unified Command.

As international civil servants, the members of the Secre-

[64] *Report of the Secretary-General on Personnel Policy,* U.N. Document A/2364, January 30, 1953, 3. Excerpts from this important document appear in *Documents on American Foreign Relations, 1952,* No. 33 (c).

tariat retain their individual nationality but are responsible to the United Nations, not to their own governments. They are debarred by the terms of the Charter from seeking or receiving instructions "from any government or from any other authority external to the Organization"; and each member government is pledged to respect "the exclusively international character" of their responsibilities and "not to seek to influence them in the discharge of their responsibilities." At the same time, members of the Secretariat are obligated to "refrain from any action which might reflect on their position as international officials responsible only to the Organization." The paramount consideration in the employment of the staff and the determination of conditions of service is "the necessity of securing the highest standards of efficiency, competence, and integrity." [65]

The authors of the Charter had further provided that "Due regard shall be paid to the importance of recruiting the staff on as wide a geographical basis as possible." But because the organization was located in a country where qualified personnel was relatively abundant, the actual membership of the staff, especially in the lower grades, was largely if not predominantly American. In a total personnel of nearly 3,500 employed at the New York Headquarters, some 1,650 or 1,675 were Americans; about 350 of these were classified as professional and the balance as clerical and mechanical employees. A somewhat smaller number of Americans were employed by the various Specialized Agencies, which were administratively independent of the United Nations, and by the special United Nations welfare and relief organizations.

The great majority of these United States citizens undoubtedly had been and remained loyal Americans. Ralph J. Bunche, perhaps the best known American member of the Secretariat, spoke for this majority when he insisted that in seven years' experience he had "never encountered any difficulty in maintaining full loyalty to my country while being devoted to the U.N." [66] But it now appeared that there were enough indi-

[65] Articles 100 and 101 (3) of the U.N. Charter.
[66] *New York Times*, November 14, 1952.

viduals of more questionable attachments to suggest that the United Nations, notwithstanding its limitations as a base for espionage and subversion, had definitely been considered a worth-while target for Communist infiltration.

In recruiting and administering his staff, the Secretary-General had followed the somewhat elastic principle that no person was eligible for employment by the United Nations if there was substantial evidence indicating subversive activities against his own or any other government. Though debarred from receiving instructions from member governments, Mr. Lie had often asked them for information about those of their nationals who had applied for or obtained United Nations employment. In the case of the United States, however, such consultations had not always achieved their purpose. Washington had been reluctant to take official responsibility for recommending or clearing American applicants; furthermore, American security procedures did not admit of furnishing the prompt and detailed information which Mr. Lie thought necessary in cases where adverse action on his part seemed indicated. The United States had apparently possessed no evidence pointing to actual espionage by any American employee of the United Nations; and Mr. Lie, though recognizing that the employment of Americans who might have Communist ties was undesirable in itself, had not felt able to dismiss employees on the sole ground that they were Communists or under Communist discipline. Over the years, a number of Americans against whom there were serious charges had been dropped, and others had been denied employment. But there remained a substantial group whose loyalty to the United States, though it could be presumed in most cases, had not been positively established.[67]

This situation had not failed to attract the notice of persons concerned with the dangers of internal Communism to the United States. On October 13, 1952, one day before the opening of the Seventh Assembly, the Internal Security Subcom-

[67] For details cf. especially the *Report of the Secretary-General on Personnel Policy*, cited, and the report on *Activities of United States Citizens Employed by the United Nations* by the Internal Security Committee of the Senate Judiciary Committee, 82nd Congress, 2nd Session (Washington, January 2, 1953).

mittee of the Senate Judiciary Committee opened a full-dress inquiry into the activities of United States citizens employed by the United Nations. The hearings, held in the Federal Courthouse in downtown New York, ran parallel to the Assembly session throughout its course and resulted in continuous unfavorable publicity for the United Nations all through the autumn and early winter. Supplementing or competing with its investigation were the endeavors of a Federal Grand Jury, also operating in the New York area, which was likewise summoning United Nations employees for questioning in connection with an investigation of possible violations of the laws against subversive activities and espionage.

The full consequences of these efforts cannot be readily assessed with historical exactitude and fairness to all concerned. On the positive side, the Senate investigation undoubtedly brought into the open for the first time the fact that some American officials of the United Nations and the Specialized Agencies either had Communist backgrounds or had been engaged in subversion or espionage or, at any rate, were unwilling to take an oath to the contrary for fear of possible self-incrimination. As a direct result of their refusal to answer pertinent questions, more than two dozen United Nations employees were eventually dismissed, and the Secretary-General secured a redefinition of his authority which would enable him to act more vigorously in the future. The situation that was thus being belatedly corrected was one which, as Secretary Acheson frankly admitted, adversely affected this country's interests and prestige—even though he personally did not share the widespread opinion that it involved the national security.[68]

These results, however, were brought about in circumstances not wholly favorable to the stability of American foreign relations. The controversial atmosphere of the inquiries and their close involvement with domestic and international politics militated against sober appraisal of the facts and their implications. The publicity accompanying the inquiries was of a character to emphasize if not to exaggerate the failure of the United Nations

[68] *New York Times*, January 1, 1953.

and the State Department to guard against the employment of possible subversives; the tendency of each of these institutions was to defend its own record and attribute any shortcomings to imperfect cooperation by the other. Amid a welter of unevaluated testimony and inference, popular reaction was molded largely by the adverse judgment of authorities who were close to the scene but had not been directly concerned with United Nations administrative problems and thus could have no interest in minimizing the significance of the discoveries.

The nearest immediate approach to an over-all evaluation was the presentment returned by the Federal Grand Jury on December 2, which mentioned no names and entered no indictment but declared that "startling evidence has disclosed infiltration into the United Nations of an overwhelmingly large group of disloyal United States citizens, many of whom are closely associated with the international Communist movement." This group, it said, "numbers scores of individuals." "Over a score" of them had refused to answer pertinent questions; "a number" of other witnesses had admitted past Communist membership and activity. In "some of the most flagrant and obvious cases of disloyalty," the Grand Jury asserted, it had been established that the State Department "gave the disloyal officials a clean bill of health of the United Nations." [69]

If some of these terms were rather indefinite, there was nothing indefinite about the Grand Jury's conclusion. "If the situation . . . is not promptly corrected," it said, "the United Nations will not enjoy the full confidence of the people of the United States." Similar opinions were being voiced in other influential quarters. Senator Wiley of the United States delegation, who was expected to become chairman of the Senate Foreign Relations Committee in the next Congress, declared that public confidence in the United Nations had already been marred by the "continued shocking disclosures about the subversive nests inside the United Nations and its specialized agencies." Unless adequate security procedures were set up "to guarantee that the United Nations and its organs do not re-

[69] *Ibid.*, December 3, 1952.

main a base for espionage and subversion," he said, Congress would in all probability refuse to appropriate further funds for the United Nations and the Specialized Agencies. Two Democratic members of the Internal Security Subcommittee publicly agreed that "It is up to the United Nations to help us purge it of spies and saboteurs, and if that can't be done, the United Nations ought not to be allowed to sit in America." [70]

Though there were differences of opinion as to the helpfulness of such comments to Mr. Lie and his advisers, their effect on the morale of United Nations employees was depressing. Loyal American employees, busy with the multiple demands of the Assembly, were naturally distressed by sweeping statements which tended to place all of them under suspicion; officials of other nationalities, including anti-Communist nationals of countries behind the Iron Curtain, were disturbed by the idea that any member state should try to exert direct influence on United Nations personnel policies. If the United States could do it, they asked, why not the Soviet Union? The strain was aggravated by the suicide on November 13 of Abraham H. Feller, the American General Counsel to the United Nations, whose own loyalty had not been questioned but who had recently suffered a nervous breakdown brought on, according to Mr. Lie, by the strain of defending American employees against "indiscriminate smears and exaggerated charges."

Three days earlier, on November 10, the Secretary-General himself had announced that he had decided to resign his post without awaiting the expiration of his term of office on February 1, 1954. This resolve, he told the Assembly, had actually been formed the previous summer and was dictated exclusively by his belief that a new Secretary-General, selected by the unanimous choice of the five great powers, could be more helpful than he in promoting the chances for peace. The consistent boycott which the Soviet-bloc states had applied to Mr. Lie since early 1951 was, no doubt, a convincing reason for retirement, and he went out of his way to emphasize that no other factors had entered into his decision. Yet few believed that he

[70] *Ibid.*, November 12, December 12, and December 26, 1952.

had been entirely uninfluenced by the difficulties which had arisen in trying to operate the United Nations in the predominantly hostile American atmosphere of 1952.

Recognizing the difficulty the great powers were sure to experience in agreeing on a successor, Mr. Lie undertook to stay on provisionally and thus see the personnel controversy through to a conclusion. Already he had appointed a panel of three legal experts—an American, a Britisher, and a Belgian—to advise him on his powers and responsibilities in a situation which had seemed to him to involve a conflict between his international obligations under the Charter and the practical necessity of maintaining a good relationship with the host country. The opinion of the Commission of Jurists, presented on November 30, was to lay unexpected stress on this second obligation, thus paving the way toward a resolution of the problem along lines that would be acceptable to this country if not to certain other non-Communist governments.[71]

The peculiar relationship between the United Nations and the United States, the three jurists pointed out, was one "which evidently requires exceptional tact and discretion on both sides." It must be recognized, they said, that an international civil service "will inevitably include persons whose political, social, economic and philosophical outlook differs from the beliefs and sentiments of many American citizens." Nevertheless they advised the Secretary-General to show great deference to the opinions of the host country, especially in security matters:

"In exercising his responsibility . . . the Secretary General should regard it as of the first importance to refrain from engaging or to remove from the staff any person whom he has reasonable grounds for believing to be engaged or to have been engaged, or to be likely to be engaged in any subversive activities against the host country." [72]

[71] U.N. Document A/2364, January 30, 1953, 21-33. The opinion was prepared by William D. Mitchell (U.S.), Sir Edwin S. Herbert (U.K), and Prof. Paul Veldekens (Belgium).
[72] In the original version the last phrase read, "any activities regarded as disloyal by the host country," by which members of the commission later explained that they had meant "activities regarded as subversive by the law of the host country." Cf. U.N. Document A/INF/51/Corr. 1, December 12, 1952.

Moreover, said the three jurists, a person who refused to answer questions about espionage or subversion against the United States was "just as unsuitable for continued employment by the United Nations in the United States as one who had actually been convicted." By similar reasoning they reached the conclusion that dismissal was also indicated in the case of individuals who refused to answer questions about membership in the Communist party or any other subversive organization.

The Secretary-General was not slow to act on this advice. On December 3 he instructed nine employees suspended as a result of their silence before the Senate subcommittee to answer on pain of losing their jobs; two days later they joined the twenty former colleagues who had already been dismissed for similar reasons. Meanwhile the International Monetary Fund had ousted its secretary (Frank Coe), the most prominent single individual involved in the disclosures, two days after he had refused to say whether he was or had been engaged in espionage against the United States. Although a dozen or more individuals on whom the United States had made unfavorable reports remained provisionally on the United Nations rolls for lack of complete evidence, arrangements were initiated for closer liaison with the United States Government and closer official scrutiny of American personnel in the future. At the end of December it was announced that Americans holding or seeking employment by the United Nations would henceforth be screened in much the same manner as Federal Government employees, with a full field inquiry by the Federal Bureau of Investigation for all except minor employees on whom no derogatory information had been developed.[73]

These arrangements did not immediately relieve the anxieties of those Americans who had shown most concern about the dangers of the existing situation. Nor were they received with much enthusiasm by the Secretariat or by the representatives of other member states, some of whom had watched the development of the controversy with considerable apprehension

[73] State Department release, December 30, 1952, in *Department of State Bulletin*, XXVIII, January 12, 1953, 61-62.

lest the independence of the world organization be compromised by what might be considered an excessive regard for American sensibilities. A number of delegates—among them those of India, Canada, Belgium, the Netherlands, and Mexico —openly questioned the Secretary-General's ready acceptance of the panel's recommendations and indicated that they would seek a more thorough airing of the problem when the Assembly reconvened in February.[74] Coming on top of the many other instances in which the United States had found itself at variance with majority opinion, it was evident that the episode had not lessened the prevalent dissatisfaction with American tactics in the world organization.

With the impending retirement of Mr. Lie and the advent of a new administration in Washington, the United States and the United Nations would soon be entering a new phase of their mutual relationship. Already familiar figures like Mrs. Roosevelt and Warren R. Austin, the titular head of the American delegation, were preparing to take leave of the organization whose vicissitudes they had shared through most of its seven-year history. The Eisenhower administration undoubtedly would be taking over at a rather low point in the fortunes of the organization. "The road is rougher than we hoped it would be when we signed the Charter in 1945," said Mr. Austin in a farewell broadcast. "We have lost some of the buoyant enthusiasm of those days, but we have gained the determined courage of a battle-tested veteran. We have found the direction, though time has not been speedy." [75] To maintain the direction and try to recapture some of the enthusiasm would be the prime task of former Senator Henry Cabot Lodge, Jr. and the new delegation which he would be heading when the Assembly reconvened in February 1953.

---

[74] U.N. Document A/C.5/SR.374, December 16, 1952.
[75] *Department of State Bulletin*, XXVIII, January 19, 1953, 107.

CHAPTER EIGHT

NATO IN THE DOLDRUMS

TOWARD THE middle of the General Assembly's fall session, the English weekly *Spectator* offered this trenchant appraisal of the situation in the United Nations as it affected the interests of the Western democracies:

"It is the conclusion forced on everyone that the United Nations is not only not united, but has no visible prospect of being. . . . No one is likely to take the responsibility for breaking up the United Nations, and no one should. But if hopes are frustrated in New York it is the more imperative that they be brought to fulfilment in Europe. If U.N.O. is doomed to be a house divided N.A.T.O. must show itself increasingly a house united." [1]

Few who looked realistically at the position of the Western world in the latter part of 1952 could have differed materially with this judgment. The United Nations, despite all disappointments, retained its value as a place where governments of every tendency could meet and transact business under common rules and, when that proved impossible, at least could probe each other's minds while seeking wider support for their own policies. As an instrument for preserving international peace and security, however, the United Nations of 1952 was remarkably unlike the organization envisaged in the Charter or even in the "Uniting for Peace" resolution of 1950. In the last analysis, that measure of international peace and security which the world still enjoyed was founded on the ability of the United States and its like-minded associates to deter aggression by methods which, though consistent with United Nations prin-

[1] *Spectator*, November 21, 1952, 649.

ciples, necessarily operated for the most part outside the United Nations machinery.

Of the several instrumentalities devised to meet these conditions, NATO alone represented a sufficient aggregation of international military power to exert a possibly decisive influence at a strategically critical point. Under the decisions approved by the NATO Council at Lisbon in February, the NATO forces in Western Europe had been scheduled to reach by the end of 1952 a level of some fifty army divisions, half of them on active duty, and some 4,000 aircraft. With the further build-up planned for 1953 and 1954, supplemented by the forces of Greece and Turkey and the prospective inclusion of Western Germany in the European Defense Community, this program was expected to "bring within measurable distance the time when even the most foolhardy man in the Kremlin will not dare risk open attack." [2]

Unfortunately, however, even the ambitious plans approved at Lisbon did not provide the solid guarantees of security which were so ardently desired by every people situated within range of Soviet striking power. Even if the theory on which NATO was being built up was correct—an assumption that remained open to vigorous challenge on both sides of the Atlantic—there remained a disconcerting gap between theory and practice. The effectives of the Atlantic alliance were being developed from virtually nothing; the Soviet Union had enjoyed an overwhelming preponderance at the outset and had continued to develop its own military strength on land, at sea, and in the air. "Although our forces today are far stronger than they were 2 years ago," General Ridgway pointed out in the course of the autumn,

". . . we are still far from the minimum we need to deal with an all-out surprise attack. . . . We have yet to reach our minimum military requirements. Until we do, military commanders . . . must face the fact that the potential aggressor is capable of moving at any time of his choosing in strength much greater than today we

[2] Message of the President on the Mutual Security Program, March 6, 1952, in *Documents on American Foreign Relations, 1952,* No. 3 (a).

can muster. We have no information which would lead us to believe that this strength has in any way diminished. On the contrary, our information indicates it has definitely grown and continues to grow." [3]

Nor was the military progress of the Soviet Union and its satellites the only hindrance to NATO's attempted correction of the military imbalance in Europe and the Atlantic world. Far more immediate difficulties arose from conditions within the Atlantic world itself. For the Atlantic powers and their West German affiliate had been among the first to experience those regressive tendencies which were so noticeable throughout most of the free world in the second half of 1952. During the early part of the year, from the Lisbon meeting to the signature of the Bonn and Paris treaties at the end of May, Atlantic affairs had seemed predominantly on the up-grade. Thereafter the tendency was reversed. Progress continued, but not in the measure demanded by the circumstances. Confidence and effort tended to slacken off. Governments and parliamentarians shrank from carrying out commitments already accepted in principle. By August the *Economist* was finding it "difficult to avoid the impression that in London and other capitals there has emerged a definite tendency to run away from NATO's plans to defend Europe." [4] Later developments offered few grounds for modifying this impression.

The causes of this general let-down were complex but easily identifiable. At bottom, nearly all of them were psychological in character—a testimony to that preeminence of "moral" factors which General Eisenhower had so often emphasized in his role as Supreme Allied Commander in Europe. "The only thing that can defeat us," the General had observed early in 1951, "is to establish a descending spiral born of suspicion, unreadiness on the part of each of us to do his job, the job that he knows in his own heart he must do." [5] But that, in brief, was exactly what seemed to be occurring in the Atlantic world of

[3] Address to the Society of Pilgrims, London, October 14, in *Department of State Bulletin*, XXVII, November 24, 1952, 816-817.
[4] *Economist*, CLXIV, August 23, 1952, 433.
[5] *The United States in World Affairs, 1951*, 54.

1952 as a good dozen nations fell into fretful contemplation of their weaknesses, their commitments, and the dispositions of their exasperating yokefellows. A quiet disposition to "wait and see" replaced the drive and determination of a few months earlier.

It is impossible to doubt that developments connected with General Eisenhower's own removal from the European scene contributed greatly to this loss of momentum. No successors could wholly fill the gaps left by his departure and by the retirement soon afterward of John J. McCloy as United States High Commissioner in Germany. Their loss was symbolic of the fact that Europe was moving from a period of optimism and imaginative creation into one of sober routine and implementation (or non-implementation) of projects that were already beginning to lose the blush of novelty. General Eisenhower's subsequent adventures in America accentuated the feeling of uncertainty induced by his departure. The man who for more than a year had acted as the conscience of Western Europe seemed somehow to have been swallowed up in the American political candidate. Europeans who tried to follow the campaign, with its calculated inattention to Atlantic problems, could not be certain what attitude the General and his party would adopt if they succeeded to the direction of American policy. In the meantime, no authority in the United States seemed able to provide the firm guidance and assurance of continuity on which the orderly progress of Atlantic affairs had come to depend.

Into this vacuum of political direction had fallen the various intimations of a possible change of "line" in the U.S.S.R. Europeans, by and large, never had fully shared the American conviction that a Soviet attack in Europe might be just around the corner. Each military decision based on this hypothesis had been extracted with difficulty on the official level and greeted with murmurs among the European public. Events in 1952— the Moscow economic conference, the Soviet notes on Germany, Stalin's article in *Bolshevik*—tended to accentuate this divergency. Americans insisted that such performances meant nothing new; Europeans refused to make light of the indications that the Kremlin was as much concerned with economic and other cleavages in the "camp of capitalism" as it was with the armaments race. "Disruption of the Atlantic alliance by some years of 'peaceful coexistence' (i.e., cold war) is the diplomatic and political formula," *The Economist* reasoned; ". . . the cold war in the West is to become colder." [6] And no one who observed the internal affairs of the Atlantic family could deny that they were rich in disruptive potentialities. Yet American policy, while abating none of its insistence on rapid execution of the various NATO military programs, still seemed hesitant to face the full economic and psychological implications for people on both sides of the Atlantic.

The most conspicuous symptoms of this general malaise were centered in Europe—in the mutual bickering of France and Germany, the delays in ratification of the Bonn and Paris treaties, the still equivocal position of Great Britain toward the Continent, the Italian-Yugoslav tension over Trieste, the general retreat from established defense production and rearmament targets. But these, to a considerable extent, were reflections of a deeper uneasiness that concerned the whole future of Europe in its relation to the world at large. The war in Indochina, the crises in Iran and Egypt, the anticolonial onslaught in the United Nations were reminders that Europe had been forced onto the defensive on all the continents, not merely its own. The signs of an impending change of emphasis in American policy were reminders that Europe by itself was still far too weak to stand against this multiplicity of troubles. For Europeans, the NATO program could be successful only if it was assumed that NATO's underlying principle of "all for one, one for all" applied equally to all the North Atlantic partners—and applied to economic and political as well as to military relations, both locally and globally. Otherwise there was no use in swallowing the many unpalatable medicines the NATO doctors had prescribed.

Was it justifiable to assume that the solidarity of the United

[6] *Economist,* CLXIV, October 11, 1952, 71.

States and its NATO partners would continue unimpaired, and broadening and deepening as circumstances might require through the years ahead? Few Americans in the autumn of 1952 would have ventured to return an unqualified affirmative. Without overlooking the shortcomings of Europe's performance to date, Americans on the whole seemed less concerned with perfecting the NATO relationship than with the possibility of diverting the East-West struggle into new channels where the importance of Western Europe would tend to diminish and the burdens of national and mutual security might weigh less heavily than they had done in the past. But what enlightened Europeans most feared—next to the old anxiety lest American actions inadvertently precipitate a war with the Soviet Union—was a refusal by the United States to give the Atlantic community that measure of continuing support which would unquestionably be needed if the good work already accomplished was ultimately to bear fruit. That apprehension would provide a key to much that was otherwise inexplicable in European behavior during our election campaign and afterward.

1. France, Germany, and the Saar

Europeans sometimes failed to realize how strongly and unfavorably American opinion was affected by the hesitations and squabbles that marked their own advance toward closer union. Progress in this direction had, indeed, become the most generally accepted criterion for judging Europe's right to continued American support. Thus far, the growth of cooperative institutions and practices in Western Europe had been sufficiently rapid to ensure public acceptance in the United States of policies which, at bottom, reflected a conviction that this country could not, for reasons of interest as well as sentiment, incur the risk of allowing Western Europe to fall under Soviet control. It was doubly unfortunate, therefore, that the process of European unification should have struck an unmistakable snag at one of the most critical turning points in the development of American foreign policy. The misfortune was compounded by the fact that a delay in European unification signified a delay in the planned build-up of the NATO military forces in Western Europe, by now directly geared to the rearmament of Western Germany in the European Defense Community.

It would be quite inaccurate to suggest that the broad movement toward closer economic, military, and political union in Western Europe was entirely halted by the reaction against the German Peace Contract and the E.D.C. treaty which set in almost immediately after their signature on May 26-27. Technical planning for the future European army went steadily forward under the auspices of an interim committee set up by the six signatory governments. Meanwhile the European Coal and Steel Community, Europe's first true supranational entity, was formally inaugurated on August 10. Jean Monnet, the inventor of the plan, became the first chairman of the High Authority, with headquarters in Luxembourg. The permanent seat of the Community, it was agreed, would be established in the Saar territory, which would be given a suitable "European" status as soon as the Franco-German quarrel over its disposition had subsided. Opening of the common European market for coal, iron ore, and scrap was scheduled for February 10, 1953; the common market for steel would be opened a few weeks later.

Preparations to crown the edifice with suitable European political institutions likewise went forward without awaiting the ratification of the E.D.C. treaty. By decision of the six foreign ministers, the task of drafting plans for a European political community was transferred from the still unborn assembly of the E.D.C. to an offshoot of the already functioning Coal and Steel assembly. Before the end of the year a draft political statute for "little Europe," embodying a nice compromise between the federal and the looser "confederal" principles, was nearly ready for submission back to the six governments. On another front, there was cause for gratification in the indications that Great Britain was prepared to accept an organic link with the new institutions through its membership in the fifteen-nation Council of Europe. In response to a suggestion from Mr. Eden, the European Assembly at Strasbourg had been actively looking into possible methods of coordinating the various European bodies and harmonizing the position of the six continental governments with that of Britain and other European countries which shared their interest in European co-operation but did not feel able to participate in any European federation.[7]

But the success of all these efforts, and of the plans for additional European ventures in such fields as agriculture and transport, depended in the first instance on the acceptance of the Bonn and Paris treaties by the prescribed constitutional processes in Germany, France, and the neighboring countries of Western Europe. That done, the essential step from the national to the European plane would have been accomplished and the further development of Europe's common life might encounter no comparable obstacles in future. Until it was taken, however, other planning for the future of Europe could amount to little more than a theoretical exercise. And the uncomfortable state of affairs in France and Germany suggested that ratification would be a long and difficult process. Indeed, a pessimist might have asked whether the bitterness of the impending struggle might not fatally impair the value of the European Defense Community when and if it became a reality.

The basic obstacle to public acceptance of the two treaties in France and Germany was the same clash of national attitudes that had hampered their negotiation: the inability of the French to accept the rearmament of Germany under conditions of real equality, and the inability of the Germans to accept collaboration with the West on anything less than equal terms. This divergence had been masked, but not eradicated, in drafting the treaties and their accompanying protocols and declarations. Amid all the verbiage about nondiscrimination and solidarity, they still left Germany in an exposed position, dependent ultimately on the will of the present occupying powers; and, with all their limitations on German freedom of maneuver, they still left France with nothing like absolute protection

[7] For details cf. especially "L'Intégration politique européenne," *Chronique de politique étrangère,* VI, May 1953, 277-320.

against its ancient adversary. In their preoccupation with these shortcomings, both peoples tended to forget the positive advantages the treaties were intended to bring them as a vital element in Europe's fight for survival.

In France, this basic dissatisfaction was directly related to the contrasting development of the two countries since Germany's defeat in 1945. As in 1918, France had emerged from the war as a nominally victorious power, only to see itself outstripped and overshadowed by the seemingly irrepressible strength and dynamism of the neighboring nation. West Germany's phenomenal economic and political recovery—which was partly attributable to its participation in the Marshall Plan and its exemption from defense burdens, but which also owed much to the native energy of its people—had been of a character to suggest that a few more years would see it the most powerful country in Western Europe. France, meanwhile, had lagged farther and farther behind, a prey to acute economic and social weaknesses, beset by the memory of past defeats and obsessed by the looming threats to what remained of its former world position.

In view of the intrinsic handicaps from which France would suffer in any postwar competition with Germany, it was not surprising that successive French governments had done their best to exploit the temporary advantages France enjoyed as one of the victorious occupying powers. Failing to achieve the original aim of a thorough dismemberment of Germany, French statesmen had fallen back on other methods of evening the scales: first, the detachment of the Saar area from Germany and its inclusion in the French economic orbit; then, after the creation of the West German government, the pooling of Europe's heavy industries on a basis that combined formal equality with a strong French voice in the oversight of European basic industry, German as well as French; finally, when it appeared that the actual rearmament of Western Germany could not be staved off much longer, the proposal to create a European Defense Community in which, once again, "discrimination" would nominally be excluded but in which France clearly aspired to play the leading military role while keeping Germany in a subordinate position.

Illustrative of the preponderance France would enjoy in the future E.D.C. was the fact that out of the forty divisions initially contemplated for the European army, France was to contribute fourteen and Germany only twelve. France, but not Germany, would have the right to maintain armed forces outside the E.D.C., and, under certain conditions, to withdraw its E.D.C. forces for service elsewhere. France clearly intended to dominate the higher command and staff functions of the European defense forces, in which Germany's right to participate at all had never been fully established. Even in the E.D.C. assembly, as in the assemblies of the Schuman Plan and the Council of Europe, the equal representation assigned to France and Germany belied the actual disparity between France's population of 42 million and West Germany's of more than 51 million.

In 1950, when the Schuman Plan and the Defense Community were first proposed, such devices had seemed less inadequate to "contain" the rising strength of Western Germany than they did in 1952. In the meantime the hope for British participation in the new institutions, to which the French had attached importance as an additional counterweight to German influence, had largely faded. As the Federal Republic continued to forge steadily ahead, France's over-all position, despite some increase in productivity and output, had failed to improve in any comparable degree. While French wealth and manpower were being drained off in Indochina, German production and exports had been booming and German political energies had been asserting themselves in ways that few Frenchmen could view without misgivings.

For German revival had not been taking place in quite so purely democratic and anti-Nazi an atmosphere as the Western Allies had hoped to establish. Despite the refusal of the Adenauer government to tolerate Nazi-like parties or organizations such as the dissolved Socialist Reich party, students of German attitudes noted a disconcerting readiness to overlook past excesses, disavow German responsibility for the war, and demand leniency for Nazi activists and war criminals. Discussion of German rearmament had encouraged a powerful and somewhat indiscriminate movement within Germany to restore "the honor of the German soldier." With growing self-confidence had gone a growing insistence on Germany's "national rights," not only to unity of the Eastern and Western parts of the country but also to the recovery of the territories detached from Germany by the U.S.S.R., Poland—and France.

Watching this powerful resurgence, not many Frenchmen could look at the proposed European army solely as a device which might potentially strengthen Western defense against the Communist bloc. Granted that their objections tended to be emotional rather than rational in character, the emotions involved were a political fact of the first order. As the time for submission of the treaties to the French parliament approached, the thinness of their political support in the country had become increasingly apparent. The opposition of the Communists and the de Gaullists was to be taken for granted; but there was little enough enthusiasm even within the middle-of-the-road parties where European conceptions were most firmly rooted. "Every official says the E.D.C. will be ratified," one observer exclaimed, "but find me a deputy who sees himself voting for it!" [8]

In Germany the opposition to the E.D.C. concept was equally intense, but somewhat differently motivated. French misgivings were rooted in the fear of Germany; but few Germans showed much real apprehension about France. Franco-German relations, they seemed to feel, were a subsidiary problem which would solve itself more or less automatically by virtue of Germany's sheer superiority in all the elements of national strength. What preoccupied them was rather the situation to the East: first, the possibility of their own engulfment by Soviet Communism, the terrors of which were already known to many Germans at first hand; and, second, the unnatural division of

[8] *Economist*, CLXIV, October 25, 1952, 238.

their own country, a state of affairs in which most Germans found it difficult if not impossible to acquiesce.

Both considerations would have militated strongly against popular acceptance of the Western policy for Germany, even if that policy had been free of other features which German opinion could find discriminatory. The prospect that the E.D.C. would really make possible an effective military defense of Western Germany and Western Europe could be made to look exceedingly tenuous; on the other hand, there was little doubt that it would definitely delay and perhaps permanently exclude the peaceful reunification of Germany by agreement with the U.S.S.R. And Moscow, through its diplomatic exchanges with the Western Allies and through the maneuvers of the East German puppet government, did not fail to encourage the notion that such an agreement might still be possible as long as the Western treaties remained unratified.

For Chancellor Adenauer and his associates, the possibility that East and West might some day come to an agreement on Germany which would not be to Germany's advantage had been one of the strongest impulses behind the policy of German integration with the West. It was somewhat ironic that the most bitter opposition to the Adenauer policy should have centered in the German Social Democratic party, whose general outlook—especially on problems of German political renewal, the elimination of Nazism, and the establishment of genuine democracy—seemed closer to that of the Western Allies than did that of some elements in the Adenauer coalition. Under the leadership of Kurt Schumacher, Adenauer's great antagonist, the German Social Democrats had largely transcended their doctrinaire origins and might easily have become the leading embodiment of national and democratic aspirations in postwar Germany. But Schumacher's decision to base his entire strategy on the issue of German reunification had committed the party to a rather negative stand in European questions which cost it some esteem in the West and was maintained without much abatement even after Schumacher's own untimely death in August 1952.

That German opposition to the E.D.C. experiment extended far beyond the ranks of the Social Democratic party, however, became more than obvious amid the complex maneuvers that followed Dr. Adenauer's submission of the treaties to the Bundestag early in the summer. True, the first reading of the treaties, which involved merely their assignment to appropriate committees of the lower house, was approved on July 10 with only the handful of Communist deputies voting in opposition. The real issues, however, were being fought out elsewhere— not primarily on their intrinsic merits but on the basis of legal and parliamentary technicalities. The essential weakness of Adenauer's position lay in the fact that his policy had few supporters outside the parties of the three-year-old government coalition, which commanded considerably less than a two-thirds majority in the Bundestag and no assured majority at all in the Bundesrat or upper house. In Adenauer's view, the approval of the treaties by a simple majority of the Bundestag alone would fulfill the legal and constitutional requirements; his opponents, however, took a very different view and set out to resist the Adenauer strategy on various fronts.

The Bundesrat, as the representative of the individual German states, put in a claim that the treaties fell within its jurisdiction, too, and could not legally be validated without its assent. Further, the question was raised as to whether a matter of such gravity did not demand the election of a new Bundestag or, at least, the approval of the treaties by an overwhelming majority of the existing lower chamber. By early July the prevalence of such doubts had impelled President Theodor Heuss, whose own political affiliations were with the Adenauer coalition, to ask the new Federal Constitutional Court for an advisory opinion on the constitutional aspects of the case. Three days later the Social Democrats also applied to the court with a request for a binding decision as to whether ratification did not require either a two-thirds majority or prior amendment of the German basic law. The political and procedural complications to which these maneuvers gave rise are far too intricate for examination here. In effect, the court was to decide that it could not at the moment make any ruling on legislation which had not yet been adopted. Thus the constitutional issue was left in suspense until after the Bundestag should have acted.

While seven special committees of the Bundestag debated the technicalities of the two treaties and the major parties girded themselves for the coming struggle, the prospect of early ratification was diminished by concurrent developments in France. There a revulsion against the treaties had been proceeding on the grand scale. In October it reached an explosive climax as the result of a speech delivered by Edouard Herriot, one of France's most respected elder statesmen, at the Radical party congress in Bordeaux. Like the famous radio address of ex-President Herbert Hoover which had precipitated the American "great debate" of early 1951, Herriot's speech of October 17 was less remarkable for its specific content than for the way it crystallized the apprehensions which had been agitating the French people, consciously or unconsciously, for months past. The E.D.C. project, Herriot roundly declared, was "not in accord with the French Constitution"; further, it gave undue advantages to Germany; it would entail serious risks for France in Europe, together with intolerable handicaps in the discharge of its overseas mission. A further vital drawback, he insisted, was the failure of the British to join directly in the treaty as the Radicals, among others, had particularly hoped they would do.[9]

Other French political leaders were quick to second Herriot's objections, and there was a widespread suspicion that his blast had been made by prearrangement with Premier Pinay himself. Pinay, an Independent in politics, had more than once dropped remarks that suggested a lack of enthusiasm for the policy of the government he headed. Challenged to clarify his position once and for all, he now assembled his cabinet and in effect reaffirmed once more his solidarity with Foreign Minister Schuman and the other supporters of the E.D.C. concept. On October 22 it was announced that the treaty would be formally

[9] *New York Times*, October 18, 1952.

submitted to parliament by the middle of November, although it was obvious that the present temper of the country, which had been further agitated by the impending discussion of North Africa in the United Nations and by various differences with the United States over European and Far Eastern questions, would necessitate a lengthy cooling-off period before there could be any hope of favorable action. At the same time it was decided to try to make the E.D.C. more palatable to French opinion by seeking additional reassurances and clarifications, with special reference to France's rights and privileges and the prospective attitude of Great Britain.

This was a guarantee of further long delays, and, in fact, the treaties had not yet been submitted to the Assembly when the Pinay government resigned on an issue of internal policy on December 23. In the meantime a new Franco-German crisis had arisen in connection with French policies in the Saar, an area that each nation regarded as the acid test of the other's intentions and as a problem which would have to be settled before the E.D.C. project could have any chance of succeeding. To that extent, their attitudes on the Saar question were similar; but there was a difference in the feelings with which the two peoples regarded this small but desirable territory. To the French it was a valuable economic prize and an essential element in the European balance of power; to the Germans it was as much a part of their national homeland as were the states in the Soviet zone and the territories east of the Oder and Neisse. Their discontent at the separation of the territory from Germany and the systematic discouragement, not to say repression, of pro-German sentiment among the Saarlanders had reached a height as the result of M. Schuman's recent proposal to "Europeanize" the Saar. The suspicion that this move was aimed at perpetuating the Saar's separate status had seemed amply confirmed by the preparations that were being made to prevent campaigning by pro-German parties in the Saar parliamentary elections set for November 30.

Through the autumn, feeling on the Saar in both France and Germany ran far too high to permit the sporadic negotiations between Messrs. Schuman and Adenauer to yield positive results. German efforts to secure a condemnation of French tactics by the Council of Europe were unsuccessful; but on November 18 the Bundestag took the bold step of formally protesting against what it called the "muzzling" of fundamental democratic rights in the Saar, and urged pro-Germans in the territory to boycott the coming elections or spoil their ballots. This incitement likewise failed to achieve its purpose; for fully 93 percent of the Saar electorate voted on November 30, and only 24 percent of the ballots cast were nullified. The French were thus enabled to claim that their policies had been vindicated by a virtual plebiscite of the Saar people. The Federal Government and the Bundestag, on their side, did not conceal their disappointment but insisted that the results were in no way conclusive.

Such recriminations could not improve the atmosphere for ratification of the treaties in either country. Nevertheless Dr. Adenauer, alarmed by portents of an unfavorable decision which was said to be in preparation by the Federal Constitutional Court, had meanwhile resolved to anticipate its action by pushing the treaties through the Bundestag as rapidly as possible. Despite that body's refusal to be hurried, the debate on the second of the three readings took place on December 3-5. Next day, in an atmosphere of almost unbearable tension, the treaties and their various protocols were approved for the second time by separate votes which averaged around 218-164 —far short of the two-thirds majority on which the court was thought likely to insist.

Contrary to expectations, Adenauer did not press for an immediate vote on the third and final reading. Instead he decided to await the result of a new maneuver by which he hoped to secure a favorable ruling from the one division of the court which was deemed sympathetic to his constitutional views. This move, however, was frustrated when the full court declared on December 9 that its pending opinion on the questions submitted earlier by President Heuss would be controlling in all respects; to which the Chancellor could find no better reply than to persuade Herr Heuss to withdraw his application and thus spare the government a probable adverse ruling.

In a country where democracy was struggling to strike root, such efforts to resolve a vital national issue by manipulating the judicial process as an instrument of party politics were scarcely more edifying than Dr. Malan's open attack on the position of the Supreme Court of South Africa. "A heap of broken china" was the expression by which one German tried to describe the condition to which the struggle had reduced German public life.[10] If the government was ultimately victorious, it would be a victory over a nation divided in more ways than one. The decision, whatever it might be, could hardly claim the broad national assent that constituted the only satisfactory basis for German membership in the Western community. Nor would it offer much reassurance to those French deputies who still wavered between acceptance and rejection of the European partnership.

2. Trade or Aid?

The over-all plans approved at Lisbon by the NATO Council had been based on two fundamental assumptions: (1) that the treaties incorporating Western Germany into the European defense system would be signed and ratified with reasonable promptitude, and (2) that the NATO member countries would succeed in carrying out the stepped-up military programs required to meet the firm goals of the alliance for 1952 as well as the more tentative targets established for 1953 and 1954. But if the first of these assumptions had soon proved overoptimistic, it was not long before the second one was beginning to look equally so.

Rather to their own surprise, the ministers who attended the tenth session of the NATO Council in Paris on December 15-18 were to discover that NATO's force goals for 1952 would, after all, be "substantially" met. So far as the further expansion of NATO's military power was concerned, how-

[10] Walter Dirks, in *Frankfurter Hefte*, VIII, January 1953, 1.

ever, it was clear that the pace would need to be considerably moderated. Well in advance of the NATO meeting, France had announced that because aid from the United States had fallen short of expectations it would be unable to carry out its plan to increase the French army from twelve to fifteen divisions during 1953. Prime Minister Churchill had disclosed that rising defense costs had necessitated the cancellation or modification of some defense contracts already placed by the British Government. Belgium had reduced its term of compulsory military service from twenty-four months to twenty-one. In Paris, the most significant action taken by the NATO Council itself was equally negative in character: it limited its authorization for the fourth "slice" of the infrastructure program to approximately one-half of the amount requested by General Ridgway for the next two years.

These and similar actions involving some of the smaller NATO members were not actually steps backward, since the over-all level of defense preparations in Western Europe continued to rise. They did, however, testify to a widespread determination to proceed more slowly until the international outlook was clarified. In part they reflected the besetting uncertainty that followed the Soviet party congress and the American election, events which made it difficult to retain the sense of urgent purpose that had prevailed at certain earlier times. More fundamentally, they represented an adjustment to economic and political realities which had proved even more intractable than had been foreseen a few months earlier. The roots of the situation had been described by Walter Lippmann in the same article in which he had stressed the necessity for renewed attention in the United States to those problems that had received so little notice during the campaign:

". . . The fundamental fact is that the key nations in the worldwide network of alliances around the Communist orbit are unable to carry out fully their obligations: their foreign commitments on the one hand, and on the other, their obligations to their own people to maintain a tolerable and, over a long period, a rising standard of life. In this sense France and Great Britain are both greatly over-extended. France cannot fight the war in Indo-China, cannot develop and support her position in Africa, cannot raise the largest ground army in Western Europe, and still maintain a standard of life at home which the French people will accept. In this sense, too, Great Britain is greatly over-extended, unable, that is to say, to support, even at what is now a very bleak and austere standard of life, the whole rearmament program and her military commitments in Germany and in the Middle East and in Southeast Asia." [11]

That there was a conflict between the requirements of European and global defense and those of economic stability and progress in Europe was, of course, by no means unrecognized in NATO planning. The attempt to keep these twin imperatives in balance was one of the oldest preoccupations of the Atlantic allies. Realization that the European members of NATO could hardly attain the desired level of military preparedness without outside help was the main reason for the American military assistance program and its concomitant of economic or "defense support" aid. But American aid, whether military or economic, was regarded as a supplement and not a substitute for what the Western European nations could do on their own account. And it was now becoming apparent not only that the realistic capabilities of the latter had been somewhat overestimated, but that the essential contribution of the United States was also falling short of earlier expectations.

With more than two million men under arms, with military expenditures standing at more than twice the pre-Korean figure and defense production at four times the level of 1949, the European partners collectively had undertaken a burden of no inconsiderable size. To sustain and expand it along the lines of the Lisbon program would have required two things: (1) a continuing growth in European production, sufficient to satisfy both defense requirements and basic civilian and export needs; and (2) the fulfillment of American intentions to provide not only great quantities of military "end-items" but also a limited amount of "defense support" aid, in the form of raw materials and other assistance needed to promote maximum

[11] *New York Herald Tribune,* November 11, 1952.

use of European resources for defense purposes. In point of fact, neither of these conditions had been realized.

Toward the end of 1951, the Western European nations had adopted the broad objective of expanding their industrial production by 25 percent during the five-year period ending in 1956. Yet the actual trend during most of 1952 was in the opposite direction: for the first time since 1947, there was an over-all decline in Western European industrial production. Throughout Western Europe, the rapid production increases of earlier years appeared to be levelling off. Talk of an economic recession, which was widespread during the spring, dwindled with a partial reemergence of more favorable trends toward the end of the year. Nevertheless, many observers feared that the flattening out of the production curves might foreshadow an exhaustion of Europe's potential for further expansion under existing conditions. This, of course, would have serious implications not only for the collective defense but also for the efforts that European countries were making to increase their exports and balance their exchanges with the rest of the world, particularly the United States.

Meanwhile the American contribution likewise failed to attain the anticipated levels. Early in 1952, the total Western European defense bill for the fiscal year 1952–53 (exclusive of Greece, Turkey, and the American and Canadian forces in Europe) had been estimated at $17.7 billion. The lion's share of this amount—$13.9 billion—represented direct defense expenditure planned by the European countries; the balance of $3.8 billion was to consist of military items to be supplied by the United States, including $1 billion allocated to "offshore procurement" of military equipment manufactured in Europe. To permit European defense expenditures to be maintained at this relatively high level, the United States had also planned to furnish an additional $1.4 billion in defense support aid.[12] But Congress had reduced the possible new outlay by this

[12] The Mutual Security Program for Fiscal Year 1953: Basic Data Supplied by the Executive Branch (Committee print, House Foreign Affairs Committee and Senate Foreign Relations Committee, 82nd Congress, 2nd Session, Washington, 1952), 9, 12-13.

country to $3.1 billion for military aid and less than $1.3 billion for defense support; and meanwhile actual shipments had fallen even lower. Largely because of delays in production, the value of *all* United States military aid shipments to Western Europe, from the beginning of the program in 1949 through November 1952, totaled only slightly over $2.6 billion out of the $11.2 billion that had been allocated to the Defense Department. Offshore procurement contracts placed during the last six months of 1952 totaled only $130 million, as contrasted with $620 million in such contracts placed through June 30, 1952.[13]

The effects of this decreased momentum were not confined to the defense field. Even more serious than the loss of impetus in production was the renewed growth of external deficits in Europe, especially with the dollar area. Although Europe's terms of trade with the outside world had tended to improve as the post-Korean raw material shortages were gradually made up and world prices of raw materials declined, the "dollar gap" with the United States persisted and seemed likely to continue at a level of $2.5 to $3 billion a year. The diversion of productive resources to rearmament had severely strained the NATO countries' ability to earn dollars by exports; and, as we have seen, there had been no effectual move by the United States to remove the domestic obstacles to European competition in the American market.

The impact of these difficulties varied from one European country to another, being perhaps least marked in Federal Germany and considerably more severe in Great Britain and France. In Britain the slowing down of industrial production was particularly noticeable, while only stringent limitations on imports plus the resumption of defense support aid from the United States made it possible to halt a new decline in gold and dollar reserves. France experienced comparable troubles

---

[13] *Third Report to Congress on the Mutual Security Program*, December 31, 1952 (Washington, 1953), 2-3. Military aid items shipped to *all destinations* from 1949 through November 30, 1952 included 18,664 tanks and combat vehicles, 98,689 motor transport vehicles, 20,095 pieces of artillery, 2,792 aircraft, 441 naval vessels, etc.

with its external deficit, and remained a prey to strong inflationary forces despite the conservative monetary and fiscal
policies of the Pinay government. As always, the French position was strongly influenced by the continuing cost of the war
in Indochina, now estimated at some $1.25 billion a year.
Although roughly one-third of this burden was being should-
ered by the United States, French authorities considered that
total American aid to France was still far from commensurate
with the French exertions in Europe and overseas. In October,
an intimation that defense support aid to France for the entire
fiscal year 1952–53 would not exceed $525 million unless
France intensified its own defense effort caused a minor explosion in Paris—a reminder that the whole field of American-
Western European economic relations was strewn with potent
psychological hazards.

For it was becoming clear that the traditional methods
of sharing the NATO defense burden could not easily be
carried on much longer, whatever SHAPE might say about
the requirements of the military situation. American programs that had already been authorized and appropriated
for would doubtless be allowed to run their course, and
would contribute substantially to the build-up of European
strength over the next couple of years. It seemed unlikely,
however, that any new programs involving the United States
would bear much resemblance to the existing Mutual Security
effort. The concept of "defense support" had never been popular with Congress or the public and seemed to be on its way out,
whether or not strictly military aid was continued on a significant scale. A good many Americans, comparing their own and
the European governments' defense expenditures, could not rid
themselves of a feeling that the latter were still carrying less
than their fair share of the load. Europeans had none of this
feeling; a really "equitable" division of burdens, they suspected, would actually require the United States to contribute
much more than it had thus far been willing to consider. But
in Europe, too, there was strong discontent with the existing
pattern, and a growing feeling that American aid must be

replaced by something less incalculable, less burdensome to the recipients and more in keeping with the spirit of national independence.

An appealing alternative was suggested by the formula of "trade, not aid"—words which implied that what Europe required from the dollar area should in future be paid for by its own exports, made possible by the removal of artificial barriers to competition in the American market. A whole row of expert studies, some of European and some of American origin, proclaimed the essential validity of this concept. Yet there were certain obvious difficulties on both sides. The experts were agreed that if Western Europe was to take full advantage of any fresh opportunities provided by the United States, its economy would have to become steadily more productive, and to produce at steadily more competitive prices. On the American side, it remained questionable how far Congress and the executive would really be willing to go in encouraging the inflow of European goods and services that competed with American enterprise. Given the probability that neither Europeans nor Americans would do everything expected of them by the other party, it seemed unlikely that the situation would ever yield to the application of this one simple formula. More probably it would continue to call for simultaneous action along several different lines on both sides of the Atlantic.

During the latter part of 1952 this problem was under active consideration in many quarters, and various new devices were suggested to accompany that liberalization of United States commercial policy to which virtually all authorities looked forward as the indispensable element in any solution that might be devised. In August, William H. Draper, Jr., the United States Special Representative in Europe and permanent representative to the NATO Council, submitted a report to the President[14] in which he emphasized the view that "we must greatly increase our imports from Europe and from other parts of the world" but conceded that it was "very unlikely that the existing gap can be closed by increased American imports

[14] *Documents on American Foreign Relations, 1952*, No. 16.

alone." Nevertheless, Mr. Draper insisted that "a better solution for Europe's chronic trade and financial problems must be found soon, or the long term consequences for the strength and solidarity of the free world could be damaging indeed." "Unless a balance can be restored," he said, "there is real danger of a deep and perhaps disastrous fissure between the economies of Europe and America."

Two possibilities to which Mr. Draper recommended close attention were (1) the chances for substantially increased overseas investment by the United States—encouraged, perhaps, by governmental guarantees against the special risks of political instability and exchange difficulties; and (2) continuation of the existing offshore procurement program "as an important and integral part of our military assistance program to Europe." The great significance of offshore procurement, he pointed out, lay in the fact "that it will contribute to the development of a production base that will make it possible for the countries of Western Europe in the future to provide more fully for their own defense requirements"; in addition, it would "contribute materially to the effective use of labor and resources in Europe and . . . help make dollars available for imports needed for defense and civilian production." In illustration of the possibilities in this field, he cited a $400 million program then being developed for the production of interceptor aircraft in Belgium, France, Italy, the Netherlands, and the United Kingdom, using funds to be provided partly by the United States and partly by the European countries.

As a step toward genuine partnership and away from the "client" relationship based on grants or loans, the commencement of the offshore procurement program had been generally welcomed in Europe despite some charges of favoritism in the awarding of contracts. Accordingly, nearly all studies of the over-all problem laid considerable emphasis on its further potentialities. One of the most widely publicized was the so-called "Green Book" prepared in the Mutual Security Administration, which was never released to the press but was known to have discussed various measures too drastic to meet with general approval either within or outside the government. Among recommendations included in this document, in addition to increased offshore procurement, were various proposals for stabilizing the world raw materials market and, more sensational, a projected "Atlantic Reserve System" or currency stabilization fund which would promote convertibility of European currencies and thus help to discourage restrictions and discriminations in trade and payments.[15]

More orthodox in approach, and somewhat less noticed by the public, was the report of an "on the ground" investigation of European business conditions carried out during the autumn by Secretary of Commerce Charles Sawyer, in company with high-ranking officials of other interested government departments and agencies.[16] Economic conditions in Western Europe, this group found, were "not hopeless or even discouraging"; in fact, they had turned out to be definitely better than expected. Although it appeared likely that substantial military aid from the United States would be needed for some time to come, the members were fairly confident that economic aid could be terminated in an "orderly" manner provided the requisite adjustments were made both in Europe and in the United States. On the American side, they emphasized, there would be a necessity for several types of action, including liberalization of trade policy, increased offshore procurement, and encouragement (though no government guarantees) for American investors. Among their other suggestions were a reduction in the number of American officials and agencies operating in Western Europe, and the avoidance of the "Olympian approach" which, they said, sometimes led Americans to "assume a responsibility on our part to direct the lives of others which we should not assume and which we have neither the wisdom, the experience, nor the resources to carry out."

But the ultimate solution to Western Europe's economic

---

[15] Cf. *New York Times*, October 29, 1952 and Klaus Knorr, "Economics for the Atlantic Allies," *Reporter*, VII, No. 10, November 11, 1952, 13-16.
[16] *Documents on American Foreign Relations, 1952*, No. 17.

problems, the Sawyer group emphatically declared, "lies not in the United States of America but in Western Europe itself." Only the Europeans could solve the problems of increasing productivity, removing restrictions and increasing incentives, and achieving financial stability and convertibility of currencies. "It is imperatively clear," they concluded, "that the most important element required for the complete recovery and future prosperity of Western Europe is its own will to survive. . . ."

While one American authority after another was arriving at virtually these same conclusions, Europeans had not been backward in advancing new ideas on their own account. Their recognition of the need for bold initiatives was dramatically attested by the great new economic program already being swung into operation by the six nations of the Coal and Steel Community. Negotiations were continuing on such related projects as the proposed European agricultural pool and European Transport Council. At the fall session of the European Consultative Assembly in Strasbourg, preliminary endorsement was given to another far-reaching program for European self-help which involved the pooling of Western European resources for the balanced development of European overseas territories, particularly in Africa. But Europeans, in seeking a basis for solution of their common problems, made no attempt to minimize the importance to them of actions that had been or might be taken by the United States in regard to tariff policy, customs barriers, import restrictions, shipping subsidies, and similar matters of mutual concern.

These problems came in for lively discussion at a series of international meetings during the autumn and early winter, most conspicuously at the seventh session of the thirty-four contracting parties to the General Agreement on Tariffs and Trade (GATT), held in Geneva from October 2 to November 10. The main achievement of this session was a waiver of certain restrictions in the General Agreement which conflicted with the obligations assumed by members of the European Coal and Steel Community. Its main preoccupation, however, was the revival of protectionist tendencies in the United States, as exemplified by such measures as the "cheese amendment" and the recently increased duties on dried figs and other imported products. A large number of countries offered specific complaints against American actions and one of them, the Netherlands, was authorized to reduce its imports of wheat flour from this country as an "offset" to American restrictions on the importation of Dutch dairy products.[17]

American actions and intentions in the economic field were likewise the central concern of a Commonwealth Economic Conference which brought the Prime Ministers of most of the British Commonwealth countries to London late in the autumn. As the years of crisis lengthened out, the Commonwealth and its economic counterpart, the sterling area, were widely felt to be approaching a decisive turning point. Either their members would advance gradually toward a broader multilateral trade and payments system in concert with the United States and other trading countries, or, if that proved impossible, they would have to fall back on their own more exclusive association as the most dependable alternative. Much of the ministers' time in London was spent in discussing the proposals which would be laid before the new American administration when Mr. Churchill and other top British authorities visited the United States early in 1953. Amid much official secrecy, it was obvious that emphasis would fall largely upon actions which this country might take in the interests of facilitating increased dollar earnings by Britain and the sterling area countries, minimizing the fluctuations in world raw material prices, and helping to restore the convertibility of the pound.[18]

Finally, in mid-December the Council of the Organization for European Economic Cooperation (O.E.E.C.) met in Paris

[17] Actions of the session are briefly surveyed in *Department of State Bulletin*, XXVII, December 1, 1952, 876-879. For further U.S. actions affecting European imports at this period cf. *ibid.*, XXVII, October 13, 1952, 569-570; November 10, 1952, 743; and XXVIII, January 19, 1953, 102-103.
[18] The communiqué of the conference, dated December 11, 1952, appears in *Department of State Bulletin*, XXVIII, March 16, 1953, 397-399.

to approve that body's fourth annual report [19]—another classic examination of the same set of problems, likewise influenced by the expectation of thorough discussions with the next American administration. Here again, Europe's dollar deficit was identified as the chronic obstacle to stable relationships, and one that would undoubtedly remain even after the expected discontinuance of most American economic aid. Here again, the possibility of a permanent solution compatible with the basic objectives of the Western governments was shown to depend on coordinated action on both sides of the Atlantic: in Europe, achievement of internal financial stability, expansion of production, and intensification of the export drive; in the United States, maintenance of economic stability, assistance in the stabilization of raw material prices, a liberal commercial policy, and a larger volume of foreign investment. Offshore purchases and other United States defense expenditures in Europe, the O.E.E.C. report noted, were a significant but inevitably temporary contribution; they afforded at best a respite while more fundamental solutions were being worked out.

The conclusion of the O.E.E.C. report, subscribed by eighteen European governments as well as by the United States and Canada, might have been appropriately applied to an even wider field of mutual endeavor:

"The appraisal of the problems now confronting the Western world emphasises above all else the need for co-operation. These problems cannot be solved by unco-ordinated action on the part of individual countries. A co-operative effort and plan of action is therefore one of the indispensable requirements. . . . The path of sound progress for the economy of the Western world requires that many difficult actions affecting special interests be taken by the various governments. The strength to take these actions and the conviction that they will lead to successful and lasting solutions of the problems will only come if they are part of an international effort."

[19] *Europe—The Way Ahead, Towards Economic Expansion and Dollar Balance: Fourth Annual Report of the OEEC* (Paris, O.E.E.C., December 1952); see especially pp. 15-31.

3. Lisbon to Paris to Ankara

With the fate of the European army treaty in suspense and the economic future of Western Europe uncertain, the NATO Council had scheduled its tenth ministerial session at a difficult moment in North Atlantic affairs. What was to be done if the E.D.C. project fell through? Would Germany be left to "stew in its own juice" for a while longer, a blank in the system of European defense and a target for every kind of antidemocratic solicitation from within and without? Or would German rearmament be deemed so essential as to demand the recreation of a real German national army, despite the violent opposition to be expected from the French? Again, by what means were the Atlantic associates to close the widening gap between defense goals and economic capabilities? By curtailing or "stretching out" their defense programs, on the chance that the adversary would remain quiet until they were better prepared to meet a sudden attack? Or by finding new resources that could still be applied to defense if the necessity were made sufficiently clear to the Atlantic peoples?

The need for a radical reassessment of Atlantic aims and policies, directed to these and similar questions, was being urged in many quarters. There was in the background, moreover, another factor of great though undefined significance that bore directly on the future of the Atlantic alliance and might be thought to cast doubt on the validity of much current NATO planning. This was the rapid progress in the field of atomic and other novel weapons that was being made on both sides of the Iron Curtain and could hardly fail to alter drastically the conditions of any future East-West conflict. While NATO had been striving to establish a system of ground defense along relatively conventional lines, and while the great powers in the United Nations Disarmament Commission had been fruitlessly debating alternative methods for the "regulation, limitation and balanced reduction of all armed forces and all armaments including atomic," there had been no lack of activity in the laboratories and proving grounds of either side. The results were such as to wrap the future of the Atlantic association, and of civilization generally, in dark uncertainty.

That the United States had maintained a substantial lead in the atomic arms race, both in the expansion of its stockpile of atomic bombs and in the development of new weapons, was not open to doubt. Frequent announcements of test explosions in Nevada and in the Pacific, and of progress in the development of guided missiles, pilotless aircraft, atomic artillery, and atomic-powered aircraft and submarines, made it clear that this country was determined to neglect no potential phase of future offensive warfare, even if preparations for its own defense against atomic attack were admitted to be virtually nonexistent. On November 1, moreover, there took place at Eniwetok Atoll in the Pacific a new kind of atomic explosion which some observers considered no less epoch-making than the first atomic detonation in 1945. The official release spoke cautiously of "experiments contributing to thermonuclear weapons research"; private authorities announced the advent of the hydrogen or "super" bomb and of an age of potentially limitless destruction. Eyewitnesses compared the diminutive "experimental" blast at Eniwetok to the light of ten suns, described a flame five miles high, and spoke of the disappearance of the mile-wide island where the detonation had occurred.[20]

The feeling of anxiety evoked by such a development was heightened by the knowledge that these new powers could not long be monopolized by the United States. The field of atomic weapons was open to all who could bring to bear the necessary material and technological resources. In October the British, despite their postwar exclusion from the exchange of pertinent scientific information with this country, had succeeded in producing their own atomic explosion in the Monte Bello Islands off northwestern Australia. Much more disconcerting was the assurance that the Russians had done even better. By early 1953 it was to become public knowledge that the U.S.S.R.

[20] *New York Times,* November 17, 1952.

had exploded three atomic bombs (one in the late summer of 1949, and two in the fall of 1951), had produced fissionable materials in quantity, and without any doubt possessed "a supply of atomic weapons." [21] Soviet scientists, too, could certainly develop the hydrogen bomb; and meanwhile it could not be many years before the U.S.S.R.'s atomic bomb stockpile and long-range bomber force had reached a level sufficient to carry out a shattering surprise attack on the United States. It was not to be wondered at that to some observers preoccupied with problems of this order, the question of a dozen divisions more or less in Western Europe looked trivial by comparison.

Although developments in this field were clearly destined to modify the whole complexion of the East-West struggle, the secrecy surrounding them was more conducive to emotionally tinged, unverified assumptions than to rational discussion and analysis. Ignorance concerning the availability and potentialities of specific types of atomic weapons was equally evident in the frequent congressional demands for the use of atomic arms in Korea and in the intense revulsion that greeted such proposals in India, Great Britain, and other countries of the free world. Much of the mistrust and fear of American intentions that prevailed in Europe and elsewhere sprang from sheer lack of information, as well as from lack of assurance that this country would use its new capabilities with wisdom and restraint. It was not inconceivable that tactical atomic weapons were the very element that was needed to close the gap in Western Europe's system of defense; conversely, it was possible that unjustified expectations in this regard were playing too large a part in the reluctance of some European countries to press their own defense programs more vigorously. Even within the higher councils of NATO, sound planning in this field was impeded by the provisions of this country's Atomic Energy Act, which forbade the disclosure of certain types of atomic information even to trusted allies.

Matters of this kind undoubtedly merited full discussion on

[21] Statement of Gordon Dean, chairman of the U.S. Atomic Energy Commission, *ibid.*, January 31, 1953.

the highest levels of NATO; but there was no possibility that they could be fruitfully discussed under the conditions of December 1952. This and every other aspect of NATO's future hinged, in the last analysis, on the intentions of the United States; and concerning these neither Secretary Acheson nor those of his colleagues who accompanied him to the NATO Council meeting could speak with much precision. Responsibility for charting the future course of American policy was already passing from the hands of Messrs. Truman and Acheson into those of General Eisenhower and Mr. Dulles, who had been designated to head the State Department in the incoming administration. Mr. Acheson could go no further than to assure his NATO colleagues that the new team would "work with you just as closely and just as enthusiastically as we have" and would prove equally loyal and devoted both to the United States and "to this great association which our country has so freely and so unanimously joined." [22]

Since the "annual review" of NATO defense programs for 1953 had not been completed, there was comparatively little for the Council to do beyond taking note of the progress achieved in various fields of work since the last session at Lisbon. By accepted NATO standards, this progress was by no means unimpressive. On the civilian side, the permanent secretariat under Lord Ismay's direction had established itself as an efficient clearing house and expediter of NATO business. Militarily, it was possible to note "a great advance in the training and effectiveness of the various national forces," "a marked improvement in cooperation between units as well as at the staff level," and "a substantial advance in the standardization of international military procedures, notably in signals." Training exercises and joint maneuvers had been held on an unprecedented scale in Germany, in the North Sea, and in the Mediterranean; "Exercise Mainbrace," a joint naval maneuver held in northern waters in September, had actually engaged

[22] *Department of State Bulletin*, XXVIII, January 5, 1953, 7. The official releases of the Council meeting appear in *Documents on American Foreign Relations, 1952*, No. 18.

200 ships, 80,000 men, and 1,000 aircraft of nine NATO countries.

Meanwhile the build-up of NATO's ground strength in Europe had been such as to establish at least a rough comparability with the Soviet forces stationed in East Germany, Poland, Austria, and Hungary. Detailed estimates of the strength of either side were difficult to draw up because of differences in the size, organization, equipment, and degree of readiness of individual units. Nevertheless it appeared that something resembling the twenty-five active divisions and 4,000 aircraft envisaged at Lisbon actually did exist in locations, chiefly in Germany, where they would be available to parry any sudden Soviet blow. Reserve divisions, on the other hand, were still painfully few. In Paris, General Ridgway "paid tribute to the high quality of the forces under his command" but emphasized, as the Council's communiqué delicately paraphrased,

"that only by a continuing increase in the forces assigned to him would he be able to carry out his responsibilities. Consequently, there could be no relaxation: on the contrary every effort must be made to increase NATO armed strength as rapidly as possible. Admiral McCormick [Supreme Allied Commander, Atlantic] spoke in similar vein."

It was at this point, however, that the military view invariably collided with that of most of the NATO governments. The United States, as always, inclined to support the military in its insistence on more rapid prosecution of the defense build-up; most of this country's partners, on the contrary, tended to question whether such a position was really justified in the light of economic circumstances, the presumptive intentions of the U.S.S.R., and the possibility of further important developments in the atomic field. Thus the discussion of military plans for 1953 echoed earlier and more strenuous contests between the United States and its allies. Most of the latter, it appeared, were still planning to increase their defense expenditure above the 1952 level, but to nothing like the extent envisaged at Lisbon. Secretary Acheson, unable to speak for the next administration in Washington, had few arguments with which to induce a change of heart.

Thus any firm decision on force goals for 1953 was quite out of the question. That was left to the next ministerial meeting of the Council, which would be held in the spring of the new year. In the meantime, the ministers "noted with satisfaction . . . that it was planned to make further individual and collective efforts in 1953 to increase, improve and strengthen the forces now in being." It was better, they agreed, to have a small force that was adequately trained and equipped than larger forces which would be unable to function effectively in an emergency:

"For the future, the Council directed that more emphasis should be given to increasing the effectiveness of the forces of the alliance and the units necessary for their support rather than to the provision of greater numbers, to the extent that resources were not available for both tasks."

As for the infrastructure program, General Ridgway had recommended a minimum commitment of $400 million for 1953 and 1954 to carry forward the construction of over 100 airfields, together with communications and jet fuel storage and distribution facilities, over a large part of Western Europe. Earlier estimates of the total cost of this "fourth slice" of the program had run as high as $744 million, but had been revised downward with the concurrence of the United States. Even $400 million, however, went far beyond the present intentions of the European governments. The most that the Council could agree upon immediately was an allocation of $229.6 million (£80 million), of which the United States undertook to pay $91.8 million or 40 percent. General Ridgway did not hide his chagrin at this decision. The Soviet Union, he pointed out, was not neglecting its own "infrastructure" in Eastern Germany and Poland. "I reject as unjustified the dangerous view that potential aggressors don't want war and won't precipitate war," he said. "We don't know how long we shall be the Kremlin's target, marked for war." [23]

Members of the Council who took a less pessimistic view of the international prospect could at least agree that "such improvement as has taken place in the general international situation" was attributable to the past efforts of the NATO governments to increase their collective strength. "If there were any relaxation in these efforts," said the communiqué, "there would be a corresponding increase in the dangers to which they are exposed." Furthermore, the Council insisted that "the increasingly successful cooperation of the fourteen member governments is a clear proof that the avowed intentions of the Soviet Government to sow dissension in the free world will not succeed." To emphasize "the sense of unity which [they said] is steadily growing among the peoples of the Atlantic Community," the Council announced two further actions of considerable importance. One was an expression of solidarity with France and the Associated States in the campaign in Indochina—an effort which, according to the Council's resolution, was "in fullest harmony with the aims and ideals of the Atlantic Community" and "deserves continuing support from the NATO governments." The other was a partial settlement of the long-standing Anglo-American dispute over the exercise of command responsibilities in the Mediterranean.

The Lisbon conference had left the command situation in the Mediterranean in a thoroughly disorganized state, with American, French, Italian, Greek, and Turkish forces falling under the nominal authority of SHAPE but with the British forces operating more or less autonomously and with hardly a semblance of effective international coordination or a recognized chain of command. Subsequent discussions had confirmed the difficulty of bringing such highly diversified land, sea, and air units into a single command system, especially at a time

[23] *New York Times,* December 20, 1952. This particular cut in the infrastructure program was restored by action of the permanent NATO Council on February 19, 1953.

when the prospects of linking NATO with a possible future Middle East Command or Middle East Defense Organization remained wholly obscure. The United States still wished to entrust Admiral Carney, the NATO Commander-in-Chief for Southern Europe, with the command of all naval as well as land and air forces in the area; the British still held out for a separate naval command, which, in their view, must retain responsibility for through communications in the Mediterranean and should be subordinate not to SHAPE but to NATO's supreme military authority, the Standing Group in Washington.

The scope of the compromise sanctioned by the Atlantic Council in Paris was officially disclosed by Prime Minister Churchill in the House of Commons on December 16. In effect, there would henceforth be not one but two recognized command organizations in the Mediterranean area, both of them nominally responsible to General Ridgway at SHAPE. The existing Southern European Command under Admiral Carney, with headquarters at Naples, would have charge of the NATO land and air forces in Southern and Southeastern Europe (Italy, Greece, and Turkey); it would also retain its authority over the heavy carriers and amphibious and support forces of the United States Sixth Fleet, which Mr. Churchill described as "primarily a force organised for the support of land campaigns in Southern Europe." Other naval forces and naval aviation would be placed under a new international command headed by Admiral Lord Mountbatten at Malta, who would be styled "Commander-in-Chief, Mediterranean" and given responsibility for the wartime security of sea communications, the protection of shipping and convoys, the coordination of logistic support, and the support of adjacent commands as well as the coordination of mine warfare and submarine and antisubmarine operations. The British, French, and Italian forces under Admiral Mountbatten's command would, however, remain responsible to their own national authorities for various tasks of a "national character"—including, in the British case, the security of British communications to the Middle East.[24]

When Mr. Churchill was asked what kind of relationship would be established between the Commander of the American Sixth Fleet and the British Commander-in-Chief, Mediterranean, he replied: "I expect they will help each other." Obviously the arrangement was not one that could operate satisfactorily unless the various commanders and their governments were determined to make it do so. With that reservation, however, the new agreement had the considerable advantage of bringing all NATO forces in the Mediterranean at least nominally into a single system of command, directly subordinate to Supreme Headquarters in Paris. So far as the member countries of NATO were concerned, SHAPE's "southern flank" could now be considered a reality. From the broader standpoint of European and global defense, however, arrangements in the Mediterranean sector were still gravely weakened by the unclarified status of Spain and Yugoslavia as well as the Arab countries farther east.

Negotiations looking toward the inclusion of Spain in the general framework of Western defense—though without direct or indirect participation in NATO—had been carried on in Madrid by United States representatives through most of the year but had not as yet reached any definite conclusion. Since other members of NATO persisted in their refusal to enter into a direct association with the Franco government, and since that government gave no indication of any fundamental change in its own political attitude, the discussions remained strictly bilateral in character. The main impetus behind the talks was the desire of the United States Navy and Air Force to secure facilities in Spain which would supplement those available in Western Europe and North Africa; the principal means of leverage on the Spanish Government, now that the $62.5 million American credit voted in 1950 had all been allocated, was the $125 million subsequently appropriated

---

[24] *Parliamentary Debates, Weekly Hansard,* House of Commons, December 16, 1952, 1204-1205.

by Congress for "military, economic, and technical assistance to Spain." Occasional disclosures from the Spanish side gave an indication of the general character of the expected agreement. There was talk of developing a major naval base at Cadiz, improving the harbor facilities at Cartagena, and establishing major and secondary air bases at various points on the peninsula. Negotiations moved slowly, however, and were far from completion at the end of the year.

In Yugoslavia the progress of events was more rapid, despite the fact that the United States had made no overt move toward including Marshal Tito's Communist but anti-Stalinist government in the Western defense system. That Yugoslavia's absence represented an unseemly breach in the line of "containment" around the Soviet bloc was, of course, apparent to anyone who glanced at the map and saw how it exposed northeastern Italy and separated Greece and Turkey from their partners in the West. The value of the twenty-five or thirty divisions which these new NATO members were contributing to the alliance was necessarily impaired by the unprotected state of their Balkan flank. Yugoslavia, which was under constant pressure from the U.S.S.R. and its satellites, was equally handicapped by the lack of defense coordination with its non-Communist neighbors; but political and ideological differences had thus far precluded any close understanding with either Greece in the south or Italy in the northwest. Although Yugoslavia's strategic importance was deemed sufficient to call for substantial American military aid as well as tripartite economic assistance by the United States, Britain, and France,[25] its defense arrangements had remained wholly uncoordinated with those of the NATO countries.

During the latter part of 1952 these conditions were modified by the development of a marked cordiality in relations among Yugoslavia, Greece, and Turkey. Before the end of

[25] Economic aid allotments to Yugoslavia for the fiscal years 1951–52 and 1952–53 totaled $120 million ($80 million from the U.S.) and $99 million ($78 million from the U.S.) respectively. The value of U.S. military aid shipments to Yugoslavia was not publicly disclosed. For details cf. *Department of State Bulletin*, XXVII, November 24, 1952, 825-826.

the year, a series of official missions by political and military leaders of the three countries had laid the groundwork for nothing less than a five-year treaty of friendship and collaboration, which was ultimately signed at Ankara on February 28, 1953.[26] This pact was to affirm not only the peaceful disposition of the parties toward each other but also their determination to "unite their efforts to strengthen the organization of defense against aggression" through regular collaboration among their general staffs. Although a treaty with two NATO members was not the same thing as Yugoslavia's direct inclusion in NATO, it did signify the end of that country's diplomatic isolation and made it more probable that the thirty-two Yugoslav divisions would act in concert with those of the Atlantic alliance in case of aggression occurring anywhere in Southeastern Europe. How long the forces of the three Balkan allies could withstand the Soviet military machine if its full weight should be brought to bear against them was, of course, a totally different question.

The formation of this new "Balkan entente" was symptomatic of the extent to which military considerations were coming to dominate government policy in all areas affected by the East-West struggle. In normal times there could have been little sympathy between the Communist regime of Marshal Tito, the stiffly republican government of Turkey under President Celâl Bayar, and monarchical Greece under the recently installed conservative administration of Field Marshal Alexander Papagos and his "Greek Rally" party. Papagos, who had owed his success in the Greek elections of November 16 to a new electoral law adopted on the urgent advice of the United States, had himself been a prominent target of the earlier Yugoslav propaganda against Greek "monarcho-fascists." The basis of the present rapprochement was not a similarity of outlook but a common concern for the maintenance of national independence against the threat from behind the Iron Curtain. Realistic appreciation of the military situation imposed a friend-

[26] Text in *Relazioni internazionali*, XVII, March 7, 1953, 228-229.

ship which might or might not continue in case the immediate peril were to be lessened.

Yugoslavia's relations with Italy, its other NATO neighbor, failed to improve in any similar degree and thus prevented any possibility of Italy's inclusion in the new treaty. Here in the north the military pressure was less immediate, and the sources of conflict were deeper. Apart from their contrasting political systems and ideologies, Yugoslavia and Italy were divided by a major territorial issue arising from their conflicting claims to the Free Territory of Trieste. Italy's position in this matter was still based on the tripartite declaration of March 20, 1948, which had held that the arrangements for Trieste provided in the Italian Peace Treaty were unworkable and that the territory should be returned to Italian sovereignty. But this section of the peace treaty could not be nullified as easily as the clauses that had limited Italy's armed forces and defense production. The objections of the U.S.S.R., which continued to insist on strict fulfillment of the peace treaty terms, might have been disregarded with impunity. But it was impossible to disregard the objections of Yugoslavia, which was also a signatory to the Italian treaty and, moreover, exercised full military and political control of the southern portion (Zone B) of the Free Territory.

The declaration of 1948 had been prompted largely by the hope of influencing the outcome of Italy's crucial parliamentary elections, and had been issued at a time when Italy and Yugoslavia belonged to opposite camps in the cold war. Now that Yugoslavia had practically come over to the Western camp, the inability of the two governments to adjust their claims was a serious embarrassment to Western diplomacy and a standing obstacle to the consolidation of Western defense. The Allies could not go back on their pledge to Italy without mortally offending public opinion and giving a lift to Communism in that country, where another parliamentary election was scheduled for the spring of 1953. Yet they could not hope to fulfill their pledge in face of Tito's resistance. They could not even move to carry out the peace treaty provisions, which were anathema to Italy and disliked in Yugoslavia and, moreover, depended on agreement with the U.S.S.R. To complete their discomfiture, the Soviet Government continued to cite the unfulfilled provisions of the Italian treaty in justification of its own refusal to complete the four-power treaty with Austria.

This radically unsatisfactory situation, combined with lesser disputes over fishing rights and other matters, produced intense friction between Italy and Yugoslavia and impaired both countries' value as members or associates of the Western coalition. During the spring of 1952 an Anglo-American-Italian diplomatic conference in London, which resulted in giving Italy virtual control of the civil administration of the Anglo-American Zone (Zone A) in Trieste,[27] was an occasion for riots and demonstrations in Rome, Belgrade, and Trieste itself. Yugoslavia retaliated by further tightening its own grip on Zone B. Meanwhile other aspects of Yugoslav-Italian relations continued to degenerate. Efforts by British and American diplomacy to assuage the bitterness won little appreciation on either side. In September, Foreign Secretary Eden went in person to Belgrade but failed to produce a solution, although foundations were laid for a more cordial relationship between the British and Yugoslav governments. Both Marshal Tito and Premier De Gasperi continued to advertise their desire for agreement but appeared unable to concur on even the procedure for reaching one, still less on the form a permanent settlement might take.

While this situation persisted it was impossible to think seriously of Yugoslavia's direct inclusion in the North Atlantic alliance system, notwithstanding the key role that Trieste and the surrounding area seemed likely to play in any European conflict. It could still be asked, moreover, whether the nature of Yugoslavia's political regime was not in reality an even more fundamental obstacle to full solidarity with the West. In the present nonviolent phase of the cold war in Europe, the existence of a dissident Communist government in Belgrade had

[27] Tripartite memorandum of understanding, May 9, in *Department of State Bulletin*, XXVI, May 19, 1952, 779-780.

obvious advantages, psychological as well as strategic, for the Western powers. But there were those who felt that Tito and his associates remained too deeply committed to a Marxist line of policy to be capable of a genuine partnership with capitalist countries. It was true that Yugoslavia's internal pattern continued to diverge more and more markedly from the Stalinist model. The pace of agricultural collectivization had been relaxed; economic life was being decentralized; various overt features of the police state system were being dropped; preparations were afoot to revise and liberalize the Yugoslav Constitution and representative organs. Yet it seemed unlikely that these changes would alter the basic character of this one-party, totalitarian regime. Even less did they promise to disarm the mutual antipathy that still persisted between the Yugoslav leaders and important circles in the West.

A sharp reminder of this antipathy was provided by Tito at the very moment of the NATO Council meeting in Paris, an occasion which the Yugoslav Marshal deemed opportune for a display of independence directed primarily against Italy and the Vatican but implicitly against the whole policy of the Atlantic alliance. Italy, Tito asserted in an important speech on December 16, was still carrying on its old imperialistic policies at Yugoslavia's expense, still dreaming not only of Trieste but of Dalmatia and "the Mediterranean," still attempting to divide and rule in the Near East, and doing everything to disrupt the growing cordiality of Yugoslavia, Greece, and Turkey. The Vatican, Tito went on, was making itself the instrument of Italian imperialism, trying to undermine the internal unity of Yugoslavia, and making anti-Yugoslav propaganda in foreign countries (accusations which were repeated next day when Yugoslavia formally severed relations with the Holy See). As for the Western powers, Tito objected sharply to their alleged support of Italy, and averred that this was no way to secure Yugoslavia as an ally:

"We shall never be anyone's allies by force. If someone or other doesn't want us for allies, we have another way out. Not by returning to the U.S.S.R. and its satellites, because they too have the knife at our throat; but we have another way out, until they see that they've taken the wrong road. I don't believe the Western Allies will accept Italy's proposal to put pressure on us, because we won't yield to any pressure. We know how far we can go, and we also know where we must stop. The West must take account of our interests just as it does of Italy's." [28]

Whether Tito's "way out" was one that would redound to the ultimate benefit of Yugoslavia might be questionable, but there was no doubt that a change of direction on Yugoslavia's part could be damaging to the Western cause. Tito's government might never become a whole-souled partner of the Atlantic allies; in the United Nations, for example, it frequently voted with the "anticolonial" bloc rather than with the West. But its continued independence had become a vital concern of the Western powers, which could not afford to let it slip back under Soviet control. Yet, at the same time, the West could not afford to buy Yugoslavia's friendship at the expense of another country whose contribution to Western defense was also essential. Nor could it fall back on the methods of compulsory adjustment of international disputes which were favored in Moscow. Adjustment was possible only by the voluntary consent of Italy and Yugoslavia; and such consent was not to be expected unless both parties could be brought to recognize that they had a common interest transcending the differences between them. To that extent the Yugoslav-Italian imbroglio typified the fundamental problem of Western diplomacy—the creation of a sense of solidarity commensurate with the dangers that actually threatened every independent nation.

4. NATO Faces a Changing World

Another international meeting which took place in the course of December provided fresh evidence that Moscow, at any rate, was banking on the inability of its antagonists to achieve and maintain the solidarity of purpose demanded by the times. No other conclusion could be drawn from the performance of the

[28] *Relazioni internazionali*, XVI, December 20, 1952, 1332.

"Congress of the Peoples for Peace," which brought 1,857 representatives from eighty-five countries to Vienna, under the usual Communist and fellow-traveling auspices, from December 12 to 19. That this gathering was designed as a counterattraction to the NATO meeting in Paris was generally recognized in Western quarters. While the NATO statesmen contemplated the dread eventuality of war, Moscow's willing servitors continued to play upon the popular longing for peace and the prevalent dissatisfaction with many phases of Western policy.

The basic insincerity and propagandistic motives of such demonstrations were well understood by the sophisticated and, as usual, had been pointed out in advance by the State Department. Nevertheless, as one Italian periodical commented,

"It would be a grave political error to underrate their importance and influence. The people of the whole world want peace, and whoever takes peace for his banner easily finds a large following, especially when he accompanies his pacifistic declarations with talk of social regeneration and presents himself as an uncompromising upholder of the national interests of every country. To combat Communist propaganda it is not enough to demonstrate its falsity; one must intensify one's efforts to modify the conditions which favor its success. In this field the Atlantic community could perform a highly useful function." [29]

The resolutions adopted by the Vienna congress followed the expected pattern. The principal demands put forward on behalf of "the peoples" concerned a five-power past of peace; an immediate end of hostilities in Korea, Indochina, and Malaya; an end of violent repression of national aspirations, especially in Tunisia and Morocco; an end of racial discrimination (this at a time when the Soviet and satellite governments were just embarking on policies of thinly veiled anti-Semitism); discontinuance of the practice of maintaining bases and troops on the soil of other countries; the conclusion of treaties of peace with Germany and Japan, and of a state treaty with Austria; immediate prohibition of bacteriological as well as atomic and

[29] *Relazioni internazionali*, XVI, December 20, 1952, 1298; cf. *Department of State Bulletin*, XXVII, November 24, 1952, 818.

other weapons of mass destruction, and universal adherence to the Geneva Protocol of 1925; immediate negotiations to end the armaments race; resumption of free commercial and cultural interchange among nations; admission of Communist China and fourteen other states to the United Nations; and a universal struggle "for the spirit of negotiation and agreement, for the right of man to peace." [30]

Thus the servants of world Communism tied up into one package all of the major objections and doubts about Western policy which had been agitating non-Communist as well as Communist world opinion during the past months. All of them, moreover, were presented as direct reflections of the basic policy of NATO, with its reliance on the creation of armed strength as the central element in the defense of peace. In Paris, the NATO Council was even then reiterating the central principle of the Atlantic alliance:

"The Council re-affirmed the purpose of their alliance as being for defence, for peace, and for security, and their resolve to extend the scope of their joint action, and collectively to preserve their common heritage of freedom. The Council welcomed the sense of unity which is steadily growing among the peoples of the Atlantic Community."

But the strategists of international Communism knew that these professions were regarded with skepticism by many in Western Europe and by still more in other lands. To those who rejected them, the Vienna congress offered an agreeable alternative:

"Free discussion has demonstrated a unanimous desire to put an end to the policy of force that has brought so much misery to mankind and risks leading mankind to catastrophe. We hold that there are no differences between states that cannot be settled by negotiation. Enough of destroying towns and countries, enough of piling up weapons of slaughter, enough of preaching hate and calling for war! It is high time to discuss, high time to agree!"

Such an idea had natural appeal not only for outright partisans of the U.S.S.R. but also for those who believed that

[30] *New Times,* No. 1, January 1, 1953, supplement, 3-4.

Soviet intentions, and the way of meeting them, had been mis-
conceived by the Western governments.

The attempt to play upon the misgivings of Western opinion
and thus disrupt the "growing unity" of the Atlantic peoples
also provided the inspiration of Stalin's last message to the
outside world. On Christmas Eve the Soviet Embassy in Washington made available the sensational replies vouchsafed by
the Soviet dictator to four questions which had been addressed
to him some days earlier by the diplomatic correspondent of
the *New York Times.* In many respects their tone seemed remarkably conciliatory. Among other observations, Stalin expressed the opinion that war between the United States and
the U.S.S.R. "cannot be considered inevitable"; indicated that
he would be willing to consider a meeting with General Eisenhower on easing world tensions; and stated that he was prepared to cooperate in a new effort to end the Korean war, an
objective in which, he said, the U.S.S.R. was "interested."

Like many earlier statements, such declarations could easily
be taken to mean that the Kremlin had at last decided to seek
a real improvement in the international situation. Coming on
top of Stalin's *Bolshevik* article and the hydrogen bomb test,
and at a moment of impending political transition in the United
States, they were so interpreted in many quarters. The nub of
Stalin's position, however, seemed to lie not in his general professions of a peaceful attitude but rather in his total rejection
of the existing Western policy. "Wherein lie the sources of
present world contention, in your opinion?" he had been asked.
To which he had replied:

"Everywhere and in everything wherever the aggressive actions
of the policy of the 'cold war' against the Soviet Union find their
expression." [31]

The Soviet Union, in other words, would be prepared to consider a new departure in East-West relations—but only if the
United States, for its part, was prepared to abandon its whole
program of defense against Soviet imperialism.

[31] *New York Times,* December 25, 1952 (*Documents on American Foreign
Relations, 1952,* No. 12).

President Truman and Secretary Acheson had sometimes been reproached for the rather stony skepticism with which they reacted to maneuvers of this character. Admitting that the Kremlin was probably animated mainly by propagandist aims, some observers had felt that the United States could have nothing to lose by displaying greater readiness to exchange views with the Russians, if only because of the effect on an anxious world opinion. The present overture, however, was directed not to the outgoing but to the incoming administration. Any reply would have to come not from the White House or the State Department but from General Eisenhower or Mr. Dulles.

The Secretary of State-designate did reply on December 26, but his answer was not one to suggest the imminence of a new departure in East-West relations or even in the "psychological strategy" which had been so heavily stressed during the autumn. If Stalin had "concrete proposals" to make, said Mr. Dulles, they would be "seriously and sympathetically received." On the possibility of an Eisenhower-Stalin meeting he made no direct comment, but contented himself with an observation frequently made by the incumbent Secretary of State:

"Diplomatic or United Nations channels of communication are always available for such purposes and for exchanges of views designed to find ways to promote peace and international goodwill." [32]

In effect, then, both main contenders in the cold war seemed to be adhering to their established policies and positions: the United States to its primary reliance on growing military power, rather than on possibly untimely negotiation, as the only fully effective restraint on Soviet ambitions; the Soviet Union, to its determination to frustrate this plan not simply through its own armament program but also by encouraging the forces of doubt and dissent within the non-Soviet world. There might be minor shifts of emphasis and method in the months ahead. The Eisenhower administration might intensify this country's own effort to sow division behind the Iron Curtain, and might work

[32] *New York Times,* December 27, 1952.

toward a somewhat different basis of association with allied and friendly countries. The Kremlin might either slacken or intensify the campaign it was conducting against the West, in different areas, by both violent and nonviolent means. There seemed little likelihood, however, that the basic strategy of either party would be materially altered. Even if open, all-out war were to result—an eventuality that both the old and the new American administrations were pledged to avoid if possible, though Mr. Dulles had described it a couple of years earlier as all too likely unless conditions underwent a drastic change [33]—the United States would still find itself relying primarily on its military and technical advantages and relegating political considerations to second place. The Soviet Union would still be using its own great military potential as one element in a broad and flexible strategy, consciously directed toward the ultimate triumph of the Communist idea.

All-out war, however, would too probably represent the defeat of everything for which the United States had striven through the years since 1945 and, indeed, throughout its history. If there had been any illusions on this point before, the new developments in the field of weapons during the year 1952 had been calculated to dispel them. The time had passed, if there had ever been such a time, when the United States could have achieved its security objectives through so-called preventive war. Not only was this country itself exposed to crippling attacks which it had no adequate means of fending off; the entire world was overshadowed by a force that was capable of blotting out the centers of civilization for many generations to come. A wholesale resort to atomic weapons, even if it eventually brought nominal success to one side or the other, would hardly be compatible with the maintenance of democratic freedoms or humane values in any part of the world. More probably it would signal the definitive breakthrough, on a global scale, of those darkly irrational forces in the human personality which had already wrought so much havoc during the preceding half-century.

[33] John Foster Dulles, *War or Peace* (New York, Macmillan, 1950), 3.

The implications of a new resort to arms were such that it was impossible to doubt that the next administration would exert itself as tirelessly as its predecessor to find other means of defending the interests of America and of free society. Whether its efforts would meet with equal or greater success depended not on the United States alone but also, in large part, on the calculations of the Soviet Government, over which this country could exert considerable influence but no control. If the men in the Kremlin were to conclude that only all-out war would protect *their* basic interests, this country and its allies would have no choice but to confront the test with what fortitude they could command. In the meantime, however, they had every interest in preventing the development of a situation in which the Soviet leaders might feel constrained to take the irrevocable step.

The chance that humanity might weather the impending crisis did not depend primarily on adventitious developments such as the expected death of Stalin or a possible momentary advantage accruing to one side or the other in a particular branch of weapons. It lay rather in the obvious preference of the Soviet leaders, deeply ingrained as it appeared to be in the whole Soviet outlook, for advancing their cause by means other than total war. Obviously, the standard-bearers of Soviet Communism had no incentive to subject their own country, or the countries they hoped to conquer for "socialism," to atomic punishment except as a last resort. And, so long as they adhered to this preference and placed their main reliance on the forces of division in the non-Soviet world, the democratic nations would retain the opportunity to combat their ambitions by constructive rather than destructive methods.

An unbiased observer of the world scene at the close of 1952 would have been forced to admit that the situation of the free nations presented ample opportunity for the further advance of Soviet-Communist interests by nonviolent means. A cynic might even have suggested that the Kremlin had no need to think in terms of all-out war against a world that was already sagging and cracking in so many places. Moscow might, of course, deem it necessary to attack with all its strength in order to anticipate an expected attack from the West; but otherwise, why should it prejudice the outcome by moving prematurely against areas which already seemed to be ripening for Soviet control? The West, in its preoccupation with possible military attack, had thus far done rather less than its utmost to eliminate its own and its neighbors' economic, social, and political weaknesses. Would it now open its eyes to the true character of Soviet strategy, as publicly advertised once again at the Moscow congress, and move to recover the lost ground while there was still time?

The problematic condition of the NATO nations in Western Europe, oppressed by the fear of war, the burdens of defense, and the persistence of old rivalries and suspicions, requires no further discussion here. Their situation was not more critical than was the growing disharmony between the NATO powers as a group and the impoverished, underdeveloped, "anti-colonial" countries of Asia, Africa, and Latin America. The instability and the basically revolutionary, neutralist, or outright anti-Western temper of many of these lands had been amply demonstrated in the General Assembly session. New reminders of the deteriorating position in this half of the world were constantly occurring—the swelling unrest in the Arab countries, the deadlocked situation in Iran, the apparent remoteness of any settlement in Palestine or Kashmir, the outbreak of a military insurrection in Indonesia, the discovery of a Communist plot in Thailand, the conclusion by Ceylon (despite urgent representations by the United States) of a long-term agreement to supply large quantities of natural rubber to Communist China.[34]

Favorable signs, of course, were not entirely absent. Great Britain and Egypt seemed likely to reach an agreement on the Sudan which might ultimately pave the way for a settlement of the Suez Canal issue and possibly for a Middle East Defense Organization. A new campaign season had opened in Indo-

[34] Problems of Economic Defense: Second Report to Congress on the Mutual Defense Assistance Control Act of 1951 (Washington, January 1953), 26-28.

china without producing any imminent threat to the French-Vietnamese position. Communist violence had waned in Malaya, Burma, and the Philippines. John M. Allison, the Assistant Secretary of State for Far Eastern Affairs, had felt able to tell a Japanese audience of the "cautious optimism" inspired by direct observation of Far Eastern trends.[35] Japan itself, with its election out of the way, had seemed receptive toward Mr. Allison's advice to conclude reparation agreements with Indonesia and the Philippines and make a beginning with its own rearmament. If no solution was in sight for the greater problems of Korea, China, and Formosa, it was at least gratifying to find so little evidence of Communist progress in other Far Eastern areas. The outbreak of general war might, of course, provoke a drastic deterioration in the Far Eastern situation from one day to the next. But the situation did not seem incapable of improvement if general war was avoided and the favorable possibilities were recognized and utilized.

Effective use of the favorable elements in the world situation would undoubtedly require a new realism and a new resolution on the part of every people that still remained free to influence its own destiny. To a quite special degree these qualities would be required of the 160 million people of the United States, who alone possessed the power, the resources, the skills and initiative which, if wisely used, might crown the adventure with a successful outcome. "A foreign policy is the face and voice of a whole people," General Eisenhower had said during the campaign. And, although the American people had now once again chosen a leader who recognized the global import of the nation's policy, he and they would still labor under important handicaps as they endeavored to chart a course between the Scylla of atomic war and the Charybdis of irresponsible retreat.

Still lacking, in the opinion of some eminent observers, was an adequate national recognition of the grave and complex problems America would continue to face after the new administration was installed. Such misgivings had recently been

[35] *Department of State Bulletin*, XXVII, December 1, 1952, 858.

expressed in unusually forthright terms by Dr. James B. Conant,
soon to be designated as the new United States High Commissioner (and, it was hoped, eventually Ambassador) to Germany:

". . . If anyone is inclined to argue that the free world has safely
turned the corner and from here on out we can relax and before
long enjoy a peaceful world, then I must dissent and dissent most
strongly. To my mind the threats to our security are only slightly
less than they were a year or two ago, and one threat seems to me
to be far greater. I refer to the failure of the American people to
face up to the long-term implications of a divided world in an
atomic age. Indeed, if I were forced to name the greatest single
threat to our national security, I would say it lay in the unwillingness of the American people to recognize the threats inherent in
the international situation, our failure to face the gravity and continuing nature of the struggle with Russian Communism." [36]

The most immediate need, in Dr. Conant's opinion, was the
development of a national military policy which corresponded
to the actual danger rather than to any arbitrary estimate of
what the country could or should afford. This in itself would
be difficult to reconcile with the demand for economy which
had played so large a part in the recent campaign. And yet there
were those who argued that normal criteria of economy were
simply not applicable to the situation in which the United States
found itself. So outstanding an authority as Paul G. Hoffman,
former Economic Cooperation Administrator and a strong
Eisenhower supporter, had flatly asserted that "the United
States cannot live within its means under conditions favorable
to the survival of a free society until genuine peace prevails
in the world." [37]

Equally critical with the material demands still to be made
on the United States was the question of the general orientation of the national policy, particularly in relation to allied and
friendly countries. Through 1952 the nation had shown a definite tendency to withdraw into itself, placing its main reliance

[36] James B. Conant, *The Threat to Our National Security* (New York, Committee for Economic Development, 1952), 5.
[37] Paul G. Hoffman, "Living Beyond Our Means," *Atlantic Monthly*, CXC,
No. 5, November 1952, 36.

on a growing military capability and shunning close contact with other nations, their ideas, and their problems. Some perspicacious observers, speaking as Americans rather than as political partisans, had expressed serious misgivings about the long-term implications of this trend. Winthrop W. Aldrich, General Eisenhower's choice as Ambassador to Britain, had argued that "we cannot decisively win even the cold war on the basis of superiority in productive capacity and military power alone." [38] Economists had insisted that a foreign policy based on maintaining a coalition of free nations could not succeed unless it was matched by an economic policy that genuinely permitted those nations to earn their way and discharge their obligations.[39] Others had cited the irritations, often petty in themselves but impressive in the aggregate, associated with the presence of large numbers of American troops and civilian officials overseas. Many had decried the increasingly inhospitable features of the national immigration policy and procedure. Still more had deprecated what they described as a prevailing atmosphere of "fear and suspicion," directed against Americans as well as foreigners, which sometimes appeared to threaten the very foundations of American democracy and of America's world position.

These were some of the problems that were bound to engage the attention of the new administration as it endeavored to carry forward and, where possible, to improve upon the work of its predecessor. The record of the preceding years, with their successes and failures, their insights and their miscalculations, would be available for its guidance. The education which Americans had already received in the responsibilities of world power would not have been wasted; nor would the basic American policies developed through the years of the Truman administration be lightly discarded. As had happened so often in the past, it was President Truman's own words that best de-

[38] Address of November 19, 1952 in *Vital Speeches*, XIX, January 15, 1953, 197.
[39] Cf. Sumner H. Slichter, "More Imports Needed," *Atlantic Monthly*, CXCI, No. 1, January 1953, 37-40.

fined America's situation as the era associated with his name drew toward its close:

"What we need in this coming period is faith in ourselves, courage to do the difficult and distasteful things, consideration and forbearance for our allies, without whose confidence and help our purposes will not be accomplished.

"To guide us on this path will soon be the responsibility of new people. No statesmen have ever had a heavier responsibility than these men will have. Let us see that they are given the type of support they need to do their work. Let us tell them frankly when we think they are wrong. But let us support them wholeheartedly when they are right. Let us work with them for peace and freedom in the world and for progress and security for our country.

"If we do these things, I am sure we can continue to move forward, with God's help, to a better and safer world." [40]

[40] Address to the National War College, December 19, 1952, in *Department of State Bulletin*, XXVIII, January 12, 1953, 46.

SELECTED BIBLIOGRAPHY

No annual bibliography of world affairs can list more than a fraction of the literature that constantly pours from the world's presses. The present selection, designed to provide a point of departure for both the student and the general reader, attempts to give due representation to all significant viewpoints but is necessarily limited to works that are both relevant and reasonably accessible. The decision for or against inclusion of particular titles has been governed solely by these criteria and not by agreement or disagreement with the views expressed. Additional materials of permanent interest will be found listed in earlier volumes of this series, and more extensive bibliographies are readily available in such specialized publications as *Foreign Affairs*, the *American Political Science Review*, and *International Organization*. A number of representative American and foreign periodicals which specialize in international affairs are included as a reminder that much of the most illuminating current material in the field appears in this medium. Except as otherwise indicated, all official United States documents are distributed by the U.S. Government Printing Office (Washington 25, D.C.). United Nations publications are obtainable in the United States from the International Documents Service, Columbia University Press, New York 27, N.Y.; official British documents, from British Information Services, 30 Rockefeller Plaza, New York 20, N.Y.

GENERAL

Periodicals

American Journal of International Law. Washington, American Society of International Law, quarterly.

Aussenpolitik: Zeitschrift für internationale Fragen. Stuttgart, Deutsche Verlags-Anstalt, bimonthly.

Chronique de Politique Étrangère. Brussels, Institut des Relations Internationales, bimonthly.

Current Developments in United States Foreign Policy. Washington, Brookings Institution, ten times a year. (Suspended 1952.)

Current History. Philadelphia, Events Publishing Company, monthly.

Department of State Bulletin. Washington, Department of State, weekly.

The Economist. London, The Economist, weekly.

Europa-Archiv. Frankfurt am Main, Verlag Europa-Archiv, semimonthly.

For a Lasting Peace, For a People's Democracy! Bucharest, Information Bureau of the Communist and Workers' Parties, weekly.

Foreign Affairs. New York, Council on Foreign Relations, quarterly.

Foreign Commerce Weekly. Washington, Department of Commerce, weekly.

440   THE UNITED STATES IN WORLD AFFAIRS

International Affairs. London, Royal Institute of International Affairs, quarterly.
International Conciliation. New York, Carnegie Endowment for International
Peace, monthly except July and August.
International Journal. Toronto, Canadian Institute of International Affairs, quar-
terly.
International Organization. Boston, World Peace Foundation, quarterly.
News: A Review of World Events. Moscow, "Trud," semimonthly.
New Times. Moscow, "Trud," weekly.
Politique Étrangère. Paris, Centre d'Études de Politique Étrangère, quarterly.
Relazioni Internazionali. Milan, Istituto di Studi Internazionali, weekly.
World Politics. New Haven, Yale Institute of International Studies, quarterly.
The World Today. London, Royal Institute of International Affairs, monthly.

Reference Works and Documents

POLITICAL HANDBOOK OF THE WORLD, 1953, edited by Walter H. Mallory
and Joseph Barber. New York, Harper (Council on Foreign Relations), 1953,
233 p.
STATISTICAL YEARBOOK, 1952. (*United Nations Publication* 1952.XVII.1.)
New York, 1952, 554 p.
DEMOGRAPHIC YEARBOOK, 1952. (United Nations Publication 1953.XIII.1.)
New York, 1952, 518 p.
DOCUMENTS ON INTERNATIONAL AFFAIRS, 1947–1948, edited by Margaret
Carlyle. New York, Oxford University Press (Royal Institute of International
Affairs), 1952, 878 p.
DOCUMENTS ON INTERNATIONAL AFFAIRS, 1949–50, edited by Margaret Car-
lyle. London, Oxford University Press (Royal Institute of International
Affairs), 1953, 796 p.
DOCUMENTS ON AMERICAN FOREIGN RELATIONS, XIII (1951), edited by
Raymond Dennett and Katherine D. Durant. Princeton, Princeton University
Press (World Peace Foundation), 1953, 626 p.
DOCUMENTS ON AMERICAN FOREIGN RELATIONS, 1952, edited by Clarence W.
Baier and Richard P. Stebbins. New York, Harper (Council on Foreign Re-
lations), 1953.

The Contemporary Crisis

THE WORLD AND THE WEST, by Arnold Toynbee. New York, Oxford University
Press, 1953, 99 p.
THE FUTURE OF THE WEST, by J. G. de Beus. New York, Harper, 1953, 178 p.
IN AN AGE OF REVOLUTION, by Cyril Garbett, Archbishop of York. New York,
Oxford University Press, 1952, 318 p.
THE PRICE OF REVOLUTION, by D. W. Brogan. New York, Harper, 1952, 280 p.
THE ANATOMY OF REVOLUTION, by Crane Brinton. New York, Prentice-Hall,
1952, 324 p.
THE TAMING OF THE NATIONS: A Study of the Cultural Bases of International
Policy, by F. S. C. Northrop. New York, Macmillan, 1952, 362 p.
IST FRIEDE NOCH MÖGLICH?: Die Verantwortung der Macht, by Hermann
Rauschning, Heidelberg, Vowinckel, 1953, 331 p.
"The Quest of Independence," by Francis B. Sayre. (*Foreign Affairs*, XXX,
July 1952, 564-579.)
INTERNATIONAL ORGANIZATION, by Norman Hill. New York, Harper, 1952,
627 p.

The Commonwealth of Man, by Frederick L. Schuman. New York, Knopf, 1952, 494 p.

Recent History

The American Road to World Peace, by Sir Alfred Zimmern. New York, Dutton, 1953, 287 p.
American Crisis Diplomacy: The Quest for Collective Security, 1918–1952, by Richard W. Van Alstyne. Stanford, Stanford University Press, 1952, 165 p.
Turbulent Era: A Diplomatic Record of Forty Years, 1904–1945, by Joseph C. Grew. Boston, Houghton Mifflin, 1952, 2 vols.
The Diplomats, 1919–1939, edited by Gordon A. Craig and Felix Gilbert. Princeton, Princeton University Press, 1953, 683 p.
Survey of International Affairs: The World in March 1939, edited by Arnold Toynbee and Frank T. Ashton-Gwatkin. New York, Oxford University Press (Royal Institute of International Affairs), 1952, 546 p.
The Challenge to Isolation, 1937–1940, by William L. Langer and S. Everett Gleason. New York, Harper (Council on Foreign Relations), 1952, 794 p.
Back Door to War: The Roosevelt Foreign Policy, 1933–1941, by Charles Callan Tansill. Chicago, Regnery, 1952, 690 p.
The Struggle for Europe, by Chester Wilmot. New York, Harper, 1952, 766 p. (Strategy and Diplomacy of World War II.)
Survey of International Affairs, 1947–1948, by Peter Calvocoressi. New York, Oxford University Press (Royal Institute of International Affairs), 1952, 581 p.
Survey of International Affairs, 1949–1950, by Peter Calvocoressi. London, Oxford University Press (Royal Institute of International Affairs), 1953, 590 p.
Lying in State, by Stanton Griffis. Garden City, Doubleday, 1952, 315 p. (Postwar diplomatic memoirs.)
Tito, by Vladimir Dedijer. New York, Simon & Schuster, 1952, 443 p. (Yugoslav account of the Tito-Cominform quarrel.)

Economic Affairs

Economic Planning for the Peace, by E. F. Penrose. Princeton, Princeton University Press, 1953, 384 p.
Economic Stability in a Changing World, by John H. Williams. New York, Oxford University Press, 1953, 284 p.
International Monetary Cooperation, 1945–1952, by Brian Tew. New York, Longmans, Green, 1952, 180 p.
World Population and Future Resources, by Paul K. Hatt. New York, American Book Co., 1952, 262 p.
International Trade and Economic Development, by Jacob Viner. Glencoe, Ill., Free Press, 1952, 154 p.
The Progress of Underdeveloped Areas, edited by Bert F. Hoselitz. Chicago, University of Chicago Press, 1952, 296 p.
Raising the World's Standard of Living: The Coordination and Effectiveness of Point Four, United Nations Technical Assistance and Related Programs, by Robert T. Mack, Jr. New York, Citadel Press, 1953, 285 p.

INTERNATIONAL TECHNICAL ASSISTANCE: Programs and Organization, by Walter R. Sharp. Chicago, Public Administration Service, 1952, 146 p.

REVIEW OF INTERNATIONAL COMMODITY PROBLEMS, 1952. (U.N. Publication 1953.II.D.1.) New York, Feb. 1953, 51 p.

REPORT ON OPERATIONS OF THE INTERNATIONAL MATERIALS CONFERENCE, Feb. 26, 1951 to Mar. 1, 1952. Washington, I.M.C., 1952, 91 p.

THE STATE OF FOOD AND AGRICULTURE: Review and Outlook, 1952. (F.A.O. Document CL 16/2.) Rome, Food and Agriculture Organization, Oct. 1952, 126 p.

Social Problems

PRELIMINARY REPORT ON THE WORLD SOCIAL SITUATION, with Special Reference to Standards of Living. (U.N. Publication 1952.IV.11.) New York, Sept. 1952, 180 p.

WHAT IS RACE? Evidence from Scientists. Paris, UNESCO, Oct. 1952, 86 p.

"The Refugee in World Affairs." (*Journal of International Affairs*, VII, No. 1, 1953, 5-92.)

Communism

SOCIOLOGY AND PSYCHOLOGY OF COMMUNISM, by Jules Monnerot. Boston, Beacon, 1953, 339 p.

DER EUROPÄISCHE KOMMUNISMUS: Seine Geschichte von 1917 bis zur Gegenwart, by Franz Borkenau. Bern, Francke, 1952, 540 p.

A CENTURY OF CONFLICT: Communist Techniques of World Revolution, by Stefan T. Possony. Chicago, Regnery, 1953, 439 p.

THE ORGANIZATIONAL WEAPON: A Study of Bolshevik Strategy and Tactics, by Philip Selznick. New York, McGraw-Hill, 1952, 350 p.

WITNESS, by Whittaker Chambers. New York, Random House, 1952, 808 p.

U.S. POLICY

FOREIGN POLICIES OF THE UNITED STATES, by Hollis W. Barber. New York, Dryden Press, 1953, 614 p.

ELEMENTS OF AMERICAN FOREIGN POLICY, by L. Larry Leonard. New York, McGraw-Hill, 1953, 611 p.

MAJOR PROBLEMS OF UNITED STATES FOREIGN POLICY, 1952–1953. Washington, Brookings Institution, 1952, 412 p.

OUR FOREIGN POLICY 1952. (Department of State Publication 4466, General Foreign Policy Series 56.) Washington, 1952, 79 p.

LET FREEDOM RING: The Struggle for a Peaceful World. (Department of State Publication 4443, General Foreign Policy Series 67.) Washington, Nov. 1952, 96 p.

THE IRONY OF AMERICAN HISTORY, by Reinhold Niebuhr. New York, Scribner, 1952, 174 p.

IDEALS AND SELF-INTEREST IN AMERICA'S FOREIGN RELATIONS, by Robert Endicott Osgood. Chicago, University of Chicago Press, 1953, 491 p.

THE NATIONAL INTEREST: Alone or With Others? edited by N. D. Palmer. (*Annals of the American Academy of Political and Social Science*, CCLXXXII, July 1952, 1-118.)

FOREIGN POLICY WITHOUT FEAR, by Vera Micheles Dean. New York, McGraw-Hill, 1953, 219 p.

ISOLATION AND ALLIANCES: An American Speaks to the British, by Walter Lippman. Boston, Atlantic-Little, Brown, 1952, 56 p.

MAJOR CAMPAIGN SPEECHES OF ADLAI E. STEVENSON, 1952. New York, Random House, 1953, 320 p.

THE CHALLENGE TO AMERICAN FOREIGN POLICY, by John J. McCloy. Cambridge, Harvard University Press, 1953, 81 p.

A FOREIGN POLICY FOR AMERICANS, by Robert A. Taft. Garden City, Doubleday, 1951, 127 p.

"A Policy of Boldness," by John Foster Dulles. (Life, XXXII, No. 20, May 19, 1952, 146-160.)

CONTAINMENT OR LIBERATION? An inquiry into the Aims of United States Foreign Policy, by James Burnham. New York, John Day, 1953, 256 p.

CITIZENS OF THE WORLD, by Stringfellow Barr. Garden City, Doubleday, 1952, 285 p.

Organization and Operations

UNITED STATES FOREIGN POLICY: Its Organization and Control, by William Yandell Elliott and others. New York, Columbia University Press, 1952, 288 p.

AMERICAN FOREIGN POLICY AND THE SEPARATION OF POWERS, by Daniel S. Cheever and H. Field Haviland, Jr. Cambridge, Harvard University Press, 1952, 244 p.

REVIEW OF BIPARTISAN FOREIGN POLICY CONSULTATIONS SINCE WORLD WAR II. (S. Doc. 87, 82nd Cong.) Washington, 1952, 48 p.

THE FUTURE OF AMERICAN POLITICS, by Samuel Lubell. New York, Harper, 1951, 285 p.

AMERICAN DIPLOMATIC AND CONSULAR PRACTICE, by Graham H. Stuart. (New ed.) New York, Appleton-Century-Crofts, 1952, 477 p.

"The United States Mission to the United Nations," by Channing B. Richardson. (International Organization, VII, Feb. 1953, 22-34.)

Legislation

SUMMARY OF THE LEGISLATIVE RECORD, EIGHTY-SECOND CONGRESS. (S. Doc. 165, 82nd Cong., 2nd Sess.) Washington, 1952, 155 p.

LEGISLATIVE HISTORY OF THE COMMITTEE ON FOREIGN RELATIONS, UNITED STATES SENATE, EIGHTY-SECOND CONGRESS. (S. Doc. 161, 82nd Cong., 2nd Sess.) Washington, 1952, 71 p.

EIGHTY-SECOND CONGRESS: Survey of Activities of the Committee on Foreign Relations, House of Representatives, Jan. 3, 1951-July 7, 1952. (Committee print.) Washington, 1952, 81 p.

JAPANESE PEACE TREATY AND OTHER TREATIES RELATING TO SECURITY IN THE PACIFIC (S. Exec. A, B, C, and D, 82nd Cong., 2nd Sess., ratified March 20, 1952).
    Hearings: Senate Foreign Relations Committee, Jan. 21-25, 1952, 182 p.
    Report: S. Exec. Rept. 2, Feb. 14, 1952, 30 p.

PROTOCOL TO THE NORTH ATLANTIC TREATY ON THE ACCESSION OF GREECE AND TURKEY (S. Exec. E, 82nd Cong., 2nd Sess., ratified Feb. 7, 1952).
    Report: S. Exec. Rept. 1, Jan. 21, 1952, 15 p.

CONVENTION ON RELATIONS WITH THE FEDERAL REPUBLIC OF GERMANY AND A PROTOCOL TO THE NORTH ATLANTIC TREATY (S. Exec. Q and R, 82nd Cong., 2nd Sess., ratified July 1, 1952).

Document: Message from the President, transmitting texts of the agreements, June 2, 1952, 328 p. *Hearings:* Senate Foreign Relations Committee, June 10-17, 1952, 267 p. *Report:* S. Exec. Rept. 16, June 28, 1952, 58 p.

MUTUAL SECURITY ACT OF 1951, AMENDMENTS (Public Law 400, 82nd Cong., approved June 20, 1952—H. R. 7005).

Documents: Message from the President, Mar. 6, 1952 (H. Doc. 382), 14 p.; Basic Data Supplied by Executive Branch (Committee print, House Foreign Affairs Committee and Senate Foreign Relations Committee), 97 p.; Selected Tables on Proposed Mutual Security Act of 1952 (H. R. 7005) (Committee print, House Foreign Affairs Committee), 63 p. *Hearings:* House Foreign Affairs Committee, Mar. 13-Apr. 29, 1952, 1136 p.; Senate Foreign Relations Committee, Mar. 13-Apr. 4, 1952, 821 p.; Senate Armed Services Committee (on S. 3086), May 8-13, 1952, 140 p. *Reports:* H. Rept. 1922, May 12, 1952, 108 p.; S. Rept. 1490 (on S. 3086), Apr. 30, 1952, 66 p.; S. Rept. 1575 (on S. 3086), May 15, 1952, 1 p. *Conference Report:* H. Rept. 2031, June 4, 1952, 22 p.

IMMIGRATION AND NATIONALITY ACT OF 1952 (Public Law 414, 82nd Cong., became law June 27, 1952—H. R. 5678).

Hearings: Senate Judiciary Committee (subcommittees) (on S. 716, etc.), Mar. 6-Apr. 9, 1951, 787 p. *Reports:* H. Rept. 1365, Feb. 14, 1952, 328 p.; S. Rept. 1137 (on S. 2550), Jan. 29, 1952, Mar. 13, 1952, 2 pts. *Conference Report:* H. Rept. 2096, June 9, 1952, 129 p. *Veto Message:* H. Doc. 520, June 25, 1952, 101 p.

DEFENSE DEPARTMENT APPROPRIATIONS, 1953 (Public Law 488, 82nd Cong., approved July 10, 1952—H.R. 7391).

Hearings: House Appropriations Committee (subcommittee), 1952, 9 pts.; Senate Appropriations Committee (subcommittee), Feb. 4-June 21, 1952, 1491 p. *Reports:* H. Rept. 1685, Apr. 3, 1952, 11 p.; S. Rept. 1861, June 27, 1952, 25 p. *Conference Reports:* H. Rept. 2483, July 4, 1952, 9 p.; H. Rept. 2495, July 5, 1952, 2 p.

STATE, JUSTICE, COMMERCE, AND THE JUDICIARY APPROPRIATION ACT, 1953 (Public Law 495, 82nd Cong., approved July 10, 1952—H.R. 7289).

Hearings: House Appropriations Committee (subcommittee), Department of State, Jan. 28-Feb. 18, 1952, 2 pts.; Senate Appropriations Committee (subcommittee), Feb. 19-June 23, 1952, 1828 p. *Reports:* H. Rept. 1665, Mar. 28, 1952, 38 p.; S. Rept. 1807, June 24, 1952, 29 p. *Conference Reports:* H. Rept. 2454, July 3, 1952, 8 p.; H. Rept. 2485, July 4, 1952, 8 p.

MILITARY AND NAVAL CONSTRUCTION ACT, 1952 (Public Law 534, 82nd Cong., approved July 14, 1952—H.R. 8120).

Hearings: House Armed Services Committee, May 12-June 10, 1952, pp. 3925-4831; Senate Armed Services Committee (subcommittee), June 17-28, 1952, 709 p. *Reports:* H. Rept. 2143, June 10, 1952, 33 p.; S. Rept. 2078, July 3, 1952, 22 p. *Conference Report:* H. Rept. 2488, July 5, 1952, 6 p.

SUPPLEMENTAL APPROPRIATION ACT, 1953 (Public Law 547, 82nd Cong., approved July 15, 1952—H.R. 8370).

Documents: Estimates of Mutual Security Appropriation (H. Doc. 510), June 17, 1952, 5 p.; Change in Supplemental Estimate (H. Doc. 512), June 18, 1952, 1 p. *Hearings:* House Appropriations Committee (subcommittees), May 21-June 24, 1952, 4 pts.; Senate Appropriations Committee, June 11-July 2, 1952, 573 p. *Reports:* H. Rept. 2316, June 26, 1952, 70 p.; S. Rept. 2076, July 2, 1952, 23 p. *Conference Reports:* H. Rept. 2494, July 5, 1952, 11 p.; H. Rept. 2499, July 7, 1952, 3 p.

AUTHORIZING ADDITIONAL IMMIGRANTS INTO THE U.S. (H.R. 7376, 82nd Cong.).
Document: Message from the President, March 24, 1952 (H. Doc. 400), 8 p. Hearings: House Judiciary Committee (subcommittee), May 22-June 3, 1952, 232 p. (Cf. also S. Rept. 1740, June 12, 1952, 2 p.; S. Res. 326, 82nd Cong., adopted June 21, 1952.)
ST. LAWRENCE SEAWAY AND POWER PROJECT (S.J. Res. 27, S.J. Res. III, 82nd Cong.).
Document: Message from the President, Jan. 28, 1952 (H. Doc. 337), 7 p. Hearings: Senate Foreign Relations Committee, Feb. 25-29, 1952, 872 p. Report: S. Rept. 1489, Apr. 28, 1952, 1 p. Application to International Joint Commission: H. Doc. 528, June 30, 1952, 9 p.
CUSTOMS SIMPLIFICATION ACT (H.R. 5505, 82nd Cong.).
Hearings: Senate Finance Committee, Apr. 22-29, 1952, 318 p.
TREATIES AND EXECUTIVE AGREEMENTS (S.J. Res. 130, 82nd Cong.).
Hearings: Senate Judiciary Committee (subcommittee), May 21-June 9, 1952, 540 p.

Economic Policy and Foreign Aid

RESOURCES FOR FREEDOM: A Report to the President by the President's Materials Policy Commission, June, 1952. Washington, 1952, 5 vols.
QUARTERLY REPORTS TO THE PRESIDENT BY THE DIRECTOR OF DEFENSE MOBILIZATION: 5th, Strength for the Long Run, Apr. 1, 1952, 48 p.; 6th, Defense Mobilization, Shield Against Aggression, July 1, 1952, 51 p.; 7th, New Resources Bring New Opportunities, Oct. 1, 1952, 44 p. Washington, 1952.
SEMIANNUAL REPORTS OF THE NATIONAL ADVISORY COUNCIL on International Monetary and Financial Problems: Oct. 1, 1951-Mar. 31, 1952, 69 p. (H. Doc. 353, 82nd Cong., 2nd Sess.); Apr. 1-Sept. 30, 1952, 74 p. (H. Doc. 60, 83rd Cong., 1st Sess.). Washington, 1952-53.
SURVEY OF UNITED STATES INTERNATIONAL FINANCE, 1951, by Gardner Patterson and Jack N. Behrman. Princeton, Princeton University Press, 1952, 325 p.
THE UNITED STATES IN INTERNATIONAL BANKING, by Siegfried Stern. New York, Columbia University Press, 1951, 447 p.
BALANCE OF PAYMENTS OF THE UNITED STATES 1949–1951: A Supplement to the Survey of Current Business. Washington, 1952, 165 p.
"The Balance of Payments in 1952," by Walther Lederer. (Survey of Current Business, XXXIII, No. 3, Mar. 1953, 7-12.)
SEMIANNUAL REPORTS TO CONGRESS OF THE EXPORT-IMPORT BANK OF WASHINGTON: 14th, Jan.-June 1952, 79 p.; 15th, July-Dec. 1952, 83 p. Washington, 1952-53.
A TRADE AND TARIFF POLICY IN THE NATIONAL INTEREST, prepared by the Public Advisory Board for Mutual Security. Washington, Feb. 1953, 78 p.
FOREIGN TRADE AND U.S. TARIFF POLICY: A Report on the Views of Leading Citizens in Twenty-five Cities, edited by Joseph Barber. New York, Council on Foreign Relations, 1953, 39 p.
FOREIGN AID BY THE UNITED STATES GOVERNMENT 1940–1951: A Supplement to the Survey of Current Business. Washington, 1952, 118 p.
"United States Foreign Aid in 1952," by E. S. Kerber. (Survey of Current Business, XXXIII, No. 3, Mar. 1953, 13-19.)
THIRTY-THIRD REPORT TO CONGRESS ON LEND-LEASE OPERATIONS: Message

from the President transmitting Report for the Period ending Dec. 31, 1951. Washington, 1952, 51 p.

REPORTS TO CONGRESS ON THE MUTUAL SECURITY PROGRAM: 2nd, June 30, 1952, 48 p.; Supplement: Statistical Data Relating to the Mutual Security Program, as of June 30, 1952, 32 p.; 3rd, Dec. 31, 1952, 15 p. Washington, 1952–53.

MUTUAL DEFENSE ASSISTANCE CONTROL ACT OF 1951: Reports to Congress by the Mutual Security Administrator. 1st, Problems of Economic Defense, Oct. 15, 1952, 107 p.; 2nd, Jan. 16, 1953, 89 p. Washington, 1952–53.

Military Policy

SEMIANNUAL REPORTS OF THE SECRETARY OF DEFENSE (with semiannual reports of the Secretaries of the Army, Navy, and Air Force): 3rd, Jan. 1-June 30, 1952, 260 p.; 4th, July 1-Dec. 31, 1952, 36 p. Washington, 1952–53.

SEMIANNUAL REPORTS OF THE ATOMIC ENERGY COMMISSION: 12th, July 1952, 125 p.; 13th, Jan. 1953, 210 p. Washington, 1952–53.

"Atomic Weapons and American Policy," by J. Robert Oppenheimer. (*Foreign Affairs*, XXXI, July 1953, 525-535.)

ANNUAL REPORT OF THE FEDERAL CIVIL DEFENSE ADMINISTRATION, 1952. Washington, 1953, 138 p.

STRATEGY FOR SURVIVAL, by John E. Kieffer. New York, McKay, 1953, 306 p.

"Military Problems of the New Administration," by Walter Millis. (*Foreign Affairs*, XXXI, Jan. 1953, 215-224.)

The Information Program

TRUTH IS OUR WEAPON, by Edward W. Barrett. New York, Funk and Wagnalls, 1953, 355 p.

IIA: The International Information Administration Program. (Department of State Publication 4939, International Information and Cultural Series 32.) Washington, Apr. 1953, 32 p.

OBJECTIVES OF THE UNITED STATES INFORMATION PROGRAM: Reply to Questions Asked by the Hon. Pat McCarran in his Letter to the Secretary of State, Sept. 13, 1951. (S. Doc. 143, 82nd Cong., 2nd Sess.) Washington, 1952, 78 p.

UNITED STATES OVERSEAS INFORMATION PROGRAMS: Background Study. (Senate Foreign Relations Committee, 82nd Cong., 2nd Sess., Subcommittee on Overseas Information Programs of the United States, Staff Study No. 1.) Washington, Nov. 17, 1952, 48 p.

OVERSEAS INFORMATION PROGRAMS OF THE UNITED STATES: *Hearings,* Senate Foreign Relations Committee (subcommittee), 82nd Cong., 2nd Sess., Nov. 20-21, 1952. Washington, 1953, 227 p. *Interim Report,* Jan. 30, 1953, 7 p. (S. Rept. 30, 83rd Cong., 1st Sess.)

SEMIANNUAL REPORTS OF THE SECRETARY OF STATE ON THE INTERNATIONAL INFORMATION AND EDUCATIONAL EXCHANGE PROGRAM: 8th, July 1-Dec. 31, 1951, 70 p.; 9th, Jan. 1-June 30, 1952, 42 p. (Department of State Publications 4575 and 4867, International Information and Cultural Series 22 and 31.) Washington, 1952–53.

REPORT ON THE OPERATIONS OF THE DEPARTMENT OF STATE (Under Public Law 594, 79th Cong.). (H. Doc. 410, 82nd Cong., 2nd Sess.) Washington, 1952, 81 p.

SEMIANNUAL REPORTS OF THE UNITED STATES ADVISORY COMMISSION ON INFORMATION: 6th, July 1952, 30 p.; 7th, Jan. 1953, 23 p. (H. Doc. 526, 82nd Cong., 2nd Sess., and H. Doc. 94, 83rd Cong., 1st Sess.) Washington, 1952–53.

SEMIANNUAL REPORTS OF THE UNITED STATES ADVISORY COMMISSION ON EDUCATIONAL EXCHANGE: 7th, July 1-Dec. 31, 1951, 8 p.; 8th, Jan. 1-June 30, 1952, 24 p. (H. Doc. 412, 82nd Cong., 2nd Sess., and H. Doc. 35, 83rd Cong., 1st Sess.) Washington, 1952–53.

Immigration Policy

MEMO TO AMERICA: The DP Story—The Final Report of the United States Displaced Persons Commission. Washington, 1952, 376 p.

THE IMMIGRATION AND NATIONALITY ACT: A Summary of its Principal Provisions, by Frank L. Auerbach. New York, Common Council for American Unity, 1952, 103 p.

"Visa Work of the Department of State and the Foreign Service: Changes under the Immigration and Nationality Act of June 27, 1952," by Eliot B. Coulter. (*Department of State Bulletin*, XXVIII, Feb. 2, 1953, 195-203; Feb. 9, 1953, 232-239.)

HEARINGS BEFORE THE PRESIDENT'S COMMISSION ON IMMIGRATION AND NATURALIZATION, Sept. 30-Oct. 29, 1952. (Committee print, House Judiciary Committee, 82nd Cong., 2nd Sess.) Washington, 1952, 2089 p.

WHOM WE SHALL WELCOME: Report of the President's Commission on Immigration and Naturalization. Washington, 1953, 319 p.

UNITED NATIONS

(See also regional headings)

EVERYMAN'S UNITED NATIONS, 3rd Edition. (U.N. Publication 1951.I.25.) New York, 1952, 388 p.

THE UNITED NATIONS: Background, Organization, Functions and Activities, by Amry Vandenbosch and Willard N. Hogan. New York, McGraw-Hill, 1952, 456 p.

UNITED NATIONS AND WORLD COMMUNITY, by A. H. Feller. Boston, Little, Brown, 1952, 153 p.

UNITED NATIONS: SUCCESS OR FAILURE?, edited by John A. Krout. (*Proceedings of the Academy of Political Science*, XXV, No. 2, Jan. 1953.) New York, 1953, 128 p.

The U.S. and the U.N.

"American National Interests and the Responsibilities of United Nations Membership," by Leland M. Goodrich. (*International Organization*, VI, Aug. 1952, 369-380.)

UNITED STATES PARTICIPATION IN THE UNITED NATIONS: Report by the President to the Congress for the Year 1951. (Department of State Publication 4583, International Organization and Conference Series III, 80.) Washington, 1952, 324 p.

ACTIVITIES OF UNITED STATES CITIZENS EMPLOYED BY THE UNITED NATIONS: *Hearings,* Senate Judiciary Committee (subcommittee), Oct. 13-Dec. 17, 1952, 434 p. *Report* of the Subcommittee (Committee print), Jan. 2, 1953, 18 p. Washington, 1952–53.

"Report of the Secretary-General on Personnel Policy." (U.N. Document A/2364, Jan. 30, 1953.) New York, 1953, 39 p.

Reports of U.N. Activities

UNITED NATIONS BULLETIN. New York, U.N. Department of Public Information, semimonthly.

YEAR BOOK OF THE UNITED NATIONS, 1951, Including an Account of the Proceedings of the Sixth Session of the General Assembly. (U.N. Publication 1952.I.30.) New York, 1952, 1030 p.

1952 ANNUAL REVIEW OF UNITED NATIONS AFFAIRS, edited by Clyde Eagleton and Richard N. Swift. New York, New York University Press, 1953, 326 p.

ANNUAL REPORT OF THE SECRETARY-GENERAL ON THE WORK OF THE ORGANIZATION, 1 July 1951 to 30 June 1952. (General Assembly *Official Records, Seventh Session,* Supplement 1.) New York, Aug. 1952, 182 p.

"Sixième Session de l'Assemblée Générale de Nations Unies." (*Chronique de politique étrangère,* V, Mar. 1952, 238-250.)

RESOLUTIONS ADOPTED BY THE GENERAL ASSEMBLY DURING ITS SIXTH SESSION, 6 November 1951 to 5 February 1952. (General Assembly *Official Records, Sixth Session,* Supplement 20.) New York, 1952, 91 p.

"Issues Before the Seventh General Assembly." (*International Conciliation,* No. 484, Oct. 1952, 361-488.)

"General Assembly." (*International Organization,* VII, Feb. 1953, 51-118.) (Reviews the first half of the Assembly's Seventh Session.)

RESOLUTIONS ADOPTED BY THE GENERAL ASSEMBLY AT ITS SEVENTH SESSION during the period from 14 October to 21 December 1952. (General Assembly *Official Records, Seventh Session,* Supplement 20.) New York, n.d., 72 p.

Political and Security

REPORT OF THE SECURITY COUNCIL TO THE GENERAL ASSEMBLY Covering the Period from 16 July 1951 to 15 July 1952. (General Assembly *Official Records, Seventh Session,* Supplement 2.) New York, October 1952, 65 p.

"Disarmament." (U.N. Document ST/DPI/SER.A/75, Feb. 20, 1953.) New York, 1953, 34 p.

"Le Problème du désarmement devant l'O.N.U." (*Chronique de politique étrangère,* V, Mar. 1952, 232-250.)

"Second Report of the Disarmament Commission." (U.N. Document DC/20, Oct. 13, 1952.) New York, 1952, 206 p.

"Report to the President by the Deputy United States Representative on the United Nations Disarmament Commission, January 12, 1953." (*Department of State Bulletin,* XXVIII, Jan. 26, 1953, 142-154.)

REPORT OF THE COLLECTIVE MEASURES COMMITTEE. (General Assembly *Official Records, Seventh Session,* Supplement 17.) New York, Oct. 1952, 23 p.

"Admission of New Members: The United Nations and the League of Nations," by Aleksander W. Rudzinski. (*International Conciliation,* No. 480, Apr. 1952, 141-196.)

"Chinese Representation in the United Nations," by Herbert W. Briggs. (*International Organization*, VI, May 1952, 192-209.)

"Die asiatisch-arabische Dreizehner-Gruppe," by Heinrich Bechtold. (*Aussenpolitik*, IV, Feb. 1953, 103-115.) (The Arab-Asian bloc in the Seventh Assembly.)

Economic and Social

REPORT OF THE ECONOMIC AND SOCIAL COUNCIL Covering the Period from 22 September 1951 to 1 August 1952. (General Assembly *Official Records, Seventh Session*, Supplement 3.) New York, Oct. 1952, 122 p.

UNITED NATIONS PROGRAMS FOR TECHNICAL ASSISTANCE, 3rd Edition. (U.N. Publication 1952.I.20.) New York, Oct. 1952, 36 p.

COMMISSION ON HUMAN RIGHTS: Report of the Eighth Session, 14 April to 14 June 1952. (Economic and Social Council *Official Records, Fourteenth Session*, Supplement 4.) New York, July 1952, 71 p.

"The United Nations and Human Rights," by Marian Neal. (*International Conciliation*, No. 489, Mar. 1953, 111-174.)

"Human Rights in the United Nations," by Charles Malik. (*United Nations Bulletin*, XIII, Sept. 1, 1952, 248-257.)

"Two Covenants on Human Rights Being Drafted," by James Simsarian. (*Department of State Bulletin*, XXVII, July 7, 1952, 20-31.)

"Freedom of Information and the United Nations," by Carroll Binder. (*International Organization*, VI, May 1952, 210-226.)

"The Refugee and the United Nations," by Elfan Rees. (*International Conciliation*, No. 492, June 1953, 267-314.)

Trusteeship and Non-Self-Governing Territories

REPORT OF THE TRUSTEESHIP COUNCIL Covering its Fourth Special Session and its Tenth and Eleventh Sessions, 18 December 1951 to 24 July 1952. (General Assembly *Official Records, Seventh Session*, Supplement 4.) New York, Sept. 1952, 298 p.

"Report of the Committee on Information from Non-Self-Governing Territories." (U.N. Document A/2219, Oct. 10, 1952.) New York, 1952, 78 p.

Related Agencies

THE WORK OF F.A.O. 1951/52: Report of the Director-General. Rome, Food and Agriculture Organization, 1952, 31 p.

INTERNATIONAL BANK FOR RECONSTRUCTION AND DEVELOPMENT: Seventh Annual Report, 1951-52. Washington, I.B.R.D., 1952, 64 p.

THE INTERNATIONAL TELECOMMUNICATION UNION, by George Arthur Codding, Jr. Leyden, Brill (New York, Heinman), 1952, 505 p.

THE END OF THE I.T.O., by William Diebold, Jr. (Essays in International Finance, 16.) Princeton, Princeton University Press, 1952, 37 p.

UNESCO Report to the United Nations, 1951-1952. Paris, UNESCO, July 1952, 206 p.

UNESCO Report of the Director-General on the Activities of the Organization from April 1951 to July 1952. (UNESCO Document 7C/3.) Paris, UNESCO, Oct. 1952, 344 p.

450   THE UNITED STATES IN WORLD AFFAIRS

U.S. NATIONAL COMMISSION FOR UNESCO: Informal Report of the United
States Delegation to the Seventh Session of the General Conference of
UNESCO, Nov. 12-Dec. 11, 1952, Paris, France. Washington, n.d., 30 p.
THE WORK OF W.H.O. 1952: Annual Report of the Director-General to the
World Health Assembly and to the U.N. Geneva, World Health Organiza-
tion, Mar. 1953, 204 p.
UNICEF (U.N. International Children's Emergency Fund): General Progress
Reports of the Executive Director. (U.N. Documents E/ICEF/205, Oct. 1,
1952, 75 p., and E/ICEF/221, Mar. 15, 1953, 75 p.). New York, 1952–53.

NORTH ATLANTIC AREA AND WESTERN EUROPE

THE ZONE OF INDIFFERENCE, by Robert Strausz-Hupé. New York, Putnam,
1952, 312 p. (Intellectual and moral tensions between the U.S. and Europe.)
REGIONAL ORGANIZATIONS: Europe and the North Atlantic Area—A Descrip-
tion of their Development and Functions. (Department of State Publication
4944, European and British Commonwealth Series 3.) Washington, Apr.
1953, 34 p.
GOVERNMENTS OF CONTINENTAL EUROPE, edited by James T. Shotwell. (New
ed.) New York, Macmillan, 1952, 881 p.
MAJOR FOREIGN POWERS: Governments of Great Britain, France, Soviet Union,
and Germany, by Gwendolen M. Carter and others. (Rev. ed.) New York,
Harcourt, Brace, 1952, 815 p.
CONVENTION ON RELATIONS WITH THE FEDERAL REPUBLIC OF GERMANY AND
A PROTOCOL TO THE NORTH ATLANTIC TREATY: Message from the President . . . Transmitting the Convention on Relations between the Three Powers
and the Federal Republic of Germany, signed at Bonn on May 26, 1952 and
a Protocol to the North Atlantic Treaty signed at Paris on May 27, 1952.
(S. Exec. Q and R, 82nd Cong., 2nd Sess.) Washington, June 2, 1952, 328 p.
(Contains also the texts of the Schuman Plan treaty, the Treaty Constituting
the European Defense Community, and related documents.)

NATO and the European Defense Community

THE DEFENSE OF WESTERN EUROPE, by Drew Middleton. New York, Apple-
ton-Century-Crofts, 1952, 313 p.
"NATO Changes Direction," by Drew Middleton. (Foreign Affairs, XXXI,
Apr. 1953, 427-440.)
NATO—NORTH ATLANTIC TREATY ORGANIZATION: Its Development and Sig-
nificance. (Department of State Publication 4630, General Foreign Policy
Series 75.) Washington, Aug. 1952, 50 p.
THE NATO HANDBOOK. London, NATO Information Service, 1952.
ATLANTIC ALLIANCE: NATO's Role in the Free World. London, Royal Insti-
tute of International Affairs, 1952, 172 p.
BULWARK OF THE WEST: Implications and Problems of NATO, by Arthur C.
Turner. Toronto, Ryerson Press (Canadian Institute of International Affairs),
1953, 106 p.
THE ARMED ROAD TO PEACE: An analysis of NATO, by Blair Bolles and
Francis O. Wilcox. (Headline Books, No. 92.) New York, Foreign Policy
Association, 1952, 62 p.
LE PRIX DE LA LIBERTÉ, by Fred Simson. Paris, Berger-Levrault, 1953, 231 p.
(A study of NATO.)

"The First Year of SHAPE," by Robert J. Wood. (*International Organization,* VI, May 1952, 175-191.)

"Activités dans le cadre du Pacte de l'Atlantique Nord." (*Chronique de politique étrangère,* V, Mar. 1952, 188-217; May 1952, 305-315; VI, Mar. 1953, 163-188.)

"Atlantikpakt under Europäische Verteidigungsgemeinschaft," by Wilhelm Cornides and Hermann Volle, parts 3-5. (*Europa-Archiv,* VII, Mar. 5, 1952, 4745-4762; July 20, 1952, 5020-5040.)

"Konsolidierung und Erweiterung der NATO: Entwicklung der Atlantikpakt-Organisation seit den Konferenzen von Lissabon und Paris," by Hermann Volle. (*Europa-Archiv,* VIII, Mar. 20, 1953, 5551-5562.)

"Background for the European Defense Community," by Clarence C. Walton. (*Political Science Quarterly,* XLVIII, Mar. 1953, 42-69.)

"La Communauté Européenne de Défense." (*Chronique de politique étrangère,* V, Sept.-Nov. 1952, 521-564.)

"Der Vertrag über die Gründung der Europäischen Verteidigungsgemeinschaft," by Johann Adolf Graf Kielmansegg. (*Europa-Archiv,* VII, July 20, 1952, 5009-5019.)

Western European Integration

EUROPE TODAY AND TOMORROW: International Bulletin of the European Movement. Paris, European Movement, monthly.

WHITHER EUROPE: UNION OR PARTNERSHIP? by M. J. Bonn. New York, Philosophical Library, 1952, 207 p.

L'EUROPE EN FACE DE SON DESTIN, by Edouard Bonnefous. Paris, Presses Universitaires de France, 1952, 386 p.

"European Integration," by John Goormaghtigh. (*International Conciliation,* No. 488, Feb. 1953, 49-109.)

EUROPE'S QUEST FOR UNITY, by Saul K. Padover. (Headline Books, No. 97.) New York, Foreign Policy Association, 1953, 63 p.

"L'Intégration politique européenne." (*Chronique de politique étrangère,* VI, May 1953, 277-320.)

COUNCIL OF EUROPE: Report on the Proceedings of the 4th Session of the Consultative Assembly of the Council of Europe, Strasbourg, May 26/30 and Sept. 15/30, 1952. (Cmd. 8701; Miscellaneous No. 15, 1952.) London, 1952.

"The Schuman Plan: Sovereign Powers of the European Coal and Steel Community," by Raymond Vernon. (*American Journal of International Law,* XLVII, April 1953, 183-202.)

"La Ratification du Traité Instituant la Communauté Européenne du Charbon et de l'Acier." (*Chronique de politique étrangère,* VI, Jan. 1953, 5-51.)

"Les Débuts de la Communauté Européenne du Charbon et de l'Acier." (*Chronique de politique étrangère,* VI, Jan. 1953, 52-77.)

EUROPEAN COAL AND STEEL COMMUNITY: Report on the Situation of the Community, by the High Authority, Jan. 10, 1953. N.p., n.d., 142 p.

"Die politischen und wirtschaftlichen Probleme der europäischen Einigung um die Jahreswende 1952/53," by Wilhelm Cornides and others. (*Europa-Archiv,* VIII, Jan. 5, 1953, 5391-5402.)

Economic Problems

ECONOMIC SURVEY OF EUROPE SINCE THE WAR: A Reappraisal of Problems and Prospects. (U.N. Publication 1953.II.E.4.) Geneva, Feb. 1953, 385 p.

EUROPE AND THE UNITED STATES IN THE WORLD ECONOMY, by Robert Marjolin. Durham, Duke University Press, 1953, 105 p.

TRADE AND PAYMENTS IN WESTERN EUROPE: A Study in Economic Cooperation 1947-51, by William Diebold, Jr. New York, Harper (Council on Foreign Relations), 1952, 488 p.

"End of the Marshall Plan," by John H. Williams. (*Foreign Affairs*, XXX, July 1952, 593-611.)

EUROPE—THE WAY AHEAD: Towards Economic Expansion and Dollar Balance; Fourth Annual Report of the OEEC. Paris, Organization for European Economic Cooperation, Dec. 1952, 358 p.

THE STRASBOURG PLAN: Proposals for Improving the Economic Relations Between Member States of the Council of Europe and the Overseas Countries with Which They Have Constitutional Links. Strasbourg, Council of Europe, 1952, 197 p.

Great Britain and the Commonwealth

(See also regional headings)

BRITAIN AND THE UNITED STATES: Problems in Cooperation, by Henry L. Roberts and Paul A. Wilson. New York, Harper (Council on Foreign Relations), 1953, 253 p.

THE UNITED STATES AND US, by Marjorie Banks and Edward Ward. New York, British Book Center, 1953, 208 p.

THE FOREIGN POLICY OF THE BRITISH LABOR GOVERNMENT, 1945-1951, by M. A. Fitzsimmons. Notre Dame, University of Notre Dame Press, 1953, 182 p.

IN PLACE OF FEAR, by Aneurin Bevan. New York, Simon & Schuster, 1952, 213 p.

REARMAMENT AND ANGLO-AMERICAN ECONOMIC RELATIONS: A Problem Paper. Washington, Brookings Institution, 1952, 64 p.

ECONOMIC SURVEY FOR 1952. (Cmd. 8509.) London, 1952, 48 p.

"Grossbritanien und die europäische Integration," by Hans Joachim Heiser. (*Europa-Archiv*, VII, Aug. 5, 1952, 5073-5084.)

BRITAIN, THE STERLING AREA AND EUROPE, by F. V. Meyer. Cambridge, Bowes, 1952, 150 p.

THE STERLING AREA: An American Analysis, published by the E.C.A. Mission to the United Kingdom. London, Her Majesty's Stationery Office, 1952, 672 p.

THE STERLING AREA, by A. R. Conan. New York, St. Martin's Press, 1952, 192 p.

CONSULTATION AND COOPERATION IN THE COMMONWEALTH, by Heather J. Harvey. New York, Oxford University Press (Royal Institute of International Affairs), 1952, 411 p.

Other Western-oriented Countries

DEMOCRACY IN FRANCE: The Third and Fourth Republics, by David Thompson. New York, Oxford University Press (Royal Institute of International Affairs), 1952, 300 p.

FRANCE UNDER THE FOURTH REPUBLIC, by François Goguel. Ithaca, Cornell University Press, 1952, 198 p.

"French Attitudes Toward Western European Unity," by Edgar S. Furniss, Jr. (*International Organization*, VII, May 1953, 199-212.)

CHRISTIAN DEMOCRACY IN ITALY AND FRANCE, by Mario Einaudi and François Goguel. Notre Dame, University of Notre Dame Press, 1952, 299 p.

"Touch-and-Go in Italy," by Ugo La Malfa. (*Foreign Affairs*, XXXI, Jan. 1953, 257-267.)

SPAIN IN THE MODERN WORLD, by James Cleugh. New York, Knopf, 1953, 339 p.

"Franco Spain: A Reappraisal," by S. Grover Rich, Jr. (*Political Science Quarterly*, LXVII, Sept. 1952, 378-398.)

THE ECONOMY OF SPAIN, by Sidney C. Sufrin and others. (Headline Books, No. 95.) New York, Foreign Policy Association, 1952, 62 p.

"Spain in Western Defense," by Lawrence Fernsworth. (*Foreign Affairs*, XXXI, July 1953, 648-662.)

THE SCANDINAVIAN STATES AND FINLAND: A Political and Economic Survey. New York, Royal Institute of International Affairs, 1952, 320 p.

GREECE: American Dilemma and Opportunity, by L. S. Stavrianos. Chicago, Regnery, 1952, 246 p.

"Greece under Papagos," by N. C. (*World Today*, IX, Mar. 1953, 109-119.)

DIE TÜRKEI AUF DEM WEG NACH EUROPA, by Friedrich von Rummel. Munich, Rinn, 1952, 177 p.

THE AUSTRIAN TREATY: A Case Study of Soviet Tactics. (Department of State Publication 5012, European and British Commonwealth Series 43.) Washington, May 1953, 16 p.

"Le Traité avec l'Autriche." (*Chronique de politique étrangère*, V, May 1952, 322-333.)

TRIESTE ED I SUOI PROBLEMI: Situazione, Tendenze, Prospettive, by Giorgio Roletto. Trieste, Borsatti, 1952, 367 p.

IL PROBLEMA DI TRIESTE, by Diego de Castro. Bologna, Cappelli, 1952, 679 p.

THE GERMAN PROBLEM

THE RETURN OF GERMANY: A Tale of Two Countries, by Norbert Muhlen. Chicago, Regnery, 1953, 310 p.

LA NOUVELLE ALLEMAGNE 1949–1951, by Henri Laporte. Paris, Charles-Lavauzelle, 1952, 202 p.

L'ALLEMAGNE DE L'OCCIDENT, 1945–1952, by Alfred Grosser. Paris, Gallimard, 1953, 340 p.

REPORT ON GERMANY, September 21, 1949-July 31, 1952. Office of the U.S. High Commissioner for Germany, 1952, 299 p.

DEUTSCHLAND IM WIEDERAUFBAU: Tätigkeitsbericht der Bundesregierung für das Jahr 1952. Bonn, Presse- und Informationsamt der Bundesregierung, [1953], 246 p.

L'ÉCONOMIE ALLEMANDE CONTEMPORAINE (ALLEMAGNE OCCIDENTALE), 1945–1952, by André Piettre. Paris, Médicis, 1952, 672 p.

"Les Accords contractuels." (*Chronique de politique étrangère*, V, Sept.-Oct. 1952, 565-587.)

REPORT OF THE CONFERENCE ON GERMAN EXTERNAL DEBTS, London, February-August 1952. (Department of State Publication 4746, European and British Commonwealth Series 38.) Washington, 1952, 59 p.

"The Struggle for German Unity," by Henry B. Cox. (*Department of State Bulletin*, XXVI, Apr. 14, 1952, 563-568.)

"Le Problème de l'unification de l'Allemagne." (*Chronique de politique étrangère*, V, July 1952, 395-439.)

DIE BEMÜHUNGEN DER BUNDESREPUBLIK UM WIEDERHERSTELLUNG DER EIN-
HEIT DEUTSCHLANDS DURCH GESAMTDEUTSCHE WAHLEN: Dokumente und
Akten. (2nd enlarged ed.) Bonn, Bundesministerium für Gesamtdeutsche
Fragen, October 1952, 112 p.
"Report of the United Nations Commission to Investigate Conditions for Free
Elections in Germany." (U.N. Document A/2122, May 5, 1952.) New York,
1952, 71 p.
EAST GERMANY UNDER SOVIET CONTROL. (Department of State Publication
4596, European and British Commonwealth Series 34.) Washington, June
1952, 95 p.
THE BERLIN STORY, by Curt Riess. New York, Dial, 1952, 368 p.

SOVIET BLOC

CHALLENGE TO THE KREMLIN, by Harry Hodgkinson. New York, Praeger,
1953, 190 p.
MARX AGAINST THE PEASANT, by David Mitrany. Chapel Hill, University of
North Carolina Press, 1952, 301 p.

U.S.S.R.

CURRENT DIGEST OF THE SOVIET PRESS. New York, Joint Committee on Slavic
Studies, weekly.
BOLSHEVISM: An Introduction to Soviet Communism, by Waldemar Gurian.
Notre Dame, University of Notre Dame Press, 1952, 189 p.
SOVIET IMPERIALISM: Its Origins and Tactics, edited by Waldemar Gurian.
Notre Dame, University of Notre Dame Press, 1953, 166 p.
AMERICAN-RUSSIAN RELATIONS, 1781–1947, by William Appleman Williams.
New York, Rinehart, 1952, 367 p.
THE END OF A REVOLUTION: Soviet Russia—from Revolution to Reaction, by
Fritz Sternberg. New York, John Day, 1952, 191 p.
THE RUSSIANS IN FOCUS, by Harold J. Berman. Boston, Atlantic-Little, Brown,
1953, 209 p.
THE KREMLIN VS. THE PEOPLE: The Story of the Cold Civil War in Stalin's
Russia, by Robert Magidoff. New York, Doubleday, 1953, 288 p.
A WINDOW ON RED SQUARE, by Frank Rounds, Jr. Boston, Houghton, Mifflin,
1953, 304 p.
POSTMARKED MOSCOW, by Lydia Kirk. New York, Scribner, 1952, 278 p.
SOVIET OPPOSITION TO STALIN: A Case Study in World War II, by George
Fischer. Cambridge, Harvard University Press, 1952, 235 p.
FORCED LABOR IN THE SOVIET UNION. (Department of State Publication 4716,
European and British Commonwealth Series 37.) Washington, 1952, 76 p.
THE SOVIET PROPAGANDA PROGRAM: A Preliminary Study. (Senate Foreign
Relations Committee, 82nd Cong., 2nd Sess., Subcommittee on Overseas In-
formation Programs of the United States, Staff Study No. 3.) Washington,
Nov. 17, 1952, 23 p.
"The Moscow Economic Conference," by Alec Cairncross. (*Soviet Studies,* IV,
Oct. 1952, 113-132.)
"Die Probleme des Ost-West-Handels auf der Internationalen Wirtschaftskon-
ferenz in Moskau," by Erwin Weghorn. (*Europa-Archiv,* VII, May 20, 1952,
4931-4936.)
CURRENT SOVIET POLICIES: The Documentary Record of the 19th Communist

Party Congress and the Reorganization After Stalin's Death, from the Trans-
lations of the *Current Digest of the Soviet Press,* edited by Leo Gruliow.
New York, Praeger, 1953, 268 p.
"The Nineteenth Party Congress," by Philip E. Mosely. (*Foreign Affairs,*
XXXI, Jan. 1953, 238-256.)
"Le XIXe Congrès du Parti Communiste d'U.R.S.S." (*Chronique de politique
étrangère,* VI, Mar. 1953, 189-214.)
MALENKOV: Stalin's Successor, by Martin Ebon. New York, McGraw-Hill,
1953, 284 p.
WHAT NEXT IN RUSSIA? by Isaac Deutscher. New York, Oxford University
Press, 1953, 230 p.

The "People's Democracies"

NEWS FROM BEHIND THE IRON CURTAIN. New York, National Committee for
a Free Europe, monthly.
REPORTS of the Research and Publications Service, National Committee for a
Free Europe, Inc. New York, N.C.F.E., 1952–53.
STALIN'S SATELLITES IN EUROPE, by Ygael Gluckstein. Boston, Beacon, 1952,
333 p.
HISTOIRE DES DÉMOCRATIES POPULAIRES, by François Fejtö. Paris, Éditions du
Seuil, 1952, 446 p.
THE CAPTIVE MIND, by Czeslaw Milosz. New York, Knopf, 1953, 251 p. (In-
tellectuals under Communism.)
ANATOMY OF A SATELLITE, by Dana Adams Schmidt. Boston, Atlantic-Little,
Brown, 1952, 512 p. (Czechoslovakia.)
LA POLOGNE D'UNE OCCUPATION À L'AUTRE (1944–1952), by Jean Malara
and Lucienne Rey. Paris, Éditions du Fuseau, 1952, 371 p.

NEAR AND MIDDLE EAST

MIDDLE EAST JOURNAL. Washington, Middle East Institute, quarterly.
MIDDLE EASTERN AFFAIRS. New York, Council for Middle Eastern Affairs,
monthly.
MIDDLE EAST DILEMMAS: The Background of United States Policy, by J. C.
Hurewitz. New York, Harper (Council on Foreign Relations), 1953, 273 p.
BACKGROUND OF THE MIDDLE EAST, edited by Ernest Jäckh. Ithaca, Cornell
University Press, 1952, 236 p.
WORLD WITHOUT END: THE MIDDLE EAST, by Emil Lengyel. New York, John
Day, 1953, 374 p.
CHALLENGE AND RESPONSE IN THE MIDDLE EAST: The Quest for Prosperity,
1919–1951, by Hedley V. Cooke. New York, Harper, 1952, 366 p.
THE MIDDLE EAST IN THE WAR, by George Kirk. (Survey of International
Affairs, 1939–1946.) New York, Oxford University Press (Royal Institute
of International Affairs), 1952, 511 p.
IL MEDIO ORIENTE. (Special issue of *Relazioni internazionali,* XVI, July 19,
1952, 693-819.)
CONSTITUTIONS, ELECTORAL LAWS, TREATIES OF STATES IN THE NEAR AND
MIDDLE EAST, edited by Helen M. Davis. Durham, Duke University Press,
1953, 541 p.
NATIONALISM IN THE MIDDLE EAST: A Series of Addresses. . . . (Washington,
Middle East Institute, 1952, 68 p.

REVIEW OF ECONOMIC CONDITIONS IN THE MIDDLE EAST, 1951–52: Supplement to World Economic Report. (U.N. Publication 1953.II.C.1.) New York, Feb. 1953, 161 p.
"Unity and Disunity in the Middle East," by J. C. Hurewitz. (*International Conciliation*, No. 481, May 1952, 197-260.)
"U.S. Foreign Policy in the Middle East," by Henry A. Byroade. (*Department of State Bulletin*, XXVII, Dec. 15, 1952, 931-935.)
"The Development of United States Policy in the Near East, South Asia, and Africa, 1951–52," by Harry N. Howard. (*Department of State Bulletin*, XXVII, Dec. 8, 1952, 891-898; Dec. 15, 1952, 936-946.)
"The Defense of the Middle East," by B. H. Liddell Hart. (*Harper's Magazine*, CCVI, April 1953, 63-70.)
"Some Aspects of the Security Problem in the Middle East," by Halford L. Hoskins. (*American Political Science Review*, XLVII, Mar. 1953, 188-198.)
"The Arabs, Israel, and Near East Defense," by Hal Lehrman. (*Commentary*, XIV, Dec. 1952, 563-574.)

The Palestine Problem and Israel

TO JERUSALEM, by Count Folke Bernadotte. New York, British Book Center, 1952, 280 p.
ISRAEL: THE ESTABLISHMENT OF A STATE, by Harry Sacher. New York, British Book Center, 1952, 332 p.
STATE IN THE MAKING, by David Horowitz, New York, Knopf, 1953, 349 p.
ISRAEL, by Norman Bentwich. New York, McGraw-Hill, 1952, 224 p.
THE NEW STATE OF ISRAEL, by Gerald de Gaury. New York, Praeger, 1952, 259 p.
"Washington Comes to Israel's Economic Rescue," by Hal Lehrman. (*Commentary*, XIV, Oct. 1952, 297-307.)
THE ARAB REFUGEE PROBLEM, by Joseph B. Schechtman. New York, Philosophical Library, 1952, 137 p.
"Twelfth Progress Report of the United Nations Conciliation Commission for Palestine . . . 1 May to 7 October 1952." (U.N. Document A/2216, Oct. 8, 1952.) New York, 1952, 11 p.
ANNUAL REPORT OF THE DIRECTOR OF THE UNITED NATIONS RELIEF AND WORKS AGENCY FOR PALESTINE REFUGEES IN THE NEAR EAST . . . 1 July 1951 to 30 June 1952. (U.N. General Assembly *Official Records, Seventh Session*, Supplement 13.) New York, Sept. 1952, 48 p.
"The Seventh United Nations Assembly and the Palestine Question," by Benjamin Schwadran. (*Middle Eastern Affairs*, IV, Apr. 1953, 113-126.)

The Arab States

THE ARABS AND THE WEST, by Clare Hollingworth. London, Methuen, 1952, 285 p.
WHAT THE ARABS THINK, by William R. Polk and W. Jack Butler. (Headline Books, No. 96.) New York, Foreign Policy Association, 1952, 63 p.
THE EMERGENCE OF MODERN EGYPT, by John S. Badeau and Richard H. Nolte. (Headline Books, No. 98.) New York, Foreign Policy Association, 1953, 62 p.
GREAT BRITAIN AND EGYPT, 1914–1951. New York, Royal Institute of International Affairs, 1952, 216 p.

"The Anglo-Egyptian Negotiations, 1950–1952," by Paul L. Hanna. (*Middle Eastern Affairs*, III, Aug.-Sept. 1952, 213-233.)

THE SUDAN QUESTION, by Mekki Abbas. New York, Praeger, 1952, 201 p.

EGYPT: Documents Concerning the Constitutional Development in the Sudan and the Agreement between the Government of the United Kingdom . . . and the Egyptian Government concerning Self-Government and Self-Determination for the Sudan, Feb. 17, 1953. (Egypt No. 2, 1953; Cmd. 8767.) London, 1953, 70 p.

"Iraqi Politics 1948–52," by S. Yin'am. (*Middle Eastern Affairs*, III, Dec. 1952, 349-360.)

THE ECONOMIC DEVELOPMENT OF IRAQ: Report of a Mission Organized by the International Bank for Reconstruction and Development. Baltimore, Johns Hopkins Press, 1952, 463 p.

"The Struggle in Lebanon," by R. Mosseri. (*Middle Eastern Affairs*, III, Nov. 1952, 328-334.)

THE ARABIA OF IBN SAUD, by Roy Lebkicher and others. New York, Moore, 1952, 179 p.

SAUDI ABABIA: With an Account of the Development of its Natural Resources, by K. S. Twitchell and Edward J. Jurji. (Rev. ed.) Princeton, Princeton University Press, 1953, 239 p.

Iran

IRAN, by Richard N. Frye. New York, Holt, 1953, 126 p.

"The Social Support of Current Iranian Policy," by T. Cuyler Young. (*Middle East Journal*, VI, Spring 1952, 125-143.)

IRAN: Correspondence between Her Majesty's Government in the United Kingdom and the Iranian Government, and Related Documents, concerning the Joint Anglo-American Proposals for the Settlement of the Oil Dispute, Aug., 1952 to Oct., 1952. (Cmd. 8677; Iran No. 1, 1952.) London, 1952, 16 p.

AFRICA

STRUGGLE FOR AFRICA, by Vernon Bartlett. London, Muller, 1953, 251 p.

LE CONTINENT AFRICAIN AU MILIEU DU SIÈCLE, by René Laure. Paris, Charles-Lavauzelle, 1952, 433 p.

AFRICA: New Crises in the Making, by Harold R. Isaacs and Emory Ross. (Headline Books, No. 91.) New York, Foreign Policy Association, 1952, 62 p.

"The United States, the United Nations, and Africa," by Vernon McKay. (*Department of State Bulletin*, XXVIII, Feb. 16, 1953, 267-273.)

North Africa

L'AFRIQUE DU NORD EN MARCHE, by Ch.-André Julien. Paris, Julliard, 1952, 416 p.

"The Tunisian Nationalist Movement: Four Decades of Evolution," by Benjamin Rivlin. (*Middle East Journal*, VI, Spring 1952, 167-193.)

"Has France a Case in Tunisia?" by Elizabeth Monroe. (*Virginia Quarterly Review*, XXIX, Winter 1953, 1-17.)

"Morocco," by Rom Landau. (*International Conciliation*, No. 483, Sept. 1952, 309-360.)

458 THE UNITED STATES IN WORLD AFFAIRS

"The French Achievement in Morocco," by General Augustin Guillaume. (*Foreign Affairs*, XXX, July 1952, 625-636.)
"The Problems of Tunisia and Morocco in the Seventh Session of the General Assembly," by Harry N. Howard. (*Department of State Bulletin*, XXVIII, Mar. 9, 1953, 359-371.)

Central and Southern Africa

AFRICA SOUTH OF THE SAHARA: An Assessment of Human and Material Resources, edited by Ann Welsh. New York, Oxford University Press, 1951, 286 p.
AFRICA: A Study in Tropical Development, by L. Dudley Stamp. New York, Wiley, 1953, 568 p.
INTRODUCING EAST AFRICA, by Mona Macmillan. London, Faber, 1952, 312 p.
THE GOLD COAST, by F. M. Bourret. Stanford, Stanford University Press, 1952, 248 p.
WEST AFRICA, by F. J. Pedler. New York, Praeger, 1951, 208 p.
MAU MAU AND THE KIKUYU, by L. S. B. Leakey. London, Methuen, 1952, 115 p.
"La Fédération de Rhodésie et du Nyasaland." (*Chronique de politique étrangère*, VI, Jan. 1953, 103-124.)
SOUTHERN RHODESIA, NORTHERN RHODESIA AND NYASALAND: Draft Federal Scheme. Report of the Civil Service Preparatory Commission, Aug. 26, 1952 (Cmd. 8673); Report of the Fiscal Commission, Aug. 25, 1952 (Cmd. 8672); Report of the Judicial Commission, July 26, 1952 (Cmd. 8671). London, 1952.
"Something New Out of Africa," by Leonard Woolf. (*Political Quarterly*, XXIII, Oct.-Dec. 1952, 322-331.) (Discusses Central African federation.)
REPORT ON SOUTHERN AFRICA, by Basil Davidson. New York, British Book Center, 1952, 285 p.

Union of South Africa

SOUTH AFRICA, by Jan H. Hofmyer, edited and revised by J. P. Cope. New York, McGraw-Hill, 1952, 253 p.
THE PEOPLES AND POLICIES OF SOUTH AFRICA, by Leo Marquard. New York, Oxford University Press, 1952, 258 p.
THE PEOPLE OF SOUTH AFRICA, by Sarah Gertrude Millin. London, Constable, 1951, 324 p.
THE DILEMMA OF SOUTH AFRICA, by John Hatch. New York, Roy Publishers, 1952, 255 p.
THE CHOICE BEFORE SOUTH AFRICA, by E. S. Sachs. New York, Philosophical Library, 1952, 220 p.
RACIAL SEPARATION IN SOUTH AFRICA, by Eugene P. Dvorin. Chicago, University of Chicago Press, 1952, 256 p.
"The Constitutional Crisis in South Africa," by Kenneth Kirkwood. (*International Affairs*, XXVIII, Oct. 1952, 432-444.)
"The South African Crisis," by C. W. M. Gell. (*Virginia Quarterly Review*, XXIX, Winter 1953, 18-35.)
"Les Indiens en Afrique du Sud." (*Chronique de politique étrangère*, V, May 1952, 334-359.)

"Question of South West Africa: Report of the Ad Hoc Committee on South West Africa to the General Assembly." (U.N. Document A/2261, Nov. 21, 1952.) New York, 1952, 101 p.

ASIA AND THE FAR EAST

FAR EASTERN SURVEY. New York, American Institute of Pacific Relations, bi-weekly.
PACIFIC AFFAIRS. New York, Institute of Pacific Relations, quarterly.
ASIA AND THE WEST, by Maurice Zinkin. New York, Institute of Pacific Relations, 1952, 300 p.
ASIAN NATIONALISM AND THE WEST: A Symposium Based on Documents and Reports of the Eleventh Conference, Institute of Pacific Relations, edited by William L. Holland. New York, Macmillan, 1952, 449 p.
"Asian Nationalism," by M. N. Roy. (*Yale Review*, Autumn 1952, 96-102.)
NATIONALISM AND COMMUNISM IN EAST ASIA, by W. Macmahon Ball. Carlton, Melbourne University Press (Institute of Pacific Relations) and New York, Cambridge University Press, 1952, 210 p.

U. S. Policy

THE UNITED STATES AND THE FAR EAST, 1945–1951, by Harold M. Vinacke. Stanford, Stanford University Press (American Institute of Pacific Relations), 1952, 144 p.
THE AMERICAN RECORD IN THE FAR EAST, 1945–1951, by Kenneth Scott Latourette. New York, Macmillan (American Institute of Pacific Relations), 1953, 208 p.
INSTITUTE OF PACIFIC RELATIONS: *Hearings*, Senate Judiciary Committee (sub-committee), 82nd Cong., July 25, 1951-June 20, 1952, 15 pts. *Report*: S. Rept. 2050, 82nd Cong., 2nd Sess. Washington, 1952, 244 p.
SPIES, DUPES AND DIPLOMATS, by Ralph de Toledano. New York, Duell, and Boston, Little, Brown, 1952, 244 p.
JOURNEY TO THE FAR PACIFIC, by Thomas E. Dewey. Garden City, Doubleday, 1952, 335 p.
BEYOND THE HIGH HIMALAYAS, by William O. Douglas. Garden City, Doubleday, 1952, 325 p.
NORTH FROM MALAYA: Adventures on Five Fronts, by William O. Douglas. Garden City, Doubleday, 1953, 352 p.
"U.S. Problems and Accomplishments in the Far East," by John M. Allison. (*Department of State Bulletin*, XXVII, July 21, 1952, 97-103.)

Economic Affairs

ECONOMIC SURVEY OF ASIA AND THE FAR EAST, 1952. (U.N. Document E/CN.11/362; *Economic Bulletin for Asia and the Far East*, III, No. 3.) Bangkok, 1953, 104 p.
COLOMBO PLAN: 1st Annual Report of the Consultative Committee on Economic Development in South and South-East Asia, Karachi, March, 1952. (Cmd. 8529.) London, 1952.
"The Colombo Plan: New Promise for Asia," by Wilfred Malenbaum. (*Department of State Bulletin*, XXVII, Sept. 22, 1952, 441-448.)

"Wirtschaftsplanung in Süd- und Südostasien: Die ersten Ergebnisse des Co-
lombo-Plans," by Franz-Hubert Demes. (*Europa-Archiv*, VII, Oct. 20, 1952,
5239-5246.)

India, Pakistan, and Ceylon

THE UNITED STATES AND INDIA AND PAKISTAN, by W. Norman Brown. Cam-
bridge, Harvard University Press, 1952, 308 p.
INDIA QUARTERLY: A Journal of International Affairs. New Delhi, Indian
Council of World Affairs, quarterly.
INDIA IN WORLD AFFAIRS, AUGUST 1947-JANUARY 1950, by K. P. Karunakaran.
London, Oxford University Press (Indian Council of World Affairs), 1952,
407 p.
FREE INDIA IN ASIA, by Werner Levi. Minneapolis, University of Minnesota
Press, 1952, 161 p.
"The Indian Elections and After," by Sir William P. Barton. (*Fortnightly*, No.
1029 N.S., Sept. 1952, 160-167.)
"India's First Five-Year Plan: A Descriptive Analysis," by V. K. R. V. Rao.
(*Pacific Affairs*, XXV, Mar. 1952, 3-23.)
PAKISTAN TODAY AND TOMORROW. Karachi, Pakistan Publications, 1951, 230 p.
"Recent Developments in the Kashmir Dispute," by Frank D. Collins. (*Depart-
ment of State Bulletin*, XXVII, Oct. 27, 1952, 663-667.)
"Fourth Report to the Security Council by the United Nations Representative for
India and Pakistan, 16 September 1952." (U.N. Document S/2783, Sept. 19,
1952.) New York, 1952, 48 p.
"The India-Pakistan Question." (U.N. Document ST/DPI/SER.A/72, Dec. 31,
1952.) New York, 1952, 32 p.
THE ECONOMIC DEVELOPMENT OF CEYLON: Report of a Mission Organized by
the International Bank for Reconstruction and Development. Baltimore, Johns
Hopkins Press, 1953, 829 p.

Southeast Asia

SOUTHEAST ASIA IN THE COMING WORLD, edited by Philip W. Thayer. Balti-
more, Johns Hopkins Press, 1953, 306 p.
SOUTHWARDS FROM CHINA, by Woodrow Wyatt. London, Hodder, 1952, 200 p.
HISTOIRE DU VIÊT-NAM DE 1940 À 1952, by Philippe Devillers. Paris, Éditions
du Seuil, 1952, 471 p.
VIÊT-NAM: Sociologie d'une guerre, by Paul Mus. Paris, Éditions du Seuil,
1952, 373 p.
"Les Événements en Indochine." (*Chronique de politique étrangère*, V, July
1952, 440-449.)
NATIONALISM AND REVOLUTION IN INDONESIA, by George McTurnan Kahin.
Ithaca, Cornell University Press (International Secretariat, Institute of Pacific
Relations), 1952, 490 p.
"Indonesia's Foreign Policy," by Mohammad Hatta. (*Foreign Affairs*, XXXI,
Apr. 1953, 441-452.)
LAND AND PEOPLE IN THE PHILIPPINES, by J. E. Spencer. Berkeley, University
of California Press, 1952, 282 p.

East Asia and the Pacific

The Mind of East Asia, by Lily Abegg. New York, Thames, 1952, 344 p.
China, Japan and the Powers, by Meribeth E. Cameron, Thomas H. D. Mahoney, and George E. McReynolds. New York, Ronald, 1952, 682 p. (Historical survey.)
"The Anzus Pact and Pacific Security," by E. D. L. Killen. (Far Eastern Survey, XXI, Oct. 8, 1952, 137-141.)
"Pacific Security as Seen from Australia," by Norman D. Harper. (International Organization, VII, May 1953, 213-228.)

China

Revolution in China, by Charles Patrick Fitzgerald. New York, Praeger, 1952, 289 p.
The Third Force in China, by Carsun Chang. New York, Bookman Associates, 1952, 345 p.
A Documentary History of Chinese Communism, edited by Conrad Brandt, Benjamin Schwartz, and John K. Fairbank. Cambridge, Harvard University Press, 1952, 552 p.
Enemy Within: An Eyewitness Account of the Communist Conquest of China, by Raymond J. de Jaegher and Irene Corbally Kuhn. Garden City, Doubleday, 1952, 314 p.
Report on Mao's Red China, by Frank Moraes. New York, Macmillan, 1953, 212 p.
God's Underground in Asia, by Gretta Palmer. New York, Appleton-Century-Crofts, 1952, 376 p.
With God in Red China: The Story of Two Years in Chinese Communist Prisons, by F. Olin Stockwell. New York, Harper, 1953, 256 p.
Formosa Under Chinese Nationalist Rule, by Fred W. Riggs. New York, Macmillan (American Institute of Pacific Relations), 1952, 195 p.
Report from Formosa, by H. Maclear Bate. New York, Dutton, 1952, 290 p.
Formosa: A Problem for United States Foreign Policy, by Joseph W. Ballantine. Washington, Brookings Institution, 1952, 218 p.

Japan

Contemporary Japan. Tokyo, Foreign Affairs Association of Japan, quarterly.
Japan, Past and Present, by Edwin O. Reischauer. (2nd ed.) New York, Knopf, 1952, 292 p.
Five Gentlemen of Japan, by Frank Gibney. New York, Farrar, Straus and Young, 1952, 317 p.
Red Flag in Japan: International Communism in Action, 1919–1951, by Roger Swearingen and Paul Langer. Cambridge, Harvard University Press (International Secretariat, Institute of Pacific Relations), 1952, 276 p.
"Japan and the General Elections," by Robert A. Scalapino. (Far Eastern Survey, XXI, Oct. 29, 1952, 149-154.)
"The Japanese General Elections of 1952," by Paul S. Dull. (American Political Science Review, XLVII, March 1953, 199-204.)

462 THE UNITED STATES IN WORLD AFFAIRS

ECONOMIC PROBLEMS OF FREE JAPAN, by Jerome B. Cohen. Princeton, Center of International Studies, 1952, 92 p.
ECONOMIC SURVEY OF JAPAN (1951-52). Tokyo, Economic Stabilization Board, 1952, 318 p.

Korea

"Special Report of the Unified Command on the United Nations Action in Korea." (U.N. Document A/2228, Oct. 18, 1952.) New York, 1952, 69 p.
"My Battle Inside the Korea Truce Tent," by Admiral Charles Turner Joy. (*Collier's*, Aug. 16, 1952, 36-42; Aug. 23, 1952, 26-31; Aug. 30, 1952, 70-72.)
"The Prisoners Stole the Show in Korea," by Demaree Bess. (*Saturday Evening Post*, CXXV, Nov. 1, 1952, 36-37 and 52-55.)
REPORT OF THE UNITED NATIONS COMMISSION FOR THE UNIFICATION AND REHABILITATION OF KOREA. (U.N. General Assembly *Official Records, Seventh Session*, Supplement 14.) New York, Oct. 1952, 41 p.
"Materials on the Work of the International Scientific Commission for Investigation of the Facts Concerning Bacteriological Warfare in Korea and China." (*New Times*, No. 39, Sept. 24, 1952, supplement.)
VERDICT IN KOREA, by Robert T. Oliver. State College, Pa., Bald Eagle Press, 1952, 207 p.
THE KOREA STORY, by John C. Caldwell and Lesley Frost. Chicago, Regnery, 1952, 180 p.
KOREAN TALES, by Lt. Col. Melvin B. Voorhees. New York, Simon & Schuster, 1952, 209 p.

WESTERN HEMISPHERE

ANNALS OF THE ORGANIZATION OF AMERICAN STATES. Washington, Pan American Union, quarterly.
INTER-AMERICAN ECONOMIC AFFAIRS. Washington, Institute of Inter-American Studies, quarterly.
MODERN AND CONTEMPORARY LATIN AMERICA, by Harry Bernstein, Philadelphia, Lippincott, 1952, 717 p.
L'AMÉRIQUE LATINE ENTRE EN SCÈNE, by Tibor Mende. Paris, Éditions du Seuil, 1952, 317 p.
THE STATE OF LATIN AMERICA, by Germán Arciniegas. New York, Knopf, 1952, 416 p.
LATIN AMERICA TODAY. (Special number of *Current History*, XXIV, Mar. 1953, 129-174.)
GOVERNMENTS OF LATIN AMERICA, by Miguel Jorrín. New York, Van Nostrand, 1953, 385 p.
LATIN AMERICA IN THE COLD WAR, edited by Walter M. Daniels. (Reference Shelf Series.) New York, H. W. Wilson, 1952, 206 p.
"Achievements of Inter-American Cooperation," by Edward G. Miller, Jr. (*Department of State Bulletin*, XXVII, Nov. 3, 1952, 702-707.)
THE FOREIGN TRADE OF LATIN AMERICA SINCE 1913. Washington, Pan American Union, 1952, 216 p.
"U.S. Exports to Latin America Decline in 1952." (*Foreign Commerce Weekly*, XLIX, No. 15, Apr. 13, 1953, 14-17.)
"United States Postwar Investment in Latin America." (*Federal Reserve Bulletin*, XXXIX, May 1953, 445-450.)

"Military Assistance to Latin America." (*Department of State Bulletin*, XXVIII, Mar. 30, 1953, 463-467.)

Mexico, Central America, Caribbean

THE UNITED STATES AND MEXICO, by Howard F. Cline. Cambridge, Harvard University Press, 1952, 452 p.

THE MEXICAN VENTURE: From Political to Industrial Revolution in Mexico, by Tomme Clark Call. New York, Oxford University Press, 1953, 273 p.

THE ECONOMIC DEVELOPMENT OF MEXICO: Report of the Combined Working Party. Baltimore, Johns Hopkins Press (International Bank for Reconstruction and Development), 1953, 392 p.

COSTA RICA: A Study in Economic Development, by Stacy May and others. New York, Twentieth Century Fund, 1952, 374 p.

THE ECONOMIC DEVELOPMENT OF NICARAGUA: Report of a Mission Organized by the International Bank for Reconstruction and Development. Baltimore, Johns Hopkins Press, 1952, 424 p.

THE CARIBBEAN: Peoples, Problems, and Prospects, edited by A. Curtis Wilgus. Gainesville, University of Florida Press, 1952, 240 p.

South America

PERÓN'S ARGENTINA, by George I. Blanksten. Chicago, University of Chicago Press, 1953, 478 p.

"Argentina After Eva Perón," by Russell H. Fitzgibbon. (*Yale Review*, XLII, Autumn 1952, 32-45.)

BOLIVIA: Land, People and Institutions, by Olen E. Leonard. Washington, Scarecrow Press, 1952, 297 p.

"The Nationalist Revolution in Bolivia," by L. L. (*World Today*, VIII, Nov. 1952, 480-490.)

BRAZIL: An Interim Assessment, by J. A. Camacho. New York, Royal Institute of International Affairs, 1952, 116 p.

"Politics and Economics in Chile," by G. J. B. (*World Today*, IX, Feb. 1953, 81-92.)

COLOMBIA: A General Survey, by W. O. Galbraith. New York, Oxford University Press (Royal Institute of International Affairs), 1953, 140 p.

"The Political Scene in Ecuador: President Velasco Ibarra Takes Over," by L. L. (*World Today*, IX, Mar. 1953, 130-138.)

Canada

CANADA'S CENTURY, by D. M. Lebourdais. New York, Praeger, 1952, 214 p.

CANADA: The Golden Hinge, by Leslie Roberts. New York, Rinehart, 1952, 288 p.

SPRINGS OF CANADIAN POWER: A Chatham House Information Paper. London, Royal Institute of International Affairs, 1953, 59 p.

CHRONOLOGY OF WORLD EVENTS

JANUARY 1–DECEMBER 31, 1952

In any such general chronology as this the selection of events to be included is necessarily somewhat arbitrary. Primary emphasis has been placed on listing the most significant international agreements, statements of policy, changes of government, and general elections, which are entered wherever possible under appropriate regional or organizational headings. The reader who desires a more detailed chronology has a choice of several convenient compilations, among which mention may be made of the *Chronology of International Events and Documents* (London, Royal Institute of International Affairs, fortnightly), *Current Developments in United States Foreign Policy* (Washington, Brookings Institution, monthly until June 1952), and the chronologies included in *Current History* (Philadelphia, Events Publishing Company, monthly) and in the *World Almanac and Book of Facts* (New York, New York World-Telegram and Sun, annual).

THE UNITED STATES

Jan. 1. The Mutual Security Agency under Director W. Averell Harriman replaces the Eeconomic Cooperation Administration established in 1948.

Jan. 14. William H. Draper, Jr. is nominated as the President's special representative in Europe for NATO and the Mutual Security Program.

Jan. 18. An International Information Administration is established in the State Department under Dr. Wilson Compton.

Jan. 21. President Truman submits a budget message for the fiscal year 1953 forecasting total expenditures of $85.4 billion, including $52.4 billion for defense and $10.5 billion for foreign aid.

Jan. 23. James E. Webb resigns as Under-Secretary of State and David K. E. Bruce is nominated to succeed him. Eric A. Johnston is nominated as Chairman of the International Development Advisory Board.

Feb. 7. The Senate approves, 73-2, a protocol bringing Greece and Turkey into the North Atlantic Treaty.

Mar. 4. Consideration of a program of universal military training is indefinitely postponed by a 236-162 vote of the House of Representatives.

Mar. 6. The President asks Congress to allocate $7.9 billion for foreign aid in the fiscal year 1953.

Mar. 20. The Senate ratifies the Japanese Peace Treaty (66-10), the U.S.-Japanese Security Treaty (58-9), and the security treaties with Australia and New Zealand and with the Philippines.

Apr. 2. George F. Kennan takes the oath as Ambassador to the U.S.S.R., succeeding Adm. Alan G. Kirk.

June 18. The Senate votes 43-40 to recommit a resolution approving the 1941 agreement with Canada relative to the St. Lawrence Seaway.

June 20. The President signs the Mutual Security Act of 1952, authorizing slightly under $6.5 billion for foreign aid in the fiscal year 1953.

June 25. President Truman vetoes the Immigration and Nationality Act of 1952, but the bill is repassed by both houses and becomes law June 27.

July 1. The Senate approves the Convention on Relations with Germany and the accompanying protocol to the North Atlantic Treaty by votes of 77-5 and 72-5 respectively.

July 10. The President signs the Defense Department Appropriation Act, providing $46.6 billion in defense funds for the fiscal year 1953.

July 15. The President signs the Supplemental Appropriation Act, 1953, carrying slightly over $6 billion for foreign aid, $2.88 billion for military public works, and $2.98 for an expanded atomic energy program in the fiscal year 1953.

July 18. Walter J. Donnelly is appointed U.S. High Commissioner to Germany, succeeding John J. McCloy.

July 24. A new constitution making Puerto Rico a self-governing "free commonwealth" is proclaimed.

Aug. 14. The President declines to authorize increased duties on imported watches as recommended by the Tariff Commission.

Nov. 4. Gen. Dwight D. Eisenhower and Senator Richard M. Nixon are elected President and Vice-President respectively; their term of office begins Jan. 20, 1953.

Nov. 1. Successful thermonuclear experiments are conducted at Eniwetok Atoll.

Nov. 20. President-designate Eisenhower names John Foster Dulles to be Secretary of State and Charles E. Wilson to be Secretary of Defense in the new administration.

THE NORTH ATLANTIC COMMUNITY

The "Big Three"

Jan. 9. President Truman and Prime Minister Winston Churchill issue a joint communiqué in Washington pledging a united policy in Europe, the Middle East, and Asia.

Jan. 17. Prime Minister Churchill stresses Anglo-American solidarity in an address to Congress. On Jan. 18, the President and Prime Minister announce agreements on the appointment of an American supreme commander for the North Atlantic and on the exchange of scarce materials.

Feb. 17-18. The Foreign Ministers of the U.S., U.K., and France meet in London. West German Chancellor Konrad Adenauer joins them Feb. 18-19.

June 27. The U.S., British, and French Foreign Ministers meet in London to discuss Germany and other common problems.

The North Atlantic Treaty Organization

Jan. 30. U.S. Admiral Lynde D. McCormick is appointed Supreme Allied Commander, Atlantic.

Feb. 18. Greece and Turkey formally accede to the North Atlantic Treaty.

Feb. 20-25. The NATO Council holds its ninth session in Lisbon, agrees on a reorganization of NATO, and adopts a goal of 50 divisions in Western Europe before the end of 1952.

Mar. 12. Lord Ismay (U.K.) is appointed Secretary-General of NATO.

Apr. 2. Gen. Dwight D. Eisenhower's first annual report as Supreme Allied Commander, Europe is released.

May 30. Gen. Matthew B. Ridgway succeeds Gen. Eisenhower as Supreme Allied Commander, Europe.

Sept. 13-24. Exercise Mainbrace, NATO's largest naval maneuver, is held in North Sea and adjacent waters.

Dec. 15-18. The North Atlantic Council holds its tenth session in Paris.

Dec. 16. Establishment of a dual command system in the Mediterranean is announced by Prime Minister Churchill.

European Organization

Jan. 27. *European Defense Community*—Foreign Ministers of the six participating countries, meeting in Paris, agree on voting procedure in the proposed community.

Mar. 19. *Council of Europe*—British Foreign Secretary Anthony Eden in an address to the Committee of Ministers outlines British views regarding closer integration of the Council of Europe with the European Coal and Steel and Defense Communities.

May 27. *European Defense Community*—The Treaty Constituting the European Defense Community, with related agreements, is signed in Paris.

May 30. *Council of Europe*—The Consultative Assembly approves the Eden proposals on association with the new federative institutions in Western Europe.

July 25. *European Coal and Steel Community*—The treaty establishing the community enters into force. Foreign Ministers of the six participating governments, meeting in Paris, decide to locate the High Authority in Luxembourg and to defer choice of a permanent headquarters pending a Franco-German settlement of the Saar problem.

Aug. 10. *European Coal and Steel Community*—The High Authority is formally established in Luxembourg with Jean Monnet of France as Chairman.

Sept. 22. *European Coal and Steel Community*—An Ad Hoc Assembly of 87 members meets in Strasbourg to draft a statute for a European political authority.

Great Britain and the Commonwealth
(See also regional headings)

Jan. 16-21. A conference of Commonwealth finance ministers is held in London.

Feb. 6. King George VI dies and is succeeded by his daughter as Queen Elizabeth II.

Feb. 28. *Canada*—Vincent Massey is installed as Governor-General, succeeding Field Marshal Viscount Alexander.

Oct. 2. *United Kingdom*—A successful atomic test is conducted in the Monte Bello Islands off Australia.

Nov. 27-Dec. 11. A conference of Commonwealth Prime Ministers is held in London.

Dec. 2. *New Zealand*—Lt. Gen. Sir Willoughby Norrie is installed as New Zealand's eighth Governor-General, succeeding Lt. Gen. Lord Freyberg.

France

Jan. 7. The coalition cabinet of Premier René Pleven is overthrown by a 341-243 no confidence vote in the National Assembly.

Jan. 22. A new coalition cabinet formed by Edgar Faure wins a confidence vote in the National Assembly.

Jan. 25. The French High Commissariat in the Saar is converted into a diplomatic mission.

Feb. 29. The Faure cabinet is overthrown by an adverse vote on its financial program.

Mar. 11. A cabinet formed by Antoine Pinay, Independent, is endorsed by the National Assembly.

May 18. Elections for one-half the seats in the Council of the Republic result in gains for the Independents and Popular Republicans (M.R.P.) and losses for the Gaullists and Socialists.

May 28. Communist demonstrations result in the arrest of Jacques Duclos and other Communist leaders.

Oct. 17. Edouard Herriot warns against French acceptance of the Treaty Constituting the European Defense Community.

Nov. 30. Parliamentary elections in the Saar result in a heavy vote in favor of an autonomous status with close ties to France.

Dec. 23. The Pinay cabinet resigns in anticipation of an adverse vote in the National Assembly.

Germany

Jan. 11. The Bundestag approves the Treaty Constituting the European Coal and Steel Community by a 232-143 vote.

Feb. 13. The East German government requests the four occupying powers to expedite the conclusion of an all-German peace treaty.

Feb. 24. The U.N. Commission invites representatives from East and West Germany to begin discussions on free elections.

Mar. 10. The U.S.S.R. in notes to the U.S., U.K., and France proposes a four-power meeting to consider a peace treaty with Germany.

Mar. 25. Replying to the Soviet note of Mar. 10, the Western powers hold that the formation of an all-German government on the basis of free elections is a prerequisite to the conclusion of a German peace treaty.

Apr. 9. The U.S.S.R. in a second note to the Western powers proposes four-power investigation of electoral conditions in Germany.

Apr. 29. A French airliner en route to Berlin is attacked by two Soviet fighter planes.

May 9. The U.N. Commission reports failure to establish contact with authorities in the Soviet zone and East Berlin.

May 13. The Western powers reply negatively to the Soviet note of Apr. 9.

May 24. The U.S.S.R. in a new note to the Western powers requests an early four-power meeting on the German question.

May 26. The Convention on Relations between the Three Powers and the Federal Republic of Germany, together with related agreements, is signed in Bonn.

June 11. President Theodor Heuss announces that he will ask the Federal Constitutional Court to decide on the constitutionality of the Treaty Constituting the European Defense Community.

June 20. The Bundesrat unanimously decides that the treaties of May 26 and 27 require its approval.

July 8. Dr. Walter Linse is abducted from the U.S. sector of Berlin by Communist agents.

July 10. The Western powers reply to the Soviet note of May 24.

Aug. 5. The U.N. Commission abandons its effort to obtain East German cooperation in a country-wide survey of electoral conditions.

Aug. 8. The London Conference on German External Debts, which convened Feb. 28, adjourns after reaching agreement on terms of settlement of Germany's external indebtedness.

Aug. 23. The U.S.S.R. again rejects the Western proposals on free all-German elections.

Sept. 10. An agreement with the State of Israel and the Conference on Jewish Material Claims Against Germany, signed in Luxembourg, provides for payments by Western Germany to a value of $822 million in indemnification for Nazi persecutions.

Sept. 23. The Western powers reject the Soviet proposal for a four-power conference on a German peace treaty prior to agreement on all-German elections.

Dec. 6. The Bundestag approves the second reading of the Peace Contract and the E.D.C. treaty.

Dec. 11. East German Premier Otto Grotewohl announces that an armed force will be established "to defend the homeland."

Austria

Jan. 18. Replying to a Western invitation to resume four-power treaty talks, the U.S.S.R. reiterates its stand on the unrelated questions of the Italian Peace Treaty and Trieste.

Mar. 13. The U.S., U.K., and France in notes to the U.S.S.R. propose an abbreviated treaty for Austria.

Aug. 14. The U.S.S.R. rejects the Western proposal for an abbreviated treaty.

Sept. 5. The Western powers in notes to the U.S.S.R. make new proposals regarding the Austrian treaty.

Sept. 27. The U.S.S.R. rejects the latest Western proposals.

Oct. 22. The coalition cabinet of Dr. Leopold Figl resigns but remains in office pending new elections scheduled for February 1953.

Dec. 20. The U.N. General Assembly appeals to the four occupying powers to agree on the terms of an Austrian treaty.

Belgium

Jan. 9. The Christian Social cabinet of Premier Joseph Phollien resigns. A new Christian Social cabinet under Jean Van Houtte is formed Jan. 15.

The Netherlands

Apr. 3. Queen Juliana pleads for international cooperation in an address to the U.S. Congress.

June 25-26. Parliamentary elections give the Labor and Catholic parties equal representation in the Second Chamber.

Sept. 1. A new coalition cabinet is formed by Willem Drees (Labor Party).

Iceland

Jan. 25. President Sveinn Björnsson dies.
June 29. Asgeir Asgeirsson is elected President and begins his four-year term Aug. 1.

Sweden

June 16. Soviet fighter planes shoot down a Swedish rescue plane searching over the Baltic for another Swedish plane which disappeared June 13.
Sept. 21. The Communists lose heavily in parliamentary elections which also reduce the strength of the Agrarian-Socialist coalition.

Spain

Mar. 12. Secretary of State Dean Acheson announces that the U.S. will shortly begin military and economic negotiations with Spain.
Apr. 15. Generalissimo Francisco Franco and Prime Minister Antonio de Oliveira Salazar of Portugal emphasize Spanish-Portuguese solidarity at the conclusion of a two-day meeting in Ciudad Rodrigo.

Greece

Jan. 1. A new constitution comes into effect.
Feb. 18. Greece becomes a party to the North Atlantic Treaty.
Nov. 16. Field-Marshal Alexander Papagos and his right-wing Greek Rally are victorious in national parliamentary elections. A new cabinet under Papagos is announced Nov. 18.

Trieste

May 9. Measures for associating Italy more closely with the administration of the Anglo-American zone are announced at the conclusion of a diplomatic conference in London which began Apr. 3.
May 13. Yugoslavia rejects the Anglo-American-Italian understanding of May 9 and initiates new administrative measures in the Yugoslav zone.

Yugoslavia

Jan. 8. A mutual security agreement with the U.S. is signed in Belgrade.
Oct. 13. The U.S., U.K., and France announce agreement to furnish $99 million in economic aid to Yugoslavia in the fiscal year 1952–53.
Dec. 17. Diplomatic relations with the Vatican are severed.

THE SOVIET BLOC

The U.S.S.R.

Apr. 2. Premier Stalin, answering questions from American newspaper editors, restates his conditions for "peaceful coexistence."

Apr. 3-12. An International Economic Conference is held in Moscow.

June 9. Soviet and U.S. representatives in Washington begin abortive discussions looking toward settlement of the Soviet lend-lease account.

June 13. Andrei A. Gromyko and Georgi N. Zarubin are named Ambassadors to the U.K. and U.S. respectively. Alexander S. Panyushkin becomes Ambassador to Communist China.

Aug. 20. A draft five-year plan for the period 1951–55 provides for a 70 percent increase in total industrial production.

Aug. 28. Valerian A. Zorin is named to replace Yakov A. Malik as Soviet delegate to the United Nations.

Oct. 2. Premier Stalin's theses on "Economic Problems of Socialism in the U.S.S.R." are published in the magazine *Bolshevik*.

Oct. 3. The Soviet Government declares U.S. Ambassador Kennan *persona non grata* and demands his recall.

Oct. 5-14. The Nineteenth Congress of the Communist party of the Soviet Union is held in Moscow.

Oct. 14. Premier Stalin addresses the Communist party congress and pledges continued support to Communist and "democratic" movements abroad.

Dec. 24. Premier Stalin informs a *New York Times* correspondent that he is willing to meet Gen. Eisenhower and favors a new approach to end the Korean war.

Soviet Satellite Countries

May 1. The U.S. State Department bans American travel to Communist-dominated countries.

Poland

Jan. 27. A draft constitution based on the Soviet constitution of 1936 is published.

Oct. 26. Parliamentary elections are held with a single list of candidates.

Nov. 20. President Boleslaw Bierut becomes Prime Minister in a governmental reorganization under the new constitution.

Czechoslovakia

Nov. 20. Rudolf Slansky, former Communist party head, pleads guilty to treason and espionage charges. Slansky and 10 codefendants are sentenced to death on Nov. 27 and the sentences are carried out Dec. 3.

Hungary

Aug. 14. Matyas Rakosi assumes the premiership, succeeding Istvan Dobi, who becomes President of the Presidium.

Rumania

May 30. The expulsion of Foreign Minister Ana Pauker from the Communist Politburo is announced.

June 2. Dr. Petru Groza becomes President of the Presidium and is succeeded as Premier by Gheorghe Gheorghiu-Dej.
July 5. Dismissal of Ana Pauker as Foreign Minister is announced.
Sept. 24. The National Assembly unanimously adopts a new constitution.
Nov. 30. Parliamentary elections are held with a single list of candidates.

Communist China

May 20. British Foreign Secretary Eden announces that most British business firms are withdrawing from Communist China.
Aug. 17. A Chinese Communist delegation headed by Prime Minister Chou En-lai arrives in Moscow.
Sept. 16. Agreements announced by the U.S.S.R. and Communist China provide for the relinquishment to Chinese control of the Chinese Changchun Railway and for joint use of Port Arthur pending the conclusion of peace with Japan.

Outer Mongolia

Jan. 26. Premier Marshal Choi Bol-san dies in Moscow; he is later replaced by Tse Den Bal.

The World Communist Movement

Feb. 22. A statement broadcast by the North Korean radio initiates a propaganda campaign charging the U.S. forces with using bacteriological warfare in Korea and Manchuria.
Mar. 31. The International Association of Democratic Lawyers formally charges the U.S. forces in Korea with using bacteriological warfare.
July 1-6. The World Peace Council meets in East Berlin.
Aug. 31. An "International Scientific Commission" completes its report on alleged bacteriological warfare in Korea and China.
Oct. 2-12. An "Asian and Pacific Peace Conference" is held in Peking.
Dec. 12-19. A "Congress of the Peoples for Peace" is held in Vienna.

NEAR AND MIDDLE EAST

Jan. 26. The U.N. General Assembly approves a $250 million resettlement program for Palestine refugees and continues the Palestine Conciliation Commission on a modified basis.
Jan. 28. The U.S.S.R. protests against the proposed Middle East Command in notes to the U.S., U.K., France, and Turkey.
Feb. 16. Jordan signs the Arab League security pact.
Aug. 23. The Arab League security pact enters into force following the deposit of ratifications by Egypt, Syria, Iraq, Jordan, and Saudi Arabia.
Dec. 18. A resolution on political aspects of the Palestine problem fails to gain the necessary majority in the U.N. General Assembly.

Israel

Nov. 9. President Chaim Weizmann of Israel dies. Dr. Itzhak Ben-Zvi is inaugurated to succeed him on Dec. 10.

Dec. 19. The cabinet of Prime Minister David Ben-Gurion resigns. A new coalition cabinet headed by Ben-Gurion is formed Dec. 22.

Egypt and the Sudan

Jan. 18. A British cruiser opens fire on Port Said in fighting between Egyptian guerrillas and British troops.

Jan. 26. Martial law is declared following major disorders. On Jan. 27, Prime Minister Mustafa al-Nahhas Pasha is dismissed and 'Ali Mahir Pasha is asked to form a government.

Mar. 1. Prime Minister 'Ali Mahir Pasha resigns and Ahmad Nagib al-Hilali Pasha is asked to form a government.

Apr. 23. A draft constitution providing for self-government in the Anglo-Egyptian Sudan is approved by the Sudan Legislative Assembly.

June 28. The cabinet of Nagib al-Hilali resigns; Husayn Sirri Pasha is asked to form a government on June 29.

July 20. Prime Minister Husayn Sirri resigns; a new cabinet formed by Nagib al-Hilali Pasha is announced July 22.

July 23. Maj. Gen. Muhammad Nagib Bey proclaims himself army commander-in-chief and asks 'Ali Mahir Pasha to form a new cabinet following the resignation of Nagib al-Hilali.

July 26. King Faruq abdicates in favor of his infant son, Ahmad Fuad, and leaves the country.

Aug. 5. Ex-King Faruq's property is placed in custody and a Council of Regency is installed to rule for the infant Fuad II.

Sept. 7. Gen. Nagib assumes the premiership after arresting numerous associates of ex-King Faruq.

Dec. 10. Prime Minister Nagib announces cancellation of the constitution and the passing of authority to a "transitional government."

Syria

June 8. Gen. Fawzi Silo declares himself Prime Minister and forms a cabinet June 9.

Lebanon

Feb. 9. The cabinet of Prime Minister Abdallah Bey al-Yafi resigns and is replaced Feb. 11 by a new cabinet under Sami al-Sulh Bey.

Sept. 9. Prime Minister Sami al-Sulh resigns; Sa'ib Salam is designated Prime Minister on Sept. 12.

Sept. 18. President Bisharah al-Khuri resigns under popular pressure; Camille Sham'un is elected President by the Chamber of Deputies on Sept. 23.

Oct. 1. A period of political crisis terminates with the formation of a cabinet by Amir Khalid Shihab.

Oct. 9. The Parliament empowers the new government of Khalid Shihab to rule by decree.

Iraq

Aug. 17. King Faysal II arrives in Washington for a visit to the President.

Nov. 22. The cabinet of Mustafa al-'Umari resigns in the midst of large-scale disorders. Martial law is proclaimed in Baghdad and a new cabinet under Gen. Nur-al-Din Mahmud, Chief of Staff, is announced Nov. 23.

Jordan

Jan. 9. A new constitution initiating responsible parliamentary government takes effect.

Aug. 11. King Talal II is deposed as mentally unfit and succeeded by his son Hussayn I under a Council of Regents.

Iran

Jan. 7. Parliamentary elections begin in outlying provinces, to continue throughout the spring.

Feb. 20. Representatives of the International Bank leave Tehran without having succeeded in negotiating a settlement of the Iranian oil problem.

June 9. Prime Minister Muhammad Mosaddeq presents the Iranian case in the Anglo-Iranian oil dispute before the International Court of Justice.

July 5. Prime Minister Mosaddeq resigns in accordance with constitutional procedure, but is asked to form a new government on July 11.

July 16. Prime Minister Mosaddeq resigns in protest against the Shah's refusal to make him Minister of War. Ahmad Qavam is appointed Prime Minister July 17.

July 21. Ahmad Qavam resigns as Prime Minister following serious riots in Tehran; Mosaddeq is reappointed July 22.

July 22. The International Court of Justice decides, 9-5, that it lacks jurisdiction in Iran's dispute with the Anglo-Iranian Oil Company.

Aug. 3. The Majlis votes full dictatorial powers to Prime Minister Mosaddeq for six months.

Aug. 30. Joint proposals for a solution of the oil problem are delivered to Prime Minister Mosaddeq on behalf of President Truman and Prime Minister Churchill.

Sept. 24. Prime Minister Mosaddeq rejects the Anglo-American proposals of Aug. 30 and demands acceptance of his counterproposals within 10 days.

Oct. 14. Great Britain rejects Prime Minister Mosaddeq's conditions for resuming oil negotiations.

Oct. 16. Prime Minister Mosaddeq announces the severance of diplomatic relations with Great Britain; relations are formally broken Oct. 22.

AFRICA

Libya

Feb. 19-Mar. 6. Elections to the lower house of the new parliament produce a large pro-government majority.

Tunisia

Jan. 18. French authorities arrest Habib Bourgiba and other nationalist and Communist leaders following a wave of nationalist demonstrations.

Jan. 26. New political proposals are dispatched from Paris following widespread disorders.

Mar. 26. The French Resident-General orders the arrest of Prime Minister Mohammad Chenik and proclaims martial law. A new Prime Minister, Salaheddine Baccouche, is appointed Mar. 28.

April 14. The U.N. Security Council decides not to consider a complaint brought by 11 Arab-Asian states regarding the situation in Tunisia.

June 20. A French program of political reforms fails to secure the approval of the French National Assembly. Thirteen Arab-Asian countries unsuccessfully request a special session of the U.N. General Assembly to consider the Tunisian situation.

Sept. 7. French reform proposals are unanimously rejected by a crown council summoned by the Bey.

Dec. 5. Discovery of the body of a murdered Tunisian nationalist leader precipitates new disorders.

Dec. 17. The U.N. General Assembly urges continued negotiations in Tunisia.

Dec. 18. The French demand acceptance of selected internal reforms hitherto rejected by the Bey, who yields Dec. 20.

Morocco

Mar. 20. The Sultan requests early revision of the protectorate treaty.

Aug. 27. The International Court of Justice defines U.S. rights in Morocco under the treaty of 1836.

Oct. 9. The Sultan announces that the French Government has placed unacceptable conditions in the way of his demand for revision of the protectorate treaty.

Dec. 8. Rioting in Casablanca causes heavy casualties and numerous arrests.

Dec. 19. The U.N. General Assembly urges a conciliatory settlement.

Tangier

Nov. 10. An eight-nation agreement restoring Spain to a role in the international administration of Tangier is concluded.

Eritrea-Ethiopia

Sept. 11. The federation of Eritrea with Ethiopia under the Emperor Haille Selassie enters into effect.

Liberia

Jan. 9. President William V. S. Tubman is inaugurated for a second four-year term.

British Africa

Mar. 21. Kwame Nkrumah becomes Prime Minister of the Gold Coast by approval of the Legislative Assembly.

Apr. 23-May 9. A conference on Central African Federation in London leads to agreement on a draft constitutional scheme for Southern and Northern Rhodesia and Nyasaland.

Oct. 20. British reinforcements are sent to Kenya to combat acts of terrorism by the Mau Mau secret society.

Union of South Africa

Jan. 19. The U.N. General Assembly adopts resolutions regretting South Africa's stand on the question of South West Africa and reiterating its opinion that the area should be placed under trusteeship.

Mar. 20. The Supreme Court invalidates the Separate Representation of Voters Bill enacted in 1951.

June 3. Action is completed on the High Court of Parliament Bill, giving Parliament authority to overrule the Supreme Court.

June 26. A nonviolent resistance campaign is inaugurated by the Indian and African National Congresses.

Nov. 13. The High Court of Parliament Bill is invalidated by the Appeal Division of the Supreme Court.

Dec. 5. The U.N. General Assembly establishes commissions on the treatment of Indians in South Africa and on racial discrimination in South Africa.

SOUTH AND SOUTHEAST ASIA

The Colombo Plan

Mar. 24-28. The Colombo Plan Consultative Committee holds its fourth meeting in Karachi.

India

Jan. 5. A five-year technical assistance agreement with the U.S. is signed in New Delhi.

Feb. 21. Voting is completed in the general elections which began Oct. 25, 1951. The Congress party wins 362 out of 489 contested seats in the new Parliament.

May 2. Rajendra Prasad is reelected President by the Parliament and the state legislatures and is inaugurated May 13; Jawaharlal Nehru is redesignated Prime Minister.

The Kashmir Problem

Jan. 29. The Security Council requests Dr. Frank P. Graham to return to the Kashmir area for further mediation efforts.

Aug. 21. The Kashmir Constituent Assembly adopts a resolution to end dynastic rule and substitute an elected Chief of State.

Nov. 14. The Constituent Assembly elects Prince Karan Singh as the territory's first Chief of State.

Dec. 23. The U.N. Security Council urges a negotiated settlement of the India-Pakistan disagreement on the basis of recommendations by the U.N. representative.

Nepal

Aug. 10. The government of M. P. Koirala resigns and King Tribhubana undertakes to govern personally.

Ceylon

Mar. 22. Prime Minister Don Stephen Senanayake dies; his son Dudley Senanayake succeeds him Mar. 26.

May 24-30. Prime Minister Senanayake's United National party obtains an absolute majority in the first general elections since Ceylon obtained independence in 1948.

Southeast Asia

Jan. 3. Soviet Foreign Minister A. Y. Vyshinsky tells the U.N. General Assembly that the U.S. is transporting Chinese Nationalist troops into Burma and Thailand and preparing to charge the Chinese Communists with aggression.

Jan. 28. A warning against any Communist aggression in Southeast Asia is delivered by U.S., U.K., and French delegates in the U.N. General Assembly.

Indochina

Jan. 11. Gen. Jean de Lattre de Tassigny, French High Commissioner and military commander, dies in Paris.

Feb. 24. French forces evacuate Hoabinh in northern Vietnam.

April 1. Jean Letourneau, French Minister for the Associated States, is named Minister Resident in Indochina.

June 2. Emperor Bao Dai of Vietnam dismisses the government of Tran Van Huu and appoints Nguyen Van Tam as Prime Minister.

June 16-18. Minister Letourneau confers with U.S. officials in Washington and obtains a promise of increased aid to France and the Associated States.

Sept. 19. The applications of Vietnam, Laos, and Cambodia for United Nations membership are vetoed by the U.S.S.R. in the Security Council.

Burma

Mar. 12. Sir Ba U is elected President by a joint session of the two houses of Parliament, succeeding Sao Shwe Thaike. A new cabinet headed by U Nu (formerly Thakin Nu) is installed Mar. 16.

Thailand

Mar. 30. Marshal Pibul Songgram forms a new government.

Nov. 10. Discovery of an alleged Communist plot leads to numerous arrests.

Malaya

Jan. 15. Gen. Sir Gerald Templer is named High Commissioner and director of military operations.

Indonesia

Feb. 22. The cabinet of Premier Soekiman resigns in protest against a bilateral aid agreement with the U.S. accepted without its knowledge by Foreign Minister Soebardjo.
April 1. A new cabinet is formed by Dr. Wilopo of the Indonesian Nationalist party.

Philippines

Oct. 27. A conference of Philippine and U.S. representatives decides on measures to strengthen Philippine and regional security.

EAST ASIA AND THE PACIFIC

Japan

Jan. 1. Soviet Premier J. V. Stalin addresses New Year's greetings to the Japanese people.
Jan. 16. The Foreign Office releases a personal undertaking by Prime Minister Shigeru Yoshida indicating that Japan will seek relations with Nationalist rather than Communist China.
Feb. 22. Anti-American riots occur throughout Japan.
Feb. 28. A U.S.-Japanese administrative agreement to implement the Security Treaty concluded in 1951 is signed in Tokyo.
Apr. 28. The Allied occupation comes to an end as the Peace Treaty and the U.S.-Japanese Security Treaty enter into force. Simultaneously, a separate peace treaty with Nationalist China is signed at Taipei and the state of war with India is ended by an exchange of notes. In Washington, the Far Eastern Commission is dissolved over a Soviet protest.
May 1. A May Day celebration in Tokyo degenerates into serious anti-American rioting.
June 9. A peace treaty with India is signed in Tokyo.
Aug. 5. The Peace Treaty with Nationalist China enters into force.
Aug. 13. Japan is admitted to membership in the International Bank for Reconstruction and Development and the International Monetary Fund.
Sept. 18. Japan's application for membership in the United Nations is vetoed by the U.S.S.R. in the Security Council.
Oct. 1. Nationwide parliamentary elections narrow the majority of the governing Liberal party and deprive the Communists of representation in the lower house of parliament.
Oct. 7. An American aircraft disappears off northern Japan; the U.S.S.R. claims that it violated the Soviet "state frontier."

Oct. 24. Shigeru Yoshida (Liberal) is designated to head the new government; formation of a cabinet is announced Oct. 29.

Korea

Feb. 9. Armistice negotiators at Panmunjom agree to recommend a post-armistice political conference on the peaceful settlement of the Korean problem.

Mar. 13. A riot among prisoners of war at Koje Island leads to the death of 12 prisoners.

Apr. 28. The U.N. armistice delegate presents a "final" proposal for solution of outstanding issues in the armistice negotiations. The Communist delegation rejects the proposal May 2.

May 7. Communist prisoners on Koje Island seize the American camp commandant and hold him as a hostage until May 10.

May 12. Gen. Mark Clark succeeds Gen. Matthew B. Ridgway as U.S. Commander-in-chief in the Far East and U.N. Commander in Korea.

June 23. U.N. aircraft bomb five hydroelectric plants in North Korea, including one on the Yalu River.

July 4. Constitutional amendments providing for popular election of the president and establishment of a bicameral congress are approved by the National Assembly of the Republic of Korea.

Aug. 5. Syngman Rhee is reelected President of the Republic of Korea by an overwhelming popular vote and begins his second term of office Aug. 15.

Sept. 28. U.N. armistice negotiators suggest new methods of implementing the principle of nonforcible repatriation of prisoners.

Oct. 8. The U.N. delegation suspends armistice negotiations after its proposals of Sept. 28 are rejected by the Communists.

Dec. 3. The U.N. General Assembly adopts recommendations on the nonforcible repatriation of prisoners of war.

Dec. 5. Completing a three-day visit to Korea, Gen. Eisenhower disclaims "panaceas" and "trick solutions."

Dec. 14. Communist China rejects the recommendations of the U.N. General Assembly. Serious disorders occur in an internment camp on Pongam Island, Korea.

The Anzus Treaty

Apr. 29. The Anzus security treaty between Australia, New Zealand, and the U.S. enters into force.

Aug. 4-7. The Anzus Council, comprising the Foreign Ministers of the U.S., Australia, and New Zealand, holds its first session in Honolulu.

LATIN AMERICA

Argentina

May 1. President Juan D. Perón opens the Congress and announces that Argentina's second five-year economic development plan will be inaugurated Jan. 1, 1953.

June 4. President Perón is inaugurated for a second six-year term following his reelection Nov. 11, 1951.

July 26. Eva Perón, wife of the President, dies after a long illness.

Bolivia

Apr. 9-11. A military coup is carried out by the National Revolutionary Movement (M.N.R.). Dr. Víctor Paz Estenssoro is proclaimed President on Apr. 16.

Oct. 31. The country's three largest foreign-owned tin mines are formally nationalized.

Brazil

Feb. 15. A military assistance agreement with the U.S. is signed in Rio de Janeiro.

July 2. Secretary of State Acheson arrives on an official visit.

Chile

Apr. 9. A military assistance agreement with the U.S. is signed in Santiago.

July 3. Ratification of the U.S.-Chilean military assistance agreement is completed.

Sept. 4. Gen. Carlos Ibañez del Campo is victor in the presidential election, and is inaugurated on Nov. 3 for a six-year term.

Colombia

Apr. 17. A military assistance agreement with the U.S. is signed in Bogotá.

Costa Rica

Sept. 26. President Otilio Ulate lays aside his functions but resumes them Oct. 12.

Cuba

Mar. 7. A military assistance agreement with the U.S. is signed in Havana.

Mar. 10. President Carlos Prío Soccarás is deposed in a military coup led by General Fulgencio Batista, who succeeds him as President.

Dominican Republic

May 16. General Héctor Trujillo Molina is elected President and is inaugurated for a five-year term on Aug. 16, succeeding his brother, Gen. Rafael Trujillo Molina.

Ecuador

Feb. 20. A military assistance agreement with the U.S. is signed in Quito.

June 1. José María Velasco Ibarra is elected President and begins his four-year term Sept. 1.

Mexico

Feb. 21. Military assistance negotiations with the U.S. are suspended as a result of Communist pressure.

July 6. Adolfo Ruiz Cortines is elected President and begins his six-year term Dec. 1.

Panama

May 11. Col. José Antonio Remón is elected President and begins his four-year term Oct. 1.

Peru

Feb. 22. A military assistance agreement with the U.S. is signed in Lima.

El Salvador

May 11-13. Congressional elections are held; the opposition parties refuse to participate.

Uruguay

Mar. 1. President Andrés Martínez Trueba assumes the chairmanship of a nine-man Council of Government, which replaces the presidency in accordance with a national plebiscite held Dec. 16, 1951.

June 30. A military assistance agreement with the U.S. is signed in Montevideo.

Venezuela

Nov. 30. Elections for a constituent congress are held; early returns show the opposition Republican Democratic Union (U.R.D.) leading.

Dec. 2. The ruling junta claims victory in the Nov. 30 elections and the army names Col. Marcos Pérez Jiménez provisional President.

UNITED NATIONS

(See also regional headings)

General Assembly

Jan. 2-Feb. 5. The General Assembly holds the second part of its Sixth Regular Session in Paris.

Jan. 11. The Assembly votes 42-5-7 to establish a new Disarmament Commission with jurisdiction over both atomic and conventional armaments.

Jan. 12. The Assembly calls on all members to keep armed forces available for use on call by the Assembly, and asks the Security Council to call a periodic meeting whenever it appears useful.

Feb. 1. The Assembly fails to adopt a Soviet resolution on U.N. membership, adopts a Peruvian membership resolution, and finds that the U.S.S.R. failed to carry out its 1945 treaty with China.

Feb. 5. The Assembly concludes its Sixth Regular Session after adopting a number of decisions on human rights, including instructions for drafting separate covenants on political and economic rights.

Oct. 14-Dec. 22. The Assembly holds the first part of its Seventh Regular Session in New York.

Dec. 10. The Assembly decides to continue the Committee on Information from Non-Self-Governing Territories for three years.

Dec. 21. The Assembly adopts a resolution on U.N. membership and rejects a Soviet proposal for simultaneous admission of 14 candidate states.

Dec. 22. The Assembly completes the first part of its Seventh Session after rejecting Soviet charges relating to the disturbances on Pongam Island in Korea.

Security Council

Feb. 6. Italy's application for membership is vetoed for the fifth time by the U.S.S.R. A Soviet proposal for the admission of 14 candidate states is rejected.

June 18. An appeal for ratification of the 1952 Geneva Protocol prohibiting bacteriological warfare is proposed by Soviet delegate Y. A. Malik. The proposal is rejected June 26.

July 3. A U.S. proposal for an impartial investigation of the Communist germ warfare charges is vetoed by the U.S.S.R.

July 9. A U.S. resolution rejecting and condemning the Communist germ warfare charges is vetoed by the U.S.S.R.

Sept. 8. The Security Council rejects a Soviet proposal to recommend 14 states for U.N. membership.

Sept. 16. Libya's application for U.N. membership is vetoed by the U.S.S.R. The application of Japan is similarly vetoed Sept. 18; those of Vietnam, Laos, and Cambodia on Sept. 19.

Economic and Social Council

May 20-Aug. 1. The Economic and Social Council holds the first part of its Fourteenth Session in New York.

Dec. 16-19. The Council holds the second part of its Fourteenth Session in New York.

Trusteeship Council

Feb. 27-Apr. 1. The Trusteeship Council holds its Tenth Regular Session in New York.

June 3-July 24. The Trusteeship Council holds the first part of its Eleventh Session in New York.

Nov. 20-Dec. 3. The Council holds the second part of its Eleventh Session in New York.

Other Activities

Mar. 14. The Disarmament Commission holds its first substantive meeting in New York.

Apr. 14-June 13. The Commission on Human Rights holds its Eighth Session in New York, and revises the draft covenants on political and civil and on economic and social rights.

Oct. 2-Nov. 10. The contracting parties to the General Agreement on Tariffs and Trade (GATT) hold their Seventh Session in Geneva.

Oct. 13-Dec. 17. The Senate Internal Security Subcommittee holds hearings in New York on activities of U.S. citizens employed by the U.N.

Nov. 10. Secretary-General Trygve Lie announces his intention to resign.

Nov. 12-Dec. 11. The Seventh General Conference of UNESCO is held in Paris.

Dec. 2. A Federal grand jury alleges extensive infiltration of the U.N. by disloyal U.S. citizens.

Dec. 3. The Secretary-General acts to oust disloyal U.S. employees in accordance with the advice of a special commission of jurists.

INDEX

435; Chinese Nationalist forces, 27, 174, 197-8
Butler, R. A., 82

Cambodia, 199, 201, 288, 333
Canada, 95, 128, 412; and U.N., 335, 337, 340-41, 384
Carney, Robert B., 129, 420
Casey, Richard G., 219
Central African Federation, 255
Ceylon, 206, 286, 434
Cheese amendment, 83, 87, 411
Chenik, Mohammed, 243
Chiang Kai-shek, 208, 210, 341-3, 345-6
Chile, 265, 270-71, 352, 360
China, 9, 16-7, 194, 435; Communist regime, 20, 172, 197, 434; expansionism, 15-6, 22, 200, 202-3; and Burma, 27, 198; aggression in Korea, 21, 173, 175-9; and U.N., 192, 429; and U.S.S.R., 288-9; see also Formosa
Chou En-lai, 35-6, 288, 341-2
Churchill, Winston S., 25, 241, 411; and Iran, 234; and NATO, 121, 402, 420-21; in U.S., 59-60, 176-7, 189
Clark, Mark W., 61, 137, 190, 376
Clementis, Vladimir, 296, 307
Coe, Frank, 383
Cohen, Benjamin V., 38
Colombia, 87, 225, 265, 335
Colombo Plan, 206-7
Communism, 6-10, 14, 53-4, 265-7, 306-7, 318
Conant, James B., 436
Congress, 53, 55, 56-7, 68, 92; and defense policy, 63-6, 73-4; and economic policy, 58, 65, 79-92; and European union, 92-3; and Far East, 60-61, 71, 217; and foreign aid, 58, 75-8, 93; and immigration, 100-106; and internal security, 54, 100; and NATO, 93-4; and presidential campaign, 52-3, 58-9; and St. Lawrence Seaway, 95; and Spain, 95; and U.N., 96-100, 378-81; and Vatican, 61-2
Connally, Tom, 78
Cooper, John Sherman, 177
Council of Europe, 111, 119, 121, 155, 391, 394, 400, 410
Cuba, 265, 267, 269
Customs Simplification Act, 84, 87

Czechoslovakia, 14, 181, 283, 296, 331, 333, 338

Defense Department, 66-7, 73-5, 185, 334
Defense Production Act, 83-4, 89-90
De Gasperi, Alcide, 117, 425
de Gaulle, Charles, 169
de Lattre de Tassigny, Jean, 194, 200
Denmark, 87, 115, 128, 292, 336
Dirksen, Everett M., 373
Dodd, Francis T., 187
Douglas, William O., 346
Draper, William H., Jr., 123, 132, 407-8
Dulles, John Foster, 327, 328, 416; and Japanese treaty, 60, 214, 309; "liberation" theory, 309-12, 317; reply to Stalin, 431-2

East-West trade, 29, 40-47, 88-9, 299-302, 434
Economic Cooperation Administration, 436
Economist, 322, 324, 387, 389
Ecuador, 265, 270-71
Eden, Anthony, 120, 124, 133, 167, 176, 192, 327, 354; and Korea, 185, 189, 339-40
Egypt, 227, 231; and U.K., 24, 229, 236-9; and U.N., 245, 257, 337, 348-9
Eisenhower, Dwight D., 50-51, 78, 107, 228, 416, 430-31; and European union, 108, 119; and NATO, 114, 121-3, 129, 133-6, 169, 387-8; presidential campaign, 277, 279, 311-13, 317-21, 323-5, 435; and U.N., 337, 344-5, 375
Ethiopia, 87, 225, 261, 335, 349
Europe, and U.S., 100-104
Europe, Western, 15, 391-3, 434; and East-West trade, 40-44; economic recovery, 116-18; political trends, 119-21, 163; rearmament problems, 127-8; strategic problems, 21-3, 108-12; and U.S., 72-3, 167, 388-90 (military support, 402-7; economic aid, 92-3, 407-12); and U.S.S.R., 30-31, 428-30
European Coal and Steel Community, 23, 93, 111, 119-20, 161-3, 391, 410; chart, 160; see also Schuman Plan
European Defense Community, 23, 93,